1968 IN CANADA

1968 IN CANADA

A Year and Its Legacies

**Edited by Michael K. Hawes,
Andrew C. Holman, and Christopher Kirkey**

MERCURY SERIES
HISTORY PAPER 61
CANADIAN MUSEUM OF HISTORY
AND UNIVERSITY OF OTTAWA PRESS

Co-published by
the Canadian Museum of History
and the University of Ottawa Press

The University of Ottawa Press gratefully acknowledges the support extended to its publishing list by the Government of Canada, the Canada Council for the Arts, the Ontario Council for the Arts, the Federation for the Humanities and Social Sciences through the Awards to Scholarly Publications Program, and the University of Ottawa.

Library and Archives Canada Cataloguing in Publication

Title: 1968 in Canada : a year and its legacies / edited by Michael Hawes, Andrew C. Holman, and Christopher Kirkey.
Other titles: Nineteen sixty-eight in Canada
Names: Hawes, Michael K., 1954- editor. | Holman, Andrew C. (Andrew Carl), 1965- editor. | Kirkey, Christopher John, 1962- editor.
Series: Mercury series. History paper.
Description: Series statement: Mercury series. History paper | Includes bibliographical references and index. | Includes two chapters in French.
Identifiers: Canadiana (print) 20200402455 | Canadiana (ebook) 20200402471 | ISBN 9780776636597 (softcover) | ISBN 9780776636603 (hardcover) | ISBN 9780776636610 (PDF)
Subjects: LCSH: Canada—Social life and customs—1945- | CSH: Canada—History—1963- | CSH: Canada—Politics and government—1963-1968. | CSH: Canada—Politics and government—1968-1979. | CSH: Canada—Social conditions—1945-1971.
Classification: LCC FC625 .A19 2021 | DDC 971.064/4—dc23

How To Order

All trade orders must be directed to the University of Ottawa Press:

>   **Web:** www.press.uottawa.ca
>   **Email:** puo-uop@uottawa.ca
>   **Phone:** 613-562-5246

All other orders may be directed to either the University of Ottawa Press (as above) or to the Canadian Museum of History:

>   **Web:** www.historymuseum.ca/shop
>   **Email:** publications@historymuseum.ca
>   **Phone:** 1-800-5550-5621 (toll-free)
>   or 819-776-8387 (National Capital Region)
>   **Mail:** Mail Order Services
>   Canadian Museum of History
>   100 Laurier Street
>   Gatineau, QC K1A 0M8

Production Team

Copy editing Trish O'Reilly Brennan (English) and Karine Lavoie (French)
Proofreading James Warren (English) and Chantal Ringuet (French)
Indexing Tere Mullin (English) and François Trahan (French)
Typesetting Édiscript enr.
Cover design Édiscript enr.
Series Editor Pierre M. Desrosiers

Cover images

Front In the thrall of Trudeaumania, fans greet Pierre Elliott Trudeau at a campaign event on 22 June 1968. Material republished with the express permission of: Montreal Gazette, a division of Postmedia Network Inc.
Back "Dancing Couple" by Normand Hudon, c.1968, McCord Museum, Montreal M997.63.171.

Printed in Canada

The Mercury Series

Strikingly Canadian and highly specialized, the *Mercury Series* presents works in the research domain of the Canadian Museum of History and benefits from the publishing expertise of the University of Ottawa Press. Created in 1972, the series is in line with the Canadian Museum of History's strategic directions. The *Mercury Series* consists of peer-reviewed academic research, and includes numerous landmark contributions in the disciplines of Canadian history, archaeology, culture and ethnology. Books in the series are published in at least one of Canada's official languages, and may appear in other languages.

La collection Mercure

Remarquablement canadienne et hautement spécialisée, la *collection Mercure* réunit des ouvrages portant sur les domaines de recherches du Musée canadien de l'histoire et s'appuie sur le savoir-faire des Presses de l'Université d'Ottawa. Fondée en 1972, elle répond aux orientations stratégiques du Musée canadien de l'histoire. La *collection Mercure* propose des recherches scientifiques évaluées par les pairs et regroupe de nombreuses contributions majeures à l'histoire, à l'archéologie, à la culture et à l'ethnologie canadiennes. Ces ouvrages sont publiés dans au moins une des langues officielles du Canada, avec possibilité de parution dans d'autres langues.

Pour commander

Les libraires et autres détaillants doivent adresser leurs commandes aux Presses de l'Université d'Ottawa :

>   **Web:** www.presses.uottawa.ca
>   **Courriel:** puo-uop@uottawa.ca
>   **Téléphone:** 613-562-5246

Les particuliers doivent adresser leurs commandes soit aux Presses de l'Université d'Ottawa (voir plus haut), soit au Musée canadien de l'histoire :

>   **Web:** www.museedelhistoire.ca/magasiner
>   **Courriel:** publications@museedelhistoire.ca
>   **Téléphone:** 1-800-5550-5621 (numéro sans frais) – 819-776-8387 (région de la capitale nationale)
>   **Poste:** Service des commandes postales
>   Musée canadien de l'histoire
>   100, rue Laurier
>   Gatineau (Québec) K1A 0M8

Abstract

The year 1968 in Canada was an extraordinary one, unlike any other in its frenetic activities and their consequences for the development of a new national consciousness among Canadians. It was a year when decisions and actions, both in Canada and outside its borders, were many and contentious, with momentous and far-reaching effects. Virtually no segment of Canadian life was untouched by the turmoil and the promise of generational change. In this volume of 16 new essays, leading scholars explore major events of 1968 and their effects on Canadian political culture, national identities, social relations, and cultural construction in the half-century that followed.

The first two chapters examine the transformative presence of Pierre Elliott Trudeau, who became both leader of the Liberal Party of Canada and prime minister in 1968. Paul Litt compares the staging of "Trudeaumania" with the presidential campaign tactics of Robert F. Kennedy, while P. E. Bryden examines how Trudeau quickly revamped the offices of the Prime Minister and the Privy Council.

A second set of chapters moves beyond Trudeau to address five themes that commanded Canadian politics in 1968: Jocelyn Létourneau reassesses the Quiet Revolution and the birth of separatism; Stephen Azzi captures the New Nationalism in English Canada through the ideas of Walter Gordon and Mel Watkins; Jane Arscott assesses the work of the Royal Commission on the Status of Women on female poverty and violence against women; Michael Temelini locates the intellectual origins of multiculturalism in the seldom-remembered "Thinkers' Conference"; and Andrew Gemmell recounts the work of Indigenous rights activists in the year before the 1969 White Paper.

A third group of chapters examines the institutions that came to be equated with Canadian identity. Ira Wagman's chapter traces the first year of the Canadian Radio-Television Commission and its efforts to manage a fragmented media landscape. Laura K. Davis examines Canadian literature and the magnetic presence of Jack McClelland and his publishing house, McClelland & Stewart. David Wright and Sasha Mullally analyze the rollout of medicare in Canada, and Graham Fraser casts 1968 as a "fork in the road," when the visions for language policy articulated in the Royal Commission on Bilingualism and Biculturalism and the cry for French unilingualism in Quebec collided.

A final section features case studies that illuminate the book's central theme. Christopher Kirkey examines Ottawa's response to the threats posed by the June 1968 discovery of oil in Alaska's Prudhoe Bay and the potential maritime transit of crude oil along Canadian coasts. Alexandre Turgeon narrates the crisis facing the Union Nationale in Quebec when the charismatic Daniel Johnson died suddenly. Andrea Chandler shifts the focus to Canadian foreign policy, assessing Canada's response to the Czechoslovak Crisis. Robin Gendron and David Tabachnick evaluate the consequences of Quebec's invitation to sit as an independent delegation at a conference of French-speaking countries in Libreville, Gabon. The last chapter returns to literature, where Will Smith follows the career and meaning of one award-winning short story by David Helwig.

Résumé

Au Canada, 1968 est une année unique, remplie d'activités frénétiques dont les conséquences ont été déterminantes pour le développement d'une nouvelle conscience nationale chez les Canadiens. Cette année-là, les décisions et les actions, tant au Canada qu'à l'extérieur de ses frontières, ont été nombreuses et litigieuses, et leurs effets se sont révélés considérables et de grande portée. Pratiquement aucun segment de la vie canadienne n'a été épargné par la tourmente et la promesse d'un changement générationnel. Dans ce volume regroupant 16 nouveaux essais, d'éminents chercheurs explorent les événements majeurs survenus en 1968 et leurs répercussions sur la culture politique canadienne, les identités nationales, les relations sociales et la construction culturelle du demi-siècle qui a suivi.

Les deux premiers chapitres examinent la présence transformatrice de Pierre Elliott Trudeau, qui est devenu à la fois chef du Parti libéral du Canada (PLC) et premier ministre en 1968. Paul Litt compare la mise en scène de la « trudeaumanie » à la tactique de campagne présidentielle de Robert F. Kennedy, tandis que P. E. Bryden examine comment Trudeau a rapidement réorganisé les bureaux du premier ministre et du Conseil privé. Une deuxième série de chapitres va au-delà de Pierre Elliott Trudeau pour aborder cinq thèmes qui ont commandé la politique canadienne en 1968 : Jocelyn Létourneau réévalue la Révolution tranquille et la naissance du séparatisme ; Stephen Azzi analyse le « New Nationalism » au Canada anglais à travers les idées de Walter Gordon et Mel Watkins ; Jane Arscott se penche sur les travaux de la Commission royale d'enquête sur la situation de la femme au Canada ; Michael Temelini situe les origines intellectuelles du multiculturalisme dans la rare « Thinkers' Conference » ; et Andrew Gemmell raconte le travail des militants pour les droits des Autochtones au cours de l'année précédant le Livre blanc de 1969.

Un troisième groupe de chapitres examine les institutions qui ont fini par être assimilées à l'identité canadienne. Ira Wagman retrace la première année du Conseil de la radio-télévision canadienne (aujourd'hui le Conseil de la radiodiffusion et des télécommunications canadiennes [CRTC]) et ses efforts pour gérer un paysage médiatique fragmenté. Laura K. Davis s'intéresse à la littérature canadienne et à la présence magnétique de Jack McClelland et de sa maison d'édition, McClelland & Stewart. David Wright et Sasha Mullally analysent le déploiement de l'assurance maladie au Canada, tandis que Graham Fraser présente l'année 1968 comme une « fourche sur la route », lorsque l'appel à l'unilinguisme français au Québec et les visions de la politique linguistique énoncées dans le cadre de la Commission royale d'enquête sur le bilinguisme et le biculturalisme sont entrés en collision.

Une dernière section expose des études de cas qui mettent en lumière le thème central du livre. Christopher Kirkey examine la réponse du gouvernement fédéral aux menaces posées par la découverte de pétrole, en juin 1968, dans la baie Prudhoe, en Alaska, et le transit maritime potentiel de pétrole brut le long des côtes canadiennes. Alexandre Turgeon raconte la crise qu'a traversée l'Union nationale au Québec lorsque le charismatique Daniel Johnson est décédé subitement. Andrea Chandler se concentre sur la politique étrangère canadienne, évaluant la réponse du Canada à la crise tchécoslovaque. Robin Gendron et David Tabachnick se penchent quant à eux sur les conséquences de l'invitation lancée au Québec à siéger en tant que délégation indépendante à une conférence des pays francophones à Libreville, au Gabon. Le dernier chapitre porte sur la littérature. Will Smith y explore la carrière et la signification d'une nouvelle primée de David Helwig.

Table of Contents

List of Figures and Tables

Acknowledgements

This collection, *1968 in Canada: A Year and Its Legacies*, began as a conversation amongst scholars and friends. In July 2017, the editors of this book participated in a colloquium, "Canada Inclusive/Exclusive: 150 Years and Beyond," convened at University College London, Institute of the Americas. A series of discussions in London, Ottawa, and Boston ensued, focusing on a common desire and plan to hold a conference on "Canada in 1968," with the best papers selected for an edited volume. The year 1968, we believe, was a landmark for Canada, and its legacies have left a significant permanent imprint on the nation.

The editors wish to extend their grateful appreciation to several individuals who are responsible for making this book a reality. First and foremost, Dr. Dean Oliver, Director of Research at the Canadian Museum of History, generously committed the Museum to host a two-day author's symposium in September 2018, provided significant underwriting, and agreed to offer the foreword to this collection. Dr. John Willis, former editor of the Mercury Series at the University of Ottawa Press, initially encouraged the development of the manuscript, while Dr. Pierre Desrosiers, current editor of the series, worked carefully with us to produce the book. Lee Wyndham and Tanya Anderson of the Canadian Museum of History and François Lavigne of the University of Ottawa Press provided invaluable assistance throughout the editing and production process. Marc Jacques, Senior Political and Economic Affairs Officer at the Canadian Consulate General in Boston, generously hosted a convivial and productive day-long editors' meeting in February 2019. Additional support for the *1968 in Canada: A Year and Its Legacies* project was contributed by Fulbright Canada, the Center for the Study of Canada at SUNY Plattsburgh, and the Canadian Studies Program at Bridgewater State University. For their support before and during the authors' symposium, we wish to thank Amy Sotherden (SUNY Plattsburgh), Alanna Blackie DeMos (Fulbright Canada), Martha Vrany (Fulbright Canada), and Susan Williams (Bridgewater State). The final manuscript benefitted appreciably from the sharp eyes and the useful comments offered by two anonymous readers recruited by the University of Ottawa Press. Our thanks go to each of them.

Finally, organizing and editing this collection of essays has allowed us the opportunity to work with an exceptionally talented group of scholars. We wish to thank them for contributing their time, energy, and scholarly output. We appreciate their patience with us as editors, and for squarely addressing the thematic focus of the book—the causes and consequences of critical events in Canada's 1968.

Michael Hawes, Andrew Holman, and Christopher Kirkey

Foreword

DEAN F. OLIVER
Senior Director (Research) and Chief Curator
Canadian Museum of History

Good ideas have rarely arrived more fully formed onto my desk than this one, a timely, well-crafted inquiry into the nature and impact of the seminal year, 1968, for Canada and Canadians. From my first conversation with the workshop's organizers (later, this book's editors) a couple of years ago, its scope was clear, its breadth dazzling, and its ambitions admirable. The resulting volume works along many vectors, from politics to publishing, from equity to oil. Not surprising, given the high-profile authors, is the collection's outstanding scholarship and contributions to knowledge. As welcome (perhaps even more welcome) are its verve and broad accessibility. There is a deep sense of professional humility; of contributors self-consciously starting conversations and following clues, rather than pronouncing or pontificating, or what, in the vernacular of museum studies, might be termed dialogic versus monologic interpretation. This is no small trick and a fine tribute to the authors' and editors' maturity and confidence at every project stage.

My colleagues and I at the Canadian Museum of History are honoured to have hosted the workshop leading to this volume and thankful for participating in its discussions. We are now privileged to be publishing, with our esteemed partner at the University of Ottawa Press, its many contributions. This book's subject is a perfect complement to the Museum's ten-year Research Strategy and the overarching directions of its Board of Trustees, which emphasize accessible history, telling important and inclusive stories, and national engagement. The Museum has pursued such goals along many tracks, not least of which are explorations of Indigenous experience, women's history, political power, and cultural representation—each of which finds skillful representation here.

The Museum has had many successful partnerships in sponsoring conferences, symposia, and publications. It has been host, for example, to the annual general meetings of the multinational Society for Military History and the Canadian Archaeological Association and supported major gatherings on musicology, folklore, heritage, Indigenous studies, public history, Canadian history, and the conservation of material culture. Our edited volumes on colonial identity, military history, and ice hockey have helped redefine their respective fields, while our monographs on war, archaeology, and folklore have become canonical texts. Individually, our Museum scholars are active in a dozen disciplines, researching, writing, teaching, and working collaboratively from Heart's Content to Haida Gwaii, but their research is aided and considerably amplified by working here, in concert with others who share common values of curiosity, authenticity, and responsibility.

Museums are far more than the collections they hold and the things they exhibit. They are these, of course, along with the professionals who maintain them and the communities of knowledge they help to construct. But museums are much more besides, from websites to town hall discussions to public programs, with various methods for informed inquiry and respectful exchange. This project, 1968 in Canada, proved many of these things, conjoining and leveraging unique scholars with unique skills into an unparalleled conversation about the importance of the past and its hold on our own time.

The Canadian Museum of History could not be prouder to have helped, to have listened, and to have learned.

Gatineau, QC
28 September 2020

A Note on Language

Several chapters in this book include terms that some readers may find offensive, discriminatory, or racist. The authors and editors have been careful to ensure that this wording is used only in direct quotations, names of associations or publication titles, and for the sole purpose of reflecting the historical context. In some cases, letters have been replaced with asterisks to avoid including an offensive word in full. This is in keeping with our understanding that history and historical study is for all of us, and that we must strive to be inclusive in the stories that we tell, and the way we tell them.

Une note sur le langage

De nombreux chapitres de ce livre contiennent des termes que des lecteurs et des lectrices pourraient juger offensants, discriminatoires ou racistes. Les auteurs et les éditeurs ont veillé à ce que ces termes n'apparaissent que dans le cadre de citations directes, de noms d'associations ou de titres de publications, et dans le but unique de bien refléter le contexte historique. Dans certains cas, les lettres d'un mot jugé offensant ont pu être remplacées par des astérisques afin d'éviter de l'afficher dans son intégralité. Cette façon de procéder s'inscrit dans notre compréhension de ce qu'est l'histoire, soit un sujet et une discipline pour tout le monde, que nous devons travailler à rendre plus inclusive, et ce, tant par les thèmes que nous abordons que par la façon de les présenter.

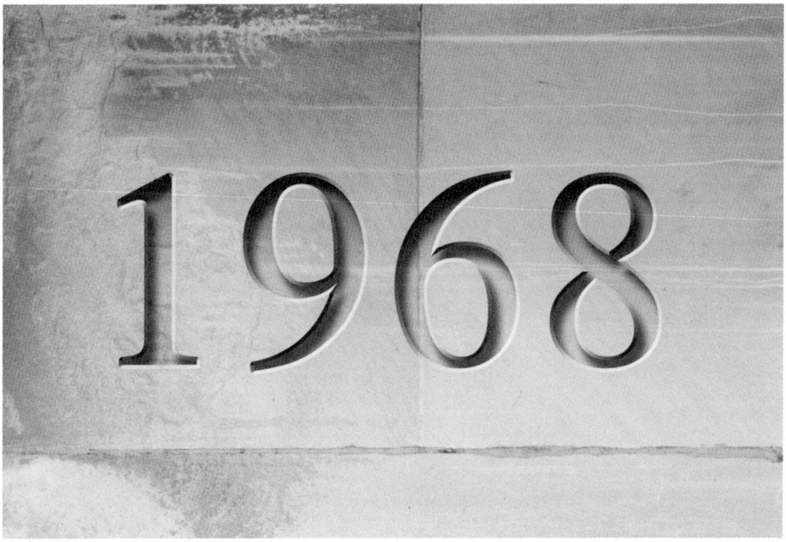
1968

Introduction

MICHAEL K. HAWES, ANDREW C. HOLMAN, AND CHRISTOPHER KIRKEY

What does 1968 hold in store for us? Who can say? We can look back to 1967 and remember our Centennial year with pride, for in many ways it brought us to the place where some at least, acknowledged for the first time that they were proud to be Canadians. Most of us can respond in a moment of glory. ... However it is a far greater test of character to be proud of our nation when it is not heightened by celebration. ...

Deaconess Wilma Sharpe,
South Nanaimo
Combined Congregation,
Nanaimo Daily News, 13 January 1968

Apprehension, fears for future stability of domestic and world order haunt the minds and disturb the spirit of the so-called civilized world today. Never ... has there been an era in which rebellion, discontent, resentment of the status quo been so alarming. ... One of the most significant things about the massive malaise which seems now to be spreading like a cancer around the globe, is that discontent is not confined to any one system of government, or even to any clearly defined class or economic group. ... This is mid-1968.

Editorial, *Lethbridge Herald*, 6 June 1968

[Nineteen sixty-eight] has been a year of violence and destruction [and] ... great suffering. ... We must learn to resolve the internal conflicts which have divided us

> and have absorbed so much of our time;
> and … to enrich the lives of those among
> us who have been deprived or ignored.
> Prime Minister Pierre Trudeau,
> Christmas Message 1968

This volume of essays examines a single year in the history of Canada. More specifically, it addresses certain events and their impact on Canadian politics, economics, foreign policy, society, and culture in the half-century that has passed in its wake.[1] The project is premised upon a straightforward assertion: 1968 was an extraordinary year, unlike any other in its activities and their significance. It was a year when decisions and actions, both in Canada and abroad, were many and contentious, with momentous and far-reaching effects. In making this preliminary assertion, we recognize its essentially apocryphal nature. How historians and others periodize the past—how they cut it up into usable parts—is always in some measure arbitrary. In theory, looking at a single calendar year is no more compelling than examining a decade or a century, the term of a government administration, or an athletic season. Yet, sometimes, the arbitrary temporal boundaries that we routinely impose upon the past hold up. Nineteen sixty-eight is one of those cases. To borrow a phrase from Edward Hallett Carr's 1961 classic *What Is History?*, a historical *period* "is like a sack—it won't stand up until you have put something in it" (Carr 1961, 11). As the content of this book demonstrates, 1968 in Canada stands up and stands out because of all that is "in it" and the importance that leading scholars of that era attach to its contents.[2]

Establishing 1968 as a year unlike others is a task unburdened by the fact that other scholars have already done so quite effectively. Outside Canada, 1968 has been recognized as a watershed year, a decisive break from the torpid postwar era of reconstruction, unbridled consumerism, and social conformity, to a world of new vibrancy, political unrest, generational rebellion, and the development of counter-culture. The examples are many. These include the

---

1. All but one of the essays in this volume were developed from selected presentations made at a two-day symposium hosted by the Canadian Museum of History (CMH) in Gatineau, Quebec, in September 2018, titled "1968 in Canada: A Year and Its Legacies," and occasioned by the 50-year anniversary of that momentous year. In addition to the CMH, the symposium's organizers and sponsors included Fulbright Canada, the Center for the Study of Canada at SUNY Plattsburgh, and the Canadian Studies Program at Bridgewater State University in Massachusetts.
2. Canada's 1968 was, of course, couched in Canada's 1960s, which has been the subject of a number of insightful, recent historical studies, foremost among them Palmer (2009); Henderson (2011); Campbell, Clément, and Kealey (2012); Donaghy (2002); and Milligan (2014).

frustration in America over the escalation of involvement in the Vietnam War and the deep discontent it aroused among young people. One can also point to public demonstrations at Columbia University and the Democratic Party's national convention, the assassinations of civil rights movement icon Martin Luther King Jr. and Democratic presidential hopeful Robert F. Kennedy, and the symbolic Black Power protests of American athletes John Carlos and Tommie Smith at Mexico City's Olympics. In Europe and elsewhere, workers, students, and poor people took to the streets en masse to argue for civil rights, environmental protection, democratic freedoms, and the reform or ouster of repressive regimes. In Poland, Italy, West Germany, Pakistan, and Mexico, student protests against institutional corruption and the concentration of power in the hands of out-of-touch elites led to violent responses, including a massacre of students in the Plaza de las Tres Culturas in Mexico City. Workers joined forces with students in Spain and in France, where a loud call for university reform blossomed into a month-long general strike, Mai 68, that all but closed down the country. In Czechoslovakia, the Prague Spring came about when leader Alexander Dubček sought to loosen restrictions on the media and travel and to broaden democratic freedoms. Ultimately, this ended in August, when Soviet tanks rolled in to assert authority. In a plethora of causes and shapes, the upheaval was everywhere: in the civil rights marches of Catholics in Northern Ireland, in the Rodney riots in Jamaica, in student demonstrations in Yugoslavia and Sweden, and many others. "What was unique about 1968," Mark Kurlansky writes in his expansive survey of that year, "was that people were rebelling over disparate issues and had in common only that desire to rebel ... a sense of alienation from the established order, and a profound distaste for authoritarianism in any form" (2004, xvii).[3]

To keen observers watching global events unfold from their perches in Canada, the world seemed to be on fire, and Canada was dangerously close to the path of the conflagration. Few of them could have been more prescient than Nanaimo's Wilma Sharpe, who saw in January 1968 that a great test of character lay ahead for Canadians (Sharpe 1968). By June, the editor of the *Lethbridge Herald* also worried that the massive malaise spreading around the globe "like a cancer" would infect Canada (1968). And by December, speaking to the nation in his Christmas message, Prime Minister Trudeau was certain that it had (*Red Deer Advocate* 1968). But to characterize Canada's 1968 as inspired and generated wholly by external events and ideas would be to miss half of the story. Some Canadians—anti-Vietnam protesters in Toronto and

---

3. The scholarly writing on 1968 is massive and impossible to capture here in its entirety. Alongside Kurlansky (2004), among the best recent volumes on this subject are Fink, Gassert, and Junker (1998); Kutschke and Norton (2013); Cottrell and Browne (2018); Gildea, Mark, and Warring (2013); and Vinen (2018).

anti-colonial separatists in Quebec—were inspired by events that took place abroad and resonated with local struggles. Still, Canada's 1968 had domestic roots, driven by its own reality. It is in the interplay of political, ideological, and social forces, both foreign and domestic, where this special year in Canadian history finds its unique character. In 1968, Canada was a nation in ferment. One might even be bold enough to argue that it was a nation in the process of remaking itself.

If in much of the world 1968 was about tearing down old, worn-out institutions and identities, 1968 in Canada was just as much about constructing new ones: new ways of doing business; new ways of administering government nationally and locally; new ways of defining identities (French, English, Indigenous, and the multicultural "Third Force"); new ways of communicating ideas in print and on the air; new ways of interacting with the world; and, in particular, new ways of dealing with the American colossus. With the wind of the Centennial celebrations under their wings and in the afterglow of Expo 67, John Saywell and Paul Stevens wrote in the *Canadian Annual Review for 1968*, Canadians were "in a mood of renewed self-confidence" (Stevens and Saywell 1969, 3). It was a time for new beginnings.

This volume traces critical Canadian events in 1968, their causes, and their long list of consequences. At the forefront of these was domestic politics, along with the transformative presence of Pierre Elliott Trudeau (PET), who won the leadership of the Liberal Party of Canada on 6 April and on 25 June was elected prime minister. "Trudeau dominated politics in 1968," Stevens and Saywell noted. "To Canadians who had become skeptical of politics and politicians during the 1960s, [his] appeal ... was irresistible" (Stevens and Saywell 1969, 3). PET appears in many of this book's chapters, but he is clearly the central focus in the first two of these. In Chapter 1, "Bobby and Pierre in '68," Paul Litt examines the phenomenon of "Trudeaumania," attributing the Prime Minister's rise to the new power of mass media, the staging of political spectacle, and the decade's celebration of youth and renewal embodied in Trudeau and in American presidential candidate Robert F. Kennedy. Penny E. Bryden's "A Very Canadian Revolution," Chapter 2 in this book, explores another transformation in politics brought about by Trudeau, one much less public but equally profound. Within a few weeks after taking office in June 1968, Trudeau revamped the structure of power in Ottawa, concentrating decision-making in the Prime Minister's Office and in Cabinet and creating a system that was "more centralized, more political, and more partisan" than ever before.

Beyond Trudeau's magnetism and machinations, five major themes dominated Canadian politics and political discourse in 1968 and the years that followed: the troubled place of Quebec in Confederation, the "new" nationalism in English Canada, the status of women, the idea of multiculturalism, and

Indigenous rights. In Quebec, 1968 was host to the establishment of the separatist Parti Québécois led by René Lévesque, a pivotal event of the decade. Jocelyn Létourneau's chapter (Chapter 3) "1968, vue du Québec" uses the lens of one year to reassess scholars' work on the Quiet Revolution and the "birth" of separatism. Rather than search for telltale turning points and investing one political movement with the spirit of an age, a fairer assessment of Quebec's 1968 emphasizes commonality—a broadly held desire for development and social justice, rather than national ambition driven by anti-colonial or socialist impulses. By contrast, Stephen Azzi argues in Chapter 4, "The Nationalists of 1968 and the Search for Canadian Independence," that 1968 marked a "decisive break" in the history of English-Canadian nationalism. Focusing on the ideas and actions of Walter Gordon and Mel Watkins, Azzi situates the new nationalism in an overriding concern about foreign investment in the Canadian economy and the need to protect it from American domination. The pursuit of equality and equity in the Royal Commission on the Status of Women in Canada in 1968 is the focus of Jane Arscott's chapter (Chapter 5). In it, she documents how that body's hearings and their coverage in the press gave voice to concerns about women's economic insecurity and poverty and about violence against women. At the same time, the Commission's ultimate recommendations revealed the limits of the state's willingness to pursue a wider range of rights issues for women and illuminated the need for continued activism. Michael Temelini's chapter (Chapter 6), titled "The 1968 Thinkers' Conference and the Birth of Canadian Multiculturalism," examines the origins of multiculturalism as an idea in the years before its inscription as government policy in 1971. Although multiculturalism was a concept current throughout the 1960s, the Thinkers' Conference elevated it to public prominence and helped trigger its adoption as policy by the Trudeau government. Andrew Gemmell's contribution in Chapter 7 examines the difficult issues facing Indigenous rights activists and government officials in the year of deliberations that preceded the Trudeau government's racist 1969 White Paper—which proposed to do away with the equally racist *Indian Act*. His chapter traces the hard-fought battles of that year, which set the parameters for federal–Indigenous relations that remain in place to this day.

The third group of chapters in this volume examines a series of institutions that have come to be equated with Canadian identity, at home and abroad: the Canadian Radio-Television Commission (CRTC), CanLit, medicare, and bilingualism. For all of these subjects, 1968 was a critical year of genesis and transition. In Chapter 8, Ira Wagman examines the first year of the CRTC's existence. He concludes that its rulings and policies reflected an overarching effort to manage a media landscape that had, by 1968, become a contested space, fragmented by public and private ventures, foreign and domestic content, and programming that balanced traditional tastes with the "new" voices of Indigenous peoples, activist students, Quebec nationalists, and "ethnic" communities. Laura K. Davis's Chapter 9 addresses the world of Canadian literature, focusing in particular on the central place of Jack McClelland's publishing house McClelland & Stewart. In a year marked by financial crisis for M&S and personal tragedy for McClelland, his company was host to an "explosion" of writers making their mark on the Canadian literary scene: Margaret Laurence, Pierre Berton, Leonard Cohen, and Farley Mowat. Just as iconic a Canadian institution as either the CRTC or CanLit was medicare. In Chapter 10, David Wright and Sasha Mullally chronicle the "rollout" of medicare in Canada on 1 July 1968, which was at once a cause of great celebration but also the source of considerable worry about the lack of trained medical professionals available to fulfill the system's needs. It is "one of the great ironies in the contemporary history of Canada," they argue, that medicare was enabled only by the influx of thousands of foreign-trained, non-Canadian professionals. In Chapter 11, Graham Fraser tackles the grand journey of language policy in Canada, calling 1968 a "fork in the road." In that year, two competing visions of language policy confronted one another: one of them crafted in the federal Royal Commission on Bilingualism and Biculturalism (1967) and later expressed in the *Official Languages Act* (1969); another generated in Quebec, where there prevailed a growing preference for official French unilingualism in government services and in schools.

A final group of chapters in *1968 in Canada* examines a variety of case studies that, in their own separate ways, illuminate the book's central theme. Christopher Kirkey, in Chapter 12, examines the Trudeau government's response to the threats posed, in the wake of the June 1968 discovery of oil in Alaska's Prudhoe Bay, by the potential maritime transit of crude oil in or adjacent to waters in the ice-laden Canadian Arctic and along the British Columbia coast. In Chapter 13, Alexandre Turgeon looks at the crisis that faced the governing Union Nationale (UN) party in Quebec when its charismatic leader Daniel Johnson died in September 1968 and was succeeded by Jean-Jacques Bertrand. Turgeon examines the factors involved in a successful transition to power and compares Bertrand's circumstances with those of UN leader Paul Sauvé, who replaced Premier Maurice Duplessis when he died in 1959. Andrea Chandler shifts the focus to Canadian foreign policy in Chapter 14, where she examines the Trudeau government's response to the Czechoslovak Crisis of 1968. The Soviet invasion, she argues, created disillusionment among Canadian political leaders in their country's abilities to influence Soviet behaviour but at the same time dampened arguments in government circles for withdrawing from its NATO commitments. Chapter 15 focuses on the issue of Quebec as an international player and the symbolism attached to its participation as an independent delegation at the conference of French-speaking countries in Libreville, Gabon. The event kicked off two years of intense debate between Ottawa and Quebec City over the meaning of sovereignty and the constitutional prerogative of foreign diplomacy. The book's final chapter returns to the literary scene, focusing on an award-winning 1968 short story, writer David Helwig's "Something for Olivia's Scrapbook I Guess," which was set in a fictionalized hippie scene in Toronto's Yorkville and published in *Saturday Night* magazine. In his close reading of the text and his examination of the larger context within which it was written and read, Will Smith sees Helwig's story as "a hinge point in local and national culture."

To alter (only slightly) Deaconness Sharpe's initial question: "What does Canada's 1968 hold in store for us?" As these chapters reveal, a great deal indeed, though we are aware of this volume's limitations. The usual caveat that accompanies all scholarly collections must appear here, as well. There is much about Canada's 1968 that these chapters do not convey. We need to know more about the importance of that year in Canada for religion, sport, the labour movement, economic change, poverty, and social class, for example. And, while we recognize the importance of these subjects, we leave those discussions for other scholars to pursue. We hope that the essays included in this volume generate a renewed interest among students and scholars in 1968 and all that is "in it."

References

Campbell, Lara, Dominique Clément, and Greg Kealey, eds. 2012. *Debating Dissent: Canada and the Sixties*. Toronto: University of Toronto Press.

Carr, Edward Hallett. 1961. *What Is History?* London: Macmillan.

Cottrell, Robert C., and Blaine T. Browne. 2018. *1968: The Rise and Fall of the New American Revolution*. Lanham, MD: Rowman and Littlefield.

Donaghy, Greg. 2002. *Tolerant Allies: Canada and the United States, 1963–1968*. Montreal and Kingston: McGill-Queen's University Press.

Fink, Carole, Philipp Gassert, and Detlef Junker, eds. 1998. *1968: The World Transformed*. Washington, DC and Cambridge, UK: German Historical Institute and Cambridge University Press.

Gildea, Robert, James Mark, and Anette Warring, eds. 2013. *Europe's 1968: Voice of Revolt*. Oxford: Oxford University Press.

Henderson, Stuart. 2011. *Making the Scene: Yorkville and Hip Toronto in the 1960s*. Toronto: University of Toronto Press.

Kurlansky, Mark. 2004. *1968: The Year That Rocked the World*. New York: Ballantyne Books.

Kutschke, Beate, and Barley Norton, eds. 2013. *Music and Protest in 1968*. Cambridge, UK: Cambridge University Press.

Lethbridge Herald. 1968. "1848—Year of Violence… 1968—Who Knows?" 6 June: 4.

Milligan, Ian. 2014. *Rebel Youth: 1960s Labour Unrest, Young Workers and New Leftists in English Canada*. Vancouver: University of British Columbia Press.

Palmer, Bryan D. 2009. *Canada's 1960s: The Ironies of Identity in a Rebellious Era*. Toronto: University of Toronto Press.

Red Deer Advocate. 1968. "Trudeau Message Stresses Poor." 26 December: 19.

Sharpe, Wilma. 1968. "A Year of Adventure." Guest Editorial. *Nanaimo Daily News*, 13 January: 4.

Stevens, Paul, and John T. Saywell. 1969. "Politics and Parliament." *Canadian Annual Review for 1968*. Toronto: University of Toronto Press.

Vinen, Richard. 2018. 1968: Radical Protest and Its Enemies. New York: HarperCollins.

Chapter 1
Bobby and Pierre

PAUL LITT

Abstract

In the spring of 1968, the political campaigns of Robert Kennedy in the
United States and Pierre Trudeau in Canada generated wild crowd scenes
featuring passionate adoration of the candidates. Both politicians were
liberals, yet their platforms, political situations, and supporters were very
different. What was it that turned their campaign events into tumultuous
love-ins? Both countries seemed threatened by fragmentation that year,
and emotions were running high. In mass-mediated national politics, the
celebrity politician offered a convenient, plausible panacea. Taking to the
streets to emote support for Kennedy or Trudeau combined elements of
sixties activism and mainstream mass culture into a form of participatory
democracy aimed at healing the nation.

In the spring of 1968, the campaigns of Robert Kennedy in the United States
and Pierre Trudeau in Canada exhibited strikingly similar characteristics. In
both cases, a celebrity politician toured the country and was mobbed by wild
throngs of fans. A politician on the campaign trail attracting enthusiastic supporters is a familiar enough political story, but these two campaigns, conducted
in the midst of the political and cultural tumult of 1968, generated successive
crowds of unusual size, passion, and intensity across each country, taking on
the appearance of popular crusades. Both Kennedy and Trudeau were liberals,
yet their platforms, political situations, and supporters were different. All of this
suggests that other factors were behind the pandemonium. What was going on?

This chapter tries to answer this question by positioning these two campaigns within the unique circumstances of 1968, in the West generally and on
both sides of the Canada–U.S. border, and, more broadly, in terms of the
possibilities available to citizens for civic engagement in the mass-mediated
national politics of these high-modern mass democracies. Both countries
seemed threatened that year. Taking to the streets to express support for a
celebrity candidate combined elements of Sixties activism and popular culture
in a form of participatory democracy aimed at healing the nation.

Figure 1.1. Campaign button 1968: GoGo Trudeau. *Source:* Canadian Museum of History Collections.

History is full of tales of charismatic figures—evangelists, performers, intellectuals, con men—attracting devoted followings and widespread fame. In the twentieth century, enhanced dissemination of print media and new media such as photography, film, radio, and television allowed such phenomena to spread further and faster.[1] When the Beatles visited North America in 1964, fans went wild to see their idols, previously known to them only through the media, live in the flesh. Exalted beings who formerly could only be imagined now materialized, however briefly, in their everyday world.

There was a similar dynamic to election campaigns by politicians in large-scale modern polities.[2] In 1960s North America, most citizens had little direct exposure to national politics because it typically occurred in far-off capital cities. The mass media naturalized and popularized the nation by continuously reporting on its leaders and politics. Still, their intangible representations of mysterious goings-on at the centre of officialdom could leave distant audiences fuzzy as to how it all related to them.[3] At election time, however, national

---

1. Celebrity has always been a part of politics. Machiavelli, for example, wrote of the importance of melding personality with performance to shape a good political persona (Van Zoonen 2005, 72). Nevertheless, celebrity seems to have become a more prominent sociological phenomenon in modern, mass-mediated mass societies, suggesting it is integral to the way they work. In his analysis of the phenomenon, John Street incorporates a definition of celebrity put forward by P. D. Marshall, concluding that the term "refers to those people who, via mass media, enjoy 'a greater presence and wider scope of activity and agency than are those who make up the rest of the population. They are allowed to move on the public stage while the rest of us watch'" (Street 2002, 437). Street is quoting from Marshall (1997, ix). For a discussion of celebrity capital as a form of Bourdieu's symbolic capital, see Davis (2010, 82–86).

2. Van Zoonen (2004) claims that "fan communities and political constituencies bear crucial similarities." Both develop in response to performances by a celebrity and maintain a discourse around their object of fascination. She goes on to argue that although fans are derided as overly emotional, in politics at least, affective investment is to be encouraged (39–52).

3. Many students of nationalism, following Benedict Anderson, see the nation as largely a construct of the media. As Gene Allen and Daniel Robinson put it: "The public sphere and the nation constitute different types of socio-political spaces,

Figure I.2. Campaign button 1968: Robert F. Kennedy.

politicians, like pop stars, went on tour and made live appearances, melding the imagined nation with local lived experience.[4]

Canada and the United States were fertile soil for salvation-by-celebrity in 1968. Cultural and political agitations that had been brewing for years came to a head that year. The protest ethos of the decade developed out of the civil rights and anti-nuclear movements of the 1950s. Throughout the early 1960s, the race issue in the United States simmered acridly, with legislative progress on civil rights offset by atrocities against activists in the South. Ghetto riots broke out in major cities every summer, leaving urban cores devastated by looting and arson. By mid-decade, a Black Power movement committed to winning social justice by whatever means necessary was challenging the non-violent tactics of the mainstream civil rights movement. The related issue of poverty also found its way onto the United States national political agenda, forcing Americans to face the fact that significant numbers of their compatriots lived in penury, ignorance, and squalor. While President Lyndon Johnson launched his Great Society assault on poverty, Black teens were being shipped to the front lines in Vietnam in disproportionate numbers. Meanwhile, the war there became increasingly controversial as the government committed more troops and casualty rates rose. Protests against it grew in size and number. Many who would never have thought of marching in an anti-war protest began to suspect that the war was unwinnable and that the government could not be trusted to admit it.

Nowhere were tensions as acute as in the United States, yet the unrest of the times was evident throughout the Western world. In Sweden, Germany, France, Spain, and Italy, student protests led to chaos in the streets in the early months of 1968. Even behind the Iron Curtain, in Poland and Czechoslovakia,

and both may be usefully linked back to the idea of dissemination. They are not only spaces to which messages are disseminated by particular media, but spaces that are *brought into existence* by this dissemination" (Allen and Robinson 2009, 9).

4. See Litt (2016, 29–31), which describes this process of "reel-to-real synthesis" as a salve for "mediation anxiety," a condition in which the citizen audience fretted that their mass-mediated knowledge of national political issues and politicians was inauthentic.

forces of liberation were generating civic strife. The public restiveness of the era played out differently from one national context to another. Canada's experience of the Sixties is a case in point. The protest spirit was evident there as well, but the big issues that rent the United States did not confront Canada so directly. While the Dominion of the North was by no means innocent of racism, social injustice, and militarism, Canadians liked to think it was. The trials besetting the United States instilled in Canadians a smug sense of national superiority. Canadian nationalism was on the upswing, in search of a new national identity and purpose (Azzi 2012). America's contemporary image problems made it a useful "Other" against which Canadian nationalists defined their country as comparatively humane, tolerant, and peaceful (Litt 2016, 74–77, 79, 91–94, 293–295).

Thanks to the baby boom, the average age of the population in both countries was less than 30 (Steigerwald 1995, 247; CBC Archive Sales 1967).[5] The prosperity and security enjoyed by the rising baby-boom generation underwrote political protest by its radical elements. As they developed loosely related organizations and tactics distinct from those of preceding left-wing movements, they became known as the New Left. On college campuses, privileged students challenged the *in loco parentis* moral strictures and complacent elitism of university authorities with protest marches, teach-ins, and sit-ins. Pictures of police facing off against young protesters appeared regularly in the news. By the late 1960s, a rising counterculture was providing more colourful conflict for the media maw. It starred long-haired hippies in anti-modern dress engaged in spiritual quests. Smoking pot or dropping acid, some of their favoured pathways to nirvana, distorted conventional sensory inputs, giving rise to a psychedelic aesthetic that problematized perception to represent all things countercultural. Such challenges to conventional behaviour were all the more threatening because middle-class values were already weakened by consumerism's siren call of self-indulgence, the sexual revolution's assault on prudery, and the defiant, hedonistic spirit of rock 'n' roll. Liberation was the byword, and it threatened to unleash all the base appetites sublimated in polite society.

Journalists were obsessed with youth, and "whither the younger generation" became a staple of feature articles and public affairs programming. The baby boomers were reared on the mass media and knew how to play them. Civil rights activists got police to beat them so they would make a bigger splash in the media, and protesters around the world emulated their tactics. Abbie Hoffman, the guru of countercultural agitation, didn't care whether his outrageous Yippie stunts made sense as long as they made news (Kurlansky 2004, 93–94; Bodroghkozy 2001, 5–9). "The establishment" often responded to

---

5. For a discussion of the contrasting life experiences and values of young and old in America, see Steigerwald (1995, 54).

radical challenges ham-handedly, overreacting with excessive force that validated protestors' accusations (Steigerwald 1995, 243). To replace it, the New Left called for participatory democracy, one of many Sixties slogans that became ubiquitous enough to gain common-sense plausibility.

Only a tiny minority, even among the young, were radicals either politically or culturally. Yet popular culture, with its insatiable appetite for novelty and titillation, amplified the Sixties' radical ethos. What was debased through commodification was simultaneously popularized through mass dissemination. Activists may have been few, but their message permeated youth culture and popular culture more generally, cultivating a latent sympathy that might, under the right circumstances, morph into a significant political force (Steigerwald 1995, 183). However, this response was not universal. In both Canada and the United States, the Sixties' radical challenges created a rift in the political mainstream. While those of a youthful or progressive disposition responded with a willingness to redress social ills through reform, others, concerned for public morality and social order, hunkered down in defence of the status quo (Anderson 1975, 120–125).

In the early months of 1968, this split was exacerbated by a series of traumatic events. The first came in January with the Tet Offensive in Vietnam, which brought American military invincibility into question and spurred the anti-war movement to greater heights in the United States and around the world. The second was the assassination of Martin Luther King Jr. on 4 April. Inner-city ghettoes immediately erupted in rioting, looting, and arson. The hope extinguished by this base act left many despairing bleakly that America was beyond redemption. The third seismic event was the Paris Spring. Student demonstrations beset cities around the world that year, but in May, student unrest in Paris led to clashes with police, which sparked days of street fighting that eventually escalated into a general strike that paralyzed the nation. It was a spectacular conflagration that came close to overthrowing the government, prompting citizens of other liberal democracies to question whether civilization as they knew it was in peril. One after another, these developments sent shock waves through an already agitated civic discourse.

In some ways, Robert Kennedy was an unlikely candidate to lead a liberal redemption of America. He was the third of four Kennedy boys groomed for careers in public life by their father, Joseph Kennedy, a rich and influential Democrat. Early in his career, Bobby had earned a reputation as a fearsome Cold Warrior. His resume was blotted by a stint hunting Reds as a junior staffer for Senator Joseph McCarthy in the early 1950s. He went on to become Assistant Counsel to the Senate Rackets Committee, where he crusaded against corruption, prosecuting Jimmy Hoffa of the Teamsters union in a relentless campaign that some saw as a vendetta against labour in general. As the campaign chair for his brother John's 1960 presidential bid, he was, depending on whose side you were on, either a highly effective organizer or a ruthless manipulator. Later, as Attorney General in his brother's cabinet, he continued the campaign against Hoffa. In that office, he also gave the FBI the go-ahead to tap Rev. Martin Luther King's phones (Tye 2016, 45–47, 82–83, 93–94, and 234–235).

Staggered and then depressed by his brother's assassination, RFK recovered sufficiently in 1964 to run successfully for the position of junior Senator from New York. He had been supportive of civil rights as a member of his brother's administration, but as a Senator he became more progressive on race issues, a rare white politician who listened and learned from leading Black activists. Kennedy also tackled the related issue of poverty, shining the national spotlight on impecunious Black sharecroppers, exploited migrant agricultural labourers, the entrenched indigence of rural Appalachian communities, and the marginalization of Indigenous peoples (Tye 2016, 159, 348–364, 346, 394; Schmitt 2009, 371–400).

By 1967, Kennedy feared that a set of intertwined, intractable antagonisms—rich against poor, whites against Blacks, hawks against doves—was ripping apart the American body politic. He watched in dismay as his older brother's replacement, President Lyndon Johnson, doubled down on a bankrupt war policy. RFK had been trying to be a loyal Democrat and put off a bid for the Democratic nomination until 1972 when Johnson would have served out his second term. Yet now America desperately needed a redemptive intervention, and he appeared to be the best available prospect for winning power and initiating progressive reform. Kennedy was in a quandary. As a placard that greeted him at Brooklyn College in January of 1968 put it: "Bobby Kennedy: Hawk, Dove, or Chicken?" (Schlesinger 1978, 836).

Then came the Tet Offensive of January 1968. The North Vietnamese Army and the Viet Cong attacked major cities in South Vietnam, surprising their defenders. The communists were supposed to be fighting a guerilla war in the jungle, not overrunning military strongholds of the world's superpower. Dramatic television footage showed the invaders inside the American embassy compound in Saigon. Though the offensive was repelled and was, in military terms, a defeat for the communist forces, it proved for them a great propaganda victory because it changed American public opinion about whether the war could be won (Halberstam 1968, 63). The split in the American body politic yawned wider, with political consequences that were soon manifest. Senator Eugene McCarthy, running on an anti-war platform, astounded everyone by almost defeating the incumbent president in the New Hampshire Democratic primary in March. Kennedy realized that he had misjudged the situation. This was the moment—he had to run.

After 16 March, when Kennedy announced his candidacy for the Democratic nomination, both Canada and the United States had celebrity politicians contesting the nation's highest office. Pierre Elliott Trudeau had emerged as a candidate for the leadership of the Liberal Party of Canada (and, by extension, the prime ministership, since the Liberals were in power) the previous December. Canada was facing a national unity crisis of its own. Quebec, the home province of most French Canadians and the only province where they were a majority, was agitating for a better deal in Confederation. With the Quiet Revolution of the early 1960s, Québécois had begun to modernize their provincial administration, retooling it as a quasi-national state that would spearhead economic development and extend social services while protecting French-Canadian culture. Nationalism was the dominant creed of the political class, with nationalists split between moderates who were comfortable with a stronger Quebec within the Canadian federation and separatists who saw an independent Quebec as the necessary vehicle of national self-determination. The latter school of thought included a radical terrorist fringe that had been bombing establishment targets in Montreal since 1963. By late 1967, the Quebec issue was constantly in the headlines, confronting Canadians with the frightening prospect that their country might break up. The conventional wisdom of political elites became that the federal government would have to negotiate a new constitutional deal with Quebec's moderate nationalists that would give the province special status in order to undermine the appeal of separatism (Litt 2016, 130, 137–140).

The Pierre Trudeau of 1967 had a long way to go to achieve the celebrity status of a Kennedy.[6] Early in the decade, he was virtually unknown in English Canada, despite having been a long-time activist and commentator on Quebec politics. Elected to the House of Commons in 1965 and mentored by Liberal Prime Minister Lester B. Pearson, Trudeau became a parliamentary secretary in 1966, then, in the spring of 1967, Minister of Justice, a position in which his star ascended still faster. He attracted notice for his principled defence of Canadian federalism and his articulate disdain for concessions that would appease Québécois nationalism at the cost of constitutional symmetry. Given this hardline approach, Trudeau might have come off as a reactionary, but all of this was offset by his fancy, jet-set, bachelor lifestyle, which gave him a

---

6. Early scholarly critiques of celebrity in politics decried it as a triumph of style over substance and bemoaned celebrities' unpreparedness for the art of statecraft. A subsequent wave of scholarship accepted celebrity as a fact of modern political life and focused instead on how it is produced and used. For an introductory overview of this literature, see "Celebrity Politics in an Era of Late Modernity," the first chapter in Wheeler (2013). In the cases of Kennedy and Trudeau, both accomplished and experienced politicians by the winter of 1968, the original complaint does not apply.

youthful image, and by his public commitment to the liberalization of divorce, abortion, and homosexuality laws. This legislative program of moral deregulation consolidated his image as a politician uniquely in step with the times.

When Prime Minister Lester Pearson announced his retirement in December 1967 and a Liberal leadership convention was scheduled for early April 1968, Party insiders and pundits who were uninspired by the regular suspects launched an extra-partisan "draft Trudeau" campaign. In the early winter of 1968, Trudeau enjoyed extensive favourable national media coverage, including numerous interviews on network news and public affairs shows, positive notices by influential columnists, and fawning profiles, despite not being a declared candidate. The media shone its spotlight on the dark horse, suggesting that the odds were against him even as they skewed the odds in his favour.

As he toured Canada on government business, Trudeau began to attract crowds curious to see him. By the time he declared himself a candidate in mid-February, he was the favourite to win the leadership. As he criss-crossed the country to woo Liberal leadership convention delegates, the crowds that greeted him grew large and rambunctious. The term "Trudeaumania," invoking "Beatlemania," was coined by right-wing columnist Lubor Zink to describe the phenomenon (Zink 1968). While the intention was to ridicule Trudeau and his supporters, the jibe backfired as Trudeau's fans joyfully embraced it. Naming the phenomenon made it a thing. Trudeau's burgeoning popularity was just enough to push him over the top at the Liberal leadership vote on 6 April.

Immediately after announcing his candidacy for the Democratic nomination, Bobby Kennedy launched a frenetic campaign. He first concentrated his attention on Indiana, the location of the next Democratic primary. On 4 April, he was heading into a Black neighbourhood in Indianapolis for a rally when news reached him that King had been assassinated. Kennedy decided to continue on to the event, where he delivered an impromptu, heartfelt address. Mentioning the loss of his brother, he asked his listeners to reject revenge and dedicate themselves instead to constructive change to redeem America (Tye 2016, 411).[7] Indianapolis was one of the few major American cities spared racial rioting in the wake of King's death. Five days later, Kennedy attended King's funeral, marching with the mourners from the church to the cemetery.

In April 1968, Simon and Garfunkel released the album *Bookends*, which included the hit song "Mrs. Robinson." Its final lines famously called on Joe DiMaggio, a hero symbolic of simpler times, for deliverance from the dislocation and bewilderment induced by the overwhelming social convulsions of the

---

7. In the nomination speeches at the Liberal convention in early April, Trudeau was the only leadership candidate to mention King's assassination the day before.

era.[8] Joe was by then beyond hailing distance, but in his place were Bobby and Pierre. The romantic spectre of John Fitzgerald Kennedy enwreathed them both. Many Americans rued nostalgically the promise denied by the assassination of their dynamic young president. Canadians had watched the myth of Camelot unfold from the sidelines, envying the JFK presidency's glamour, and hoping they too might one day have a leader like him. RFK naturally inherited his brother's mantle, whereas PET was the Kennedy that Canadians had always wanted but never dreamed they would get.[9]

Both candidates were youthful—an eminently desirable attribute in the Sixties. Both grew their hair a little long as a gesture of solidarity with the younger generation. A closely related attribute was sexiness. Although the early Sixties had given rise to the sexual revolution, in 1968 second-wave feminism, with its challenge to male dominance and traditional gender roles, was still in its infancy. The construction of the potential national patriarch as a sex symbol was relatively uncontested in this interval. Pierre was a bachelor playboy, whereas Bobby was the father of ten children (with another on the way). Young women with connections wangled positions on their campaign teams. Those who were not so fortunate strove for a momentary encounter. One chronicler of Kennedy's campaign noted that he often "was surrounded by teenage girls in Day-Glo toreador pants emitting 'Beatle' squeals." He then listed various other ways in which the fan response to him reflected either sexual arousal or something very much like it.[10] Trudeau enjoyed similar adulation. Young women seeking a kiss from Trudeau, and getting it, was a signature of his campaign. "When young girls with long hair

---

8. "Mrs. Robinson" had been part of the soundtrack of the feature film *The Graduate*, which was released the previous year. Its lament for a Joe DiMaggio can be heard at https://www.youtube.com/watch?v=9C1BCAgu2I8.

9. For more background on Canadians' yearning for a Kennedy, see Cook (1969) and Clarkson and McCall (1990, 97). It is interesting to note, too, that Trudeau, like the Kennedys, had inherited wealth, which raises the question of whether this was a significant attribute they had in common because it gave them the freedom to engage in politics in a relatively disinterested fashion, because it set them above the common throng, signalling exceptionality, because the wealthy were glamorous and/or aspirational figures—or some combination of these factors. This attribute is considered below in an analysis that contemplates all of these factors but places particular weight on their significance as symbols of upward social mobility.

10. Thurston Clarke argues that the Kennedy campaign was suffused with a sexual energy that aroused both fans and celebrity alike (Clarke 2008, 212). The word orgasm was used to describe fan responses in both campaigns (Clarke 2008, 212; Peacock 1968, 259). Its deployment, though enabled by the sexual revolution's liberalization of discourse on sex, was still quite risqué for the times, and represented commentators' attempts to find appropriate words to describe the atavistic potency of the rapture they were observing.

and short skirts elbow one another to get close enough to the Canadian Prime Minister to touch him and, preferably, to kiss him, that is a phenomenon," marvelled one national political journalist (Bain 1968). "The whole country needs a cold shower," concluded a reader writing in to a national magazine (Letter 1968).

An attractive image was one prerequisite of political success. An ingratiating performance was another (Street 2003). In 1968, a progressive candidate needed to take to the streets to signal solidarity with the people. Kennedy's campaign appearances featured motorcades in which he stood in the back of a convertible, waving to crowds. The one in Indiana on 6 May, the day before that state's primary, went on all day, weaving through three steel towns, from suburb to downtown to suburb, then onward to the next city. People turned out all the way along, lining the streets for mile after mile (Witcover 1969, 173–176). As the throngs closed in on him, arms reaching out to make contact, all Kennedy could do in response was hold out his hands, bouncing them from one outstretched hand to the next like he was dragging them along a picket fence.

North of the border, Trudeau dissolved Parliament and called a national election in late April. The Liberals planned their campaign to take full advantage of Trudeau's flowering celebrity. Like Kennedy, Trudeau flew into a city where he would leave the airport in a motorcade, waving from a convertible en route to a rally where a crowd was waiting for him.[11] There he would mingle, slowly making his way through the surging, adoring multitude. When he took the stage, a phalanx of arms bristled upwards from below. The crowds grew in size and intensity in the weeks leading up to election day on 25 June: 10,000 in Victoria, 12,500 in Vancouver, 40,000 in Toronto, and 35,000 in Montreal. Canadians fixated on a national phenomenon the likes of which they had never seen before: a relative political newcomer rocketing to fame and being mobbed by hordes of excited supporters.

When Kennedy campaigned in California in late May and early June, wild crowd scenes were the norm in one urban centre after another. His advance

---

11. The similarities between the two campaigns prompted fears north of the border that Canadian electioneering was becoming Americanized. See, for instance, *La Presse* (1968); Zolf (1968). There was, though, no direct American influence on Trudeau's campaign in the form of backroom Democratic talent imported to advise the Liberals. The Pearson Liberals had brought in JFK presidential pollster Lou Harris as a consultant in 1961. They kept him under wraps, however, fearing that any indication of outside interference in Canada's domestic politics by the superpower next door could unleash Canadian paranoia about Americanization (English 1992, 234–235). Trudeau, for his part, had no interest in drawing upon U.S. expertise, and by the late 1960s America's growing image problems would have greatly heightened the risk of doing so (email communication to the author from John English, 17 January 2019).

team set up rallies in inner-city neighbourhoods where Black and Hispanic people turned out in droves to demonstrate their support. Knowlton Nash, covering the campaign for the Canadian Broadcasting Corporation, believed that the crowds Kennedy was generating were unprecedented in U.S. political history (CBC Television National News Library 1968). Was it something about the times? The candidate tried to explain it in political terms, telling Nash, "People are concerned about the poverty, the violence, and Vietnam." But Kennedy added, "Others have seen your picture on the cover of magazines and think it's a lark" (CBC Television Newsworld 1968).

What did these two candidates offer to their supporters to generate such enthusiasm? They were both liberals in the contemporary sense of the term. They supported a capitalist economy based on competitive individualism balanced by government social programs to ensure equality of opportunity. But such thinking was centrist at the time and did not distinguish them from the pack. Their more significant similarity was that they promised national deliverance in parlous times. Trudeau mused publicly about participatory democracy and declared that Canada must be a "just society," acknowledging the legitimacy of contemporary dissent and promising to accommodate it through official channels. Meanwhile, his principled opposition to the idea of special constitutional status for Quebec was music to the ears of English Canadians. He had arrived on the scene at a critical juncture when national unity was in peril and, with admirable sangfroid, promised to keep the body politic whole. Kennedy offered much the same. Rather than playing the politics of division, he was the only viable presidential candidate who called out the issues of race, poverty, and war that were tearing the United States apart. He tackled them head-on, challenging Americans to heal their nation by drawing on their shared values of fairness and generosity. Both candidates pointed towards the potential of the nation when unified, invoking a bright future as inspiration for resolving present challenges.[12]

---

12. John Hutchinson has written about how saving the nation by remaking it in pursuit of a higher meaning and purpose is a common feature of nationalist movements. See Hutchinson (1994, 122–131). Moral rebirth is also a defining characteristic of religious revivals. Although the iconoclastic spirit of the Sixties rejected traditional Christian worship, it featured a spiritual questing that has prompted some scholars of religion to call it a modern "Great Awakening" (Ahlstrom 1980, 510–511; McLoughlin 1978, 179–216). The venerable North American tradition of revival meetings, at which charismatic religious leaders inspire their followers by revealing the path to salvation, was still very much alive in the postwar period. The new electronic media had given rise to figures like Billy Graham, a thoroughly modern televangelist whose popular religious crusades won him millions of devoted adherents. A recent study observed that "In every culture and every historical period, the way to arrest a decline from a mythical

In May, just as Kennedy's and Trudeau's campaigns were hitting full stride, university student protests in Paris spiralled out of control. Violent police repression of the protesters mobilized progressives who joined the students in the streets, clashing with gendarmes in pitched battles. Televised scenes of police brutality won the protesters still more sympathy and further reinforced their ranks. On Monday, 13 May, more than a million people marched through the capital. Workers across the country joined in, occupying factories, until about two-thirds of the total national workforce, some ten million people, were on strike by late May. There were fears that the communists would use the unrest as a springboard to revolution. When President de Gaulle unexpectedly left the country for two days, the government was visibly shaken, and at one point, it looked to be collapsing. Things began to calm down later in the month, when Prime Minister Georges Pompidou orchestrated a dissolution of the National Assembly, bringing on a national election. These events, widely publicized as they unfolded throughout May, suggested that one possible outcome of Sixties liberations was anarchy.

Trudeau's and Kennedy's rallies seethed with the anarchic potential of masses of humanity. Kennedy sometimes had to beg his supporters to back off because children were in danger of being crushed.[13] During motorcades, a Kennedy aide, a former college football player and FBI agent, crouched beside him, arms wrapped around his legs, to keep him from being pulled over (Witcover 1969, 113). Even so, he was often yanked off his feet. In Mishawaka, Indiana, a woman tackled him off the back of the convertible. He tumbled against the curb, chipping a tooth and getting a fat lip (Clarke 2008, 212; Witcover 1969, 173). Trudeau's crowds were generally better behaved, but often they too pressed in, pinning the candidate, requiring his handlers to pry him out of the crush. In Edmonton, thousands gathered at City Hall to see Trudeau presented by the mayor with a Klondike hat and a cane. As he left, the crowd rushed him. At first police managed to hold people off, but as he tried to gain his car, the throng closed in, pushing and shoving to get at him. Two of his aides were thrown against the car as Trudeau barely squeezed in the door

---

golden age is always the same: rededication to the values and restoration of the practices that were present in the golden age. This was exactly Graham's timeless prescription" (Finstuen, Wills, and Wacker 2017, 178). Note too that Graham and his ilk practiced the "reel-to-real synthesis" mentioned above (note 4). These parallels explain the common journalistic trope of comparing election rallies to evangelical revivals. The relationship between spiritual and sexual transport at such events (note 10) is fascinating to contemplate.

13. As the multitude pressed in at one Los Angeles rally, a baby was torn from the arms of its mother and went airborne. Apparently, it was caught by a press photographer (Harwood 1988).

(Fairburn 1968; *Edmonton Journal 1968*).[14] A couple of days later, in Toronto, Trudeau emerged from a meeting into a waiting mob that immediately swept him away from his handlers. In both campaigns, the crowds reeled and lurched with powerful, random menace.

Danger lurked in another way as well. With King's death, the ever-present possibility of assassination escalated. Both candidates received death threats yet refused to prioritize security if it limited their contact with voters. "I've got to give the people who love me a chance to get at me" Kennedy explained (Witcover 1969, 119, 147). Ignoring anonymous threats on his life, Trudeau accepted an invitation to attend the Saint-Jean-Baptiste parade in Montreal on election eve. Separatist protestors confronted police and a full-scale riot ensued, with projectiles flying at Trudeau in the reviewing stand. He held his ground (Sullivan 1968, 12).

Kennedy was already famous when his campaign started. Trudeau came out of nowhere. His rise had a fairy-tale quality that captured the imagination. Along the way he became a pop culture icon in a way that Kennedy did not. If you could not make it to a Trudeau rally, Trudeau-themed cultural goods, rendered in peak-Sixties mod style, offered other ways to embrace the candidate. Posters of the great man adorned university dormitory walls to celebrate his appeal in a personal, intimate context and were plastered in public spaces to proclaim his political relevance. Fashion designers marketed the "Trudeau look." Trendsetters styled their hair like his. Trudeau tumblers and ashtrays adorned the shelves of souvenir shops. Trudeau-inspired pop tunes made the Canadian hit parade that spring. There were Trudeau ties, sweatshirts with his image proclaiming slogans like "Go Go Trudeau" or "Justice Will Triumph," cotton prints with his image on them made into ponchos, pillowcases, and dresses. In 1968, paper dresses were in vogue, and political campaigns generated versions of the ephemeral garb sporting their candidates' images to generate publicity. Every campaign staged photo ops of women dressed in the candidate's image, but the gimmick worked better for Trudeau than others, catching on enough that pictures of women wearing Pierre appeared frequently in the media (Litt 2016, 256–261). The Kennedy campaign deployed all the usual campaign ephemera: ads, buttons, posters—even a psychedelic poster of RFK—but it did not generate Trudeaumania's combustive synergy of politics and mod fashion. Kennedy was a Kennedy, but Trudeau was a fad.

In this regard, it is interesting to note that by declaring himself an anti-war candidate for the Democratic nomination while Kennedy dithered, McCarthy had won over educated middle- and upper-class liberals, including fervently anti-war students. They could have been Kennedy supporters, but they subsequently stuck with McCarthy (Halberstam 1968, 9). Kennedy's initial appeal

---

14. The crowd was estimated variously as 3,000 and 5,000.

included his opposition to Johnson's war policy, but in a move unprecedented for a sitting president, Lyndon Johnson announced at the end of March that he had decided not to run for re-election rather than risk splitting his party over the war issue. His war on poverty in the United States had been undone by his war on the spectre of communism abroad. Kennedy's campaign then had to shift, as the war was no longer the defining electoral issue. He increasingly depended on a coalition of white and minority working-class voters, while simultaneously hoping to win back some of his lost white-collar supporters by demonstrating that he was the only reform candidate with a real shot at the presidency (Kahlenberg 2018). It was hard slogging. Despite his celebrity, he had to battle for each of his primary victories and came up short in Oregon in late May. His campaign was not the triumphal progress that Trudeau enjoyed. He was running hard and running from behind. The stakes were immense. Kennedy was engaged in a desperate, agonizing crusade.

In contrast, Trudeaumania was a bit of a romp—triumphal progress animated by an ironic, self-aware spirit of fun. Unlike Kennedy's base, Trudeau's most fervent fans came from the educated, urban, upwardly mobile middle class who wanted to see Canada move ahead to embrace the bright future they expected for themselves. Trudeau's privileged supporters identified more with the community of nation than their rural or working-class compatriots who, in contrast, clung more tightly to allegiances traditional, local, and ethnic (Meisel 1975, 38; Liberal Party of Canada fonds 1968).[15] Surfing a cresting wave of Canadian nationalism, they embraced him, a cosmopolitan sophisticate with a liberated lifestyle, as an appropriate personification of their new Canada. This group included the cultural producers who proved so effective in promoting Trudeau. Not just journalists, but cartoonists, artists, musicians, advertising creative directors, fashion designers and the like put their talents to work, adeptly associating Trudeau with the Sixties ethos.[16] Hence the mod fashions, the kitsch and the posters, the tunes, and the cartoons. Energized by the buzz of the chattering classes, Trudeau's rise was not just farther and faster, it was more of a cultural phenomenon than Kennedy's.

It had to be. If the forces of progressive reform were to prevail, they had to coalesce around one candidate and hype him as the only hope for change. Kennedy, as a Kennedy, came to the fray already eminently electable. Canadians

---

15. Ontario was a bit of an exception; larger numbers of the upper class and the better educated supported the Conservatives there.
16. Pierre Bourdieu characterized the "new petite bourgeoisie" as consisting of "all the occupations involving presentation and representation." He included "'the cultural intermediaries' of advertising, journalism, marketing, public relations and the modern—or rather, postmodern—media and culture generally" (Bourdieu 1984, 359).

didn't have a Kennedy so they had to manufacture one of their own. Endowing Trudeau with such celebrity capital involved a lot of cultural work.[17] Fortunately, the ground was prepared by opinion-makers who had already been cultivating a progressive new Canadian identity. Trudeaumania was Sixties reformist liberalism turbocharged by cultural nationalism. As was their wont, Canadian nationalists demonstrated their difference from the United States in a decidedly American fashion.[18]

Both Trudeau and Kennedy were controversial figures who provoked strong reactions, pro and con. The lines along which support for them coalesced differed slightly, however. While Trudeau was the darling of the progressives, he was deeply distrusted by those who were out of step with the modern world and bewildered by its recent gyrations (Litt 2016, 315–320). As his popularity grew, disaffected reactionaries launched a smear campaign that portrayed him as a communist and a homosexual. The allegations first appeared in mid-winter and circulated in obscure newsletters and other marginal media with growing intensity during the federal election campaign in May and June. They confirmed the worst suspicions of those put off by Trudeau's trendy image, and it cost the Liberals votes, mostly in rural areas, and particularly in Quebec (Litt 2016, 197–204). Kennedy inspired antipathy for different reasons. Opponents on the left saw him as a ruthless opportunist who had jumped into the race after McCarthy did the initial heavy lifting, a late-to-the-party progressive with a retrograde past (Tye 2016, 93–94). Business leaders detested him for promising to tax the rich to feed the poor and portrayed him as a dangerous demagogue whose populist campaign was emboldening the underclasses and encouraging anarchy in the streets. In regard to the central rift between reformers and reactionaries, however, both Kennedy and Trudeau came down squarely on the side of progressive reform. They were not radicals advocating systemic change, but rather willing negotiators who believed that common sense had to be liberalized and concessions made if the system was to survive.[19]

Indeed, far from threatening the status quo, both Trudeau and Kennedy were poster boys for it. A significant component of contemporary unrest in both countries stemmed from a large minority group's determination to liberate itself from subjugation. If the issue was analyzed in Marxist terms (as

---

17. Street (2002) identifies two basic types of celebrities. Some, like Robert Kennedy, are born into celebrity as members of a famous family. Others, like Trudeau, become celebrities through their "charismatic public performances" (437).
18. For other examples of this phenomenon, see Litt (1992, 288, n5); Litt (1991, 384); and Brison (2005, 6). See also Cain (2019, chap. 5).
19. This is a classic feature of ideological hegemony as theorized by Antonio Gramsci (1971). The ruling order negotiates with subaltern groups and makes concessions to their interests, but the essential underpinnings of the political economy are never on the table.

"ethnic proletarianization"), the obvious remedy, as was evident in postwar decolonization movements around the world, was national liberation.[20] This collectivist solution informed both Quebec separatism and Black nationalism in the U.S. (even though lack of access to an ancestral homeland bedevilled the latter). In contrast, the celebrity campaigns of Trudeau and Kennedy showcased individual exemplars of upward social mobility. Granted, neither had made it on their own, Horatio Alger–like. In both cases, their parents had started from solid (if modest) socio-economic family platforms and built fortunes that had given their sons privileged upbringings. Nevertheless, the end product represented how members of an oppressed minority—Irish in Kennedy's case, French Canadian in Trudeau's—could realize the American Dream.[21] They were inspiring examples to be emulated. The message was that the system was essentially sound, it only needed some tweaking to ensure access so that anyone who was willing to work hard to improve themselves would be rewarded.

In this sense at least, Kennedy and Trudeau were men of the people. They leveraged this perception by appealing to voters in the spirit of participatory democracy. Both had a shot at power but would need the support of the people to get there. Bobby Kennedy was up against the Democratic Party machine, which Johnson had redirected in support of the candidacy of his vice-president, Hubert Humphrey. Trudeau joined the race for the Liberal leadership as a media darling, but with no significant base in a party in which his rivals had been organizing delegate support for years. They each had to convince their party to switch to them, and the only way to do that was to demonstrate to leadership convention delegates that they were the party's best chance to win the upcoming election. Mobilizing popular support and demonstrating that support through the mass media did an end run around machine politics, local bosses, and established client–patron relationships. By railing against the establishment—at least in the limited sense of the party establishment—they exhibited some affinity with the radicalism of the Sixties.

The uphill battle facing them also gave their supporters a meaningful role in the drama. In mass democracies, most voters follow national politics at a distance, engaging directly with it only sporadically. However, in the troubled context of 1968, any voter with a sense of civic obligation felt compelled to do something to help out. But what exactly could they do? The answer came in the form of a live appearance from a celebrity politician who promised to

---

20. Radical separatist Pierre Vallières's manifesto *Nègres blancs d'Amérique* (1968) equated French Canadians' condition in Canada with that of Black people in the U.S.

21. The distinction here, or course, was that Trudeau was a member of the minority currently aggrieved, whereas Kennedy was not, even though he was recognized by Black people as a rare white politician who was truly sympathetic to their plight.

cure all of the nation's ills. Turning out to express support enthusiastically was a convenient way to discharge one's civic obligations, "takin' it to the streets" in the fashion of the day.

These celebrity politicians' campaigns offered a simple solution to complex, intractable problems that confounded the average voter. Both Trudeau and Kennedy promised to rescue their nation from crisis and lead it to the promised land. It was expedient to cheer them on. The commitment was modest, the potential payoff high. Their rallies fell somewhere in between Tupperware party and riot, with the candidate as a panacea: an off-the-shelf, all-purpose, one-stop-shopping solution to the demands that civic life had imposed on the busy modern citizen.[22] Maximum crisis resolution for a modest outlay was too good a deal to pass up. It was bargain day in the local political marketplace, and the hordes converged.

Turning out for Bobby or Pierre also quieted anxieties about the mediated nature of national politics. The celebrity politician's fans engaged tangibly with an otherwise frustratingly impalpable national community by seeing one of its principal actors live in the flesh. The need to make it real was evident in the souvenir hunting that harried both candidates. Trudeau was kissed incessantly, lost his watch and the odd hair to an overenthusiastic fan, and had the lapel of his jacket ripped by someone trying to swipe his boutonniere. Kennedy lost his watch, jacket, shoes (more than once), even socks. Their fans wanted proof of contact with the exalted figure. As they gazed on, screamed at, grabbed and smooched, or stole a souvenir from him, the abstract nature of national life was reified.[23]

This engagement in civic affairs, however fleeting, engendered feelings of agency and catharsis. Swept up in the crowd, fans experienced emotions of

---

22. In light of the earlier discussion of the affinities between evangelical and election rallies, it is interesting to note that in North America religion was also deeply integrated with commercial culture. See Moore (1994, 256). For Moore, the mass media were critical agents in a commercialization of religion that extended back at least as far as the revivalism of the early nineteenth century.

23. John Thompson argues that being a fan, whether of a sports team, a performing artist, or a politician, provides an "intimacy with distant others" that is a defining and necessary characteristic of life in modern mass society (Thompson 1995, 220). According to Paolo Mancini and David Swanson, as modernity breaks down traditional familial and local relationships, celebrity is one of the new "symbolic realities" that develop to take their place (Mancini and Swanson 1996, 1–28). These points are consistent with Benedict Anderson's concept of the nation as an imagined community and suggest that celebrity is integral to such communities because it humanizes an otherwise alienating modernity. The imagined community (McLuhan's "global village" on a national scale) is imagined as a virtual premodern village populated by celebrities, a form and size of community readily comprehensible to the ordinary citizen.

solidarity, loyalty, and collective power, enacting the nation in microcosm. They knew what was expected of them because they had seen earlier episodes on TV, and the significance of it all was confirmed by ongoing media coverage. At each stop, television crews recorded the action to play it back to the mass audience, stitching one community after another into the national fabric and embroidering a plot line that pointed upwards toward a glorious climax. The suspense continued as the serial drama unfolded in successive daily episodes throughout the spring of 1968.[24]

This chapter began with the observation that three major shocks rocked an already turbulent world in the first half of 1968. Bobby Kennedy's assassination on 5 June was another. Thereafter, the Kennedy factor was raw and nationalized: Canadians had a Kennedy and Americans did not.[25] The United States ended up electing Republican Richard Nixon in the ensuing presidential election. When Trudeau won a majority government, the two countries seemed headed in very different directions.

Political narratives of the United States and Canada see 1968 as a pivotal moment that generated trends that characterized each nation's politics for decades. Whereas Johnson's Great Society programs of the Sixties emphasized economic equality, Nixon's victory ushered in a right-wing moment in which elite economic interests were masked and facilitated by playing on popular prejudices and resentments, portraying government as a threat to freedom, and using dog-whistle racist and macho appeals to set poor white people against poor minorities and obscure their shared economic interests. The Republicans blamed any and all economic woes on big government and undermined the Democrats' narrative of progress towards social justice by demonizing them as feather-nesting, unpatriotic, soft-on-crime, tax-and-spend liberals. Fear of this caricature eventually led Democrats to work within rather than challenge the emergent neo-liberal orthodoxy. They expressed progressive credentials instead through an identity politics that, however noble and just, tended to fragment their constituency into disparate contending interests, thereby playing into the Republican divide-and-conquer electoral strategy. This scenario still has resonance in U.S. party politics today. In this sense "it's never stopped being 1968."[26]

In contrast, the liberal reformer won and stayed in power for most of the subsequent 16 years in Canada. Trudeau's promises of participatory democracy

---

24. Sociologist Victor Turner developed the concept of "social drama" to describe the way in which societies work through problems in ways that seem to imitate art. See Bell (2008, 87–92, 105–110). Leadership campaigns and general elections have customary stages with which the public is familiar, providing greater than usual structure for the unfolding plot.

25. In the documentary *Just Watch Me: Trudeau and the 70's Generation* (Annau 1999), one interviewee remarks that "Trudeau was our Kennedy that didn't get shot."

26. This phrase is the title of the concluding chapter of Cohen (2016).

and a Just Society came just after major components of the modern Canadian welfare state, including medicare, were put in place. His election symbolized that Canada was now a more progressive society than the United States, offering Canadians a new way to define their national identity. The political events of 1968 exemplified and reinforced the myth of Canada as a Peaceable Kingdom in tune with the Sixties' values of peace and love.

Yet this narrative of divergence conceals an underlying similarity. Although Canada, channelling its new identity, was initially resistant to neo-liberalism, in the long term it was inexorably driven by economic logic towards policy harmonization with its trading partners. In time its politics came to be dominated by the right-wing agenda of trade liberalization, monetarism, deregulation, and debt reduction. No major new social programs would be introduced in Canada after 1968, and by the new millennium many of the signature pieces of the Peaceable Kingdom getup were threadbare.[27] On the other hand, the

---

27. Arguably Canadians' self-satisfaction with their supposed moral superiority to the United States has instilled a complacency that has impeded further reform. In this regard it is interesting to consider the chequered legacy of the Sixties in the two countries. The decade's assault on traditional morality had enduring effects. As social mores liberalized, the state retreated from moral regulation of matters such as sex, recreational drug use, or reproduction, ceding them to the private purview of the individual or family. Environmentalism enjoyed some success in raising public consciousness and generating laws to regulate pollution and development processes. Meanwhile, Sixties movements against discrimination on the basis of race, gender, sexual orientation, and other personal characteristics grew in strength and influence in ensuing decades. This "identity politics" made public attitudes and government policies more accommodating of diversity. Progress on these fronts created the impression that the legacy of the decade was vital and salutary. Thanks to the Sixties, people today seem freer to do what they want and be who they are. On issues such as these Canada has consistently maintained its identity differentiation by liberalizing ahead of the U.S. The recognition of same-sex marriage and the legalization of marijuana are recent examples.

In other areas, however, significant enduring effects of the Sixties are difficult to discern. The anti-nuke and anti–Vietnam War movements enjoyed some short-term success, but in the long term neither the arms race nor America's proclivity towards military adventures abroad were substantially diminished, and Canada remained more or less its loyal junior partner in international affairs. To the dismay of the radical left, in both countries the political system retained its legitimacy and capitalism emerged from the decade unscathed. Indeed, the progressive agenda of the Sixties incited a neo-liberal counteroffensive that stopped welfare-state formation dead in its tracks.

Why did some Sixties causes thrive while others stagnated? Those that were most successful presented no threat to the system and could be accommodated easily within the liberal capitalist political economy. Lifestyle liberation enabled by moral deregulation was entirely consistent with the liberal conception of society

United States was never quite as mean and lean as Canadian nationalist imaginings made it out to be. The Republican ascendancy may have halted the growth of the welfare state, but it did not dismantle it. Identity myths aside, the legacy of 1968 was a flash-freezing of the agenda of twentieth-century liberalism that left Canada just slightly to the left of the United States.

It is an engaging counterfactual exercise to contemplate what the current political scene would look like if the outcomes of the Trudeau and Kennedy campaigns had been different. For students of Canadian nationalism, it is intriguing to consider how Canada would have differentiated itself from the U.S. had Bobby Kennedy lived, become president, and made America kinder and gentler. South of the border the retrospective gaze of the progressive-minded views his assassination as a cruel tragedy that left the nation to lose its way.[28] There are still hopes it will find its way back. Amidst Democrats' soul-searching following their embarrassing loss to Donald Trump in the 2016 presidential election, the colour-blind working-class coalition Kennedy was attempting to forge is being invoked as a way forward by which the Party can redeem its soul and recover its fortunes (Kahlenberg 2018). It will be interesting to see how that project goes. In the meantime, we need only point to the contrasting images of Donald Trump and Justin Trudeau to see how they are keeping up appearances.

References

Ahlstrom, Sydney E. 1980. "The Traumatic Years: American Religion and Culture in the '60s and '70s." *Theology Today* 38, no. 4 (January): 510–511.

Allen, Gene, and Daniel Robinson, eds. 2009. *Communicating in Canada's Past: Essays in Media History.* Toronto: University of Toronto Press.

Anderson, Terry. 1975. *The Sixties.* New York: Pearson Longman.

---

as a collection of autonomous individuals, and consumer capitalism was happy to provide those individuals the things, services, and experiences they needed to fulfil themselves. Righteous battles against racism, sexism, homophobia, and other prejudices were harmless diversions as long as they did not entail any redistribution of wealth. The discursive work of the keyword "identity" was particularly useful in this regard. By investing group characteristics in the individual, it diverted attention from economic issues and minimized the danger of collective action on the basis of class interests. As suggested above, the legacy of the Sixties is Gramscian insofar as it unfolded hegemonically: in the ongoing negotiations of quotidian politics, concessions were continuous, but the fundamentals of the system were never on the table. The myth of the Peaceable Kingdom only made Canada more susceptible to and hypocritical about this process.

28. For an extended meditation on this theme, see Cohen (2016), particularly its concluding chapter. For differing analyses of the legacy of Trudeaumania, see Gwyn (1980, 71), Duffy (2002, 244), and Litt (2016, 335–338).

Annau, Catherine, dir. 1999. *Just Watch Me: Trudeau and the 70's Generation* [film]. Produced by Yves Basaillon and Gerry Flahive. Montreal: National Film Board of Canada.

Azzi, Stephen. 2012. "The Nationalist Movement in English Canada." *In Debating Dissent: Canada and the Sixties*, edited by Lara Campbell, Dominique Clément, and Gregory S. Kealey, 213–230. Toronto: University of Toronto Press.

Bain, George. 1968. "Canada Has a Case of Trudeaumania," *New York Times*, 16 June: SM10.

Bell, Elizabeth. 2008. *Theories of Performance*. London: Sage.

Bodroghkozy, Aniko. 2001. *Groove Tube: Sixties Television and the Youth Rebellion*. Durham, NC: Duke University Press.

Bourdieu, Pierre. 1984. *Distinction: A Social Critique of the Judgement of Taste*. Cambridge, MA: Harvard University Press.

Brison, Jeffrey. 2005. *Rockefeller, Carnegie, and Canada: American Philanthropy and the Arts and Letters in Canada*. Montreal and Kingston: McGill-Queen's University Press.

Cain, Matthew. 2019. "'What Shadows We Are, and What Shadows We Pursue': A Study of Edmund Burke's Influence on Canadian Political Culture." PhD diss., Carleton University.

CBC Archive Sales/Archives Radio-Canada. 1967. Twenty Million Questions, "The Young Contenders," 30 March.

CBC Television National News Library. 1968. Canadian Broadcasting Corporation records, no. 68 [Kennedy Campaign], 28 March, consultation copy, V18310-0100, Library and Archives Canada.

CBC Television Newsworld. 1968. Off-Air, Sense of History (re-broadcast of a *Newsmagazine* segment from 1968), Canadian Broadcasting Corporation records, ISN 284680, Library and Archives Canada.

Clarke, Thurston. 2008. *The Last Campaign: Robert F. Kennedy and 82 Days That Inspired America*. New York: Henry Holt.

Clarkson, Stephen, and Christina McCall. 1990. *Trudeau and Our Times*, Vol. 1, *The Magnificent Obsession*. Toronto: McClelland & Stewart.

Cohen, Michael A. 2016. *American Maelstrom: The 1968 Election and the Politics of Division*. New York: Oxford University Press.

Cook, Ramsay. 1969. "Of Instant Books and Instant Prime Ministers," *Tamarack Review* 49:64–80.

Davis, Aeron. 2010. *Political Communication and Social Theory*. London: Routledge.

Duffy, John. 2002. *Fights of Our Lives: Elections, Leadership, and the Making of Canada*. Toronto: Harper Collins.

Edmonton Journal. 1968. "Giggling Youngsters Mob PM." 13 May: 1.

English, John. 1992. *The Worldly Years: The Life of Lester Pearson*, Vol. II, 1949–1972. Toronto: Knopf.

Fairburn, Joyce. 1968. "Trudeau Big Draw at Edmonton Stop." *Winnipeg Free Press*, 13 May: 1.

Finstuen, Andrew, Anne Blue Wills, and Grant Wacker, eds. 2017. *Billy Graham: American Pilgrim*. New York: Oxford University Press.

Gramsci, Antonio. 1971. *Selections from the Prison Notebooks of Antonio Gramsci*, edited and translated by Quinton Hoar and Geoffrey Novell Smith. London: Lawrence and Wishart.

Gwyn, Richard. 1980. *The Northern Magus: Pierre Trudeau and Canadians*. Toronto: McClelland & Stewart.

Halberstam, David. 1968. *The Unfinished Odyssey of Robert Kennedy*. New York: Random House.

Harwood, Richard. 1988. "With Bobby Kennedy on That Last Campaign." *The Washington Post*, 5 June. Accessed 28 November 2020. https://www.washington-post.com/archive/opinions/1988/06/05/with-bobby-kennedy-on-that-last-campaign/cf20b8be-588d-4f63-924b-0d849b63eb0c/.

Hutchinson, John. 1994. "Cultural Nationalism and Moral Regeneration." In *Nationalism*, edited by John Hutchinson and Anthony Smith, 122–131. Oxford: Oxford University Press.

Kahlenberg, Richard. 2018. "The Inclusive Populism of Robert Kennedy." The Century Foundation, 16 March. https://tcf.org/content/report/inclusive-populism-robert-f-kennedy/?session=1.

Kurlansky, Mark. 2004. *1968: The Year That Rocked the World*. New York: Ballantyne Books.

La Presse. 1968. "Variations sur le thème 'Kennedy.'" 2 April: 4.

Letter to the editor. 1968. *Maclean's*, 1 July: 55.

Liberal Party of Canada fonds. 1968. A Survey of Voter Opinion in Canada – Research Services Ltd. R5727-2-5-E, vol. 1120, June, Library and Archives Canada.

Litt, Paul. 2016. *Trudeaumania*. Vancouver: University of British Columbia Press.

———. 1992. *The Muses, the Masses, and the Massey Commission*. Toronto: University of Toronto Press.

———. 1991. "The Massey Commission, Americanization, and Canadian Cultural Nationalism." *Queen's Quarterly* 98, no. 2 (Summer): 375–387.

Mancini, Paolo, and David Swanson. 1996. "Politics, Media, and Modern Democracy: Introduction." In *Politics, Media, and Modern Democracy*, edited by David Swanson and Paolo Mancini, 1–28. Westport, CT: Praeger.

Marshall, P. D. 1997. *Celebrity and Power: Fame in Contemporary Culture*. Minneapolis: University of Minnesota Press.

McLoughlin, William G. 1978. *Revivals, Awakenings, and Reform: An Essay on Religion and Social Change in America, 1607–1977*. Chicago: University of Chicago Press.

Meisel, John. 1975. *Working Papers on Canadian Politics*, 2nd cd. Montreal and Kingston: McGill-Queen's University Press.

Moore, Robert Laurence. 1994. *Selling God: American Religion in the Marketplace of Culture*. Oxford: Oxford University Press.

Peacock, Donald. 1968. *Journey to Power: The Story of a Canadian Election*. Toronto: Ryerson.

Schlesinger, Arthur M., Jr. 1978. *Robert Kennedy and His Times*. Boston: Houghton Mifflin.

Schmitt, Edward R. 2009. "The Appalachian Thread in the Antipoverty Politics of Robert F. Kennedy." *The Register of the Kentucky Historical Society* 107, no. 3 (Summer): 371–400.

Steigerwald, David. 1995. *The Sixties and the End of Modern America*. New York: St. Martin's Press.

Street, John. 2003. "The Celebrity Politician: Political Style and Popular Culture." In *Media and the Restyling of Politics*, edited by John Corner and Dick Pels, 85–98. London: Sage.

———. 2002. "Celebrity Politicians: Popular Culture and Political Representation." *British Journal of Politics and International Relations* 6, October: 435–452.

Sullivan, Martin. 1968. *Mandate '68: The Year of Pierre Trudeau*. Toronto: Doubleday.

Thompson, John. 1995. *The Media and Modernity: A Social Theory of the Media*. Cambridge, UK: Polity.

Tye, Larry. 2016. *Bobby Kennedy: The Making of a Liberal Icon*. New York: Random House.

Vallières, Pierre. 1968. *Nègres blancs d'Amérique*. Montreal: Éditions Parti pris.

Van Zoonen, Liesbet. 2005. *Entertaining the Citizen: When Politics and Popular Culture Converge*. Oxford: Rowman and Littlefield.

———. 2004. "Imagining Fan Democracy." *European Journal of Communication* 19, no. 1 (March): 39–52.

Wheeler, Mark. 2013. *Celebrity Politics: Image and Identity in Contemporary Political Communications*. Cambridge, UK: Polity.

Witcover, Jules. 1969. *85 Days: The Last Campaign of Robert Kennedy*. New York: G. P. Putnam's Sons.

Zink, Lubor. 1968. "Trudeaumania Seems to Be Fading on Parliament Hill." *Toronto Telegram*, 4 March.

Zolf, Larry. 1968. "Trudeau Ran for President—and Won." *Toronto Daily Star*, 26 June: B7.

Chapter 2
A Very Canadian Revolution: The Transformation of Backroom Power in Canada's 1968

P. E. BRYDEN

Abstract

Pierre Elliott Trudeau was the embodiment of Canada's 1960s: young, hip, and impatient with the status quo, he bounded onto the political scene with fresh ideas and an image to match. Voters in June 1968 embraced Trudeaumania. But behind the scenes, this chapter argues, Trudeau's personal mania was for administrative control, and he moved quickly to introduce a series of structural and institutional changes that would have a lasting effect on the Canadian political environment. In the summer of 1968, Trudeau fundamentally restructured cabinet governance and reorganized his own office into a much more powerful locus of partisan power. The balance of power between non-partisan advisors, who reported to the Privy Council Office, and partisan advisors within the Prime Minister's Office, began to shift in favour of the latter. It was a peculiarly Canadian revolution.

As historian Mark Kurlansky has written, 1968 was "the epicenter of a shift, of a fundamental change, the birth of our postmodern media-driven world" (Kurlansky 2005, 351). Fifty years on, it still seems that way: viewed through the rear-view mirror, when revolutions and cultural shifts and rights movements are all visible in the same frame, 1968 looks like the moment everything changed. And Canada was right there with the rest of the frenzied world, thanks in good part to the elevation of Pierre Elliott Trudeau into the Prime Minister's Office. "There's a new infatuation that's been sweepin' the nation," went the song, "Shakin' the roots in the ground; Of an old generation, a new inspiration; Takin' a new look around; But he's quickly disarming and utterly charming; Quite enough to make you let down your hair ... Regardez PM Pierre" (Allan Ryan, quoted in Litt 2008, 39).

They mobbed him, kissed him, and wrote songs about him—about a politician, of all things, and one who championed reason over passion, yet

Figure 2.1. Marc Lalonde: Trudeau's "SOB." *Source:* Antoine Desilets 1960–1970. Bibliothèque et Archives nationales du Québec, BAnQ Vieux-Montréal, 06M, P697, S1, SS1, SSS16, D60.

nevertheless inspired that selfsame passion. Pierre Elliott Trudeau was contradictory. To the public, he was the embodiment of Canada's 1960s: young, hip, and impatient with the status quo, he bounded onto the political scene with fresh ideas and an image to match. Voters in June 1968 were thrilled not only about the phenomenon of a modern prime minister, but also at what that said about Canada as it embarked on its second century. This new Canada was mature enough to be mod, and Trudeaumania was an essential manifestation of that coming of age.

The Trudeau phenomenon was more than just flash, however. Voters seemed to see in the former justice minister a solution to the genuine problems that were vexing the federation at its centennial. This bilingual Quebecker, a staunch federalist, would bring peace to the intergovernmental—and particularly to the interlingual—acrimony that had been growing over the previous decade. Trudeau's capacity to solve the Quebec problem was less recognized in Quebec, but even there, he attracted support. If Trudeaumania was about style, that style revolved around a modern approach to contemporary fissures in the federal system.

In both style and substance, Trudeau represented something new and in keeping with the spirit of the 1960s, a Canadian revolution along the same lines as those revolutions reverberating elsewhere around the world in 1968. But there was more to Trudeau's revolution than just image and essence; further behind the scenes, he redesigned the very shape of the state, making changes that would have far longer and far greater effects on the machinery of governance than any mere platform plank or publicity stunt could have. Far from the Trudeaumania of the streets, the new prime minister's personal mania was administrative control, the only way to impose his agenda on a government that had not seen a majority in the last three elections and was used to functioning somewhat messily. In the aftermath of his electoral victory in 1968, Trudeau moved quickly to introduce a series of structural and institutional changes that would have a lasting effect on the Canadian political environment.

In a concerted effort to avoid the sort of chaos that had mired previous governments in scandal and inaction (Gwyn 1965; Bryden 1997, 145–169), the Trudeau team began to reorganize the machinery of governance in such a way that there could be little opportunity for unravelling. The Trudeau revolution—the real one, not the one for show in front of the cameras—occurred in the central agencies of government. In the summer of 1968, Trudeau oversaw fundamental changes in the organization of the Prime Minister's Office (PMO), in the Privy Council Office (PCO), and in cabinet organization. The balance of government power between non-partisan and partisan advisors began to shift in favour of the latter. Rooted in Trudeau's desire to rationalize decision-making, put his own stamp on government, and solidify control, these administrative shifts within the central offices of government fundamentally altered the Canadian political landscape. In the end, they changed the way decisions are made, the way elections are fought, and the way democracy functions. It was a peculiarly Canadian revolution: ostensibly dull, and easily overlooked, rooted not in street protest or bloodshed, but administrative change. It was nevertheless profound in its implications for the role of the state and the exercise of power (Greer and Radforth 1992; Curtis 2001).

★★★

Trudeau's revolutions were possible because, for the most part, they were undertaken using the existing institutional framework. The changes he introduced were mere tweaks to the system, revisions to offices that had long existed; he neither eliminated nor added anything new. Both the PMO and the PCO had long histories, often intertwined; Cabinet, of course, had been in existence since long before John A. Macdonald's first administration. Various prime ministers had introduced changes to the way each of the institutions operated, sometimes intentionally and sometimes more inadvertently. None, however, introduced such fundamental changes as Trudeau.

The modern PMO and PCO have Mackenzie King to thank for their existence. Each had existed informally since Confederation—in that there was *always* an office in which the prime minister sat, and always an office in which cabinet member, or privy councillors, did their business. However, under King, each developed into a more formal and more institutional presence. From the outset, the relationship between the two was both fraught and interconnected, reflecting their origin in the murky thinking of Canada's longest-serving prime minister, who had wanted a secretary but got a secretary of cabinet instead (Mallory 1976; Robertson 2000, 216).

Initially, it was the PCO that was by far the more important office, and in a formal capacity that remains the case today. The Clerk of the Privy Council is Canada's top bureaucrat, and often the most potent non-elected member of the Ottawa pantheon. In the early years, the movement of personnel between the PMO and the Cabinet secretariat underlined how close the connection between the two offices was. There were never more than about ten staff members in either of the central offices during this period, and some of those were quite junior. At the more senior level, however, not only did the first Clerk of the Privy Council, Arnold Heeney, himself move from the PMO to the PCO at the beginning of the decade, but Gordon Robertson took the same path at the beginning of the St. Laurent administration in 1948, and Jack Pickersgill followed along in 1953. It was all a bit incestuous, and it spoke to the value attached to having similar skills in each of the two offices.

The PCO is comparable to other departments, with the clerk equivalent to a deputy minister, and the prime minister, in his or her role as head of Cabinet, equivalent to the minister. But because the PCO is essentially the prime minister's personal department, it occupies an ambiguous position in the federal state, despite the similarities to other government departments. Rather than being charged with a particular set of public policy issues, the PCO is concerned instead with securing consensus in Cabinet, monitoring the progress of Cabinet work, advising on timing, and keeping track of the external considerations to be addressed (Hay 1982, 10–12). Without the same sort of policy mandate that departments like Finance or Health and Welfare have enjoyed, the PCO has earned a reputation as something of a super-department, ultimately familiar with, if not responsible for, virtually all the work of government. And within that department, the clerk is a "superbureaucrat," not only the administrative leader of the PCO itself who reports directly to the prime minister but also head of the public service of Canada (Campbell and Szablowski 1979; Bourgault 2008, 42). The potential to exert power and influence is enormous but dependent on the way power is shared across the rest of the government.

The Prime Minister's Office is not an administrative office at all. Not formally part of the government, it is more comparable to the office occupied by every Member of Parliament; the PMO is the prime minister's office, whereas the PCO is his or her department. Each, in many ways, is the other's opposite and, as such, casts light on the nature of its contrasting office by ostensibly illustrating what the other is not. Gordon Robertson, the former Clerk of the Privy Council, has explained the two offices in such a way as to highlight their opposing qualities: "The Prime Minister's office is partisan, politically oriented, yet operationally sensitive. The Privy Council Office is non-partisan, operationally oriented yet politically sensitive" (Robertson 1971, 506). They are the two sides to the advisory structure built around the prime minister and occupy positions of extraordinary privilege as a result. In other ways, too, the spaces are each other's opposite. The Privy Council is the space for the nation's business, the public side of governance, even if little that transpires within it is ever made particularly public; conversely, the Prime Minister's Office is the private space for his or her reflection. In this way, the PMO bears more similarity to "home" than to "office," in that it is a "private realm" that "offers freedom and control, ... security, ... and scope for creativity and regeneration" (Mallett 2004, 71). Appreciating the PMO as sanctuary, as well as recognizing the fluid movement of personnel between the two central offices, enables us to realize how changes made to the organization of the haven had significant but perhaps unintentional consequences for the more public space of the PCO.

Similar to the way that the PCO came into being, the creation of the PMO essentially formalized a longstanding practice in Ottawa. The prime minister had always had a personal staff and an office within which they worked; in the early days of Confederation, that staff might only have consisted of one secretary or clerk to deal with the mail and serve as a receptionist in the office itself. As the work of the country grew, so too did the size of the office staff. Usually, these people were seconded from the civil service. However, occasionally prime ministers brought in particular individuals with whom they had developed a trust, such as Arnold Heeney, whom King decided to appoint to the PMO in 1938 (Axworthy 1988, 257). The office was a small one: R. B. Bennett had a staff of 12, and King, Louis St. Laurent, and John Diefenbaker each had PMOs with about 30 members (Lalonde 1971, 519).

Over time, the tasks that the PMO undertook increased. Diefenbaker used his PMO to protect him from the Liberals he saw behind every door and at every desk in the civil service of 1957. He could appoint his advisors to the PMO, reducing his reliance on those about whom he was suspicious. Pearson increased the size and also used it as a place to develop policy. In naming Tom Kent his "Co-ordinator of Programming," Pearson took a big leap toward shifting the role of the PMO from a friendly buffer around the prime minister to an un-elected, un-vetted, un-trained policy-generating unit (Kent 1988, 225). But his successor pushed the revolution even further.

In part, Trudeau was able to do this because he was an outsider, in part because he had a bit of insider leverage. The PMO was perhaps the easiest office to clean up because it was the one where the prime minister exerted the most independent authority; no one would need to upend the bureaucratic structure to fix the PMO. Trudeau was not alone in thinking that the PMO needed an overhaul. Key members of the Trudeau team, following his victory on the fourth ballot at the Liberal leadership convention of April 1968, included Marc Lalonde and Michael Pitfield. They had worked, respectively, in the PMO and the PCO for the Pearson government, and both were appalled at the level of disorganization that had been allowed to develop (English 2009, 17–18). Lalonde, in particular, was a key advocate for change in the office system, having been attached to the Pearson PMO for little more than a year as a "special advisor" with both policy and political sides to his responsibilities (Hodgson 1968a). He later described the office during Pearson's tenure as a train station that anyone could walk into, but only one person knew where the trains were heading. It was, he said, perpetually in "a nice state of disorganization" (Lalonde in Bothwell and Granatstein 2017, 16). Lalonde was also widely thought to have "played an important backstage" role in Trudeau's campaign. Hence, the combination of his views on the PMO, and his proximity to the new prime minister, pointed to his crucial role in the bureaucratic revolution (Stevens 1968a, 25).

Lalonde was not alone in pushing for change. Pearson's principal secretary, Jack Hodgson, had prepared a transition document for the next prime minister, outlining not only how the office worked, but also how it did not (Hodgson 1968a). Hodgson, a former Rhodes Scholar with an Oxford PhD in economic history, had meandered his way into Pearson's inner sanctum through the navy and then the Department of National Defence, where he had been an assistant deputy minister (*National Defence Headquarters Directorate of History and Heritage*, n.d.). His PMO appointment was a civil service appointment and his primary concerns were about the workload. In addition to outlining the "day-to-day cooperation" between the PCO and the PMO, and the responsibilities of the main officers in the latter—particularly his own—the transition document raised some areas for potential reform. For example, he thought that a "case could be made" for dividing the types of work done at PCO and PMO more clearly, perhaps by making the principal secretary a political appointment. The problem with such a shift, however, was that "such a change could be misrep-resented as implying a purely partisan approach to public affairs" (Hodgson 1968a). Nevertheless, the fact that the principal secretary came through the ranks limited the prime minister's maneuverability in staffing the PMO, and probably explains Pearson's habit of appointing other special advisors from outside—including both Kent and Lalonde.

Hodgson also laid out for the new prime minister—whoever it might be—other positions in the PMO and proposed some areas for growth. Key players included the executive assistant, in charge of "the operations side of the office," and the policy secretary, who had "a wide-ranging mandate." It was so comprehensive, in fact, that "a high calibre Task Force" composed of three people needed to be struck to assist with the responsibilities. None "should ... be attached to any department or have any continuing desk work in order to ensure their complete mobility and freedom from bias" (Hodgson 1968b). Other areas where reforms might be implemented included the relationship between the House Leader in the Commons and the PMO, and the "overall public information policy of the government" (Hodgson 1968b). The incoming prime minister might consider introducing new positions, including a legislative assistant, who would serve as the new prime minister's "watchdog on [the] House" and "on progress of legislation being drafted," and an "Office of Government Co-ordination" that would coordinate "ministerial activities in order to ensure that the business side of government and the political responsibility of the Cabinet can be realized in the most effective manner possible" (Hodgson 1968b). Hodgson clearly found the Pearson PMO wanting in its ability to oversee the government's legislative agenda, and in its general organizational capacity.

There is nothing surprising about members of an experienced office staff taking the opportunity offered by a change in administration to suggest reforms, but these particular proposals served as a springboard for the far more sweeping reforms Trudeau envisioned. The new prime minister quickly moved to put his own stamp on government following the legitimation of his leadership victory through the federal election of June 1968. Following the general logic of the transition document, Trudeau clearly agreed that there were ways that the PMO could be streamlined, that the relationship between the PCO and the PMO could be clarified, and that the way information was delivered to the public could be made more effective. The result was an overwhelming centralization of power at the centre.

Once in office, Trudeau worked quickly to rearrange the people around him. In order to do so, he instituted one of the most significant, unnoticed changes in Canadian governmental history: he made the PMO openly political, removing the artifice of the office being staffed with civil service appointees, and giving all positions the status of order-in-council appointments. The transition document had raised this possibility, but had not warned about what it would mean. The significance of the shift was consistently downplayed: at the time, no media outlet took notice; it may have been regarded as mere administrative housekeeping. Ottawa-based political correspondent Geoffrey Stevens noted in August 1968 that Trudeau had begun his reorganization by appointing a staff of 20—about twice the size of the PMO staff under Pearson—with further appointments anticipated. While this was causing stress on office space and telephone lines and the physical capacity of the East Block, there was no suggestion that Trudeau's reforms were anything more significant than new office furniture (Stevens 1968b). According to Tom Axworthy, Trudeau's principal secretary, Trudeau was simply legitimizing a longstanding practice: he "made the system honest by acknowledging what always had been the case—politics was part of the Prime Minister's Office. It had been duplicitous to paper over this function with the screen of civil service impartiality" (Axworthy 1988, 258).

In this initial period of reorganization, it was the separation of functions that really signalled changes to the way decisions were made. In the PMO, this separation was achieved by establishing two distinct lines of authority. One could trace its origins to the early days of parliamentary government; Trudeau's personal staff was no different than the staff employed by every prime minister since John A. Macdonald. Trudeau had an executive assistant, Gordon Gibson, who was in charge of staff handling the daily routine of prime ministerial activity—"appointments, travel, public engagements and correspondence" (Stevens 1968b). What was distinct about the Trudeau PMO was that the personal office was separated from the policy office, where the new prime minister followed some of the advice offered by Pearson's principal secretary in the transition document. Trudeau appointed a legislative assistant, for example, who would "advise the Prime Minister on Parliamentary procedure and the conduct of Parliamentary business generally," and extended the responsibilities of the press secretary to "the press and information policy of the government as a whole, whether reflected at the ministerial or departmental level" (Trudeau 1968b). Ivan Head was a somewhat odd choice for legislative assistant in that he had previously served Trudeau as a legal advisor, but his appointment sent the message that Parliament was a legal entity; Roméo LeBlanc's appointment was more obvious, having occupied a similar position in the Pearson PMO. At the very top of the pyramid was a new principal secretary.

Marc Lalonde was a natural choice for Trudeau's principal secretary once the position itself had been redefined as a political appointment. Thus, Hodgson was shifted to Deputy Minister of Veterans Affairs, a position suited to both his civil service seniority and his skills, and in his place arrived a logical, Cartesian thinker like the boss. With the change in appointment category came a change in role. Now officially responsible for advising "the Prime Minister on policy matters" and "on the political platform of the Party," the principal secretary's position had suddenly become considerably more powerful. As Lalonde later explained it, the role of the PMO included such things as "the budgeting of the prime minister's time on a daily, weekly and monthly basis" and "the preparation of speeches and other public statements to be delivered by the prime minister himself." Determining what the prime minister spends time on, or what the prime minister says about government priorities, can clearly foreshadow government policy just as easily as it can follow it. While the PMO was not a "mini-cabinet" and was not "directly or indirectly a decision-making body" according to Lalonde (1971, 520–521), it nevertheless was the source of an increasing amount of information amassed for the use of the Prime Minister in Cabinet, caucus, and Parliament and in communications with the public. And as a result, it was regarded with suspicion by lowly MPs, who "began to complain about the pervasive influence of the PMO" and the "tight little group of officials who surround the PM" (McCall-Newman 1982, 123).

These changes mirrored some of the transformations that John F. Kennedy had implemented in Washington in the earlier part of the decade. In noting the academic credentials of Trudeau's new policy advisors, for example, parallels were drawn by some journalists "with the young Harvard intellectuals President John Kennedy recruited in 1961" (Cumming 1969). Trudeau's PMO had more in common with the American system than just the Camelot of Kennedy: in introducing his new office staff, for example, Pierre Trudeau underlined that "the Principal Secretary is my Chief of Staff," taking a title common in the White House but not on Parliament Hill. Indeed, even in Washington the chief of staff was a fairly recent innovation, having been first proposed to Franklin Roosevelt during the Depression. Dwight Eisenhower was the first to appoint a truly powerful chief, Sherman Adams, rather than simply a friend to offer support, but the position was entrenched in the American model by the time Trudeau emulated it (Whipple 2017, 18, 303).

Despite the appearance of a Kennedy-esque intellectual PMO, it was actually with the administration of his contemporary, Richard Nixon, that Trudeau shared the most. Nixon, like Trudeau, formalized and, arguably, perfected a system that had been functioning in an ad hoc way for the previous decade or more. Building on the hierarchical structures of government management favoured by Republican administrations in the past, Nixon built a pyramid of power with himself at the top and Bob Haldeman as chief of staff. The two ran an increasingly centralized White House Office, with a larger staff and a broader range of tasks than ever before. Like foreign policy, which had traditionally been designed at the executive level, now domestic policy— with the shift from the Bureau of the Budget to the Office of Management and Budget—also came under the purview of the expanded White House Office. Nixon also introduced the Domestic Council, the Council on International Economic Policy and the Council on Economic Policy, all policy-oriented bodies within the White House Office and all elements of the centralization that characterized the Nixon administration (Hult and Walcott 2004, 18, 165, 171). While in foreign policy, this centralization of power in the hands of the president and his staff constituted an "imperial presidency" according to Arthur Schlesinger (1973), a similar shift in the management of domestic affairs has been described as the emergence of an "administrative presidency" (Nathan 1975).

It is unlikely that either Nixon or Trudeau ever appreciated how closely their two administrative structures mirrored each other, but the similarities only continued for a few years. In Washington, the outrages of Watergate soon led to a dismantling of the administrative edifices; that no such scandal plagued Trudeau's PMO meant that the Canadian version of an administrative overhaul was allowed to continue unchecked well into the twenty-first century. There was nothing underhanded about Trudeau's preoccupation with renovating the central agencies in Ottawa; he was obviously enamoured with the new study of systems, of managerial methods, and of efficiency, and wanted his office to reflect this new managerial style (Trudeau 1993, 113). Thus, on the advice of a coterie of assistants, Trudeau moved in the direction of his neighbours to the south, and empowered his principal secretary with the responsibility to "relieve the pressures upon the Prime Minister to the greatest possible degree" (Trudeau 1968b). As Eisenhower had advised Nixon, everyone needs "to have his own SOB" (Whipple 2017, 303); Marc Lalonde would be Trudeau's "son of a bitch."

When Trudeau changed the nature of the principal secretary's appointment from the civil service to an order-in-council, it could not help but have implications for the functioning of the Privy Council Office and the Cabinet secretariat as well. No longer would it be possible for the occupant of one office shift to the other; the PCO was henceforth to remain an administrative appointment while the PMO would be staffed with political appointees. Trudeau noted that "close and friendly working relations" between the two offices would continue to be "imperative." He then went on to note that each ultimately served *him*: "members of my personal staff must work hand in hand with the staff of the Privy Council Office and, as a general rule, make contact with other departments ... after first consulting" PCO officials; on the other side, members of the Cabinet secretariat would assist "my staff ... in working closely with them in the assessment and elaboration of ideas regarding government policies and programs old and new" (Trudeau 1968b).

Gordon Robertson had been Clerk of the Privy Council during Pearson's prime ministership, and he would remain so under Trudeau. Some continuity, in the midst of massive change, was important, and Robertson had considerable experience in the position. Appointed in 1963 on the recommendation of the incumbent, Robertson arrived in the office with "good judgement, a temperament compatible with the prime minister's"—in this case, Mike Pearson—"and complete reliability" (Robertson 2000, 215). Nothing had happened in the intervening five years to suggest that that initial judgement was inaccurate, and Robertson remained in his post following the transition.

Robertson developed a positive relationship with Trudeau. The two met every morning with Marc Lalonde, bringing the PMO, the PCO and the PM into daily conversation; they also frequently met for lunch to discuss matters that needed "more time than was possible" in the morning meetings (Robertson 2000, 215). While the threesome seems to have generally operated smoothly, it was clear that Lalonde was the dominant advisor; he was in receipt of the Cabinet minutes and agendas, as well as being familiar with the political priorities, and doled out information to Robertson as he determined was appropriate. Lalonde, then, was "the judge of what was political and what was policy" (Robertson in Bothwell and Granatstein 2017, 26). One of the first pieces of advice Robertson offered the new prime minister was on the timing of the next election: "I don't see how the situation in a few months could be better than it is right now, and it could be worse. I would go as soon as possible." Robertson probably voiced the same opinion Trudeau had been hearing from many quarters in those first few months after his leadership win in April 1968, but the fact that the Prime Minister asked for Robertson's opinion underlined something important. Even though it was Trudeau's goal to separate the policy matters from the political issues through a clearer division between the staff of the PCO and the PMO, he was nevertheless as guilty as all his predecessors had been in politicizing the policy function of the Privy Council. Managerial man he may have been, but politics slipped into even the purest of policy positions.

With Trudeau at the helm, Robertson now had the task of "implementing the changes the prime minister wanted" (Robertson 2000, 255). For the most part, those changes revolved around the Cabinet structure itself, the one element of the Trudeau revolution that has received some scholarly attention. In addition to changing the make-up of the PMO, and subsequently influencing the way in which the PCO affected policy, Trudeau also introduced sweeping changes to Cabinet committees and to Cabinet decision-making procedures in the summer of 1968. He announced these early in July. In the interest of having "fewer meetings of Cabinet" and being able to "deal effectively and quickly" with an ever-increasing workload, Trudeau proposed a streamlined committee process. The PCO would direct memoranda to Cabinet—generally prepared by departmental bureaucrats to introduce problems and propose decisions—to the appropriate committees for their consideration. Committee agendas would be widely circulated to ensure adequate preparation and participation, and any interested member of Cabinet was free to attend. The new system was designed to enable the committees "to take decisions in a wide area of activity" and thereby share the burden formerly carried by the Cabinet as a whole (Trudeau 1968a).

These changes reflected Trudeau's desire to implement a system of "rational management" within the central executive. Believing that "knowledge would increasingly become the basis for political power," he sought to increase the policy decision-making capacity of Cabinet by emphasizing focused, collegial discussion (Aucoin 1986, 6–9). A better-briefed, better-prepared, more engaged Cabinet would go a long way toward wresting control over policy from the bureaucracy, the Prime Minister assumed. He had frequently noted that "cabinet is less easily captured by the bureaucracy than are ministers operating independently" (French 1979, 365). In other words, there was strength in numbers, and the civil service needed, somehow, to be contained.

Although Trudeau wanted little to do with the Liberal Party as an institution, he acknowledged that it needed a role. Thus, the final innovation that occurred in that heady summer of 1968 was an attempt to compartmentalize politics within the centre. Building on a proposal from Gordon Gibson, the Prime Minister's new executive assistant (and therefore ostensibly responsible for such things a scheduling and appointments), Trudeau introduced a "political cabinet." Not really a cabinet in any formal sense, this was a group of Cabinet ministers and Liberal Party officials and regional watchdogs who met to discuss "the public sentiments of the day, likely trends for the future" and how each "can, or should, be modified through the political process" (Gibson 1968).

The political cabinet system was an effort to integrate the Liberal Party into Ottawa, on the one hand, and use the Party as a conduit into the regions, on the other. Topics that were discussed by this super-cabinet included reviews of "the government and Party's present and future programs and priorities," of various expenditures related to elections, of the relationship between the national and provincial Party wings, of policy proposals (Wylie 1969). Key to its functioning was the "troika," a group of three ministers and Party officials responsible for each region; through this body, information would flow between Ottawa and the provinces. The goal was "to improve consultation and communication between the parliamentary and organizational wings of the Party," something that was perceived to have been lacking during the 1960s (Wylie 1969). It would also, not incidentally, shield a prime minister with a stated aversion to party duties from dealing with the Liberal Party directly.

Each of the Trudeau innovations pointed to an aversion to disorder and a distrust of power centres. In politicizing the PMO and creating the political Cabinet, he was announcing that there was a place—a carefully defined space—for politics in government. Outside that space, though, the responsibility of government was to design policy. That had to be done in an environment of open discussion and rational thought. The cabinet committee structure was built in order to facilitate debate over policy, and to turn the Cabinet into a more efficient, less political, more thoughtful and authoritative decision-making body. That move ended up stripping the PCO, and the bureaucracy more generally, of some of the power that it had come to exercise, shifting it more markedly towards administration rather than decision-making.

In the summer of 1968, these were viewed as housekeeping innovations, no more revolutionary than the changes introduced by any of Trudeau's predecessors. A few years later, however, it all looked quite different. Most of Trudeau's own goals in introducing the changes remained unmet: government remained inefficient, not really any more "rational" than it had been before, and partisanship had not been compartmentalized into one corner of government. Indeed, quite the opposite had occurred. The Prime Minister's Office had become increasingly powerful in practice, the Privy Council Office had become, ironically, more political, and the cabinet committee structure had done nothing to ease the burden of work or streamline decision-making.

By 1972, the PMO had grown larger, and was increasingly used to figure out where Trudeau's allies were; the office had a new reconnaissance role (Davey 1973). It also began to take on more of a public relations role. There were already six people in the press office of the PMO in 1970, with a further 41 in charge of correspondence, all of whom were clearly in charge of the "message" that was being delivered, but staff in other positions were also responsible for the message. Joyce Fairbairn, the special legislative assistant with responsibilities for the House, explained her job in 1972 as "briefing the PM" on everything from the position of ministers, the Whip, the House Leader, and the members of caucus (a job, she noted that had "not been well done in the past"). Moreover, she was responsible for the "coordination of press relations in connection with the House of Commons," an "area which was somewhat hit and miss in the days of majority government" but one that needed renewed attention (Fairbairn 1972).

Others in the office, like Ivan Head, were now taking on a far greater policy-development role than their original appointment documents suggested. At the Commonwealth meeting of 1969, Head found Trudeau "ill-prepared to cope." Although generally "the domain of the PCO," Gordon Robertson took little interest; Trudeau turned to Head in the PMO to "produce material that sounded like him" (Head in Bothwell and Granatstein 2017, 49–62). Even more ominously, the PMO, and Head in particular, weighed in on one of the major initiatives of the early Trudeau government, and in doing so announced the extent of its authority. Uneasy with what he regarded as the complacent, tradition-bound approach of the Department of External Affairs to Canada's place in the world, Trudeau sought to stir the foreign policy pot. With Ivan Head from the PMO in charge, and a "Non-Group" of advisors pulled from Treasury

Board and the PCO (but not from External Affairs) acting as assistants, Trudeau's own office put together a "Study of Defence Policy" that proposed a drastic reduction in both Canada's NATO commitment and nuclear weapon capacity. The document was dropped into a Cabinet meeting in the spring of 1969, to considerable surprise, telegraphing the Prime Minister's position and manipulating debate on the forthcoming foreign policy review (Bothwell and Granatstein 1990, 19–24). And so the PMO moved stealthily, out of necessity or out of comfort, into a role normally associated with the neutral bureaucracy.

The Privy Council Office also changed. The Trudeau variations had been designed to isolate the bureaucracy to some extent, limiting the power of senior deputy ministers and the Clerk of the Privy Council by arming Cabinet itself with more tools to propose, discuss, and decide upon policy. But with the 1975 appointment of the young, untested Michael Pitfield as clerk, chosen for the position over far more senior bureaucrats, it seemed that the politicization of all branches of the executive was complete. As the *Ottawa Journal* complained, the problem was "the politicization of the public service at the highest level in the most dangerous and insidious ways. Mr. Pitfield bears the mark of a Trudeau man" (quoted in Robertson 2000, 309). But by 1975, the revolution was well underway and too late to stop.

Canadians could be convinced that they were participating in the global protests of 1968 in part because they elected a man who seemed to personify the new age. Trudeau was young, hip, comfortable with the new media, fluent in the politics of image and performativity, and clearly designed for a revolutionary age (Litt 2016). Looking like he belonged in it, he promised to tackle revolutions that were threatening national stability: his platform stressed a solution to Quebec separatism, an answer to demands for greater participation—indeed a new Just Society. But if the appearance and content of the Trudeau campaign suggested a departure from what had gone on before, it was the form of what happened once he was elected in the spring of 1968 that was truly revolutionary. With the nation still swooning over the effects of Trudeaumania, the Liberal government moved quickly to revamp the structure of power in Ottawa. With changes to the appointment process in the Prime Minister's Office, the decision-making process in Cabinet, and the personnel in both—all made within a few weeks of taking office in June 1968—government was now more centralized, more political, and more partisan than it had ever been before. In formalizing the informal, Trudeau laid the groundwork for a much more aggressive move into centralized power. Successive leaders of both parties, and premiers of all provinces, have subsequently followed suit, arming their executive offices with policy-generating capabilities and decision-making responsibilities that would have been unthinkable in the middle of the 1960s. The role of elected legislators, and the public that elected them, has declined. Whether

Trudeau could have imagined where his reforms would lead is perhaps the dilemma of all revolutionaries.

References

Aucoin, Peter. 1986. "Organizational Change in the Machinery of Canadian Government: From Rational Management to Brokerage Politics." *Canadian Journal of Political Science* 19, no. 1 (March): 3–28.

Axworthy, Tom. 1988. "Of Secretaries to Princes." *Canadian Public Administration* 31, no. 2 (Summer): 247–264.

Bothwell, Robert, and J. L. Granatstein. 2017. *Trudeau's World: Insiders Reflect on Foreign Policy, Trade and Defence, 1968–84.* Vancouver: University of British Columbia Press.

———. 1990. *Pirouette: Pierre Trudeau and Canadian Foreign Policy.* Toronto: University of Toronto Press.

Bourgault, Jacques. 2008. "Clerks and Secretaries to Cabinet: Anatomy of Leadership." In *Searching for Leadership: Secretaries to Cabinet in Canada*, edited by Patrice Dutil, 41–81. Toronto: University of Toronto Press.

Bryden, Penny E. 1997. *Planners and Politicians: The Liberal Party and Social Policy, 1957–1968.* Montreal and Kingston: McGill-Queen's University Press.

Campbell, Colin, and George Szablowski. 1979. *The Superbureaucrats: Structure and Behaviour in Central Agencies.* Toronto: Macmillan of Canada.

Cumming, Carman. 1969. "Efficiency, Independence—Not Hominess—Mark PM's Office." *Globe and Mail*, 15 January: 9.

Curtis, Bruce. 2001. *Politics of Population: State Formation, Statistics, and the Census of Canada, 1840–1875.* Toronto: University of Toronto Press.

Davey, Jim. 1973. Letter to Trudeau. P. E. Trudeau fonds, MG 26 O19, vol. 271, file: Joyce Fairbairn - Corr and Memo - Memo for PM from Jim Davey (pt 1) - 1970–1974: 23 March, Library and Archives Canada.

English, John. 2009. *Just Watch Me: The Life of Pierre Elliott Trudeau, 1968–2000.* Toronto: Knopf.

Fairbairn, Joyce. 1972. Letter to Martin O'Connell. P. E. Trudeau fonds, MG 26 O19, vol. 272, file: Joyce Fairbairn - Corr and Memo - Memo for PM from Joyce Fairbairn - Sept–Dec 1972 – 1972: 17 November, Library and Archives Canada.

French, Richard. 1979. "The Privy Council Office: Support for Cabinet Decision-Making." In *The Canadian Political Process*, 2nd ed., edited by Richard Schultz, Orest M. Kruhlak, and John C. Terry, 363–394. Toronto: Holt, Rinehart and Winston.

Gibson, Gordon. 1968. Letter to Pierre Elliott Trudeau. P. E. Trudeau fonds, MG 26 O11, vol. 60, file *312, Government - Federal Executive - The Cabinet - Personal and Confidential 1968 - Sept. 1969: 9 August, Library and Archives Canada.

Greer, Allan, and Ian Radforth. 1992. "Introduction." In *Colonial Leviathan: State Formation in Mid-Nineteenth Century Canada*, edited by Allan Greer and Ian Radforth, 3–16. Toronto: University of Toronto Press.

Gwyn, Richard J. 1965. *The Shape of Scandal: A Study of a Government in Crisis.* Toronto: Clarke, Irwin.

Hay, Murray A. 1982. "Understanding the PCO: The Ultimate Facilitator" *Optimum* 13 (1): 1–14.

Hodgson, J. S. 1968a. Letter to O. G. Stoner. Roméo LeBlanc fonds, R 12069, vol. 402, file 10: 1 April, Library and Archives Canada.

———. 1968b. Memorandum re: Organization of Office of Prime Minister. Roméo LeBlanc fonds, R 12069, vol. 402, file 10: 4 April, Library and Archives Canada.

Hult, Karen M., and Charles E. Walcott. 2004. *Empowering the White House: Governance under Nixon, Ford and Carter.* Lawrence: University of Kansas Press.

Kent, Tom. 1988. *A Public Purpose: An Experience of Liberal Opposition and Canadian Government.* Kingston and Montreal: McGill-Queen's University Press.

Kurlansky, Mark. 2005. *1968: The Year That Rocked the World.* New York: Random House.

Lalonde, Marc. 1971. "The Changing Role of the Prime Minister's Office." *Canadian Public Administration* 14, no. 4 (Winter): 509–536.

Litt, Paul. 2016. *Trudeaumania.* Vancouver: University of British Columbia Press.

———. 2008. "Trudeaumania: Participatory Democracy in the Mass-Mediated Nation." *Canadian Historical Review* 89, no. 1 (March): 27–53.

Mallett, Shelley. 2004. "Understanding Home: A Critical Review of the Literature." *The Sociological Review* 52 (1): 62–89.

Mallory, J. R. 1976. "Mackenzie King and the Origins of the Cabinet Secretariat." *Canadian Public Administration* 19, no. 2 (June): 254–266.

McCall-Newman, Christina. 1982. *Grits: An Intimate Portrait of the Liberal Party.* Toronto: Macmillan.

Nathan, Richard P. 1975. *The Plot That Failed: Nixon and the Administrative Presidency.* New York: John Wiley and Sons.

National Defence Headquarters Directorate of History and Heritage. n.d. https://www.archeion.ca/j-s-hodgson-fonds.

Robertson, Gordon. 2000. *The Memoirs of a Very Civil Servant: Mackenzie King to Pierre Trudeau.* Toronto: University of Toronto Press.

———. 1971. "The Changing Role of the Privy Council Office." *Canadian Public Administration* 14, no. 4 (Winter): 488–508.

Schlesinger, Arthur M., Jr. 1973. *The Imperial Presidency.* Boston: Houghton Mifflin.

Stevens, Geoffrey. 1968a. "PM Takes Assistants from 6 Ministers, Keeps Pearson Aides." *Globe and Mail,* 30 July: 25

———. 1968b. "Trudeau's Expansion of Staff Means Accommodation Problem." *Globe and Mail,* 1 August: 3.

Trudeau, P. E. 1993. *Memoirs.* Toronto: McClelland & Stewart.

———. 1968a. Letter to all Ministers. P. E. Trudeau fonds, MG 26 O11, vol. 60, file ★312, Government - Federal Executive - The Cabinet - Personal and Confidential 1968 - Sept. 1969: 10 July, Library and Archives Canada.

———. 1968b. "Memorandum to the Staff of the Prime Minister's Office." P. E. Trudeau fonds, MG 26 O11, vol. 60, file 7, correspondence, Inter-office, 7-12/1968: 18 July, Library and Archives Canada.

Whipple, Chris. 2017. *The Gatekeepers: How the White House Chiefs of Staff Define Every Presidency.* New York: Crown.

Wylie, Torrance. 1969. Letter to Michel Vennat. James Coutts Papers, R13437, vol. 134, file 12 – Political Cabinet Agenda 1969–1970: 16 December, Library and Archives Canada.

Chapitre 3
1968, vue du Québec

JOCELYN LÉTOURNEAU

Résumé

L'année 1968 s'inscrit dans la continuité d'une période évolutionnaire plus que révolutionnaire. Il s'agit d'un moment traversé par des questionnements, des bouillonnements et des emportements. Au lieu de reprendre le mythistoire selon lequel les années 1960, au Québec, coïncident avec une période de dissolution et de transmutation tous azimuts, l'auteur montre que la décennie est traversée par la volonté de trouver des solutions concrètes aux problèmes qui marquent le Québec, Montréal et les francophones au Québec et au Canada. Raplomber la situation de la province, de sa métropole et de sa majorité démographique, tel est le défi qui se présente aux Québécois. Comment y parvenir ? Voilà la question à laquelle groupes et parties tentent de répondre à leur façon en s'empoignant verbalement ou violemment dans l'espace public. 1968 marque un moment charnière de leur affrontement, à travers les personnes de Pierre Elliott Trudeau et de René Lévesque notamment, qui entreprennent alors leur croisade respective. Éventuellement, le peuple tranchera, se faisant éclectique, paradoxal et ondoyant dans ses choix, à la manière québécoise…

L'année 1967 avait été extraordinaire à plus d'un titre : ouverture d'Expo 67 le 27 avril par Lester B. Pearson, Daniel Johnson et Jean Drapeau, entourés de 7 000 invités provenant des quatre coins du monde ; visite du général De Gaulle à Québec et à Montréal, où il avait lancé son désormais célèbre, mais controversé « Vive le Québec libre ! » ; célébration du centenaire du Canada en présence de Sa Majesté la Reine, qui avait prononcé le tiers de son discours en français ; dépôt de la loi créant les collèges d'enseignement général et professionnel, les cégeps ; inauguration de l'autoroute Décarie, de l'échangeur Turcot, du tunnel Louis-Hippolyte-La Fontaine et de la ligne jaune du métro de Montréal ; adoption, lors des deuxièmes assises des États généraux du Canada français tenus à Montréal, en novembre, d'une résolution portant sur le droit à l'autodétermination du peuple canadien-français sur le territoire du Québec, celui-ci étant déclaré « territoire national et milieu politique fondamental de cette nation ». On pourrait en ajouter d'autres. Une seule ombre au tableau :

Figure 3.1. Allumettes du Parti Québécois.
Source: *Collections du Musée canadien de l'histoire.*

en mai de cette année-là, les Maple Leafs de Toronto avaient éliminé les Canadiens de Montréal en six parties lors de la finale de la Coupe Stanley !

Comment 1968 pouvait-elle dépasser, en réalisations, en controverses et en tensions, ce que l'année précédente avait apporté à une population en phase avec les changements du monde, donc ouverte à de nouvelles stimulations et désireuse de se repositionner avantageusement dans l'économie politique du Canada, à coups de grands événements, certes, mais sur une base moins spectaculaire et plus solide aussi, quitte à jouer la carte autonomiste – et même plus – à l'endroit d'Ottawa ?

Révolution tranquille

Depuis quelques années déjà, la société québécoise vivait ce qu'on avait fini par appeler une «révolution tranquille[1]». Bien qu'elle soit consacrée, l'expression doit être utilisée avec nuance. Tout au Québec n'a pas (re)commencé avec l'arrivée au pouvoir des libéraux de Jean Lesage, en juin 1960, et la province n'a pas attendu ce moment pour se «moderniser». Si, dans les années 1950, certaines traditions persistaient et si la parole cléricale commandait le respect sans pour autant imposer la vénération – la distinction est importante –, les Québécois, qui s'identifiaient alors comme des Canadiens français, s'étaient entichés depuis le milieu des années 1940 de tout ce que la société de consommation apportait d'agréments à leur vie : automobile, bungalow, téléviseur, biens ménagers, vêtements prêts-à-porter, loisirs nouveaux genres, sorties grâce aux vacances payées, etc. Certes, Maurice Duplessis, premier ministre du Québec sans interruption depuis 1944, en menait large. Mais il ne s'opposait pas à l'investissement de capital non plus qu'au développement industriel, bien que les orientations économiques qu'il privilégiait pour le Québec, favorables à la croissance à court terme et fondées sur les avantages comparatifs traditionnels de la province (ressources naturelles, abondance d'une

---

1. Sur les origines du terme, voir la note de Warren (2016).

main-d'œuvre peu mobile, spécialisation dans l'industrie légère), consolidaient la place du Québec dans le système productif et la division continentale du travail, avec les inconvénients qui en découlaient et les problèmes qui se profilaient à l'horizon. Cela dit, le Québec sous Duplessis n'était pas en retard ou décalé par rapport aux tendances observables ailleurs au Canada. À l'époque, la pauvreté était répandue et mal jugulée d'un océan à l'autre ; les « communistes » et autres « gauchistes » faisaient l'objet d'une surveillance étendue ; les femmes plaisaient dans la mesure où elles étaient d'abord mères au foyer ; l'éducation supérieure ne concernait qu'une minorité de gens ; les valeurs morales conservatrices portées par les Églises ou par d'autres institutions ou groupes traditionnels étaient les plus valorisées ; et ainsi de suite. Il y aurait lieu, un jour, d'insister sur les similitudes historiques des deux solitudes canadiennes plutôt que sur leurs différences.

Vers la fin des années 1950, au Québec comme dans d'autres provinces, et surtout à Ottawa, on ne se satisfaisait plus, toutefois, d'un mode de régulation simplement réactif pour orchestrer le développement économique et social des espaces institués et gouvernés. Au Québec, les critiques et les suggestions pour changer la donne fusaient de toutes parts (Roy, 1973) : des associations patronales, qui pestaient contre la déficience des infrastructures matérielles, le manque de formation de la main-d'œuvre et l'absence de planification générale de la part de l'État provincial ; des associations syndicales, qui fulminaient contre la dureté des législations ouvrières, la protection minimaliste dont bénéficiaient les travailleurs et le manque de soutien aux personnes vulnérables ; et des penseurs, y compris de nombreux clercs réformateurs (Gauvreau, 2008), qui vitupéraient contre les abus de pouvoir du chef de l'Union nationale, son contrôle autoritaire des institutions et sa fermeture à l'égard de l'innovation sociale et culturelle.

Au tournant de la décennie, les inconvénients, empêchements et goulots d'étranglement générés par la gouvernance duplessiste, accentués par la petite récession de la fin des années 1950, dépassaient nettement les avantages liés au mode de régulation préconisé par le « Chef » et ses acolytes. Cela dit, l'Union nationale n'était pas unanimement décriée, loin de là.

On le sait, Duplessis mourait subitement le 7 septembre 1959, laissant son parti aux mains de Paul Sauvé, successeur capable, mais décédé brutalement lui aussi après 114 jours au pouvoir, plaçant les « bleus » dans une situation politique trouble. Malgré tout, l'Union nationale était loin d'être rayée du paysage politique québécois. Aux élections générales de 1960, elle obtenait un score enviable, 100 000 votes seulement séparant le parti de Jean Lesage, figure de proue du monde politique québécois, de celui d'Antonio Barrette, travailleur essoufflé et leader éteint, qui démissionnait à titre de chef de l'Union nationale le 15 septembre 1960.

Morale de l'histoire ? Ce qu'on appelle la Révolution tranquille ne marque pas une volonté de rupture radicale des Québécois avec la période antérieure, réduite par plusieurs à l'image d'une grande noirceur, un cliché repris *ad nauseam* depuis. Elle ne traduit pas davantage la volonté des intéressés, galvanisés dit-on par le désir de s'affranchir d'une condition historique qui les faisait souffrir, de changer drastiquement le cours de leur destinée, bien que certains intervenants, animés par différentes idéologies, le souhaitaient effectivement. En fait, la période qui s'amorce avec l'arrivée au pouvoir des libéraux témoigne bien plus de la recherche, par des décideurs pragmatiques appuyés par une population aux penchants réformistes, de solutions concrètes aux maux de la province à une époque où il appert que les remèdes connus étaient inaptes à guérir quoi que ce soit.

De ce point de vue, l'année 1968 s'inscrit dans la continuité d'une période évolutionnaire dans laquelle les transformations, reconversions et réorientations (à distinguer des révolutions, transmutations et dissolutions) sont nombreuses dans la province. Dans les années 1960, les Québécois ne souhaitent pas construire leur avenir à rebours du passé ; ils envisagent seulement de poursuivre leur histoire différemment.

1968 : les faits

Si l'année 1968 s'inscrit dans la continuité de ce qui se déroulait au Québec depuis quelques années, elle constitue aussi, à travers les événements qui lui donnent vie, un moment où certains enjeux dormants et certaines interrogations latentes se manifestent explicitement dans la cité ou sont directement exposés par des personnalités de premier plan, mobilisant par le fait même une bonne partie de la population et amplifiant les débats. Que s'est-il donc passé en 1968 qui soit si important du point de vue de l'Histoire ?

Bouillonnements

Reconnaissant l'effet des réussites d'une «équipe-nation» (Laurin-Lamothe et Moreau, 2011) sur l'humeur populaire, certains rappelleront la victoire des Canadiens de Montréal en finale de la Coupe Stanley, le 11 mai de cette année-là, sans oublier le 500ᵉ but de Jean Béliveau le soir du 20 octobre. Autre bonne nouvelle pour les sportifs de la province : l'octroi, par la Ligue majeure de baseball, d'une concession à Montréal. L'équipe est alors nommée «Expos de Montréal», ce qui en dit long sur les traces laissées par l'Expo 67 dans l'imaginaire populaire.

Plus intéressés par l'art ou les choses de l'esprit, d'autres insisteront sur des épisodes témoignant de l'effervescence qui régnait alors au Québec sur les plans scientifique (incluant le domaine médical et celui de l'ingénierie), artistique et culturel : première greffe du genou à être tentée au monde par le Dʳ André

Gilbert, de l'Hôpital Saint-François d'Assise à Québec ; première transplantation cardiaque effectuée au Canada par le Dr Pierre Grondin, de l'Institut de cardiologie de Montréal ; première édition du Festival d'été de Québec ; inauguration du barrage Manic-5, cependant assombrie par le décès *in situ* du premier ministre Daniel Johnson ; première représentation de la pièce *Les Belles-Sœurs*, de Michel Tremblay, au Théâtre du Rideau vert à Montréal ; première diffusion, à la télévision de Radio-Canada, de la revue de fin d'année *Bye Bye* (sans la participation de Dominique Michel toutefois !) ; première présentation, au Théâtre de Quat'Sous de Montréal, de *L'Osstidcho,* un spectacle emblématique de la contre-culture québécoise.

Fascinés par l'activité des décideurs et des gouvernants, d'autres encore dresseront une liste de faits à caractère plus politique : abolition, sous l'égide du gouvernement Johnson, du Conseil législatif et modification du nom de l'Assemblée législative du Québec, désormais appelée – très symboliquement – Assemblée nationale du Québec ; création de Radio-Québec (un geste interprété par certains comme une manifestation autonomiste du Québec face à Ottawa dans le domaine des télécommunications, une compétence fédérale en vertu de la disposition sur les pouvoirs résiduels dans la *Loi constitutionnelle du Canada de 1867*) ; modification du nom de la Sûreté provinciale du Québec, qui devient la Sûreté du Québec ; création du ministère de l'Immigration, avec la mission d'accroître la reconnaissance de l'État-nation québécois et d'attirer des immigrants de langue française en contexte d'inquiétude démographique dans la province ; lancement d'*Option Québec*, livre-programme-manifeste de René Lévesque ; publication par Pierre Vallières de son essai influent *Nègres blancs d'Amérique*.

Emportements

En 1968, tout n'est cependant pas de l'ordre de la loi, du verbe dialogique et de la joute politique sereine. Voici quelques exemples.

Le 24 juin, à la veille des élections fédérales et pendant le défilé de la Saint-Jean-Baptiste qui a lieu à Montréal en présence de Pierre Elliott Trudeau, Daniel Johnson et Jean Drapeau, assis à l'estrade d'honneur, des indépendantistes, dont plusieurs membres du Rassemblement pour l'indépendance nationale (RIN), débordant d'enthousiasme ou de colère, selon le point de vue privilégié, sont chargés par des policiers à cheval. Au terme de l'échauffourée, 290 personnes sont arrêtées et l'on rapporte de nombreux blessés. (Trudeau, cependant, refuse d'obéir au personnel de sécurité, qui l'exhorte à quitter son siège [2].)

La rage de certains, plus radicaux dans leurs manières de faire de la politique, car inspirés par l'idéologie de l'anticolonialisme ou par celle du socialisme

---

2. Voir une vidéo de la scène à l'adresse www.youtube.com/watch?v=uk7Qsrm34Bo.

révolutionnaire, deux crédos alors en vogue, s'exprime de manière plus brutale encore dans les mois qui suivent. Le 20 août, trois bombes éclatent presque simultanément à Montréal, vraisemblablement l'œuvre de Pierre-Paul Geoffroy, militant du RIN et du Front de libération du Québec (FLQ). Le 4 novembre, une charge de dynamite détruit un garage de la Murray Hill, une entreprise associée au « capitalisme monopoliste sauvage et anti-français ». Le 31 décembre, des bombes explosent près de l'hôtel de ville de Montréal et d'un édifice du gouvernement fédéral [3]. À ces événements violents s'ajoutent, bien qu'il ne s'agisse pas d'actes de nature criminelle, des affrontements à Saint-Léonard, en banlieue de Montréal, qui opposent francophones et Italiens à la suite de la décision de la commission scolaire locale d'éliminer plusieurs écoles bilingues et d'imposer des cours de français aux enfants d'immigrants allophones. Chez les non-francophones, on s'inquiète sérieusement, à l'époque, de l'excitation que suscite la question linguistique, laquelle, quelques mois plus tard, prendra la forme d'une véritable exaltation à travers l'opération « McGill français » (mars 1969) et les contestations issues de l'adoption de la loi 63 (octobre et novembre de la même année).

Questionnement

Tous ces épisodes montrent que la société québécoise, en 1968, est interpelée de manière générale par une question cardinale qu'aucun habitant de la province – francophone, anglophone ou allophone – ne peut éviter. Cette question, que l'on peut formuler de manière spectaculaire : « Comment se libérer des jougs qui nous affligent ? », mais qu'il est préférable d'énoncer sur un mode réaliste correspondant aux expectatives de la population au milieu des années 1960, s'articule à peu près comme suit : compte tenu de ce que nous avons été et de ce que nous sommes devenus, quel chemin doit-on emprunter pour poursuivre notre route ?

À cette question, les réponses divergent selon les uns et les autres. Il y a bien sûr les extrémistes, présents dans toutes les communautés qui forment la collectivité québécoise. Ceux-là prônent, suivant la société qu'ils envisagent de façonner, l'idée du statu quo (radicalisme de l'inaction et de la perpétuation des choses) ou celle de révolution (radicalisme de la refondation tous azimuts). C'est ainsi qu'à côté des traditionalistes purs et durs qui s'inquiètent des évolutions que connaît une société dans laquelle ils ne se reconnaissent plus, on trouve une bonne partie de l'élite anglophone désireuse de conserver ses privilèges et de maintenir le mur symbolique qui la sépare des « naturels [entendre ici les primaires] du pays québécois », pour reprendre les termes

---

3. À noter que ces déflagrations n'étaient pas les premières ni ne seraient les dernières. Entre 1963 et 1968, plusieurs attentats à la dynamite, dans le Grand Montréal surtout, ont provoqué la mort d'au moins six personnes. Voir Laurendeau (1990).

d'André Laurendeau dans son célèbre éditorial « La théorie du roi nègre »
(1958). En face figurent les terroristes du FLQ et autres insurgés ou séditieux,
qui estiment que rien ne peut être construit si tout n'est pas d'abord brisé.

Ces deux clans, situés aux extrêmes du spectre politique québécois, forment
évidemment des groupes fort minoritaires, le premier (les « perpétualistes ») se
terrant dans le silence et le lobby, le deuxième (les subversifs) s'exprimant dans
le bruit et le complot. Loin d'être suivis par les masses, ils sont désavoués par
elles, y compris par la jeunesse, réformiste plus qu'anarchiste (Warren, 2008).
Quant aux politiciens, ils s'en détournent. L'exemple de René Lévesque est
éloquent, lui qui fustige les « Rhodésiens blancs » de Westmount[4] autant que
les irréductibles du RIN et les activistes du FLQ, dont il ne cherche ni ne veut
la présence au sein du mouvement qu'il s'efforce d'initier et auquel se joignent
plusieurs leaders du mouvement étudiant en 1968, notamment Bernard Landry,
Louise Harel et Claude Charron.

Si les masses fuient les extrêmes et les extrémistes, qu'il s'agisse des apôtres
de l'inertie ou des disciples de l'agitation, où se trouvent-elles donc ? Elles sont,
suivant la culture politique propre aux Québécois qui, sur ce plan, ne se dis-
tinguent pas fondamentalement des Canadiens, dans le changement qui s'accorde avec la continuité. Précisons-le, il s'agit d'un lieu qui n'est pas facile à
découvrir, d'autant moins qu'il est imprécis, instable ou mobile, et qu'il n'existe
pas de carte absolument fiable pour le trouver.

Au cours de l'année 1968, alors que Pierre Elliott Trudeau est élu à la tête
du Canada ; que René Lévesque fonde le Parti Québécois ; que Daniel Johnson,
jusqu'à son décès tragique survenu le 26 septembre à Manicouagan, maintient
la pression sur les politiciens fédéraux pour que l'expérience canadienne per-
mette l'épanouissement des deux nations qui la composent ; que les « pages
bleues » du premier livre du rapport de la Commission royale d'enquête sur le
bilinguisme et le biculturalisme, véritable testament politique d'André
Laurendeau (décédé subitement le 1er juin 1968), sont dans l'air (Lapointe-
Gagnon, 2018) ; et que Québec et Ottawa se livrent une joute politico-
diplomatique acerbe pour déterminer les limites des prétendues prérogatives
internationales du Québec[5], les politiciens, sans égard à leur parti et à leur
capitale d'allégeance, s'attellent à dégoter le fameux point « Q », soit l'empla-
cement de la raison et de l'émotion québécoise qui, une fois déniché, permet-
trait de répondre adéquatement à cette question à la fois lancinante, opiniâtre
et inévitable : que veulent vraiment les Québécois ?

---

4. Formule utilisée par Lévesque en avril 1970 et rapportée dans le *Montreal Star* du
   23 avril 1970.
5. Voir le texte de Robin Gendron et David Tabachnick dans cet ouvrage,
   p. 325-341.

Dans ce contexte, 1968 marque un moment où l'arène de la province, inséparable du théâtre canadien, se peuple de joueurs qui occuperont, pendant 20 ans, le forum du pays. L'année 1968 est incontestablement importante dans l'histoire du Québec.

La conjoncture 1968

Rappelons la question qui, taraudant les citoyens comme les politiciens, se fait particulièrement insistante au Québec en 1968 alors que l'évidence antérieure du cours des choses (d'où venons-nous ? qui sommes-nous ?) s'est brouillée : quel chemin doit-on emprunter pour poursuivre notre route ?

Le mot « notre », qui renvoie bien sûr à un « nous » implicite ou sous-jacent, est ici ambigu. S'agit-il des Canadiens français du Québec (en voie de se renommer Québécois), des Canadiens de langue française ou des Canadiens français de partout au Canada ? Le « notre » en cause inclut-il les habitants du Québec qui ne sont pas d'héritage canadien-français, par exemple les anglophones et les allophones (à l'époque, les Autochtones sont clairement ou négligemment exclus du « nous ») ? Ce « notre » se réfère-t-il à la réalité ou à la possibilité d'une route commune suivie ou à suivre par les Canadiens de langue française (parmi lesquels figurent les francophones du Québec) et les Canadiens de langue anglaise ? Par le Québec et le « reste du Canada » ?

À la question « quel chemin doit-on emprunter pour poursuivre notre route ? », différentes réponses sont offertes par les uns et les autres, sans toutefois qu'une thèse ou une vision particulière s'impose. Les années 1960 à 1968 correspondent à une période de recalibrage des enjeux, d'intensification des rapports de force et d'établissement des positions respectives des acteurs politiques dans le cadre d'un paradigme discursif et actanciel qui, du côté québécois, devient celui de l'autonomisme franc et, du côté canadien, tourne autour de l'idée de fédéralisme coopératif, une notion mise de l'avant par Pearson, avec plus ou moins de limites, durant ses deux mandats minoritaires.

À partir de 1968, cependant, la donne change : Pearson quitte la vie politique, Johnson trépasse et Lesage n'est plus l'ombre de lui-même – il exprime d'ailleurs sa volonté de démissionner de son poste de chef du Parti libéral du Québec (PLQ) dès le mois d'août 1969. Entrent alors en scène deux figures majeures du paysage politique québéco-canadien : René Lévesque et Pierre Elliott Trudeau, qui entreprennent de proposer aux Québécois et aux Canadiens deux options d'avenir qui se révèlent aussi fortes qu'irréconciliables tandis que le souhait de la majorité des Québécois (tenons-nous-en aux francophones pour le moment) est de conjuguer ces options dans une forme politico-constitutionnelle mitoyenne. Voyons les choses de plus près.

René Lévesque

L'année 1968 est importante pour René Lévesque. En rogne contre les membres du PLQ, qui ne veulent pas appuyer la position constitutionnelle qu'il favorise pour permettre à la socioéconomie québécoise de se développer au diapason de ses possibilités : celle de faire du Québec un État souverain associé au reste du Canada[6], Lévesque, en octobre 1967, quitte son parti tout en demeurant député indépendant de Laurier. Un mois plus tard, il fonde le Mouvement souveraineté-association (MSA), profitant d'une conjoncture politique qu'il estime favorable à la promotion de son idée, qu'il ne perçoit pas, précisons-le, comme une position radicale et qu'il entend promouvoir dans la cité par le biais d'un processus politique entièrement démocratique.

La lecture que fait Lévesque de la situation québécoise – soit que les Québécois sont en majorité ouverts à l'idée d'indépendance – est-elle juste ? On peut le penser, à priori.

Aux élections de 1966, deux partis résolument indépendantistes, le Rassemblement pour l'indépendance nationale (RIN) et le Ralliement national (RN), avaient en effet obtenu, ensemble, près de 9 % des votes exprimés. Sous la direction de Daniel Johnson, l'Union nationale, qui formait le gouvernement depuis juin 1966, défendait par ailleurs une position constitutionnelle empreinte d'autonomisme et flirtant allègrement, sur le plan discursif tout au moins, avec l'idée d'autodétermination, voire avec celle d'indépendance. En 1965, le premier ministre n'avait-il pas publié son fameux ouvrage *Égalité ou indépendance*[7] ? Et, depuis son accession au pouvoir, ne cherchait-il pas à étendre les compétences et les prérogatives de l'«État du Québec», quitte à durcir les rapports de force avec Ottawa[8], voire à provoquer franchement le gouvernement fédéral,

---

6. À l'époque, la position constitutionnelle du Parti libéral du Québec, toujours dirigé par Jean Lesage, se situe quelque part entre la pratique de l'autonomie provinciale et la recherche d'un statut particulier pour l'État du Québec. À ce sujet, voir Boismenu (1989) et Morin (1989).

7. Dans son livre, Johnson revendiquait, pour les minorités francophones du Québec, une égalité semblable à celle dont bénéficiait la minorité anglophone du Québec. En plus de plaider pour le droit à l'autodétermination des Québécois, il défendait leur droit de s'épanouir normalement selon leur entité ethnique et culturelle distincte, dans un cadre juridique, politique et institutionnel clairement défini. Il exigeait la reconnaissance effective des Canadiens français comme l'un des deux peuples fondateurs du Canada, avec les conséquences en découlant pour le Québec, foyer national du Canada français. Tout en précisant que la Confédération n'était pas une fin en soi, il militait enfin pour la reconnaissance élargie du français comme l'une des deux langues officielles au Canada.

8. En février 1968, lors de la conférence constitutionnelle fédérale-provinciale nommée «Confédération de demain», initiée par le premier ministre ontarien John Robarts et influencée par les travaux de la commission Laurendeau-Dunton, dont le rapport préliminaire avait été publié en 1965, Daniel Johnson s'était opposé à

ce qui à l'évidence répondait aux attentes des Québécois, du moins à celles des francophones, qui formaient la majorité de la population?

Mais il y avait plus. Depuis quelques années déjà, les décideurs québécois, appuyés par une panoplie de brillants technocrates [9], avaient entrepris de s'attaquer de manière originale, sans céder à quelque dogmatisme fumeux ou furieux, aux problèmes structurels qui touchaient la socioéconomie québécoise. Ces problèmes se résumaient à six: la détérioration relative de la position du Québec dans l'espace économique canadien et nord-américain; le déclassement de Montréal dans l'économie politique du Canada; la position de dépendance de l'économie du Québec envers le capital étranger et la place résiduelle occupée par les entreprises à propriété canadienne-française parmi les compagnies établies au Québec [10]; la situation défavorable des francophones dans l'échelle des revenus au Québec, et ce, par rapport à toutes les autres catégories ethniques à l'exception des Italiens et des Autochtones; le manque de main-d'œuvre spécialisée et de professionnels pour assurer le roulement optimal d'une socioéconomie reposant sur la production et la consommation de masse; la persistance de foyers de pauvreté ainsi que de phénomènes d'inégalité et de disqualification sociale au cœur d'une société économiquement mature.

On se souvient des solutions mises de l'avant par les gouvernants pour résoudre ces problèmes ou rattraper les retards: utiliser l'État du Québec comme support de redressement économique et levier de développement pour la collectivité afin de compenser la difficulté qu'avaient les entrepreneurs locaux, en particulier les entrepreneurs canadiens-français, à exercer ce rôle et à infléchir les dynamismes de marché en faveur de la zone québécoise; investir massivement dans la formation, l'entretien et la reproduction de la force de travail, de manière notamment à impulser la mobilité sociale ascendante des

---

l'adoption d'une charte des droits de la personne enchâssée dans la Constitution canadienne. La thèse des deux nations formulée par Johnson n'avait par ailleurs pas plu à certains fédéralistes, Pierre Elliott Trudeau en particulier, alors ministre de la Justice, qui avait répliqué au premier ministre du Québec que «[s']il faut reconnaître aux Canadiens français des droits linguistiques et culturels, il n'y a pas de place, dans un Canada à dix, pour un Canada à deux».

9. Contentons-nous de mentionner Jacques Parizeau, Claude Morin, Michel Bélanger, Roger Marier, Guy Coulombe, Louis Bernard, André Marier et Arthur Tremblay.

10. On se rappelle la fameuse étude d'André Raynauld ayant pour titre «La propriété des entreprises au Québec: les années 1960», dont les conclusions sont publiées dans le livre III du *Rapport de la Commission royale d'enquête sur le bilinguisme et le biculturalisme* (1967, ch. IV, p. 53-60). L'ensemble du travail de l'économiste a pris la forme d'un livre intitulé *La propriété des entreprises au Québec: les années 1960*. Voir Raynauld (1974).

francophones; instaurer des mécanismes de protection sociale permettant aux disqualifiés de toutes natures, sans égard à leur origine ethnique bien sûr, de participer à la «société de demain» (Fortin, 1970).

C'est dans le but de stimuler et de redéployer la socioéconomie québécoise que sont créées, durant les années 1960, une foule de sociétés publiques et parapubliques; qu'Hydro-Québec est promue au rang de vaisseau amiral de l'entrepreneuriat québécois; que la Caisse de dépôt et placement est fondée pour administrer les fonds accumulés au titre du régime des rentes du Québec; que l'État, dont les fonctions sont étendues comme appareil d'orchestration, de régulation et de représentation, accueille des masses de fonctionnaires (de langue française surtout, qui peinaient à trouver de bons emplois dans une économie privée fonctionnant largement en anglais[11]); que certaines entreprises sont ciblées pour tirer vers l'avant l'économie québécoise en vue d'installer le capital local dans des créneaux ou des filières d'avenir (aéronautique, ingénierie, pharmaceutique, alimentation, télécommunications); que les cégeps et le réseau de l'Université du Québec sont créés; et que, dans la foulée des recommandations de la commission Castonguay-Nepveu, dont le premier tome du rapport paraît en 1967, sont instaurés un ensemble de programmes à caractère social visant le mieux-être de la population.

Or, pour Lévesque comme pour plusieurs autres intervenants, Jacques Parizeau par exemple, homme à la raison implacable, ces mesures, bien qu'elles fussent opportunes et bienvenues, n'étaient pas suffisantes pour atteindre l'objectif. Le moyen le plus efficace et le plus rapide pour solutionner les maux du Québec, liés au passé bien sûr, mais qu'il était possible de résoudre dans le présent en vue de bâtir un avenir meilleur, se trouvait dans l'indépendance, seule façon d'offrir aux Québécois, tirés par leur État (national), les dispositifs nécessaires à leur progrès collectif à long terme.

L'idée n'était pas insensée, loin de là. Encore fallait-il en convaincre les Québécois, au premier chef les francophones, qui à l'évidence étaient les plus facilement mobilisables aux fins du projet. C'est à ce dessein que s'emploie Lévesque à partir de 1968. Le 11 octobre de cette année-là, au terme de négociations fructueuses avec Gilles Grégoire, président du RN, un nouveau parti politique est fondé, le Parti Québécois (PQ), qui regroupe les militants du MSA et du RN, ces deux formations politiques étant aussitôt sabordées. Peu de temps après, dans le but de favoriser la convergence des forces indépendantistes, le chef du RIN, Pierre Bourgault, cautionne la dissolution de son parti dont les membres, à titre individuel seulement et s'ils le désirent, peuvent intégrer le PQ. Et c'est ce que font plusieurs d'entre eux, aux conditions cependant posées par Lévesque, très soucieux de protéger les droits des

---

11. Au cours des années 1960, le nombre de fonctionnaires employés par l'État du Québec passe de 36 000 à 70 000.

anglophones (qui, pour lui, font partie du « nous », les Québécois), opposé à toute forme de violence ou de déchaînement, et désireux de libérer le projet d'indépendance du Québec de tout relent de ressentiment et de toute idée revancharde ou intention de vindicte. Le but de Lévesque, soyons clairs, n'est pas de mener une offensive contre qui que ce soit, qu'il s'agisse des anglophones, d'Ottawa ou des fédéralistes. Il aspire plutôt à poursuivre une démarche en faveur du Québec et de tous les Québécois, animée par une finalité noble et désirable : assurer la prospérité et l'épanouissement d'une nation historique.

À partir de 1968, le mouvement indépendantiste québécois acquiert, grâce à Lévesque et sous sa direction, une crédibilité, une respectabilité et une notoriété sans pareil. Aux élections de 1970, les premières auxquelles participe le PQ, le parti obtient d'ailleurs 23,1 % des voix exprimées, soit plus que l'Union nationale (19,7 %), ce qui n'est pas rien. Trois ans plus tard, 30,2 % des Québécois appuient le PQ ; en 1976, il recueille plus de 40 % des voix et prend le pouvoir après qu'il eut, il est vrai, adouci sa position politico-constitutionnelle.

Pierre Elliott Trudeau

1968 n'est toutefois pas qu'une année de grâce pour Lévesque. Élu chef du Parti libéral du Canada (PLC) le 6 avril de cette année-là, Pierre Elliott Trudeau est assermenté comme premier ministre deux semaines plus tard, en remplacement de Lester B. Pearson, démissionnaire. Désireux d'affermir sa légitimité, Trudeau déclenche immédiatement des élections. Profitant de l'engouement qu'il suscite par sa personne – jeune, énergique, anticonformiste et progressiste [12] : autant d'ingrédients qui nourrissent ce qu'on appelle alors la « trudeaumanie » –, il remporte haut la main les élections générales de 1968. Sa victoire est particulièrement impressionnante au Québec, où il recueille 53,6 % des voix et rafle 56 comtés sur 74 (76 %).

Montréalais de naissance et grandement interpelé par la place des francophones au pays et par celle du Québec dans le Canada, Trudeau se situe toutefois aux antipodes de Lévesque quant à l'évaluation qu'il fait de l'avenir du Canada, du Québec et du fait français au pays. À ses yeux, l'indépendance du Québec représenterait une perte pour les Québécois puisqu'ils ont contribué à bâtir le Canada, qui est également leur pays de plein droit et de plein espoir. Ainsi, renoncer au Canada serait pour eux une façon de se départir d'un capital qu'ils possèdent et d'une ressource dans laquelle ils ont beaucoup investi. (À noter que l'inverse est aussi vrai, selon Trudeau : perdre le Québec constituerait

---

12. Peu de temps après son élection, le gouvernement Trudeau fait adopter la *Loi légalisant le divorce au Canada*. Moins d'un an plus tard, le 14 mai 1969, il décriminalise les activités homosexuelles entre adultes consentants et légalise l'avortement sous certaines conditions.

pour le Canada une privation, une aliénation, une mutilation, peut-être même le début d'une perdition.) Selon Trudeau, qui voit grand pour les siens et qui a combattu ardemment ce qu'il appelait le «petit nationalisme de repli et anti-démocratique de Duplessis[13]», l'indépendance du Québec ne ferait par ailleurs que projeter les Québécois, en particulier les francophones, dans une situation de régression collective, contribuant à leur isolement et consolidant leurs réflexes de pauvres, de petits et de perdants alors même que leur défi est de prendre la place qui leur revient, hors du syndrome de la seule survivance ethnique et de son horizon défensif, au sein du pays qu'ils ont bâti et qui peut ou pourrait être le lieu de leur épanouissement dans une démocratie renouvelée à laquelle il convie tous les Canadiens, à l'époque (Létourneau, 2004). Si l'on ajoute à ces raisons le fait que Trudeau aimait bien ramer à contre-courant des consensus[14], on comprend que sa croisade contre les «séparatistes», au moment où l'idée d'indépendance prenait du galon au Québec, n'allait pas perdre de son ardeur.

Évidemment, Trudeau ne se contente pas d'établir des diagnostics et de dénigrer l'indépendantisme québécois, qu'il associe arrogamment à un cul-de-sac politique. Il donne suite à sa vision des choses, qui est d'amener les francophones du Canada à se faire maîtres chez eux et à s'épanouir en français dans un Canada renouvelé par l'entremise du gouvernement fédéral, qu'il utilise comme vecteur de transformation du pays – d'où ses tendances à majorer les compétences du gouvernement central contre toute prétention des provinces, en particulier le Québec, à étendre leurs pouvoirs ou leurs attributions.

C'est en conséquence que, fort des conclusions préliminaires de la commission Laurendeau-Dunton qu'il interprète à sa manière, Trudeau enclenche, dès 1968, un processus politico-législatif menant à l'adoption, un an après son arrivée au pouvoir, de la *Loi sur les langues officielles*, qui fait de l'anglais et du français les langues officielles de l'État canadien. On se rappelle qu'au milieu des années 1960, seulement 9 % des postes dans la fonction publique fédérale

---

13. Voir en particulier son texte «La Province de Québec au moment de la grève», dans Trudeau (1956).
14. «Il ne faut pas chercher, écrit Trudeau, d'autre constante à ma pensée que celle de s'opposer aux idées reçues.» (Trudeau, 1967) À cet égard, on sait que Trudeau, dans les années 1950, à une époque où il estimait que la gauche entière demandait à Ottawa de redresser la situation au Québec, était farouchement partisan de l'auto-nomie provinciale. «Dès 1962, toutefois, le gouvernement Lesage et l'opinion publique québécoise, ajoute-t-il, avaient fait de l'autonomie un absolu et tentaient de réduire à rien le pouvoir fédéral; c'est pour défendre le fédéralisme que je suis entré en politique en 1965.» Peut-on penser que si le rouli-roulant de la politique québécoise avait amené la province du côté du fédéralisme à tout crin, Pierre Elliott Trudeau, fidèle à sa pensée et à sa pratique contrariantes, se serait fait le champion de la cause souverainiste?

sont occupés par des francophones, qui forment pourtant le quart de la population du pays. Trudeau va cependant plus loin dans sa promotion du fait français au pays. À compter de 1968, il accorde à des francophones des postes clés au sein de ses cabinets successifs et de l'administration fédérale. Il privilégie la construction d'un deuxième aéroport international à Montréal, plus précisément à Mirabel, façon de lier davantage la région de l'Outaouais (incluant Ottawa) à la zone montréalaise. Soucieux de (re)construire une capitale nationale représentative des deux nations fondatrices du Canada, il décide que le quart des travailleurs fédéraux installés à Ottawa doit déménager à Hull, suscitant amertume et angoisse chez bien des fonctionnaires pour qui traverser la rivière des Outaouais était comme passer du côté «sombre [15]». Désireux de faire de l'État fédéral le garant et le protecteur du fait français au pays, en remplacement du gouvernement du Québec qui, à l'époque, ne sait plus où se situer à ce chapitre, et des péquistes, qui semblent ne plus croire au Canada français [16], il défend sans ambages les minorités de langue française au pays, dont il cherche à garantir les droits dans une Constitution renouvelée au moyen d'une charte des droits qui en ferait partie.

Or, ces actions plaisent généralement aux Québécois. Aux élections de 1972, le PLC réussit à se maintenir au pouvoir (bien que dans le cadre d'un gouvernement minoritaire), grâce au Québec surtout qui, à lui seul, élit plus de députés libéraux (56) que toutes les autres provinces réunies (53). Pour autant, les Québécois, de plus en plus divisés sur leur avenir politico-constitutionnel (en dehors ou au sein du Canada? comme une province ou un État avec un statut spécial? dans le cadre d'un fédéralisme renouvelé ou sur le mode de deux États souverains, mais associés?), ne mettent pas tous leurs œufs dans le panier de l'option Canada que leur propose Trudeau. Cela est particulièrement vrai pour les francophones, qui forment la majorité des électeurs. Fidèles à une espèce de constante de leur culture politique, ceux-ci refusent de s'intégrer à une structure (par exemple, le Canada) s'ils y perçoivent

---

15. C'est en février 1969, à l'occasion d'une conférence des premiers ministres du pays, que les gouvernements fédéral et provinciaux s'entendent sur une nouvelle définition de la capitale fédérale. Dorénavant, la ville de Hull et ses environs feront partie intégrante de la région de la capitale canadienne. Le 20 mai 1969, le gouvernement Trudeau, sous l'égide de Jean Marchand, ministre responsable de la capitale nationale, décrète le transfert d'une partie considérable de l'administration fédérale du côté québécois de la rivière des Outaouais.

16. On se souviendra que le 15 octobre 1968, soit quatre jours après la fondation du Parti Québécois, René Lévesque avait qualifié les francophones hors Québec (sans inclure les Acadiens du Nouveau-Brunswick dans son propos) de «dead ducks» dans une entrevue à l'émission *Twenty Million Questions* de la CBC. Cette formule malheureuse fait oublier que Lévesque, une fois élu premier ministre, a soutenu de diverses manières les francophonies nord-américaines.

un risque d'incorporation ou d'assimilation, au même titre qu'ils regimbent à se séparer de cette même structure s'ils appréhendent la possibilité d'être marginalisés ou exclus. Cette dynamique paradoxale s'applique tout autant à leur relation avec le Québec : pour la majorité, la seule appartenance à cette entité apparaît périlleuse (risque d'isolement) à l'instar d'une situation dans laquelle ils s'en trouveraient éloignés (risque d'égarement) (Létourneau, 2006).

Jusqu'à un certain point, l'année 1968 constitue le moment initial d'une dynamique politique qui marquera fondamentalement les années 1970, alors que deux options majeures seront offertes aux Québécois – celle de la canadienneté de Trudeau [17] et celle de la souveraineté-association de Lévesque –, qu'ils refuseront (ou accepteront?) également !

Conclusion

Il est habituel d'inclure l'année 1968 telle que vécue au Québec dans une conjoncture d'effervescence politique, sociale et culturelle témoignant de la transformation rapide, catégorique et générale d'une société qui se déleste (enfin) de ses figures identitaires traditionnelles et qui, forte de ses nouvelles dispositions et ambitions, entreprend de s'affranchir de ses tutelles pérennes tout en s'élançant vers des lendemains meilleurs. Si pareille interprétation n'est pas irrecevable, elle n'est pas pour autant la plus juste qui soit, et ce, pour au moins quatre raisons.

D'abord, plusieurs transformations que connaît la province au cours de la décennie sont sensiblement les mêmes que celles qui surviennent dans d'autres provinces du Canada (Igartua, 2007) et ailleurs dans le monde. À bien des égards, au cours des années 1960 comme précédemment, le Québec continue d'être marqué par des changements et des processus largement semblables à ceux de ses voisins, ce que l'historiographie québécoise récente a fait ressortir avec acuité – exagérément au dire de certains (Rudin, 1992). Une chose est sûre, la thèse de l'« exceptionnalisme québécois » mérite d'être nuancée.

Ensuite, il est contestable d'affirmer que la société se révolutionne littéralement dans les années 1960. Le changement est plutôt graduel et partiel. Il est aussi tâtonnant (Morin, 1991). Il est enfin inspiré et impulsé de l'extérieur, en particulier par le gouvernement fédéral (Dion, 2000), autant qu'il découle d'idées originales et d'initiatives locales.

---

17. On peut ainsi définir la canadienneté (à distinguer de la canadianité) : projet/ processus de reconstruction du Canada en tant que société multiculturelle dans laquelle l'esprit civique dame le pion aux logiques ethniques ; dans laquelle des droits fondamentaux sont constitutionnalisés dans une charte des droits et libertés de la personne ; et dans laquelle la citoyenneté et la liberté individuelle sont rehaussées par rapport à la nationalité culturelle et l'identité collective. Voir Létourneau (2006, p. 158).

En outre, il est excessif de laisser croire que toute la société québécoise est, au cours des années 1960, emportée par la fièvre du changement. De manière générale, la population, irréductible à un seul type identitaire, s'ouvre à de nouveaux référents en se délestant lentement de certains de ses anciens repères ou en les investissant de nouvelles significations. La question du sentiment religieux des Québécois est intéressante à aborder sous l'angle du changement progressif plutôt que du point de vue de la déchirure soudaine. En 1968, la grande majorité des Québécois (limitons-nous ici aux francophones) est croyante, à défaut d'être pieuse (si tant est que cette piété soit mesurée par l'assistance à la messe dominicale, qui est en baisse). Avec le temps, ils prennent toutefois leurs distances par rapport à certaines prescriptions religieuses, plusieurs fidèles trouvant justification à leur démarche dans les réformes lancées par le concile Vatican II. Toujours animés par la foi, d'autres acteurs cherchent hors du canon traditionnel des réponses spirituelles à leurs interrogations existentielles. Le rejet par les fidèles, y compris par les femmes, des préceptes d'*Humanae vitae*, encyclique du pape Paul VI lancée en 1968 et interdisant la régulation des naissances par la pilule contraceptive, témoigne allègrement d'un tel phénomène. Cependant, ce n'est que dans la première moitié des années 1970 que l'Église perd vraiment sa fonction référentielle au sein de la société et auprès des masses, le catholicisme ne disparaissant toutefois pas pour autant à titre de «ressource identitaire» (Laniel, 2016).

Enfin, il est tout aussi abusif de prétendre que l'ensemble des Québécois est excité par l'idée d'indépendance ou par celle de nationalisme. Ce n'est manifestement pas le cas des non-francophones (Québécois aussi!), qui continuent massivement à se dire fédéralistes en plus d'appuyer le PLQ ou le PLC à chacune des élections provinciales ou fédérales. Chez les francophones, la situation est compliquée : s'il se trouve des indépendantistes radicaux, impétueux ou modérés, ils ne forment pas, en 1968, la majorité de l'électorat, loin de là. La majeure partie des Québécois francophones oscille plutôt entre la thèse des «deux États séparés, mais associés» et celle – qui, à l'évidence, rejoint la portion prédominante de l'électorat – d'une espèce de statut particulier pour le Québec dans le cadre d'un fédéralisme renouvelé. C'est cette thèse, qui trouve son fondement dans la représentation de la canadianité, forte depuis toujours chez les Canadiens puis chez les Canadiens français, qu'Yvon Deschamps rendra en 1978 par une tirade aussi éloquente que succulente : «Le vrai Québécois sait qu'est-ce qu'y veut. Pis qu'est-ce qu'y veut, c't'un Québec indépendant dans un Canada fort.» (Deschamps, 1998) Dans ce contexte, l'usage du concept de nationalisme pour décrire le fondement et la forme politiques de l'humeur populaire des Québécois (francophones) dans les années 1960 est peut-être inapproprié, sauf si l'on dilue le terme pour lui permettre d'accueillir à peu près toute volonté de faire progresser le Québec et de modifier la situation de la province (qui n'en est pas simplement une, de l'avis de la majorité!) à l'intérieur du Canada.

Dans le Québec des années 1960, il se trouve une grande majorité de gens qui, prenant acte de la situation pâlissante du Québec au Canada, déclinante de Montréal au pays et désavantageuse des francophones au sein de l'appareil d'État fédéral, dans les provinces et au Québec même, décident de s'attaquer au problème qui gangrène l'idéal alors en vogue de justice sociale et qui pose un défi à l'unité nationale. Épousant différents horizons politiques et provenant du monde anglophone ou francophone, ces gens sont animés par une ambition développementale bien plus que mus par un élan nationaliste, anticolonialiste ou socialiste. La prospérité du Québec et sa reconstitution en tant que zone économique forte, le repositionnement de Montréal au Canada, la redynamisation des entreprises québécoises, la mobilité ascendante des francophones, le souci d'égalité des citoyens au pays, la protection des minorités, le soutien aux individus et aux familles (dans la perspective d'une égalisation des chances entre tous), voilà ce qui les intéresse et les motive. Comment y parvenir avec le maximum d'avantages et le minimum d'insuccès, voilà ce qui les sépare.

En dépit d'erreurs de parcours qu'il est facile de diagnostiquer après coup, les décideurs, luttant contre les contingences de ce qui vient et advient, ont dans les années 1960 et subséquemment permis de faire évoluer les situations pour le mieux, encore qu'il soit difficile de déterminer ce qui découle de l'action des gouvernants et ce qui tient aux dynamismes intrinsèques de la socioéconomie. Toujours est-il qu'en 2018, la condition générale des francophones au Québec est nettement meilleure qu'il y a 50 ans (celle des minorités francophones au Canada reste cependant préoccupante, sauf en Acadie, et encore!). La position de Montréal dans l'économie du pays a non seulement cessé de s'enfoncer, mais la métropole québécoise, mondialisation et nouvelle économie aidant, a repris du poil de la bête par rapport à Toronto, dont la grandeur actuelle traduit peut-être davantage la croissance passée que sa performance récente. Enfin, si la position politique du Québec au sein de la fédération canadienne ne s'est pas améliorée pour la peine, se détériorant même à la Chambre des communes[18], le Québec et l'Ontario, dont les intérêts et les cultures politiques sont proches malgré leurs concurrences épisodiques, continuent à jouer un rôle névralgique dans l'évolution des affaires politiques du Canada[19], sans compter le fait que le Québec se présente et existe comme société globale distincte maintenant plus que jamais. Évidemment, personne ne

---

18. En 1968, la Chambre des communes du Canada comptait 264 sièges, dont 72 accordés au Québec (27,3 %). En 2016, le nombre de sièges était passé à 338, dont 78 au Québec (23,1 %).

19. Ensemble, les députés du Québec et de l'Ontario occupent toujours une majorité de sièges (199 sur 338, soit 58,9 % des places) à la Chambre des communes.

peut pronostiquer l'avenir. Il appert cependant que 1968, qui marque l'arrivée dans le décor québéco-canadien de figures majeures, aura permis aux Québécois de tenir leur bout dans un jeu de tensions où les positions unilatérales ou monovalentes, quoi qu'on dise, se seront révélées être les seules vaincues.

Références

Boismenu, Gérard (1989). « La pensée constitutionnelle de Jean Lesage », dans Comeau, Robert, et Gilles Bourque (dir.). *Jean Lesage et l'éveil d'une nation*, Montréal, Presses de l'Université du Québec, p. 76-107.

Deschamps, Yvon (1998). « La fierté d'être Québécois », monologue, *Tout Deschamps. Trente ans de monologues et de chansons*, Montréal, Lanctôt, p. 253-262.

Dion, Stéphane (2000). « Le rôle moteur du gouvernement fédéral dans la Révolution tranquille », dans Bélanger, Yves, Robert Comeau et Céline Métivier. *La Révolution tranquille : 40 ans plus tard : un bilan*, Montréal, VLB éditeur, p. 49-61.

Fortin, Gérald (1970). « La société de demain ses impératifs, son organisation », Québec, Commission d'enquête sur la santé et le bien-être social, Annexe 25, p. 31-42 et 77-99.

Gauvreau, Michael (2008). *Les origines catholiques de la Révolution tranquille*, Montréal, Fides, 464 p.

Igartua, José (2007). *The Other Quiet Revolution: National Identities in English Canada, 1945–71*, Vancouver, University of British Columbia Press, 288 p.

Laniel, Jean-François (2016). « La laïcité québécoise est-elle achevée ? Essai sur une petite nation, entre société neuve et république », dans Meunier, É.-Martin (dir.). *Le Québec et ses mutations culturelles. Six enjeux pour le devenir d'une société*, Ottawa, Presses de l'Université d'Ottawa, p. 423-474.

Lapointe-Gagnon, Valérie (2018). *Panser le Canada : une histoire intellectuelle de la Commission Laurendeau-Dunton*, Montréal, Boréal, 416 p.

Laurendeau, André (1958). « La théorie du roi nègre », *Le Devoir*, 4 juillet, p. 4.

Laurendeau, Marc (1990). *Les Québécois violents*, Montréal, Boréal, 352 p.

Laurin-Lamothe, Audrey et Nicolas Moreau (dir.) (2011). *Le Canadien de Montréal : une légende repensée*, Montréal, Presses de l'Université de Montréal, 146 p.

Létourneau, Jocelyn (2006). *Que veulent vraiment les Québécois ? Regards sur l'intention nationale au Québec (français) d'hier à aujourd'hui*, Montréal, Boréal.

———. (2004). « Penseurs, passeurs de la modernité dans le Québec des années cinquante et soixante », dans Michaud, Ginette et Élizabeth Nardout-Lafarge (dir.) *Construction de la modernité au Québec*, Montréal, Lanctôt éditeur, p. 53-64.

Morin, Claude (1991). *Mes premiers ministres : Lesage, Johnson, Bertrand, Bourassa, Lévesque*, Montréal, Boréal, 640 p.

Morin, Jacques-Yvan (1989). « Jean Lesage et le rapatriement de la Constitution », dans Comeau, Robert et Gilles Bourque (dir.). *Jean Lesage et l'éveil d'une nation*, Montréal, Presses de l'Université du Québec, p. 116-136.

Raynauld, André (1974). *La propriété des entreprises au Québec : les années 1960*, Montréal, Les Presses de l'Université de Montréal, 160 p.

Roy, Jean-Louis (1973). *La longue marche des Québécois : le temps des ruptures (1945–1960)*, Montréal, Leméac, 383 p. [En ligne] http://classiques.uqac.ca/contemporains/roy_jean_louis/roy_jean_louis.html.

Rudin, Ronald (1992). « Revisionism and the Search for a Normal Society : A Critique of Recent Quebec Historical Writing », *Canadian Historical Review*, vol. 73, n° 1, p. 3061.

Trudeau, Pierre Elliott (Dir.) (1967). *Le fédéralisme et la société canadienne-française*, Montréal, Hurtubise HMH, 227 p.

———. (1956). *La grève de l'amiante*, Montréal, Les Éditions Cité libre, 448 p.

Warren, Jean-Philippe (2016). « L'origine d'un nom. D'où vient l'expression Révolution tranquille ? », *HistoireEngagée.ca*, 14 septembre. [En ligne] http://histoireengagee.ca/lorigine-dunnom-dou-vient-lexpression-revolution-tranquille/

———. (2008). *Une douce anarchie. Les années 1968 au Québec*, Montréal, Boréal, 312 p.

Chapter 4
The Nationalists of 1968 and the Search for Canadian Independence

STEPHEN AZZI

Abstract

The year 1968 marked a decisive break in the history of English-Canadian nationalism. An older generation of nationalists, mostly located in rural Canada and concerned with the loosening of Canada's bond to Britain, found itself overtaken by a movement known as the New Nationalism. Young, well-educated, and concentrated in the urban centres of southern Ontario, the New Nationalists were preoccupied with U.S. economic control of Canada. Their concerns were propelled to the forefront of Canadian public debate in 1968 with the publication of the Watkins Report, a study of foreign investment in Canada. The two key figures in producing that report, Cabinet Minister Walter Gordon and economist Mel Watkins, also represented the two distinct factions of the New Nationalist movement, mainstream and radical. Their 1968 collaboration helped channel Canadian anxieties about the United States into an effort to reduce American economic influence in Canada.

The year 1968 marked a decisive break in the history of English-Canadian nationalism. A movement known as the New Nationalism pushed aside an older generation of nationalists. Young, well-educated, and concentrated in the urban centres of southern Ontario, New Nationalists were alarmed by the level of American economic control over Canada. Their ideas had been percolating since the mid-1950s. They were propelled to the forefront of Canadian public debate in 1968 with the publication of the Watkins Report,[1] a government-sponsored study of foreign investment in Canada. The report appeared just as Canadians were developing profound apprehensions about the United States, fuelled by the war in Vietnam and racial conflict in the United States. These anxieties were channelled into an effort to reduce American influence—especially economic influence—in Canada. The next

---

1. This was widely referred to as the Watkins Report; its official name when published was *Foreign Ownership and the Structure of Canadian Industry* (Canada 1968).

Figure 4.1. University of Toronto political scientist Stephen Clarkson (*right*) looks on as Mel Watkins (*left*) and Walter Gordon (*centre*) examine Clarkson's book *An Independent Foreign Policy for Canada*, 14 March 1968. *Source:* Bob Olsen, *Toronto Star.* Courtesy of Getty Images.

decade showed the impact of the New Nationalism, as a reluctant federal government created an agency to screen foreign investment, a national oil company, and a large Canadian-owned corporation to increase the Canadian presence in the domestic economy. The New Nationalism was evidence of the intellectual impact, beyond the borders of the United States, of the Vietnam War and the struggle for Black equality. Canada's 1968 experience was unique, but at the same time it was intimately linked to the issues that defined 1968 in the United States.

Although connected to events abroad, the English-Canadian experience lacked much of the radicalism that characterized 1968 in Paris, Prague, and elsewhere. Canadian students and workers did not declare a general strike, race riots did not erupt in Canada's cities, and police and protesters did not clash violently in the streets—at least not outside Quebec. English-Canadian nationalism in the period was mild. Most nationalists were not seeking to overthrow Canada's political and economic system. Instead, they wanted the government to enact some measures to discourage further American invest-ment in the economy and, perhaps, to promote Canadian culture. A radical branch of the movement, the Waffle, sought more fundamental changes, including a socialist system to replace the market economy, but these ideas never won widespread support. Suffering possibly from 1968 envy, Canadian historians have emphasized the radical fringe at the expense of the mainstream, giving a distorted image of both the New Nationalism and of Canada's insipid 1968 experience.[2]

Countless English Canadians espoused nationalist ideas in the 1960s and 1970s, but two individuals stand out. Liberal Cabinet Minister Walter Gordon and economist Mel Watkins were not only the two most prominent leaders of the movement, they also represented the two distinct varieties of nationalism that resonated in English Canada at the time. It was their work together in 1968 that proved a catalyst for the nationalist movement.

Walter Gordon

Walter Lockhart Gordon was a pillar of the Canadian establishment. Born to a wealthy Toronto family, he was a senior partner in both Clarkson Gordon, the country's largest firm of chartered accountants, and Woods Gordon, Canada's leading management consulting firm. He was the founding president of Canadian Corporate Management, a conglomerate that grew to become one of the country's 100 largest firms. Although he had a talent for business, Gordon was bored by the day-to-day grind of corporate life. His real interests lay in his side projects: he worked during the Second World War in the federal Department of Finance, took on consulting contracts for the provincial and federal governments, and chaired two royal commissions. In the 1950s, Gordon turned down an invitation to join the federal Cabinet, but only because he doubted that he could wield much power as a junior minister—no doubt a shrewd assessment, as no one understood power better than Walter Gordon. Following the defeat of the Liberal government in 1957 and Louis St. Laurent's resignation as prime minister and Party leader, Gordon began devoting an increasing amount of time to politics. He helped his friend Lester Pearson win the Liberal leadership, and, when Pearson struggled to reorganize the Party, Gordon took on the task himself. He restructured the Party, hired and fired staff, recruited candidates, and raised funds—acting throughout as though he were Party president. Keith Davey, Judy LaMarsh, and many other Party activists later remembered that Pearson would never have become prime minister but for Walter Gordon (Peter Stursberg fonds 1977, 17; Peter Stursberg fonds 1976a, 44; Library of Parliament fonds 1984, 83; Library of Parliament fonds 1986, 12; Davey 1986, 114; LaMarsh 1969, 63).

When Pearson took office as prime minister in 1963, Gordon was able to choose his reward. He decided that he would become minister of finance, a portfolio that would allow him to implement his political ideas, including his

---

2. The scholarly literature on the Waffle is extensive and ever-growing. It includes Hackett (1979); Bullen (1983); Brodie (1985); Watkins (1990); John Smart (1990); Mahon (1990), Patricia Smart (1990, 2009); Burstyn (1990); Levine (1990); Borch (2005); Webber (2009), Lexier (2013, 2017); Blocker (2018, 2019); Chiarello (2020).

goal of restricting foreign investment in Canada. In his 1963 budget, Gordon proposed a 30 percent tax on the foreign takeover of Canadian firms and an increase in the tax on dividends paid to non-residents by companies that were not at least 25 percent Canadian owned. The business community reacted with outrage, and Gordon found himself without support within the Cabinet, whose members did not share his nationalist views. He withdrew the contentious elements of the budget, never to reintroduce them. Two years later, he resigned from the Cabinet after recommending that Pearson call an election, one in which the Liberals failed to win a majority. For one year, he languished on the backbenches, frustrated at the government's disorganization and at its failure to address the foreign investment issue. In late 1966, he decided to resign his seat in Parliament and return to corporate life. Ontario's Liberal MPs, fiercely loyal to Gordon, reacted with alarm. They urged Pearson to find a way to keep Gordon in Ottawa.

The final act of Gordon's political career began in late 1966 and early 1967 when he negotiated his return to Pearson's Cabinet. Gordon had several conditions. He insisted on having the power to supervise Cabinet business, as well as control over the Privy Council Office, the prime minister's government department. Gordon suggested that his title be deputy prime minister or president of the Privy Council. Pearson agreed to the position of President of the Privy Council and to the powers that Gordon demanded, which would have made him de facto co–prime minister. Gordon also stipulated that the government issue a policy statement on foreign investment and introduce legislation requiring all companies to sell a portion of their shares to Canadians, with a goal that at least two-thirds of any major company be owned by Canadians after 25 or 30 years. Pearson rejected this idea but agreed that Gordon could chair a Cabinet committee that would supervise the work of a task force of experts charged with examining the foreign investment issue. In turn, this study would lead to a government policy statement, a *white paper* in the language of official Ottawa. On this understanding, which—despite Gordon's repeated efforts—was never put in writing, Gordon returned to Cabinet on 9 January 1967. Later, he was angered by not being given control over Cabinet business or the Privy Council Office. His frustrations grew when Pearson appointed the Cabinet foreign investment committee, which included several ministers whose views were diametrically opposed to those of Gordon, the committee chair.

Mel Watkins

As chair of the Cabinet Committee on Foreign Investment, Gordon was responsible for recruiting an economist to head the task force that would prepare a study on the issue. This was a more challenging task than it appeared on the surface: Gordon knew few economists, and most of them disagreed with his views on foreign investment. In fact, Gordon knew only one economist with nationalist views. In 1964, Gordon had written to University of Toronto economist Abraham Rotstein to commend him for an article that criticized Harry Johnson, the most influential economist of the era and a caustic critic of nationalist thought (Abraham Rotstein fonds). Later, Gordon and Rotstein met and began a friendship. In early 1967, Gordon asked Rotstein to chair the task force, but Rotstein refused, fearing that his nationalist views would undermine the report's integrity. Instead, Rotstein suggested his friend and University of Toronto colleague Mel Watkins, a recommendation Gordon accepted (Watkins 1994a). "I told him I was not a Liberal but a New Democrat," Watkins (1987) later recalled. "He said not to worry, that many of his strongest supporters were similarly misguided and that he couldn't afford to be choosy."

At the time, Watkins was on the road to Damascus, in transition from being a classical economist to a Marxist. One year earlier, he had written a sympathetic piece on Gordon's policy manifesto *A Choice for Canada: Independence or Colonial Status*. Although Watkins (1966) criticized elements of the book, he concluded that "Mr. Gordon's case against foreign investment is … a strong one based on political experience and premise" (77). Few other Canadian economists found Gordon's argument so compelling.

Watkins encountered Gordon during a two- or three-year period when the views of the two men overlapped. Previously, Watkins had rejected Gordon's position as economic nonsense, mocking the 1963 budget as not just pre-Keynesian but also pre-Cambrian (Bothwell, Drummond, and English 1989, 303; Drummond 1988, 12). In 1965, Watkins wrote that "there is no convincing evidence that foreign ownership is a threat either to Canadian independence in general or to our ability to exercise effective domestic economic policy in particular." For that reason, the federal government should "stop harassing foreign owners" (Watkins 1965, 76, 78). But by 1966, Watkins's views had begun to change, moving more closely in line with Gordon's. Beginning in 1968, Watkins shifted far to the left, parting ways with Gordon. While Gordon's views remained remarkably constant, Watkins became convinced that socialism was more important than nationalism.

Watkins's background contrasted starkly with Gordon's. Watkins was born in 1932, near the lowest point of the Great Depression, on a farm outside McKellar, a small community in central Ontario. The family struggled to survive: Watkins's father logged in the bush and worked in the local sawmill to support his six children.[3] "We weren't poverty-stricken—in the sense that you could always grow your own food—but there was a distinct shortage of cash,"

---

3. Christina Newman (1970, 24) reported that there were five children in the family, but the *Globe and Mail* obituary (Obituary 2020) written by Watkin's son Matthew, recounted that there were six.

Watkins (1972, 68) remembered. The meagre, small-town upbringing had a lasting effect on Watkins. "To grow up in such a community, you begin to sense at an early age where the power lies and where it doesn't lie," he later said. "A feeling of powerlessness hangs over you like a smog. ... [McKellar] was poor to begin with, [then came] the Great Depression, then the war came along, a war plant came in and everyone left the farms to manufacture cordite, the war ended, the plant closed" (Watkins 1972, 68–69). At the age of 16, Watkins and his twin brother headed to the University of Toronto, where they funded their education with summer jobs, scholarships, and money their father had earned in the cordite plant during the war. Back home in the summers, Watkins worked in a tourist hotel, carrying bags for Americans. He enjoyed giving them inaccurate directions so they would get lost. "It was the kind of area where it was no sin to be suspicious of the Americans. It's a tory part of the world" (Watkins 1972, 68).

Almost all of the rest of Watkins's life was spent in the academic world. Originally intending to become an accountant, he studied commerce and finance at the University of Toronto. His trajectory changed when he heard lectures by Harold Innis, the leading Canadian economist of the 1930s and 1940s. By the 1950s, Innis was, in Watkins's words (1972, 69), "no longer an economist anymore, in any conventional sense of that term." Instead, Innis had become an anti-imperialist: "He was looking at all the great empires and why they fell. Innis was very much a liberal, profoundly suspicious of great aggregations of power. And he was very opposed, as an intellectual, to American imperialism." After working one year as an accountant at Price Waterhouse, Watkins yearned for more. He returned to the University of Toronto as a graduate student, before heading off to Boston to attend the Massachusetts Institute of Technology (MIT). There he married an American, became active in the Democratic Party, and picked up a hint of the local accent.

While becoming an American liberal in Boston, Watkins missed the bubbling up of nationalism in English Canada during the 1957 and 1958 elections. Under the leadership of John Diefenbaker, the victorious Conservatives had tapped into a general disenchantment with the United States, fuelled by concerns over American economic influence in Canada and revulsion at the way innocent Americans—and some Canadians—were caught up in the anti-communist purges known as McCarthyism. "I was first conscious of what had happened to me when I came back ... and found great difficulty in understanding what Diefenbaker was about. ... I had a really predictable American liberal reaction to that 'clown'" (Watkins 1972, 70).

Returning to Canada in 1958, Watkins began teaching at the University of Toronto. He became friends with fellow economist Rotstein, who Watkins later described as "the most important single influence on my thinking of any man I've met" (Newman 1970, 24). By the mid-1960s, Watkins was also shaped by events in the United States: the Black Power movement, unrest on American college campuses, and, most significantly, protests against the American war in Vietnam. These struggles between the powerful and the powerless reminded Watkins of life growing up in McKellar (Stewart 1970, 33).

Watkins Task Force

On 1 February 1967, the ministerial Committee on Foreign Investment agreed to hire Watkins to head up the task force, with the rest of the members being appointed on 9 March. The task force was composed of eight university economists: Watkins, Rotstein, Stephen Hymer (an expert on the operations of multinational corporations), Ed Safarian (the only Canadian to conduct empirical research on the performance of foreign-owned firms), Gideon Rosenbluth (to represent the West), William Woodfine (to represent the Atlantic provinces), Bernard Bonin and Claude Masson (to represent Quebec). The members were young: not one of them was older than 46, and six of the eight were still in their 30s. All the anglophones had pursued graduate studies in American universities: Rotstein at Chicago and Columbia, Hymer at MIT, Safarian at the University of California Berkeley, Rosenbluth at Columbia, and Woodfine at MIT. Still, the task force membership represented a wide range of opinions, and there were, as Bonin (1994) later recalled, "some lively debates." While preparing the task force report, Watkins met every week with Gordon, later recalling that Gordon had "a considerable influence" on his ideas (Watkins 1994a).

Relations between the task force and senior bureaucrats were tense. Bonin (1994) remembered the economists being called "Gordon's bright boys" and being treated with disdain by the officials. The problem, according to Bonin (1994), was that "the civil service at the time was certainly well disposed toward the United States and not well disposed towards any kind of economic nationalism." Watkins was annoyed that the Deputy Minister of Industry, Simon Reisman, was urging him to take his time and get it right, no doubt hoping to delay the task force report until after Pearson and Gordon had left office (Watkins 1994b, 31). Indeed, when Pearson announced his resignation in December 1967, senior civil servants told task force members, "You guys are dead now: your task force will be forgotten" (Bonin 1994). But the tensions went both ways. Marshall Crowe, Deputy Secretary to the Cabinet, remembered that Watkins was contemptuous of the officials, treating them as though they were idiots. He seemed to have "a big chip on his shoulder" (Crowe 1995). In the view of Gerald Stoner, Deputy Secretary to the Cabinet, Watkins was "wild" and "harum-scarum" (Stoner 1994).

The task force submitted its final report to Gordon on 12 January 1968, during a foreign-exchange crisis. Officials tried to prevent publication of the report, fearing it would hinder a negotiated solution to Canada's exchange problems with the United States (Stoner 1994). Worried that the government would try to block the report's release, Brian Land, Gordon's former executive assistant, went to the Queen's Printer in Hull, Quebec, and took a couple of boxes of the document (Land 1994). Gordon threatened to resign if the task force report was not published (Stoner 1994). For his part, Watkins leaked the report to Beland Honderich, publisher of the *Toronto Star*, and then told government officials that the *Star* would publish it if the government did not (Watkins 1994a). On 22 January, the ministerial committee agreed to table the report in the Commons, which Gordon did on 15 February.

The Liberal government ignored the report. Members of the Cabinet committee did not feel bound by the views of a group of unelected university economists and would not endorse the report (Gordon 1977, 312). With Pearson leaving office in three months, there was no time to draft a policy statement—and, in any case, there was no chance that ministers with strongly conflicting views could agree to any common position on the issue. According to Maurice Sauvé, "There was no enthusiasm at all [in Cabinet] for the Watkins Report" (Peter Stursberg fonds 1976b). With no experience in government, Watkins had the naive view that the Cabinet should be bound by the recommendations emanating from his team of economists. When the report was submitted, Watkins was surprised by the response, which he summarized as "What? What? I'm not going to advocate that!" (Watkins 1972, 76). He later described himself as "pissed off with the system I'd always worked so dutifully for that I figured something radical had to be done" (Newman 1972, 58). In the end, Cabinet could not agree on a position on the report. The matter would be held for Pearson's successor. Having completed his work, Gordon resigned from Cabinet on 11 March 1968. Pierre Trudeau replaced Pearson as Liberal Party leader on 6 April and as prime minister on 20 April.

The task force report was a moderate document, much more anodyne and less controversial than officials had feared (Stoner 1994). The choice of language was revealing. A compromise among eight economists, it avoided the jargon of the New Left and the Old Left. At no point, did the report talk about American imperialism or the other issues that would preoccupy Watkins for the rest of his life. Reflecting the American training of most of its authors, the report spoke of the *multinational firm*, drawing from the most recent American literature on that issue, rather than referring to the *branch-plant economy*, as Canadian economists had traditionally framed the issue.

The report began with the premise that Canada had benefitted from foreign investment and would continue to do so in the future. Still, there were problems with foreign capital that demanded government attention. Foreign-owned firms paid too little tax, sold their products for too high a price in

Canada, imported too many parts from abroad (instead of using Canadian components), charged too little for their exports (especially natural resources), and did not offer shares to the public, depriving Canadians of a cut of the profits. The task force rejected any suggestion that the government force a large-scale replacement of foreign with domestic investment. Still, the members did recommend that the government create incentives to encourage foreign firms to sell some of their shares to Canadians. The task force was particularly concerned with extraterritoriality: the application of foreign law to foreign-owned subsidiaries operating in Canada. The report recommended both legislation to prevent foreign-owned firms from following directives from foreign governments and the creation of a Crown corporation that would buy goods from foreign-owned firms in Canada and sell them to other countries to get around the U.S. *Trading with the Enemy Act.*

Another problem was the inefficiency of Canadian industry, which in turn explained why companies tended not to export. The productivity of Canadian firms could be improved by creating a more competitive economic environment, which could be accomplished by lowering Canadian tariffs and strengthening the country's competition policies. The task force also recommended the creation of the Canada Development Corporation, a large holding company that would pool domestic capital (some public, some private) to increase the Canadian presence in the domestic economy. These proposals were not outside the mainstream of thought among Canadian economists but were out of harmony with Walter Gordon's views. Gordon had wanted a far-reaching initiative to replace foreign with domestic capital, an idea the task force rejected. The task force also favoured a move toward freer trade, a proposal that was an anathema to Gordon (Canada 1968).

Generally hostile to nationalism, economists gave the report mixed reviews. Typical were the views of Harry Johnson, who described the report as "a useful, sensible, and important document on the whole" (Johnson 1968, 615). He was particularly favourable toward the task force's recommendations to improve the information made available to the government on the operations of foreign-owned firms, the proposed measures to counteract extraterritoriality, and the report's overall emphasis on increasing the benefits and reducing the costs of foreign investment, rather than restricting future foreign investment or encouraging foreigners to sell their business to Canadians. Johnson was more critical of the analysis of capital markets, the politics of foreign investment, and the balance of payments implications of foreign investment.

The 1968 Context

All this occurred against a backdrop of upheaval in the United States. In the same month that the Watkins Report was released, the Kerner Commission, appointed by President Lyndon Johnson after the race riots of 1967, issued its report, predicting further polarization in U.S. society and a breakdown of democracy if the government did not move quickly to help bridge the social and economic gap between Black people and white people (United States 1968). February 1968 was also a turning point in the public's view of the war in Vietnam, as events convinced increasing numbers of Canadians and Americans that the United States was betraying its principles in that conflict. The month began with the United States defending against the Tet Offensive, a series of attacks by the North Vietnamese Army and the South Vietnamese Vietcong rebels. Tet revealed the disingenuousness of American leaders, who had long insisted that the United States was on the verge of winning the war. On 2 February, newspapers across the world ran a dramatic Associated Press photograph of the South Vietnamese police chief, Nguyen Ngoc Loan, carrying out the summary execution of a Vietcong guerrilla on the streets of Saigon.[4] On 8 February, newspapers ran a report from the devastated city of Ben Tre in South Vietnam, where a U.S. major was quoted as saying, "It became necessary to destroy the town to save it," a phrase that came to represent the senselessness of the American position.[5] During the week of 11–17 February, 543 Americans were killed in action and 2,547 were wounded, the highest weekly American casualty toll during the war (Buckley 1968). On 27 February, CBS aired a 30-minute special report on Vietnam, in which news anchor Walter Cronkite concluded that the war was "mired in stalemate" and that a negotiated settlement was the best way out (Cronkite 1998, 582). In the following months, Martin Luther King Jr. and Robert Kennedy would be assassinated, riots would break out in more than 100 American cities, and mass protests against the Vietnam War would erupt around the world.

This context—in which Canada's neighbour seemed to represent violence at home and abroad—had a profound impact on English-Canadian nationalism. Stephen Clarkson, a young political scientist at the University of Toronto, edited *An Independent Foreign Policy for Canada?*, a collection of academic essays (1968), several of which argued that Canada should withdraw from the NATO and NORAD alliances. These views crossed partisan lines (Donaghy 2002, 113–114). Others argued that the Canadian government should promote and protect Canadian culture by establishing content quotas for Canadian radio and televisions stations, by providing funding for Canadian films, and by preventing foreign magazines from establishing editions aimed at the Canadian market. Still others insisted that federal and provincial governments should work to

---

4. See, for example, the front page of the 2 February 1968 editions of the *New York Times*, the *Globe and Mail*, the *Washington Post*, the *Times* of London, and the *Manchester Guardian*.

5. The story was widely reported. See, for example, *New York Times* (1968); *Globe and Mail* (1968); *Ottawa Citizen* (1968); *Montreal Gazette* (1968).

ensure both a minimum number of Canadian professors in the country's universities and a significant level of Canadian content in university programs. At times, the nationalists veered into xenophobic silliness, as when Carleton University English professor Robin Mathews (1970) mocked Prime Minister Trudeau for dating Barbra Streisand instead of a Canadian: "Pierre-baby is a realist. He knows where it's at. The name of the game is power. When you're the prime minister of a colony, you appear with one of the princesses of the empire."

Throughout the discussion, nationalists focused on the economic realm. Yes, there were concerns over Canadian content on radio and television, over the nationality of university professors in Canada, over Canada's military alliance with the United States—but all these issues paled next to economic matters. The economy was "the key," according to book publisher and English professor Dave Godfrey. "Before you could have cultural freedom, before you could have real political freedom, especially in foreign affairs, before you could have your own military policy, you had to have a national economy that was controlled by your own people" (Godfrey, Watkins, and Gordon 1970, 158). For media commentator Laurier LaPierre (1968, 59), Canada could not solve its social, political, and economic problems "until the absentee landlords stop dominating the country." Countless nationalists repeated this sentiment. In 1972, when pollsters asked 5,000 Canadians which was more important—economic, political, or cultural independence—48 percent chose economic, while only 27 and 16 percent chose political and cultural independence, respectively (*Toronto Star* 1972b).

The major political parties all struggled to respond to the foreign investment issue. Walter Gordon had long been open about his nationalist views, but now other prominent Liberals joined him. In 1968, while seeking the Liberal Party leadership, John Turner declared himself a nationalist and announced his support for the objectives of the Watkins Report (Walter L. Gordon fonds 1968). The victor of that contest, the new prime minister, Pierre Trudeau, had assured Walter Gordon that he was sympathetic to the cause, but once in office he turned out to be mostly indifferent. "It's a non-concern with him," said Barney Danson, a Toronto-area Liberal MP (Tower 1970). As a result, several Liberal MPs worked to force the Prime Minister to act. The Conservatives also began talking about restrictions on foreign investment. The issue emerged as a contentious topic at a five-day Conservative policy conference in 1969, when Eddie Goodman, a senior party organizer, pushed for a party policy to limit foreign ownership (Westell 1969). In 1971, party leader Robert Stanfield proposed that the government classify industries according to the "degree of Canadian control necessary to maintain our independence." Some sectors would be entirely Canadian-owned, while others could have some foreign ownership or, presumably, could be entirely foreign-owned (*Toronto Star* 1971). Of the major parties, the New Democrats were the most favourable to nationalist policies. Party officials asked Watkins if he would tour with leader Tommy Douglas during the 1968 election campaign. "The NDP embraced me like a long lost brother," Watkins (1994a) later recalled.[6] Watkins sought the advice of Walter Gordon, who reminded his protégé of his promise to stay out of politics for one year after the Watkins Report's publication (Watkins 1994a). As a result, Watkins did not take part in the campaign, but Douglas still spoke frequently about the report, warning that the New Democrats would "make life unbearable for any government" that did not implement the recommendations (Stevens and Saywell 1969, 59).

Watkins's prominent position in public debate was very much the result of his alliance with Walter Gordon. When Gordon first met Watkins, he was a little-known 35-year-old associate professor of political economy. Afterward, he was a national figure. In part, this was because of Watkins's position as task force chair, but it was also a product of Gordon's strong ties with the *Toronto Star*, the largest circulation newspaper in Canada. The *Star* published an extraordinary eight-page supplement on the Watkins Report the day after it was released (1968). Afterward, the paper gave prominent coverage to Watkins's pronouncements, however mundane. When Watkins proposed an international conference on foreign investment, for instance, the story ran on the front page of the *Star* (1969). Once, at a cocktail party, *Star* reporter Val Sears snapped at Watkins: "Shut up, Watkins. You wouldn't exist if I hadn't invented you" (Berton 1997, 69).[7] Sears was exaggerating—but not much.

The Waffle

Preparing the report radicalized Watkins (Watkins 1994b, 31). As he later recalled, "Working for Walter Gordon certainly made me more of a nationalist" (Watkins 1994a). His initial agreement with Gordon was that he would work to promote the report for 12 months after its release, accepting media interviews and speaking engagements, always championing the report's recommendations. "Defending the report pushed me towards socialism," he remembered (Watkins 1972, 82). He was particularly troubled by his speeches to business audiences: "I ... learned to experience the hostility engendered from those guys simply for being a nationalist" (Watkins 1972, 76).

Vietnam played a significant role in Watkins's intellectual transformation. In the fall of 1967, as he was finishing the task force report, he attended a

---

6. See also Watkins's comment that he was welcomed in the NDP "with open arms" (Watkins 1972, 76).

7. See also the various articles by Val Sears in the *Toronto Star*: (1968a); (1968b); (1968c); (1968d); and (1969).

meeting at the University of Toronto on whether to allow on-campus recruitment by Dow Chemical, which produced the napalm used in American bombs and flamethrowers that destroyed Vietnamese villages. "By the end of the debate," he later wrote, "I was voting to throw Dow Chemical and every other war company off the campus … but you're never allowed to do anything, to change anything … When I get thrown into that kind of political situation, I inevitably get radicalized" (Watkins 1972, 74). Canada, he concluded, had to live outside the American economic orbit if it were "to escape the political horrors of American imperialism of the kind we are witnessing in Vietnam" (Newman 1972, 58).

Watkins was also heavily influenced by the New Left, a movement of radical intellectuals who rejected the old-style communist parties and their traditional critique of capitalism. Watkins began to favour "democracy at every level of decision-making: … the students and professors should run the universities, the workers should run the factories, the residents … should run the neighbourhood." This put him at odds with the NDP establishment. "From my brief encounters with the NDP I knew that the party was closer to the Old Left position of considering hierarchical power structures inevitable" (Watkins 1972, 82).

Watkins quickly came to believe that the task force report did not go anywhere near far enough. The solution to Canada's problems, he wrote in the spring of 1969, was "socialism, and radical socialism at that" (Watkins 1969, 2). At a meeting of the Canadian Bar Association in September 1969, he proposed the complete socialization of industry in Canada (*Toronto Telegram* 1969). But what could he do as one person? After all, he did not know many others who shared his views.

At the time, Watkins was president of the University League for Social Reform, an organization of young, mostly left-leaning University of Toronto academics dedicated to debating public policy issues. The group was considering publishing a book on socialism in Canada. In search of contributors to the project, Watkins came across a group of a dozen radical New Democrats who were grappling with the issue of Canadian independence and were troubled by what they perceived as their Party's migration toward the centre of the political spectrum. Watkins joined the group and discovered that his views were closely in line with those of James Laxer, a University of Toronto history PhD student.

Laxer had drafted a manifesto to present at the NDP's annual convention, to be held in Winnipeg in November 1969. Watkins rewrote the statement, which had originally been cast in the obscure prose of the academy. The group's other members—including Ed Broadbent, Gerald Caplan, Lorne Brown, and Giles Endicott—then made further revisions. At some point, when debating a particular part of the manifesto, one of the group members said, "I'd rather waffle to the left than waffle to the right" (Lavoie 1970). From that offhand remark, the group became known as the Waffle movement.

The manifesto was circulated to New Democrats in the summer of 1969 and was released publicly at a press conference in Ottawa on 4 September. "From the beginning, we were surprised at the amount of interest the manifesto created both in the media and in the party," Watkins (1972, 83) later wrote. "When we called meetings to discuss it, 50–60 party members would show up regularly. We were also getting letters and phone calls from NDPers across the country." The events of 1968–1969 were crucial. According to Watkins (1979, 42), "The Waffle was possible because of widespread dissent within the United States against the war in Vietnam."

The manifesto began with the statement that its goal was to "build an independent socialist Canada" and to make the NDP "a truly socialist party." According to the Waffle, "The most urgent issue for Canadians is the very survival of Canada," and the main threat was American economic control. Yet replacing American owners with Canadians was not enough. The Canadian corporate elite could not be counted upon to defend Canada's interests as it had "opted for a junior partnership" in the American empire, reducing Canada "to the position of an economic colony of the United States." As a result, efforts to assert Canada's economic independence were a "sham" unless they were accompanied by socialism. The manifesto attacked both the United States and capitalism. Canada's neighbour was "an empire characterized by militarism abroad and racism at home." The capitalist economy fostered "superfluous individual consumption" and provided inadequate funding for "housing, education, medical care, and public transportation." Capitalism had to be replaced by socialism, "by national planning of investment and by the public ownership of the means of production in the interests of the Canadian people as a whole" (*Canadian Dimension* 1969). But, it was not clear how this goal would be accomplished.

Rotstein was troubled by his friend's intellectual trajectory. The idea of buying out American owners "boggles the mind," he wrote. A further problem was "how to retain access to the stream of new technology generated by the multi-national corporation" (Rotstein 1969, 146). And then there was the Waffle's presentism. Rotstein wondered what would happen if the United States solved its problems. "Is the raison d'être of Canadian independence to be based on the permanent victory of violence and the permanent failure of the American left?" he asked. "If by chance America were to change course and become a social democracy would the authors of the manifesto logically be required to go continentalist?" Rotstein's conclusion was prescient: "A manifesto which pivots on a reaction to America at a low point in its history is, in my view, not an enduring basis on which to construct the edifice of Canadian independence" (Rotstein 1969, 147).

At the NDP convention in November 1969, the Party establishment produced a counter-manifesto, "For a United and Independent Canada," which became known as the Marshmallow Resolution. Drafted by Deputy Leader David Lewis—who had called the Waffle manifesto "horrible, indigestible rubbish" (Newman 1970, 27)—and philosopher and former NDP candidate Charles Taylor, the resolution was supported both by Party elders, including leader Tommy Douglas, and by the labour movement. The debate in Winnipeg's Civic Auditorium was televised nationally. On the key vote, the Waffle was defeated 499 to 268.[8] Although disappointed with the result, Waffle leaders were pleased to have won the support of one-third of the delegates and to have elected Watkins as one of the Party's vice presidents. Waffle members decided to continue as a group and to elect their own steering committee. Soon they would begin distributing a newsletter to a growing mailing list. Within one year, the Waffle had a mailing list of 1,500 (Newman 1970, 27).

Waffle supporters tended to be university professors and students. Few of them had run for office, let alone won an election. Watkins came from a humble background, but most of the Waffle members seemed to have sprung from the suburban middle class. Half of them were under the age of 35 (*Canadian Dimension* 1971a, 25; *Canadian Dimension* 1971b, 24). Virtually none of the members lived in Quebec or the Atlantic provinces (Newman 1970, 27). A few came from the western provinces, but the vast majority lived in southern Ontario.

The Waffle continued to generate publicity after the convention. The group hosted a teach-in on the Americanization of Canada at the University of Toronto in March of 1970, with a range of speakers, including Walter Gordon. In June, Watkins published *Gordon to Watkins to You*, an idiosyncratic book about the struggle against foreign investment (Godfrey and Watkins 1970). The book was co-edited by Dave Godfrey, a University of Toronto English professor who was a founder of House of Anansi Press, one of Canada's leading independent publishers. In August of that year, the Waffle held its first national convention at the University of Toronto. In September, it organized a rally outside the Ontario legislature at Queen's Park to protest the sale of natural gas to the United States. At the Ontario NDP's October 1970 convention, the Waffle candidates for Party president (Krista Maeots) and secretary (John Smart) were handily defeated, but both were elected to the Party executive, along with two other Waffle members, Bruce Kidd and James Laxer.

---

8. The vote was on Watkins's motion that the Marshmallow Resolution be referred back to the resolutions committee. The vote was 268 in favour and 499 against.

In 1971, the Waffle reached its apogee. In April, Laxer ran as the Waffle candidate for the NDP leadership at the Party convention at the Ottawa Civic Centre. He placed second on the final ballot, receiving about one-third of the votes. But the NDP establishment was losing its patience, and the labour movement was increasingly hostile. Murray Cotterill (1972) of the United Steelworkers published an opinion piece in the *Toronto Star* titled "Why We Must Stop the Waffle." Later, he called the Waffle members "posturing academics" (McQueen 1971). Dennis McDermott of the United Auto Workers described the Waffle as a "haven for every social misfit in the party" and "an ego trip for many of the Waffle leaders" (List 1971).

In March 1972, Ontario NDP leader Stephen Lewis condemned the Waffle as a party within a party. Two months later, a party committee described the Waffle as a direct challenge to the NDP and recommended that Waffle be dissolved as a distinct organization. At an Ontario party council meeting in June, the Waffle was ordered to disband, though the individual members were welcome to remain in the NDP. Most Waffle leaders strode out of the Party, their heads held high, not realizing how badly they had been battered and bruised.

Outside of the NDP, the Waffle became the Movement for an Independent Socialist Canada, which quickly split into nationalist and socialist factions. Margaret Atwood (1976, 233–234) later parodied them in *Lady Oracle*: "They were deciding the future of the country. Should it be nationalism with a socialist flavour, or socialism with a nationalist flavour?" In 1973, Watkins left to work in the North among the Dene. James Laxer remained as leader of the organization's nationalist wing, now wanting to reach out and forge alliances with nationalists in the Liberal and Conservative parties. In the July 1974 federal election, Laxer ran under the Movement for an Independent Socialist Canada banner in the Toronto-area riding of York West, where he won fewer than 700 votes, about one percent of the total. In October of that year, Laxer lost control of the organization to younger members who wanted their socialism pure and undiluted. Now merely the remnants of a group of refugees from Canada's distant third-place party, the Waffle had disintegrated by the end of 1974. It had once been powerful enough to destabilize the NDP, but never had the strength to make an impact on Canadian politics beyond the party and the university seminar room. Watkins (1979, 42) later attributed the Waffle's demise to the end of both the Vietnam war and rioting in U.S. cities. "In due course, the U.S. pasted over the worst of the cracks, and Canadians went back to sleep. The Waffle, born to widespread media coverage, died unnoticed."

Much of the historiography of the late 1960s and early 1970s sees the nationalist movement as a force from the left, using the terms *New Nationalism* and *left nationalism* interchangeably.[9] The movement had support from "maverick Liberals like Walter Gordon," as Joan Sangster (2006, 50) has written, but it was, in her telling, primarily a socialist struggle.[10] Yet the New Nationalism was a broad, cross-partisan movement, not an exclusive preserve of the far left. It began in the mainstream with Walter Gordon and others. When the Waffle tried to marry nationalism to socialism, a battle for the nationalist movement began and continued until the movement began to decline. Despite the widespread attention the Waffle has received in the historiography, the group had little impact outside universities. Even at its peak, the Waffle won the support of only one-third of New Democrats, a party which in turn had about 20 percent of public support.

The Committee for an Independent Canada

Less innovative but more representative of Canadian opinion was the Committee for an Independent Canada (CIC), an organization founded in reaction to the Waffle. Horrified that the Marxist left was seizing control of the nationalist movement, Gordon and Rotstein collaborated with *Toronto Star* editor Peter C. Newman to create a new organization. Launched in September 1970, the Committee for an Independent Canada spanned the political spectrum. The 13 members of the founding committee included prominent members of the main political parties: Liberals Walter Gordon and Dorothy Petrie (a party organizer), Conservatives Eddie Goodman (the party's national director of organization) and Alvin Hamilton (a former Cabinet minister), and New Democrat Eamon Park (past president of the party).

From the start, the Waffle was antagonistic toward the CIC, seeing it as a lobbying group for big business. Watkins, Laxer, and other Waffle leaders refused to join. Waffle members resented that CIC received considerably more than they did. As much as the *Toronto Star* had provided extensive coverage to Watkins, it now afforded even more to the CIC.

The CIC was active in its first five years. It recruited prominent individuals from a variety of fields: the media (*Chatelaine* editor Doris Anderson, TV personality Adrienne Clarkson), book publishing (publishers Mel Hurtig and Jack McClelland, and author Pierre Berton), politics (Liberal senator Keith Davey, Conservative organizer Flora MacDonald, former Liberal Cabinet minister Judy LaMarsh, former NDP Member of Parliament Max Saltsman), and the

---

9. See, for example, Squires (2013), esp. 104, 143–145. For Squires, the liberal Walter Gordon and conservative George Grant were part of the "long pedigree" of left nationalism.

10. Similarly, Carabuccia (2016–2017) asserts that the most influential nationalist movements in English Canada in the 1960s and 1970s "were the product of the New Left" (117).

labour movement (Ed Finn of the Brotherhood of Railway, Transport and General Workers). It opened branches in more than 30 communities and held conferences in Thunder Bay, Edmonton, Toronto, and Ottawa. In 1972, it raised funds through a 27-hour weekend telethon on Toronto's City-TV. The organization produced two books (Rotstein and Lax 1972; 1974) and enjoyed prominent and sympathetic coverage from the country's large-circulation periodicals, the *Toronto Star*, *Maclean's*, and *Saturday Night*.

The Trudeau Government

The Trudeau government reacted to growing nationalist sentiment, slowly at first, with tentative steps. In the September 1968 throne speech, the government promised the creation of the Canada Development Corporation, though it would take the government another two years to introduce the legislation. In 1970, Cabinet agreed that Herb Gray, minister without portfolio, would establish a working group of officials to draft a policy statement on foreign investment, the white paper that Gordon had wanted back in 1967–1968. Gray's group was composed of several bureaucrats, with most of the work being carried out by Harvey Lazar, Joel Bell, and Roberto Gualtieri.

Pressure mounted as the government dawdled. The Pearson government had referred the Watkins Report to the Standing Committee on External Affairs and National Defence. In August 1970, the committee, chaired by Liberal MP Ian Wahn, issued its report. It recommended tariff reductions, the creation of a Canada Development Corporation, and the establishment of a government office to collect information, coordinate policy on foreign investment, combat extraterritoriality, and screen foreign takeovers. The report also urged the government to adopt a policy that the largest firms operating in Canada should have at least 51 percent of the shares owned by Canadians. This idea came directly from Walter Gordon (Wahn 1994). In January 1971, the government finally introduced legislation to create the Canada Development Corporation (CDC). The act was passed in June, though the company's mandate was to make a profit for its Canadian shareholders, not to purchase companies that might otherwise fall into foreign hands, as Walter Gordon had initially proposed.

In addition, in June 1971, Gray submitted his report to Cabinet. Its main recommendation was the establishment of an agency to screen incoming foreign investment. Gray and some of his colleagues favoured the creation of such an entity, but others in the Cabinet were opposed, including Foreign Minister Mitchell Sharp, Minister of Regional Economic Expansion Jean Marchand, Minister of Manpower Otto Lang, Treasury Board President Bud Drury, and Minister of Public Works Arthur Laing. In July, the Cabinet agreed in principle to create a screening agency, but then nothing happened. The issue appeared on the Cabinet agenda repeatedly, but little progress was made on the details of the proposal. Finally, in November 1971, two leaks broke the deadlock. On 12 November, *Canadian Forum* published an early draft of Gray's report, and on 15 November, the *Montreal Gazette* published a record of the Cabinet's July decision to create a screening agency. Cabinet now agreed to release the Gray Report. Finally, in May 1972, the government introduced legislation to screen foreign takeovers. It would take another 19 months before Parliament passed the legislation to create the Foreign Investment Review Agency (FIRA).

"You know, I'm not a nationalist, and this is a form of nationalism, which I find suspect," Trudeau had told Alistair Gillespie, the minister responsible for the legislation. According to Gillespie (2009, 144), Trudeau came around in 1971, when an election was approaching, not because he was won over by economic arguments, but because of the "significance of the issue in vote-rich Ontario and at the insistence" of many of members of the Liberal caucus.[11] In 1969, polls had shown that 34 percent of Canadians saw U.S. investment in a negative light, while 43 percent had a positive view. By the end of 1972, the sides had switched. Fully 47 percent now had a negative view of U.S. ownership, and 38 percent viewed it positively (*Toronto Star* 1972b). In February 1972, a Gallup poll showed that 69 percent of Canadians were in favour of the screening agency, and only 15 percent were opposed (*Toronto Star* 1972a).

There were other effects of the nationalism that bubbled up in 1968. In the middle of the 1972 election campaign, fearing that the Liberals were about to lose, the government published the Options Paper, a statement that outlined three choices for Canada's international economic policy: the country could maintain the status quo, pursue closer ties with the United States, or seek to expand commercial links with other countries to lessen Canada's dependence on the American market. The paper made it clear that the government would choose what became known as the Third Option. Then in 1975, the government created Petro Canada, a domestic oil company that would lessen the country's reliance on large multinationals.

Conclusion

Most of these measures would have been unthinkable before 1968, and all of them flowed from that year's events. In 1968, the two strands of the nationalist movement, personified by Walter Gordon and Mel Watkins, found common cause. Gordon was already a national figure, and he transformed Watkins into one too. By appointing Watkins as task force chair, Gordon legitimized the young academic in the eyes of Canada's major media outlets, particularly the

---

11. See also Trudeau's comment: "I think the times have changed a bit and that in four years Canadians have become a lot more nationalist economically than they were before" (Resnick 1977, 147).

Toronto Star. Together Gordon and Watkins worked to raise the alarm about foreign investment in Canada. This collaboration occurred precisely when Canadians were coming to question Canada's close relationship with the United States, a country engaged in a vicious war abroad and beset by violent conflict at home. Gordon and Watkins were able to take Canada's anxieties about the United States, focus them on economic issues, and, in the process, launch the New Nationalism.

Not long after the New Nationalism was born, it was riven by internal conflict between conventional nationalists and the radicals of the Waffle movement. Conservatives, Liberals, and some New Democrats found common cause against the nationalists from the far left. Ultimately, the socialist approach failed, unable to win over significant numbers of Canadians. Though often overlooked in the historiography, the mainstream nationalists were victorious, convincing the government to adopt much of their program.

Still, it was only a limited victory. The CDC and FIRA did not take the form that the nationalists had envisaged. FIRA was, in Abraham Rotstein's view, "a very ineffective agency" (Croft 1979). And the victory did not last long. In the late 1970s and early 1980s, the Liberals began backing away from FIRA and talking about sectoral free trade with the United States. In 1984, the Conservatives under Brian Mulroney came to office and began dismantling the nationalist legacy. By then, the sun had set on the nationalism of 1968.

Yet nationalist concerns remain. The silhouette of the globalization debate of recent years was sketched by the New Nationalists in the late 1960s. So long as the American economy has been a powerhouse that dwarfs Canada's, and so long as Canadians have had cause to recoil at the behaviour of American leaders—whether Richard Nixon, George W. Bush, or Donald J. Trump—Canadians will crave greater independence from their powerful neighbour. They will engage in passionate debate over how much distance that should be.

Casting the birth of the New Nationalism in an international context reveals much. The triumph of moderate nationalists over the radicals illustrates the degree to which Canada's 1968 lacked the ardour that animated that year around the globe. It also speaks to the historiographical debate over whether 1968 was a national or international experience. The story of the New Nationalism suggests that Canada was less a part of an international 1968 experience than a North American one, albeit one with many distinctive Canadian elements. English-Canadian nationalists paid much less attention to liberation movements erupting around the globe than they did to the news from the United States and from American reporters in Vietnam.

Acknowledgements

The author is grateful to Tim Greenough for assistance with the research and to Norman Hillmer for reading the manuscript and offering sound advice.

References

Abraham Rotstein fonds. 1964. Gordon to Rotstein, 30 July, MG31 D73, vol. 4, file 61, Library and Archives Canada.

Atwood, Margaret. 1976. *Lady Oracle*. Toronto: McClelland & Stewart.

Berton, Pierre. 1997. *1967: The Last Good Year*. Toronto: Doubleday.

Blocker, David G. 2019. "To Waffle to the Left: The Waffle, the New Democratic Party, and Canada's New Left during the Long Sixties." PhD diss., University of Western Ontario.

———. 2018. "Waffling in Winnipeg and London: Canada's New Left and the NDP, 1965-75." In *Party of Conscience: The CCF, the NDP and Social Democracy in Canada*, edited by Roberta Lexier, Stephanie Bangarth, and Jon Weier, 72-81. Toronto: Between the Lines.

Bonin, Bernard. 1994. Interview with author, Ottawa, 15 April.

Borch, Peter. 2005. "The Rise and Decline of the Saskatchewan Waffle, 1966–1973." MA thesis, University of Regina.

Bothwell, Robert, Ian Drummond, and John English. 1989. *Canada since 1945: Power, Politics, and Provincialism*, rev. ed. Toronto: University of Toronto Press.

Brodie, M. Janine. 1985. "From Waffles to Grits: A Decade in the Life of the New Democratic Party." In *Party Politics in Canada*, 5th ed., edited by Hugh G. Thorburn, 205–217. Scarborough, ON: Prentice–Hall.

Buckley, Tom. 1968. "U.S. Dead at 543 in Week, a Record." *New York Times*, 23 February: 1.

Bullen, John. 1983. "The Ontario Waffle and the Struggle for an Independent Socialist Canada: Conflict within the NDP." *Canadian Historical Review* 64 (2): 188–215.

Burstyn, Varda. 1990. "The Waffle and the Women's Movement." *Studies in Political Economy* 33 (Autumn): 175–184.

Canada. Task Force on the Structure of Canadian Industry. 1968. *Foreign Ownership and the Structure of Canadian Industry*. Ottawa: Privy Council Office.

Canadian Dimension. 1971a. "Profile of the Waffle." April: 25.

———. 1971b. "Wither Waffle?" April: 24–25.

———. 1969. "For an Independent Socialist Canada." August–September: 8–10.

Carabuccia, Chloé. 2016–2017. "A Distinct and Independent Canada: The Fear of the United States and the National Unity Project under the Liberals (1963–1984)." *Cultures of the Commonwealth* 19/20/21 (Winter): 117–134.

Chiarello, Michael. 2020. "The Course and Canon of Left Nationalism in English Canada, 1968-1979." PhD diss., Carleton University.

Clarkson, Stephen. 1968. *An Independent Foreign Policy for Canada?* Toronto: McClelland & Stewart.

Cotterill, Murray. 1972. "Why We Must Stop the Waffle." *Toronto Star*, 22 June: 6.

Croft, Roger. 1979. "Foreign Investment Chief Caught in a Crossfire." *Toronto Star*, 9 November: B8.

Cronkite, Walter. 1998. "We Are Mired in Stalemate …" In *Reporting Vietnam, Part 1, American Journalism, 1959–1969,* 581–582. New York: Library of America.

Crowe, Marshall. 1995. Interview with author, Ottawa, 22 March.

Davey, Keith. 1986. *The Rainmaker: A Passion for Politics.* Toronto: Stoddart.

Donaghy, Greg. 2002. *Tolerant Allies: Canada and the United States, 1963–1968.* Montreal and Kingston: McGill–Queen's University Press.

Drummond, Ian. 1988. *The Canadian Debate about Foreign Investment, 1945–1972,* Canada House Lecture Series no. 37. London: Canadian High Commission.

Gillespie, Alastair W., with Irene Sage. 2009. *Made in Canada: A Businessman's Adventure in Politics.* Montreal: Robin Brass Studio.

Globe and Mail. 1968. "Allies Decided Ben Tre Must Die to Be Saved." 8 February: 4.

Godfrey, Dave, with Mel Watkins, eds. 1970. *Gordon to Watkins to You, Documentary: The Battle for Control of Our Economy.* Toronto: New Press.

Godfrey, Dave, Mel Watkins, and Walter Gordon, 1970. "Gordon to Watkins to You: Press Conference," transcribed and edited by Susan Turner. *Canadian Forum,* July–August: 158–160.

Gordon, Walter. 1977. *A Political Memoir.* Toronto: McClelland & Stewart.

Hackett, Robert. 1979. "The Waffle Conflict in the NDP." In *Party Politics in Canada,* 4th ed., edited by Hugh G. Thorburn, 188–213. Scarborough, ON: Prentice-Hall.

Johnson, Harry G. 1968. "The Watkins Report." Review of *Foreign Ownership and the Structure of Canadian Industry: Report of the Task Force on the Structure of Canadian Industry. International Journal* 23, no. 4 (Autumn): 615–622.

LaMarsh, Judy. 1969. *Memoirs of a Bird in a Gilded Cage.* Toronto: McClelland & Stewart.

Land, Brian. 1994. Interview with author, Toronto, 13 September.

LaPierre, Laurier. 1968. "Vive le Canada Libre." In *The New Romans: Candid Canadian Opinions of the U.S.,* edited by Al Purdy, 59–61. Edmonton: Hurtig.

Lavoie, Michael. 1970. "Public Ownership of Oil, Natural Gas Endorsed by NDP." *Toronto Star,* 30 October: 7.

Levine, Gilbert. 1990. "The Waffle and the Labour Movement." *Studies in Political Economy* 33 (Autumn): 185–192.

Lexier, Roberta. 2017. "Two Nations in Canada: The New Democratic Party, the Waffle Movement and Nationalism in Quebec." *British Journal of Canadian Studies* 30 (1): 1–22.

———. 2013. "Waffling towards Parity in the New Democratic Party." In *Mind the Gaps: Canadian Perspectives on Gender and Politics,* edited by Roberta Lexier and Tamara A. Small, 64–75. Halifax: Fernwood.

Library of Parliament fonds. 1986. Tom Earle interview with Richard Stanbury, 27 May, R1026, vol. 2565, file 10, Library and Archives Canada.

———. 1984. Tom Earle interview with Mitchell Sharp, 2 February, R1026, vol. 2562, file 14, Library and Archives Canada.

List, Wilfrid. 1971. "A Union Roadblock for Waffle." *Globe and Mail,* 12 April: 1.

Mahon, Rianne. 1990. "The Waffle and Canadian Political Economy." *Studies in Political Economy* 32 (Summer): 187–194.

Mathews, Robin. 1970. "Should the PM's Date Have Been a Manitoban?" *Ottawa Citizen*, 30 January: 6.

McQueen, Don. 1971. "The Waffle Lives On." *Commentator*, June: 14–15.

Montreal Gazette. 1968. "Viet Town Wiped Out to Save It." 8 February: 19.

Newman, Christina. 1972. "Growing Up Reluctantly—How a Political System Failed: The Birth and Brutal Death of the New Nationalism," *Maclean's*, August: 21–22, 56, 58–60.

———. 1970. "True Compromise, Good and Sane: How Mel Watkins Brought Socialism to the NDP." *Saturday Night*, September: 23–27.

New York Times. 1968. "Major Describes Move." 8 February: 14

Obituary for Mel Watkins. 2020. *Globe and Mail*. 6 April: B18.

Ottawa Citizen. 1968. "'Always a Pity': City Destroyed 'to Save It.'" 8 February: 1.

Peter Stursberg fonds. 1977. Peter Stursberg interview with James Coutts, 22 April, R5637 (MG31 D79), vol. 28, file 15, Library and Archives Canada.

———. 1976a. Peter Stursberg interview with Lionel Chevrier, 17 August, R5637 (MG31 D79), vol. 28, file 9, Library and Archives Canada.

———. 1976b. Peter Stursberg interview with Maurice Sauvé, 15 December, R5637 (MG31 D78), vol. 31, file 18, Library and Archives Canada.

Resnick, Philip. 1977. *The Land of Cain: Class and Nationalism in English Canada, 1945–1975*. Vancouver: New Star Books.

Rotstein, Abraham. 1969. "The Search for Independence." *Canadian Forum*, October: 146–148.

Rotstein, Abraham, and Gary Lax, eds. 1974. *Getting It Back: A Program for Canadian Independence*. Toronto: Clarke Irwin.

———. 1972. *Independence: The Canadian Challenge*. Toronto: Committee for an Independent Canada.

Sangster, Joan. 2006. "Remembering Texpack: Nationalism, Internationalism, and Militancy in Canadian Unions of the 1970s." *Studies in Political Economy* 78, no. 1 (Autumn): 41–66.

Sears, Val. 1969. "Watkins Report Stalks U.K. in U.S. Investment Debate." *Toronto Star*, 21 November: 15.

———. 1968a. "The Big Trick: Getting Most Benefits at Least Cost." *Toronto Star*, 16 February: 25.

———. 1968b. "Does Economic Control Lead to Political Control?" *Toronto Star*, 16 February: 25.

———. 1968c. "We Need Muscle to Meet 'Invasion' of U.S. Law." *Toronto Star*, 16 February: 29.

———. 1968d. "Issue: Can We Afford to Let the U.S. Keep Buying Us Up?" *Toronto Star*, 1 June: 8.

Smart, John. 1990. "The Waffle's Impact on the New Democratic Party." *Studies in Political Economy* 32 (Summer): 177–186.

Smart, Patricia. 2009. "Queen's University History Department and the Birth of the Waffle Movement." In *The Sixties in Canada: A Turbulent and Creative Decade*, edited by M. Athena Palaeologu, 310–318. Montreal: Black Rose.

————. 1990. "The Waffle and Quebec." *Studies in Political Economy* 32 (Summer): 195–201.

Squires, Jessica. 2013. *Building Sanctuary: The Movement to Support Vietnam War Resisters in Canada, 1965–73.* Vancouver: University of British Columbia Press.

Stevens, Paul, and John Saywell. 1969. "Parliament and Politics." In *Canadian Annual Review for 1968*, edited by John Saywell, 3–114. Toronto: University of Toronto Press.

Stewart, Walter. 1970. "Captain Canada of 1971," *Maclean's*, November: 31–35.

Stoner, Gerald. 1994. Interview with author, Rockcliffe Park, ON, 28 November.

Toronto Star. 1972a. "69% Favour Screening Agency for New Foreign Investment." 16 February: 7.

————. 1972b. "Survey: More Canadians Oppose U.S. Ownership." 30 December: 1, 13.

————. 1971. "Stanfield Says Ottawa 'in Sea of Ambiguity' on Foreign Investment." 31 March: 9.

————. 1969. "Watkins Urges World Talks on Takeovers." 4 September: 1.

————. 1968. Special Report. 16 February: 23–30.

Toronto Telegram. 1969. "The Watkins Way Is Chaos." 8 September: 6.

Tower, Courtney. 1970. "The Heartening Surge of a New Canadian Nationalism," *Maclean's*, February: 1–2.

United States. National Advisory Commission on Civil Disorders. 1968. *Report of the National Advisory Commission on Civil Disorders.* Washington: n.p.

Wahn, Ian. 1994. Interview with author, Toronto, 18 May.

Walter L. Gordon fonds. 1968. John Turner press release, 16 March, vol. 24, file 14, Library and Archives Canada.

Watkins, Melville H. 1994a. Interview with author, Toronto, 2 March.

————. 1994b. "Foreign Ownership 94: Buy, Bye Canada." *This Magazine*, April/May: 30–32.

————. 1990. "The Waffle and the National Question." *Studies in Political Economy* 32 (Summer): 173–176.

————. 1987. "Principles, Not Power, Came First for Gordon." *Toronto Star*, 25 March: A27.

————. 1979. "Where Is the Waffle Now That We Need It?" *This Magazine*, November–December: 38–42.

————. 1972. "Learning to Move Left." *This Magazine Is about Schools*, Spring: 68–92.

————. 1969. "Nationalism vs. Socialism." *Canadian Dimension*, April/May: 2.

————. 1966. "Is Gordon's Game Worth the Candle?" *Canadian Forum*, July: 77–78.

————. 1965. "Canadian Economic Policy: A Proposal." In *The Prospect of Change: Proposals for Canada's Future*, edited by Abraham Rotstein, 63–82. Toronto: McGraw–Hill.

Webber, Patrick. 2009. "'For a Socialist New Brunswick': The New Brunswick Waffle, 1967–1972." *Acadiensis* 38, no. 1 (Winter/Spring): 75–103.

Westell, Anthony. 1969. "Tory Report Urges Curbs on Foreign Investment." *Toronto Star*, 14 October: 3.

Chapter 5
Equality, Equity, and the Royal Commission on the Status of Women

JANE ARSCOTT

Abstract

In 1968, Canadian women addressed women's equality in the spotlight of a royal commission's public hearing process. Predominantly white, married women spoke truth to power in unprecedented ways. Their spokespersons were filmed for television, recorded for radio, and their views reported in newspaper and magazine articles across the country; women made news. The sole Black women known to have addressed the Royal Commission on the Status of Women (RCSW) spoke up in support of the one of the largest, long-established, vocal, and nationally recognized Black communities in Canada at the time. Carrie Best, a Black Nova Scotian journalist, pointed to the economic insecurity of local Black communities and Indigenous communities. Their long-standing grievances ought to have been front and centre in any meaningful discussion of gender equality in her view. Such an analysis was marginalized in the RCSW's public consultation that ran from April through October. Best called for equity through community development and the intentional elimination of racial discrimination. She challenged the RCSW study's liberal approach that focused on white women by pointing to the need to uproot structural inequality originating in enslavement and colonization to identify racism as the primary cause of poverty and human degradation in Canada. The chapter summarizes the creation of the RCSW, its purpose, and scope, followed by a discussion of the public-engagement process and then, briefly, long-lasting legacies of the royal commission's work that began the shift from equality of opportunity to considerations of equity as a way station on the long, lonesome road toward substantive social justice.

Nineteen sixty-eight was a tumultuous year in a rebellious era (Kurlansky 2004, 305–308; Palmer 2009). Civil rights protesters marched against racial

Figure 5.1. Royal Commission on the Status of Women hearing in Montreal, 1 June 1968. *Source:* Rita Cadieux 1966–1969. Bibliothèque et Archives nationales du Québec. BAnQ Vieux-Montréal, Fonds *La Presse* 06M, P833, S2, D853, P4-1.

discrimination in the United States in 1968, student protesters took to the streets in France, and anti-immigration rallies occurred in Britain. Feminists protested the Miss America pageant by crowning a pig and throwing their bras into the garbage. Canadian women addressed injustice in more than 1,000 letters, 400 briefs, and at least 100 hours of testimony at 37 days of public hearings. This public engagement disrupted the status quo, challenged societal complacency, and produced a robust public discussion about equality as a remedy for gender injustice.

A Royal Commission about women considered as a social problem (Morris 1982) by the federal government came about due to a confluence of factors. The NDP held the balance of power in a minority Liberal government. Gender imbalance had been criticized in the planning of the celebrations for the country's centennial. An international conference to be held in Montreal to celebrate the twentieth anniversary of the United Nations' (UN) *Universal Declaration on Human Rights* (*UDHR*) had also not named any women to its planning committee. National women's organizations entreated the federal government to follow the example of the United States and other countries by studying the status of women at the behest of the UN Commission on the Status of Women. The absence of gender in the work of the Royal Commission on Bilingualism and Biculturalism in public life and society had been noticed. Women's marginal presence in politics, especially at the national level unsettled gender politics. Prominent politicians regarded a sole woman in the Cabinet as sufficient, and the male-dominated media satirized women's demands for gender equality. National women's organizations enjoyed a history of success in using their brief and lobby strategy to encourage government to change laws and policies affecting them. In addition to explaining some of these framing conditions, this chapter points attention to the sole Black woman known to have addressed the issues facing women in the Black community of Nova Scotia, which was historically the largest and most well-organized, vocal, and nationally recognized Black community in Canada until the mid-1960s.

Human rights activist Carrie Best, a Black Nova Scotian journalist, advised the Royal Commission on the Status of Women (RCSW) to analyze the effects of economic insecurity on Black women, Indigenous women, and their communities. She drew attention to the absence of both groups at the RCSW's public hearing in Halifax on 11 September 1968 (Library and Archives Canada [LAC] 1968m). Invited to the national hearings in Ottawa, Best addressed injustices, such as the legacy of slavery, that continued to oppress Black women as the "Mammy in the kitchen of her Mistress" and the "Mother in her home." Presentations were recorded and that artefact survives (LAC 1968k). In her view, unemployment among men in her community and substandard housing on local First Nations reserves were relevant social problems. Best wanted to see the members of disadvantaged communities employed, racism ended, group identities respected, intercultural understanding promoted, and human rights championed. However, the RCSW disregarded her clarion call for equity and the elimination of racial discrimination due in part to the standards of social scientific objectivity that it had adopted, which regarded her views as beyond the scope of the inquiry's purview, as was institutionalized racism.

Best's presentation affirmed women's voice and agency by challenging the RCSW's approach to its study of women. She recommended that Canadian society uproot the causes of structural inequality, remediate the legacies of slavery and colonization, and identify racism as the primary cause of poverty and human degradation. Best subsequently received national honours, including the Order of Canada, though her critique of the RCSW's lack of diversity and inclusion is virtually unknown. Although the RCSW's influence has lasted half a century, confrontation of societal injustice the way Best wanted to see done has yet to occur.

The RCSW has been criticized widely since the 1960s. No one appointed to the RCSW was associated with organized labour (*Canadian Labour* 1967, 26).

The *Report* lacked a structural analysis of the causes of the persistence of women's inequality (*Globe and Mail* 1970, 15). Looking back, former RCSW Executive Secretary Monique Bégin identified silences that should have had more attention (1988, 31). Almost all of the contributors were heterosexual, white Euro-colonial settlers, though it must be acknowledged that in Canada, in 1968, homosexual men or women and persons of colour were small demographic minorities compared to the present day. The voices of Black women (Williams 1990), Indigenous women (Monture-Okanee 1992; Turpel-Lafond 1997), immigrant women, and other racialized women (Agnew 1996, 113; St. Lewis 1997) were barely present.

The first part of this chapter explains initial resistance to the creation of the RCSW and then summarizes the RCSW's formal purpose and national scope. The second part considers the public hearings as the process that awakened popular consciousness to women's demands. The legacies are then discussed briefly, such as the creation of agencies recommended by the Commission and implemented subsequently, which altered the idea of equality over time from its originally narrow definition of equality of opportunity between two complementary genders to encompass more robust conceptions of equity. More recent conceptions focus on substantive, multiple, and overlapping impacts that disproportionately effect populations of women. Intersectional analysis of the differential impacts of racism, indigeneity, disability, class, sexual orientation, gender identity, and gender expression reveals the existence of concurrent societal inequities. For many women, inequity is compounded to the detriment of their health and their quest for economic sufficiency, and exacerbated by incidents of violence against them. These results tend to be more frequent, prolonged, and severe for women than those experienced in Canadian society overall. In Best's autobiography, *That Lonesome Road* (1977), she elaborated her aspiration to see all forms of discrimination eliminated and to bring to the fore the dignity of persons, human rights, and equity, seeing the experiences of Black Nova Scotians as a microcosm of the sorts of long-standing injustices that needed to be redressed.

Background

In 1968, the RCSW's public hearing process asked what the federal government could do "for women to ensure equal opportunities with men in all aspects of Canadian society" (PCO 1967). The idea of bringing equality to bear on Canadian society involved the work of changing attitudes, institutions, law, policy, practices, and procedures. From the creation of the RCSW by Order-in-Council 16 February 1967 until the tabling of its *Report* 7 December 1970, the RCSW considered all aspects of Canadian women's experiences in society's "cultural mould" (*Report* 1970, 10–18). The United Nations had designated 1968 as International Human Rights Year to mark the anniversary of the UN's *Universal Declaration of Human Rights* (*UDHR*) and ad hoc national women's organizations pushed Canada to take action on the status of women to demonstrate a strong commitment to the human rights of women.

The Canadian Federation of Business and Professional Women's Clubs (CFBPWC), the Canadian Federation of University Women (CFUW), the National Council of Women of Canada (NCWC), and the Voice of Women (VOW) were among the most active national women's organizations. They joined forces to lobby the federal government for a high-profile national study of Canadian women, such as had occurred in the United States (1961–1963), and as had been recommended by the UN Commission on the Status of Women (UNCSW) in 1967. In the United States, President John F. Kennedy had created such a Presidential Commission on the Status of Women (PCSW), chaired by international human rights champion Eleanor Roosevelt (Executive Order 10980 1961). In 1962, the UNCSW called on member states, especially the more affluent nations, to advance the status of women by raising the international profile of matters related to women. Countries like Canada were encouraged to produce national studies. As the resolution of the UN General Assembly stated, such reports could be prepared by governments, national women's organizations, or other agencies already available or created for that purpose (United Nations General Assembly 1962).

The publication of the PCSW's *American Women* in 1965 affirmed for many Canadians the relevance of a similar study in Canada. The American report made 48 recommendations on topics such as child-care services; equal opportunity for women in hiring, training, and promotion; security of basic income; and equal pay for comparable work (Mead and Kaplan 1965, 210–213). Beyond the United States, countries such as West Germany (1962–1966), Denmark (1965), and France (1966) provided additional points of comparison (ICCACSW 1965, 56; Committee for the Equality of Women in Canada 1966), which Canadian women adapted when they lobbied the Prime Minister for a Canadian study. Internationally, discourse about the status of women in society was in the air in the mid-1960s, and it was only a matter of time until Canada, like Sweden (Sandlund 1968), produced its own report.

In Canada, Judy LaMarsh, the Member of Parliament for Niagara Falls, floated the idea of a Canadian status-of-women commission to Prime Minister Lester Pearson shortly after being appointed to Cabinet in the spring of 1963. She maintained that the PCSW had alleviated "unrest among women" in the United States (LaMarsh 1969, 301). Might Canada do something similar? Her first request went nowhere, though the idea was reiterated by the CFBPWC in its brief to Prime Minister Pearson on 11 July of that year (CFBPWC 1963). At the CFBPWC's national convention held in Ottawa the next July, LaMarsh spoke favourably about the PCSW and the good that might come from such a study in Canada (LaMarsh 1964). The NCWC included a similar rationale for study of the status of women in Canada in its meeting with the Prime Minister that year (National Council 1964), but its request fared no better. Initially, high-level national women's organizations were the principal vehicles of women's collective agency, pressuring the federal government by submitting briefs and lobbying the Prime Minister. That they had elite access to the Prime Minister reflected the organizations' considerable membership base but also pointed to the negligible number of women who had been elected to any Canadian legislature, and their tiny presence in public life more generally.

According to LaMarsh, the Prime Minister seemed prepared to move forward early in 1965. But again, the effort failed. Pearson reacted "as if stung with a nettle," she opined, when he was criticized in the local press (LaMarsh 1969, 301). Journalists tended to believe that women already enjoyed a "pretty good status" (CBC 1967). However, the VOW, women members of Parliament, senators, and the indomitable Laura Sabia, president of the CFUW, coordinated their efforts in 1966 and garnered media attention that ultimately aided the success of their call.

In the spring of 1966, Winnipeg activist June Menzies asked the VOW national president located in Halifax what might be done to expedite government action on the status of women. After the question was circulated in the VOW's spring newsletter, Sabia called together representatives of women's organizations, who met in Toronto at the offices of the CFUW in May. Canada had not lived up to the UN's *UDHR* and its Convention on the political rights of women, Sabia told the gathering. In advance of the International Human Rights Year, and because women's rights are human rights, she maintained, the demand for government-sponsored action was timely (CEWC 1966). The point was brought home by the announcement in 1966 of a planning committee for a national event to celebrate the anniversary of the *UDHR*, a committee comprised exclusively of men (*Globe and Mail* 1966, W2). Calling themselves the Committee for the Equality of the Women in Canada (CEWC), representatives of 32 women's organizations got to work (McGuire 1966).

In this effort, the CEWC had the support of women politicians such as LaMarsh, the sole woman in Cabinet; Grace MacInnis, NDP MP for Vancouver Kingsway; New Brunswick Senator Muriel Fergusson; and Thérèse Casgrain, who had run for the CCF, established the Voice of Women in Quebec, and recently founded the Fédération des Femmes du Québec. Their support indicated cross-party and regional representation from Ontario, British Columbia, the Maritimes, and Quebec. The CEWC submission on 15 September 1966 was formally presented to the Prime Minister on 10 November, accompanied by an unprecedentedly large delegation of 50 women representing two million members, in addition to several women representing unions. The Prime Minister delegated the ministers of Labour and Justice to stand in for him when he was called away unexpectedly on government business.

By early January 1967, there was still no response from the government, perhaps in part because the PM had announced on 14 December his forthcoming retirement in April. When a reporter phoned Sabia late one evening, she impulsively suggested that women might take to the streets if their demands were not met (Craig 1967, 1). The media ran the story that envisioned millions of women protesting in Ottawa. This excitement renewed public interest. LaMarsh had been "pushing hard," Pearson told the House, and when she did that "something almost inevitably happens—something" (Canada 1966, 7665). That something would be the RCSW; even LaMarsh continued to counsel activists like Sabia to be patient. Pushing too hard on a door that was open could backfire (Platiel 1967, 13).

Female fury was constructed as a threat—a fantastical one, perhaps—but a threat nonetheless (Whalley 1968). The announcement of the RCSW occurred on 2 February 1967. Canadian Broadcasting Corporation (CBC) reporter Tom Earle asked the Prime Minister if the women were demanding a Charter of Equality. Pearson replied that the government had been hearing representations from women's organizations "for quite a long time." A satirical opinion piece about "an army of 2 million women" ready to storm Ottawa followed the newscast. Sabia had been quoted as saying that women would use violence if necessary. In a similar vein, Frank Tumpane, a reporter for the *Toronto Telegram* addressed the problem of pacifying "militant females; necessitating men's walking on eggshells when talking about women's rights" (CBC 1967). Another newspaper columnist jibed that Canada's constitution made no provision for two founding sexes, drawing a parallel to the debate over Quebec nationalism and suggesting that women were agitating for a bi-gendered state (Bain 1967, 7).

The RCSW had been several years in the making. The delegation representing organizations that had a combined membership of more than two million women was hopeful that the report could be completed in time to mark 1968 as International Year of Human Rights (CFBPWC 1967, 3). The new body spent the remainder of the year hiring staff and planning its activities. In 1967, Canada's centennial, that nation had hosted the World's Exhibition (Expo) called "Man and His World." Nineteen sixty-eight would be the year of Woman and Hers.

Purpose of the RCSW

The CEWC requested a Royal Commission format due to its recognized prestige and resources, as well as its capacity to consult public opinion by holding hearings across the country. Royal commissions sat atop the hierarchy of public inquiry models available to the federal government (Hodgetts 1964, 476). In keeping with the CEWC's request, the RCSW was mandated to "inquire into, report upon," and recommend "steps" the Federal Government might take "*to ensure for women equal opportunities with men in all aspects of Canadian society*, having regard for the distribution of legislative powers under the constitution of Canada" (my emphasis). The general items were listed for the RCSW's consideration included:

1. the political rights of women,
2. their role in the labour force,
3. better use of their skills and education,
4. federal labour law as applied to women,
5. their employment and promotion by federal employers,
6. federal taxation pertaining to women,
7. marriage and divorce,
8. criminal law in relation to women,
9. immigration and citizenship with respect to women; and
10. other matters in relation to the status of women in Canada as may appear to the Commissioners to be relevant (PCO 1967).

The items closely aligned to those suggested in the CEWC submission, though with an explicitly federal focus.

The Committee was chaired by Florence Bird, a print and broadcast journalist who wrote under the name Anne Francis. Bird had covered international affairs, women's rights, and social conditions for the International Services of the CBC. She led a group of six other commissioners, which included one each from the Maritimes and the West and two each from Ontario and Quebec. Among them were political scientist Donald Gordon Jr. of the University of Waterloo, who was interested in rapidly changing communications and technology, and Professor Jacques Henripin, a demographer at the Université de Montréal, whose research concerned falling birth rates in Quebec. McGill law professor John P. Humphrey had recently retired from the directorship of the UN Human Rights Commission in Geneva. Lola Lange, who with her husband had a mixed-farming operation near Claresholm northeast of Lethbridge, had been involved in rural community development and continuing education. Professor Jeanne Lapointe was a French and French-Canadian literature specialist at L'Université Laval and had served the Quebec government previously on the Parent Commission on modernization of the education system. Elsie MacGill, trained as an aeronautical engineer, had been the national president of the CFBPWC from 1962 to 1964. Finally, Doris Ogilvie was a lawyer who had recently been appointed a juvenile court judge in Fredericton. Until the end of 1967, the newly created body hired personnel, planned its activities, and developed its research program. "The Commission is listening" to Canadian women was the initial message communicated in its first press release on 15 May (LAC 1967).

Public Engagement Begins

Public engagement began with the receipt of submissions and the circulation of a brochure about the work of the RCSW. In addition, commissioners made public appearances and attended conferences, conventions, and other public events. "What do you have to say about the status of women?" asked the RCSW brochure inviting written opinions from the public—a publication available in supermarkets and public libraries, and through women's organizations (*What Do You* 1967; Bird 1974, 269). In response, nearly one thousand women wrote personal communications to the Royal Commission or to Bird, comprising two-thirds of all the submissions received. The rest were briefs, often presented in the style of legal factums.

The first meeting of the RCSW in 1968 took the form of a seminar attended by commissioners, staff, and consultants on women's voluntary organizations, a topic of special interest to Commissioner Lange. Facilitator Gladys Dunn knew about brainstorming (Dunn to Bégin 1968) and other new methods of inquiry to gather the disaggregated views of women who normally had not been listened to by society. They tended to experience discrimination and were not members of women's organizations, Dunn noted; they also tended to occupy positions in the lowest third of the socio-economic scale. Some among them were first-generation immigrants; others included Inuit women, married women deserted by their spouses, Métis women, mothers in low-income families, mothers who used child-care facilities, new Canadians such as women domestic workers from the West Indies, single mothers, status Indian women living on and off reserves, unemployed women, widows, women in prisons and reformatories, women living in isolated communities such as Fogo Island, Newfoundland and Labrador, women living in public housing, and women supported by social assistance (RCSW 1968b).

As it turned out, Dunn's outreach strategy was the road not taken. Had it been accepted for use, the contrast between organized women's groups and disaggregated women in the bottom socio-economic strata would have been made visible. Women "who don't know how to write a formal brief" or what to say in it had their own opinions to contribute, if only they were asked, Dunn noted (RCSW 1968b). Another consultant (possibly from the PCO) maintained it was not the job of the RCSW to gather opinions from women. And so, the initial discussion was inconclusive. The aspiration to conduct effective outreach to women at the grassroots of society had reached an impasse. Lange continued to solicit opinions from focus groups and other informal activities, which she organized and documented. However, a narrower preference for the use of objective social-science techniques gave more attention and authority to the contributions from formal women's organizations thereafter. By the end of January 1968, that course of procedure had been determined. What remains to be explained is why.

Activities associated with consciousness raising—meeting women where they were and on their own terms—would have been a useful complement to formal briefs and public hearings. Such methods would have further contributed to the modernization of the government's traditional techniques used in public inquiries. The dismissal of such deep-listening initiatives can be explained by factors related to research, human rights, and timing. First, the research program had already prioritized social-scientific modes of inquiry that discounted qualitative methodologies that were associated with feminist scholarship and oral history. Second, the RCSW deferred to the view that human rights bodies were the entities most suited to adjudicate equality claims. Finally, in the matter of timing, the RCSW was initially set by the government to take place over 12 to 18 months, which made some commissioners cautious about taking on activities they saw as beyond what it was formally required to do. These factors are discussed below.

First, after the initial seminar, the executive secretary and research coordinators indicated in a memo to Lange that "scientific information" along with citizens' opinions had already been gathered and would stimulate interest and participation in the Royal Commission's work (RCSW 1968a). Its principal function was to prepare for the implementation of its recommendations and formulate a plan of action. Two remaining gaps identified by the seminar would be addressed by funded research contracts on immigration that were pending (Ferguson 1970) and by special invitations from commission staff to populations that had yet to communicate with the RCSW, including Indigenous (status and non-status Indians on and off reserve), Métis, and Inuit women (Sangster 2016, chap. 6), and other underrepresented populations. Taking into consideration age, geographic distribution and religion would also broaden the representativeness of the views received (even though commissioners recognized that "Women of the second generation want to be considered as Canadian women" (RCSW 1968b). In addition to contracted research studies, the views of women of Chinese, Greek, Portuguese, and Caribbean heritage, for example, could be solicited through the media and outreach to prepare and submit briefs.

Second, the arrival of a new commissioner decisively shifted the RCSW's focus and tone. John Humphrey joined the RCSW to replace Donald Gordon Jr. in February. Humphrey's presence strengthened the human-rights orientation of the Royal Commission and its alignment with international conventions, declarations, and treaties. Humphrey's influence on RCSW deliberations reinforced the legalistic orientation of the RCSW's activities. Lange's community-development perspective diminished thereafter, with the balance of power among the commissioners resting squarely on a liberal human-rights orientation familiar to Bird (1950) and supported by Humphrey.

A third factor militating against further experimentation with new methods of public engagement was the rapid approach of the public hearing dates, which were scheduled to begin on 16 April. In addition, the transition of a new prime minister in office delayed the RCSW's research program (RCSW 1969): Pierre Trudeau won the leadership of the Liberal Party on 6 April, became prime minister on 20 April, and won a majority in the general election on 25 June. A time squeeze, then, worked against the possibility of incorporating additional and alternative methods of inquiry into a schedule that was already set.

The RCSW's public hearings began on the West Coast, and continued eastward to Winnipeg, Toronto, and Montreal, from the end of May to mid-June 1968. During a summer break, Lange, Bird, and Bégin travelled to Whitehorse and Yellowknife, as well as several smaller settlements (Sangster 2016, chap. 6). Full sessions resumed in the Maritimes in September and wound up in Ottawa on 4 October, with commissioners having heard nearly 400 presentations.

Several of the hearing sessions were held in atypical venues—a shopping centre in Vancouver, a college gymnasium in Halifax, a public library in Edmonton, and a YWCA and college in Montreal—in addition to more typical settings in upscale hotels. In addition to northern outreach, commissioners aimed to make the sessions accessible to women by using locations close to public transportation and by scheduling evening sessions that mothers and other working women could readily attend. The public hearings also held several telephone hotline sessions in conjunction with the first session held in Victoria, which helped to cultivate interest in its proceedings. For example, the hotline informed participating commissioners that divorcees, spinsters, and widows could not obtain mortgages without a male guarantor and that banks would not promote women above the position of head teller (LAC 1968l). Like the hotline experiment, media coverage in newspapers and public broadcasting amplified interest in the Royal Commission's work, and reinforced the RCSW's commitment to engage with the Canadian public.

In Vancouver, mature women pointed out the need for universities to adapt their courses, programs, and schedules to the needs of non-traditional students, many of whom were married women (LAC 1968a). In Calgary, farm and ranch women advocated for the legal recognition of the financial value of their contributions to family-run agri-businesses (LAC 1968b). In Edmonton, women journalists who had experienced intimate partner violence advised the commissioners to look to the records of police and family courts for documented cases of domestic violence (LAC 1968c; RH Edmonton 1968). The need for cost-shared child-care programs was proposed by the Director of the Women's Bureau on behalf of the Saskatchewan Ministry of Labour (LAC 1968d). The availability of medically safe abortions was discussed in Saskatoon (Mahood 1968). The situation of sole-support mothers raised previously in other locales received intense media attention in Winnipeg (LAC 1968e).

The CFBPWC's presentation on 3 June 1968 led off the public hearings in Toronto, which principally covered legal problems encountered by women, such as lack of equal pay for equal work and pension discrimination. The work of remediation, it was argued, could be sustained by a permanent commission on the status of women to assist in the implementation of the recommendations of such a study (LAC 1968f). In Montreal, the VOW presented its national brief proposing to reallocate funds for the provision of daycare and employment retraining from money currently allocated by the Canadian government to cover its commitments to the North American Treaty Organization (NATO) and the North American Air Defense Command (NORAD) (LAC 1968h). This delegation included Thérèse Casgrain and Muriel Duckworth, who had consulted with Sabia in the creation of the CEWC and the RCSW. The presentation advised the RCSW to make use of the UN Declaration on the Elimination of Discrimination against Women (DEDAW) adopted by the General Assembly on 7 November 1967 as the basis for its recommendations.

Two francophone organizations that had joined the CEWC's delegation lobbying in Ottawa for a Royal Commission presented their briefs in Montreal. L'Association féminine d'éducation et d'action sociale (AFÉAS) promoted improved employment conditions for women to enable them to either join the paid labour force or qualify for an allowance for the invisible work (such as child care) they contributed to their households (LAC 1968k). The Fédération des Femmes du Québec exhorted the federal government to establish free daycare centres throughout the country and to provide the same education and training to women in rural areas as were available in urban settings (LAC 1968g).

In Atlantic Canada, the RCSW heard a good deal about the gender wage gap that contributed to small pensions and the likelihood of poverty among abandoned, divorced, separated, single, and widowed older women. In Halifax, Carrie Best observed the absence of Indigenous or Black women, who should have been encouraged to attend (LAC 1968m). Best's invited presentation at the national hearings in Ottawa was summarized as "a personal brief on behalf of Negro women" (LAC 1968k) by staff and is preserved on audiotape, however (RH Ottawa 1968).

Finally, in Ottawa, the CFUW presentation cast doubt on the achievement of equality between spouses until the responsibility for child care and household work was fairly distributed at a time when increased numbers of women were working for pay outside the home. The completion of university degrees by part-time studies was championed and a call was made by the CFUW for the end to quotas for the admission of women applicants to medical schools (LAC 1968j). Women from the Caughnawaga Reserve near Montreal informed the RCSW about the effects of the *Indian Act* on Indian women, especially as it regarded married women's status as band members (LAC 1968i). But the discussion never strayed very far from subjects outlined in the official terms of reference. The presentations made by national women's organizations served to elaborate the themes already identified by the CEWC and the RCSW's Terms of Reference, and this focus was reflected in the content of the final *Report*.

Public Attention Shifts

The public hearings attracted mainstream media attention. Ridicule and grudging forbearance that had been reported in newspapers, magazines, and broadcast media throughout 1967 took a decisive turn once the public hearings began (Malkin 1968; Freeman 1994, n23). The hearings gained a national audience with their accounts of women's experiences of discrimination, poverty, and sexism. Stories about women moved from the women's section of newspapers to those devoted to news and public affairs (Freeman 1994). Evidence mounted that turned what had previously been characterized as women's complaints, gripes, and personal stories into what Morris (1982, 1) called "legitimate social problems" in need of solutions.

In addition, the Canadian Security Intelligence Services operated by the Royal Canadian Mounted Police undertook preliminary investigations of some groups that had submitted briefs (CSIS 1968). Three kinds of perceived threats were most concerning to them: leftist ideology expressed by socialist and communist-influenced groups; coalitions built between Indigenous women and other activists; and the potential for violence incited by peace and civil liberties groups who opposed the war in Vietnam and the U.S.-led military industrial complex. In each case, memos were written and sent up the service's chain of command.

Ideological groups such as the Young Communist League and the Labour Youth Federation in Toronto, the Canadian Congress of Women in Winnipeg, and the socialist Quebec Women's League in Montreal were of particular interest (CSIS 1968). So, too, were chapters of the VOW in the West and in Halifax, and one informant reported on its national annual convention held in Calgary. Passing interest was shown in the activities of the United Fisherman and Allied Workers' Union (UFAWU) and the United Electrical, Radio and Machine

Workers, possibly concerning radicalization and coalition-building over such issues as women's unionized work being paid less than men's (Sangster 2010, 249). VOW members and women of the Cowesses Reserve met at the Indian and Métis Friendship Centre in Regina in February, which suggested the possibility of an alliance between "militants" and Indigenous women. The unredacted material provides no guidance as to which groups were feared as potentially violent, though it was felt that any of the groups could be susceptible to infiltration by provocateurs fomenting civil disobedience that could escalate into anti-state violence. The surveillance of the organizations involved in the RCSW did not continue after the public hearings concluded. The RCMP security investigation file remained dormant until 1977 when it was closed due to inactivity. Overall, the investigation appears not to have turned up anything justifying the creation of the file in the first place; the RCSW participants posed no real threat to peace, order, and good government.

With the end of the public hearings in October, the RCSW's public engagement wound down. Its attention then turned to drafting, editing, and translating chapters for its report. That process lasted nearly two years. Speaking at an International Conference on Human Rights in Montreal on 1 December 1968, Secretary of State Gérard Pelletier indicated that the completed RCSW report would receive close attention, especially with regard to the under-utilization of women in paid employment. The *Report* was completed in October 1970, the Commission's final meeting was held on 1 December 1970, and the *Report* was tabled in Parliament six days later.

The RCSW's coordinated approach to raise awareness, educate the public, and advocate for change was not, in the end, revolutionary. Having set the direction for social change by emphasizing women's free choice to decide matters for themselves, the multiple vectors for change listed in the individual chapters—society, the economy, education, the family, and others—set the course for that change over time. Disagreements over the pace, extent, and urgency of societal transformation animated new social actors that became the heirs of the RCSW *Report*, especially women's liberation and progressive social movement organizations, and pushed them to pressure government for action on multiple fronts.

The public hearing process raised more matters for consideration than a single public inquiry could possibly have done with the resources available to and the timeline imposed on it. Affirmative action, child care, citizenship status, conflict with the law, equal pay, equality in employment, electoral representation, the *Indian Act*'s mistreatment of Indigenous women, leadership, pornography, poverty, reproductive rights, the rights of Indigenous Peoples, violence against women, and women's health—all of them required further study and dedicated resources.

Legacies

The RCSW put women on the political agenda as the *subject* as well as the *object* of public policy (Findlay 1993, 217). The *Report*'s published recommendations principally recommended updating laws, policies, practices, procedures, and regulations. The *Report* concluded with a Plan for Action that envisaged status-of-women agencies such as implementation committees, Human Rights Commissions, and a perennial Status of Women Council with permanent funding (like the Canada Council for the Arts or the Economic Council of Canada). A network of loosely organized agencies and institutions evolved that operated under authorities at different levels of government, with the federal-, provincial- and territorial-based status-of-women councils being the best known. Similar to the United States and other countries that had studied the status of women, Canada developed its own array of status-of-women machinery (Geller-Schwartz 1995). Such entities were recognized by governments as being authorized to do this work and to promote equality of opportunity in society (Ashworth 1994). The conception of equality between women and men continued to evolve to encompass, first, gender equality, and then, more explicitly, matters of equity that extended beyond gender. Among them was an attempt to identify the multiple sources of oppression, name inequity, and establish inclusivity throughout society grounded in mutual respect and reciprocity.

The most important entities that resulted from the implementation of the RCSW recommendations were the federal status of women agency and an advisory council. Within the federal government a new body reported to Parliament through a Minister Responsible for the Status of Women, which was established in 1971. That portfolio later became a full department, renamed the Ministry of Women and Gender Equality in 2018. Created in 1973, the Canadian Advisory Council on the Status of Women (CACSW) was an autonomous agency designed to educate and inform the public and to provide advice to the federal government (Lipkin 2006). CACSW reported in 1974 that a third of the RCSW's 167 recommendations had been achieved, a third only partially completed, and a final third remained undone (ACSW 1974, 30). A national child-care program remained one item on the list of changes still to be made; however, that item was never delivered before funding cuts resulted in CACSW's closure on 1 April 1995.

The women's movement formed the National Action Committee on the Status of Women (familiarly known as NAC) in 1971 to advise, berate, cajole, demand, and exhort action from various levels of government (Vickers, Rankin, and Appelle 1993), and it wielded considerable power during the process that led to the patriation of the constitution in 1982. The inclusion of women's equality rights in sections 15 and 28 of the *Charter of Rights and Freedoms* (1982) put in place solid constitutional protections for women (Newman and White

2012, 75, 123). The RCSW's aim to achieve "equality of women and men in all aspects of Canadian society" received formal and enduring affirmation from constitutional entrenchment. Once governments withdrew operational financial support from women's organizations, including status-of-women agencies in favour of short-term project funding, the NAC effectively ceased to exist by 2010, ending the education and advocacy phase of women's empowerment that the implementation phase of the RCSW's Plan of Action had initiated. As Cheryl Collier has argued, a resurgence of a national women's movement is unlikely (2014).

A decline in the movement's prominence and the transfer of its energies to other, more specialized, and newer social organizations has since followed. Nevertheless, the pursuit of gender justice continues to amplify the strength of women's voices and social movements to mobilize over issues surrounding ability, citizenship status, Indigeneity, racialization and racism, and the elimination of *all* forms of discrimination that involve gender. Though indirect and unforeseen, the on-going legacies of the RCSW include equity demands to increase economic security, end violence, and address legacies of colonization and racism. Few ideas have had such far-reaching consequences.

Conclusion

Voices like that of Carrie Best contributed to an evolving understanding of equality that has sought to eliminate gender-based discrimination and articulate a broader consideration of equity. However, women who were Black, Indigenous, and persons of colour received minimal attention, little that was immediately actionable, and no substantive change management plan. However, the unmet needs of Indigenous women, including the treatment of women under the federal *Indian Act*, and separate mentions of Métis and Inuit women, along with racialized women and women's problematic immigration and citizenship status were flagged as placeholders for further study and analysis. Overall, the efforts and results were welcome—yet insufficient for the complexity and magnitude of the social problem (Morris 1982) and the ability of subject experts in all manner of public policy to address them. Dissatisfaction with the RCSW's approach and analysis and the limitations of the recommendations prompted women and other equality-seeking groups to mobilize. This activity has sustained the direction, trajectory, and momentum of women's equality for decades.

The groundwork laid and seeds sown by the RCSW continue to point to the Commission's aspiration to end all forms of discrimination as injustices consistent with UN human rights conventions and declarations. It is true that the application of the RCSW's internal logic has still to be applied to the intersections of racial and gender injustice. Social movements that execute a pincer movement from several directions at once (Bashevkin 2009) tend to be effective. The pressure of the twin pincers of the Truth and Reconciliation Commission of Canada's *Calls to Action* (TRC 2015) and Black Lives Matter (BLM 2020; BLM Canada 2020) offer compelling rationales to pursue equity toward justice.

Resistance to studying women's status gave way twice: first, from 1961 to 1966, the years leading up to the appointment of the RCSW in February 1967, and again from April through October 1968, when the media began presenting women's voices and experiences as newsworthy. There was Trudeaumania in advance of that year's general election, the assassination of American civil rights activist Martin Luther King Jr. on 4 April, month-long demonstrations of students and workers in Paris in May, and the assassination of U.S. presidential candidate Robert Kennedy on 6 June. These events occurred concurrently with the RCSW public hearings that spring. Popular protests that summer accelerated social change through civil rights and social movement activism ranging from women-only pickets for peace to confrontations between police and protesters in the lead-up to the presidential election. Then, in the fall, the National Organization of Women and women's liberation groups in the United States joined forces to disrupt the Miss America Beauty Pageant, suggesting that unrest among women was growing. In Canada, women addressed the RCSW's final public hearings where they continued to attest to their own dignity, demand respect, claim equality, recount injustices, and seek fairness. In the turmoil of the times, Canadian women's demands as presented to the RCSW seemed reasonable, respectful, moderate, and non-threatening. Arguably, the moderation that led progressive women to form the NAC provided direction for a perennial public dialogue. NAC then took up contested policy subjects, such as abortion, pornography, reproductive technology, violence, missing and murdered women, truth and reconciliation, gender identity and expression, and institutionalized racism in its own organization. The fruit of the RCSW has fed a long discussion about gender equality in a free and democratic Canada, which resonates, most recently, in the Royal Commission on Truth and Reconciliation's *Calls to Action* (TRC 2015) and Black Lives Matter (BLM 2020; BLM Canada 2020).

Beginning in the 1960s, national governments initiated equality-seeking studies of women's status in the United States and elsewhere. In Canada, the creation of the RCSW unsettled the status quo; the public hearings gave women standing to speak their truths. Once the Canadian public heard about women's economic insecurity, poverty, and violence against women, public attitudes began to shift, though views like those held by Carrie Best remained peripheral. The RCSW did accept an invitation in early 1970 to address the Senate Committee on Poverty and its effect on the working poor, the elderly, Black Nova Scotians living in the Halifax area, and Métis people (RCSW 1970). The RCSW's recommendation 135, to implement a guaranteed annual income, had it been adopted, would have initiated far-reaching structural remediation of economic injustice for people living on insufficient incomes. Equality and equity remain strong demands for the further transformation of society today. One of the lessons of the RCSW is clear: the voices that speak and are heard must be as diverse and inclusive as the people who inhabit this land. Best described the lonesome road to recover her own cultural identity and that of her community as being carried forward across generations. Nineteen sixty-eight disrupted the status quo through public speech; it was transformational, too, for the public discussion that followed. Here, Carrie Best showed the way. In retrospect, the RCSW fell short of the aims of current social movements' demands for anti-racist justice and reciprocity as equity. Although her voice was ignored at the time, nevertheless she spoke up for equality toward equity. Voices like hers sought respect, inclusion, and justice. In rejecting historical amnesia, she drew on the collective memory of the past to call for human-rights advocacy, equality toward equity and justice. She spoke truth to power in her time, and her clarion call exhorts each of us take up that call.

References

ACSW (Advisory Council on the Status of Women (Canada)). 1974. *What's Been Done?: Assessment of the Federal Government's Implementation of the Recommendations of the Royal Commission on the Status of Women: A Report*. Ottawa: Advisory Council on the Status of Women.

Agnew, Vijay. 1996. *Resisting Discrimination: Women from Asia, Africa, and the Caribbean and the Women's Movement in Canada*. Toronto: University of Toronto Press.

Ashworth, Georgina. 1994. "Model Actions to Strengthen National Women's Machineries." Paper written for the Commonwealth Secretariat. London: Change.

Bain, George. 1967. "The Battle of the Sexes." *Globe and Mail*, 6 February: 7.

Bashevkin, Sylvia. 2009. *Women, Power, Politics: The Hidden Story of Canada's Unfinished Democracy*. Toronto: Oxford University Press.

Bégin, Monique. 1988. "Debates and Silences: Reflections of a Politician." *Daedelus* 117 (Fall): 335–352.

Best, Carrie M. 1977. *That Lonesome Road: The Autobiography of Carrie M. Best*. Halifax: Clarion.

Bird, Florence. 1974. *Anne Francis: An Autobiography by Florence Bird*. Toronto and Vancouver: Clarke, Irwin.

———. 1950. "The Rights of Women." *Behind the Headlines Series* 10 (4). Canadian Association for Adult Education and Canadian Institute for International Affairs.

BLM (Black Lives Matter). 2020. https://blacklivesmatter.com.

BLM Canada (Black Lives Matter Canada). 2020. http://blacklivesmatter.ca.

Canada. 1966. *House of Commons Debates*, 14 July.

Canadian Labour. 1967. "No Working Women on Royal Commission." 12 March: 26.

CBC (Canadian Broadcasting Corporation). 1967. "Why Call the Bird Commission on the Status of Women?" [television broadcast]. Aired 2 February. https://www.cbc.ca/player/play/1724212893.

CFBPWC (Canadian Federation of Business and Professional Women's Clubs). 1967. *Business and Professional Woman* (Jan–Feb.): 3.

———. 1963. Marion V. Royce Papers, vol. 2, file 20, Library and Archives Canada.

Collier, Cheryl. 2014. "Not Quite the Death of Organized Feminism in Canada: Understanding the Demise of the National Action Committee on the Status of Women." *Canadian Political Science Review* 8 (20): 17–33.

Committee for the Equality of Women in Canada. 1966. "Submission to the Government of Canada from the Committee for the Equality of Women in Canada." Royal Commission on the Status of Women in Canada fonds, RG33-89, R1170-0-7-E, vol. 37, file: "Report of the Royal Commission Outlines." 15 September, Library and Archives Canada.

Craig, Barry. 1967. "Women's March May Back Call for Rights Probe." *Globe and Mail*, 5 January: 1.

CSIS (Canadian Security Intelligence Service). 1968. Records, 1968–1977, vol. 2713, file 93-A-00009, Library and Archives Canada.

Dunn, Gladys, to Monique Bégin. 1968. 13 February. In RCSW Minutes, Seventh Meeting, 15–16 February. Elsie Gregory McGill fonds, RG33-89, R1170-0-7-E. Library and Archives Canada.

Executive Order 10980 (United States). 1961. Establishing the President's Commission on the Status of Women. The American Presidency Project webpage. https://www.presidency.ucsb.edu/documents/executive-order-10980-establishing-the-presidents-commission-the-status-women.

Ferguson, Edith. 1970. *Immigrant Women in Canada: A Report Prepared for the Royal Commission on the Status of Women.* [mimeograph].

Findlay, Sue. 1993. "Problematizing Privilege: Another Look at the Representation of 'Women.'" In *And Still We Rise: Feminist Political Mobilizing in Contemporary Canada*, edited by Linda Carty, 207–224. Toronto: Women's Press.

Freeman, Barbara M. 1994. "The Media and the Royal Commission on the Status of Women in Canada, 1966–1972: Research in Progress." *Resources for Feminist Research* 23 (3): 3–9.

Geller-Schwartz, Linda. 1995. "An Array of Agencies: Feminism and State Institutions in Canada." In *Comparative State Feminism*, edited by Dorothy McBride Stetson and Amy G. Mazur, 40–58. Thousand Oaks, CA: Sage.

Globe and Mail. 1970. "Feminists Criticize Report on Status of Women as Upholding Status Quo." 8 December: 15.

———. 1966. "Women Protest All-Male Committee." 29 June: W2.

Hodgetts, J. E. 1964. "Should Canada Be De-Commissioned? A Commoner's View of Royal Commissions." *Queen's Quarterly* 70:475–490.

ICCACSW (Interdepartmental Committee and the Citizens' Advisory Council on the Status of Women). 1965. "Report on Progress in 1965 on the Status of Women. Second Annual Report of the Interdepartmental Committee and the Citizens'

Advisory Council on the Status of Women." Washington, DC: ICCACSW. https://files.eric.ed.gov/fulltext/ED014570.pdf.

Kurlansky, Mark. 2004. *1968: The Year That Rocked the World*. New York: Ballantine Books.

LAC (Library and Archives Canada). 1968a. Exhibit 22. University Women's Club of Vancouver. Brief no. 234, Vancouver, 17 April. Royal Commission on the Status of Women in Canada fonds, RG 33/89.

———. 1968b. Exhibit 52. Izette Mitchell. Brief no. 259, Calgary, 23 April. Royal Commission on the Status of Women in Canada fonds, RG 33/89.

———. 1968c. Exhibit 67. Karen Harding. [Brief no. 377], Edmonton, 25 April. Royal Commission on the Status of Women in Canada fonds, RG 33/89.

———. 1968d. Exhibit 88. Mary Rocan, Director of the Women's Bureau on behalf of the Hon. Lionel Coderre, Minister of Labour, Government of Saskatchewan, Regina, 30 April. Royal Commission on the Status of Women in Canada fonds, RG 33/89.

———. 1968e. Exhibit 111. The Minus Ones. Brief no. 146, Winnipeg, 30 May. Royal Commission on the Status of Women in Canada fonds, RG 33/89.

———. 1968f. Exhibit 121. The Canadian Federation of Business and Professional Women's Clubs. Brief no. 147, Toronto, 3 June. Royal Commission on the Status of Women in Canada fonds, RG 33/89.

———. 1968g. Exhibit 208. Fédération des Femmes du Québec. Brief no. 155, Montreal, 11 June. Royal Commission on the Status of Women in Canada fonds, RG 33/89.

———. 1968h. Exhibit 243. National Voice of Women. Brief no. 348, Montreal, 13 June. Royal Commission on the Status of Women in Canada fonds, RG 33/89.

———. 1968i. Exhibit 344. Women from the Caughnawage [*sic*] Reserve. Brief no. 245 [Mary Two-Axe Earley], Ottawa, 2 October. Royal Commission on the Status of Women in Canada fonds, RG 33/89.

———. 1968j. Exhibit 358. Canadian Federation of University Women. Brief no. 192, Ottawa, 3 October. Royal Commission on the Status of Women in Canada fonds, RG 33/89.

———. 1968k. Exhibit 363. Carry Bess [*sic*]. Ottawa, 3 October. Royal Commission on the Status of Women in Canada fonds, RG 33/89.

———. 1968l. "Precis of the Public Hearings." General Discussion. Victoria, 16 April. Royal Commission on the Status of Women in Canada fonds, RG 33/89.

———. 1968m. "Precis of the Public Hearings." General Discussion. Halifax, 11 September. Royal Commission on the Status of Women in Canada fonds, RG 33/89.

———. 1967. "Press Release." 15 May. Elsie Gregory MacGill Papers, RG33-89, R1170-0-7-E.

LaMarsh, Judy. 1969. *Memoirs of a Bird in a Gilded Cage*. Toronto: McClelland & Stewart.

———. 1964. "Speech to CFBPWC." 16 July, Ottawa. MacGill Papers, vol. 2, file 10, Library and Archives Canada.

Lipkin, Mary-Jane. 2006. "Canadian Advisory Council on the Status of Women." In *The Canadian Encyclopedia*. Historica Canada. https://www.thecanadianencyclopedia.ca/en/article/canadian-advisory-council-on-the-status-of-women.

Mahood, Margaret C. to the RCSW. 1968. 3 May. Royal Commission on the Status of Women in Canada fonds, RG 33/89, vol. 10, file: Letters of Opinion: Saskatchewan, Library and Archives Canada.

Malkin, Ben. 1968. "…On the Rights of Women." *Ottawa Citizen*, 22 April: 6.

McGuire, Patricia. 1966. "The Worm's About to Turn." *Ottawa Journal*, 30 June: 36.

Mead, Margaret, and Frances B. Kaplan. 1965. *American Women: The Report of the President's Commission on the Status of Women and Other Publications of the Commission.* New York: Scribner's Sons.

Monture-Okanee, Patricia A. 1992. "The Violence We Women Do: A First Nations View." In *Challenging Times: The Women's Movement in Canada and the United States*, edited by Constance Backhouse and David Flaherty, 193–200. Montreal and Kingston: McGill-Queen's University Press.

Morris, Cerise. 1982. "No More Than Simple Justice: The Royal Commission on the Status of Women and Social Change." PhD diss., McGill University.

National Council of the Women of Canada. 1964. "Brief for presentation to the Prime Minister." In Marion V. Royce Papers, vol. 2, file 20, Library and Archives Canada.

Newman, Jacquetta, and Linda A. White. 2012. *Women, Politics, and Public Policy: The Political Struggles of Canadian Women.* Don Mills, ON: Oxford University Press.

Palmer, Bryan. 2009. *Canada's 1960s: The Ironies of Identity in a Rebellious Era.* Toronto: University of Toronto Press.

PCO (Office of the Privy Council, Canada). 1967. Privy Council Office fonds, RG106, R728-0-9-E. 16 February. 1967-312, Library and Archives Canada.

Platiel, Rudy. 1967. "Stop Harping about a Royal Commission on the Status of Women: Judy LaMarsh Warns Women's Groups." *Globe and Mail*, 9 January: 13.

RCSW (Royal Commission on the Status of Women). 1970. Minutes, Thirty-seventh Meeting. 7–9 January. Elsie Gregory MacGill Papers, MG31 K7. Library and Archives Canada.

———. 1969. Sixteenth Meeting. 21–22 January. Elsie Gregory MacGill Papers, MG31 K7. Library and Archives Canada.

———. 1968a. Eighth Meeting, Appendix J, 13–15 March. Appendix Seminar. Elsie Gregory MacGill Papers, MG31 K7. Library and Archives Canada.

———. 1968b. "Seminar" [on Women and Voluntary Associations]. Appendix. RCSW Minutes, Seventh Meeting. 15–16 February. Elsie Gregory MacGill Papers, MG31 K7. Library and Archives Canada.

Report of the Royal Commission on the Status of Women. 1970. Ottawa: Queen's Printer. https://epe.lac-bac.gc.ca/100/200/301/pco-bcp/commissions-ef/bird1970-eng/bird1970-eng.htm.

RH (Regional Hearings) Edmonton. 1968. [audiotape]. 25 April, Exhibit 67 [Brief no. 377]. Royal Commission on the Status of Women in Canada, Library and Archives Canada.

RH (Regional Hearings) Ottawa. 1968. [audiotape]. 2 October, Exhibit 363. Royal Commission on the Status of Women in Canada, Library and Archives Canada.

Sandlund, Maj-Britt. 1968. *The Status of Women in Sweden: Report to the United Nations.* Stockholm: Swedish Institute.

Sangster, Joan. 2016. *The Iconic North: Cultural Constructions of Aboriginal Life in Postwar Canada.* Vancouver: UBC Press.

———. 2010. *Transforming Labour: Women and Work in Post-war Canada.* Toronto: University of Toronto Press.

St. Lewis, Joanne. 1997. "The Entire Woman: Immigrant and Visible-Minority Women." In *Women and the Canadian State/Les femmes et l'État canadien,* edited by Caroline Andrew and Sanda Rodgers, 262–267. Montreal and Kingston: McGill-Queen's University Press.

TRC (Truth and Reconciliation Commission of Canada). 2015. *Truth and Reconciliation of Canada: Calls to Action.* Winnipeg: Truth and Reconciliation Commission of Canada. https://trc.ca/assets/pdf/Calls_to_Action_English2.pdf.

Turpel-Lafond, Mary Ellen. 1997. "Patriarchy and Paternalism: The Legacy of the Canadian State for First Nations Women." In *Women and the Canadian State/Les femmes et l'État canadien,* edited by Caroline Andrew and Sanda Rodgers, 64–77. Montreal and Kingston: McGill-Queen's University Press.

United Nations General Assembly. 1962. Resolution 17777. 17th Session (1962–1963). United Nations Assistance for the Advancement of Women in Developing Countries. A/RES/17777, 7 December. http://research.un.org/en/docs/ga/quick/regular/17.

Vickers, Jill, Pauline Rankin, and Christine Appelle. 1993. *Politics as If Women Mattered: A Political Analysis of the National Committee on the Status of Women.* Toronto and Buffalo: University of Toronto.

Whalley, Peter, prod. 1968. Take 30 [television program], "Big Sister Is Watching." Aired 14 October on CBC. https://www.cbc.ca/archives/entry/big-sister-is-watching.

What Do You Have to Say about the Status of Women? Quel est votre avis sur la situation de la femme? 1967. Ottawa: Queen's Printer.

Williams, Toni. 1990. "Reforming 'Women's Truth:' A Critique of the Report of the Royal Commission on the Status of Women in Canada." *Ottawa Law Review* 22 (3): 725–759.

Chapter 6
The 1968 Thinkers' Conference and the Birth of Canadian Multiculturalism

MICHAEL TEMELINI

Abstract

From 13 to 15 December 1968, a meeting took place in Toronto that should be considered among the most important contributions to the birth of Canadian multiculturalism: the Thinkers' Conference on Cultural Rights—A Conference to Study Canada's Multicultural Patterns in the Sixties. Despite this meeting's significance, its legacy receives too little academic attention. Of course, it's well known that the 8 October 1971 multiculturalism policy is a constitutive feature of Canada's national identity. But there's surprisingly little attention addressing the question of its political origins: specifically, where did the policy come from? Some mistakenly suggest the Royal Commission on Bilingualism and Biculturalism recommended it, but it did no such thing. On the contrary, its commissioners steadfastly refused to abandon the long-standing position that Canada was bicultural. To answer the origins question, we must examine the successful pressure tactics of an organized political movement, of which the 1968 Thinkers' Conference was a critical aspect, and a key impetus for the policy. Initiated by Senator Paul Yuzyk, the conference was co-sponsored by the Government's Citizenship Branch and several ethnocultural organizations, with over 150 delegates and 50 observers representing 20 linguistic backgrounds discussing papers by university professors and prominent Canadians like journalist and eventual Québec Liberal leader Claude Ryan, and high-ranking politicians like Ontario Education Minister (and future Premier) Bill Davis. This is important because some downplay the political significance of this multicultural movement. Will Kymlicka, for example, argues that the emergence and success of multiculturalism are explained by luck (timing and geography). Others deny that multiculturalism was the outcome of an organized political movement at all. But the best way to explain the 1971 policy is to understand, in the vocabulary of political theory, this popular struggle over recognition, and a key aspect of this struggle for hearts and minds was the 1968 Thinkers Conference.

Ethnic groups reject
biculturalism concept
but back bilingualism

Spokesmen for 20 major eth- Government aid for expanded
nic groups in Canada yester- work by the sponsoring Cana-

Thinkers favor multiculturalism

English-French Canada vetoed

TORONTO (CP) — Dele- Leon Kossar, conference co- advisory body to assess the dian Folk Arts Council, credit
gates to a weekend thinkers ordinator, said the resolution needs and interests of courses in third languages to
conference on cultural rights means that all conference was Canada's ethnic groups "to matriculation level, and aid
Sunday rejected th "standardized history
of a French-Englis ls" reflecting factually the
Spokesman for tributions of all Canadians.
ethnic groups fav

Multicultural

society

favored

TORONTO (CP) — Delegates

Thinkers For 'Multiculture'

TORONTO (CP) — Delegates | ment to set up an advisory body | at least 50 more languages are
to a weekend thinkers' confer- | to assess the needs and inter- | spoken here."
ence on cultural rights Sunday | ests of Canada's ethnic groups | Other resolutions called for
rejected the concept of a | "to ensure their full participa- | government aid for the Cana-
French-English Canada. Spokes- | tion in the cultural development | dian Folk Arts Council, credit
man for 20 major ethnic groups | of Canada " | courses in third languages to
favored the rec
multicultural soci

Leon Kossar,

Conference rejects concept
of French-English Canada

Canadian Press | In the resolution, the 151 | organizations, churches and so
Province News Services | delegates urged the federal gov- | on, and at least 50 more langu-

Figure 6.1. Canadian newspaper headlines from 16 December 1968. *Source:* (Top to bottom) *Globe and Mail, Windsor Star, Edmonton Journal, Calgary Herald, Vancouver Province.*

From 13 to 15 December 1968, a meeting took place in Toronto that must be considered among the most important contributions to the birth of Canadian multiculturalism. It was called the Thinkers' Conference on Cultural Rights—A Conference to Study Canada's Multicultural Patterns in the Sixties. This meeting has received too little academic attention, despite its long-term legacy of shaping one of the most historically significant and widely recognized public policies: the 8 October 1971 policy of "multiculturalism within a bilingual framework."With that announcement, the Government of Canada became the first in the Western world to adopt as official state policy the recognition of cultural and ethnic pluralism. It was premised on the fact that "although there are two official languages, there is no official culture, nor does any ethnic group take precedence over any other," that "cultural pluralism is the very essence of Canadian identity," and "every ethnic group has the right to preserve its own culture and values within the Canadian context" (Canada 1971, 8545, 8580–8581). Eleven years later, Canada became the first state in which *multiculturalism* was mentioned in its written constitution.

Multiculturalism within a bilingual framework is of course a well-known aspect of Canadian civic life.[1] But there is surprisingly little attention addressing the question of its political origins: Where did the 1971 policy come from? Whose idea was it? Some point to Prime Minister Pierre Trudeau (or his bureaucrats) as its mastermind. But the idea of multiculturalism was discussed long before his civil servants and government recognized it. And at least one Canadian province had adopted such a policy a few months before Trudeau's federal government did.[2] Others mistakenly suggest the Royal Commission on Bilingualism and Biculturalism (RCBB) recommended it,[3] but it did no such thing. On the contrary, its commissioners steadfastly refused to abandon the emerging consensus that Canada was essentially bicultural.

To answer the origins question, to properly understand the emergence and state recognition of multiculturalism in Canada, we must consider the successful pressure tactics of a vocal and organized political movement. One of the best ways to explain why the 1971 policy was adopted is to see it as the response to this popular *struggle over recognition*.[4] This is one of the reasons why it is

1. Elsewhere I distinguish the Canadian policy from Québec's policy of interculturalism (see Temelini 2012).
2. At the June 1971 First Ministers' Constitutional Conference in Victoria, British Columbia, Alberta Premier Harry Strom declared that, "Alberta is a multi-cultural Province, and Canada is a multi-cultural country. And we cannot accept any proposal which does not give that fact full recognition." At an "Alberta multicultural conference" on 16 July 1971, Strom announced a policy of multiculturalism. On 9 September 1971, Ontario Premier William Davis announced a major conference to discuss the concept and its implications in Ontario (Jaworsky 1979, 66; Lupul 2005, 139–145; Alcantara, Levine, and Walz 2014, 99).
3. For example, Iacovetta (2011, 61) mistakenly claims that a "critical development" in the sea change in public opinion included "the federal Royal Commission on Bilingualism and Biculturalism, which would endorse multiculturalism within a bilingual framework."
4. I employ this term following its use by the Canadian political philosophers James Tully (2000; 2008) and Charles Taylor (1994).

important to examine the 1968 Thinkers' Conference, because it played a key role in the development of this famous Canadian public policy. The first of its kind, this conference was a pivotal moment in a struggle for hearts and minds by gathering some 200 people for the express purpose of seeking official constitutional recognition of multiculturalism. Since the policy was in part a response to a popular political movement, any explanation about its origins must also include the motivations behind this political movement. It must explain why so many people actually liked the idea—what the appeal was and why people found it inspiring.[5] And this is another reason to study the conference in that it offers clues to the public reasons people gave to promote multiculturalism.

There is no evidence that the conference alone, it must be underscored, had a direct causal relationship with the 1971 policy. But there is intriguing evidence that the conference discussions did play a principal role in that policy, because it articulated the novel idea that multiculturalism and bilingualism were compatible as a single public policy. This innovation essentially became the official government policy, and important actors who implemented that policy were either at the conference or admitted to having studied its reports, and went on record to acknowledge its significance. This was the long-term legacy of the 1968 conference. It also had an immediate impact in capturing the attention of policy-makers, academic theorists, and the wider public, thereby putting the issue of multiculturalism into the public spotlight at a time when it was being ignored or downplayed. Examining the conference helps us better understand the successful pressure put on the politicians, policy-makers, and bureaucrats who eventually implemented the policy.

Background/Context: The Emerging Consensus of Biculturalism

An historically accurate understanding of Canadian multiculturalism policy requires explaining this concept in the context of a series of interconnected and overlapping developments beginning sometime in the early 1960s (Palmer 1976, 515–517; Troper 1979).[6] Before then, federal and provincial governments showed little interest in addressing the demands of new immigrant groups for

---

5. This approach to explaining and understanding the modern identity draws inspiration from Charles Taylor's historical approach articulated in his magisterial work *Sources of the Self: The Making of the Modern Identity* (1989, 202–203).

6. The commonly accepted understanding of the public policy of multiculturalism is that it underwent at least two distinct phases. The first phase of its articulation emphasized ethnocultural diversity and the celebration of differences. This dates roughly from the launch of the Royal Commission on Bilingualism and Biculturalism in 1963 to the implementation of the 1971 policy. The second phase (announced in late 1975) emphasized race relations and serving the interests of visible minorities (Jaworsky 1979; Fleras and Elliott 2002, 62–67).

assistance, or helping established non-Anglo-Saxon and non-French ethnic groups retain their linguistic or cultural heritage. This changed in the 1960s when established ethnic groups, initially from central and eastern European communities, became increasingly assertive. The most prominent and organized were Canadian-born Ukrainians who legitimately feared the loss of their language and culture, and sought guarantees to protect them. Others who were among the first to organize included members of the Jewish-Canadian community, German-Canadian Mennonite societies, as well as Canadians of Polish, Slovakian, Finnish, and Dutch descent (Burnet 1975, 37; Troper 1979, 13; Jaworsky 1979, 48–51, 55, 63–65; Lupul 2005; Kymlicka 2007a, 70; Temelini 2007).[7] As Jaworsky aptly observed, these ethnic groups found "a ready forum in the hearings of the Royal Commission on Bilingualism and Biculturalism [RCBB]" (Jaworsky 1979, 44).

This story is fairly well-rehearsed. It is generally accepted that the policy of multiculturalism emerged when citizens spoke out against the RCBB's terms of reference, and demanded their own recognition. The formal hearings of the RCBB provided a timely and convenient forum for these groups to articulate long-felt grievances. And it was during these very popular public hearings that the demands of these ethnic groups and their supporters became more vocal and vehement and received considerable public attention.

In Canada, the concept of multiculturalism thus emerged as a political protest movement between 1963 and 1971. In fact, there was a series of issues debated at this time, sparked by the Quiet Revolution and the rise of Quebec nationalism and secessionism. In this context, the idea of multiculturalism was mobilized by Canadian citizens with cultural origins other than British or French in a simmering contest with anglophones, Québécois(es), and French Canadians outside of Quebec. Various issues were disputed: whether French Canadians and Québécois(es) formed distinct nations (compact versus unitary theories of Confederation); whether to accommodate Quebec with special linguistic and cultural guarantees or distinct status (symmetrical versus asymmetrical federalism); and whether the other ethnic groups deserved comparable guarantees (assimilation/biculturalism versus multiculturalism).

What was gaining considerable traction at this time was the idea expressed in the RCBB's terms of reference that Canada was defined essentially and exclusively as bicultural and bilingual, which is to say an "equal partnership" of "two founding" races, peoples, or nations. The RCBB *Preliminary Report* described this conflation of bilingualism and biculturalism as "duality," "dualism," and a "dualistic" concept of Canada (RCBB 1965, 45–50). As the political

---

7. For brevity, and following the usage of the RCBB terms of reference, I employ the term "ethnic groups" and "other ethnic groups" to refer to these various groups struggling for multicultural recognition.

scientist Kenneth McRoberts explains, this concept of dualism allowed no role for Indigenous peoples, and it denied any distinct status to non-Indigenous Canadians of neither French nor British origin, presuming instead that they were assimilated into one or the other culture (McRoberts 2003, 86).

The concept of multiculturalism had a distinctly political purpose during this time in that it challenged the emerging consensus among Canadians of French and British origins regarding this dualism and its presumption about Canada's essential biculturalism. Multiculturalism was a political strategy not of immigrants (or new Canadians), but of the established ethnic groups who shared francophones' fears of loss of identity, and their aspirations for cultural survival.[8] Nevertheless, as historian Harold Troper (1979) warns, it is unfair and incorrect to dismiss multiculturalism as simply an "ethnic spin-off" of French-Canadian national resurgence. While the influence of the Quiet Revolution cannot be denied, the roots of multiculturalism weave through "a tangle of historical forces," including the global movements of ethnic self-awareness, as well as the decline of Britain's power and prestige and its Anglo-conformist model of citizen assimilation (Troper 1979, 7–13; Burnet 1976, 200–201). We can also take into account the rise of a distinctly Canadian nationalism, and the yearning for an authentic Canadian identity to buttress the domineering political and economic influence of the USA.

In the context of Quebec's increasingly emphatic demands for special constitutional recognition, and in response to André Laurendeau's editorials in *Le Devoir*, various members of Parliament in the Canadian House of Commons launched a campaign between the fall of 1962 and spring 1963 for a Royal Commission on Bilingualism. Prime Minister J. G. Diefenbaker refused, but the leader of the opposition, Lester B. Pearson, championed the idea. In the House on 17 December 1962, Pearson expressed his concern about "a serious crisis of national unity," and he promoted an interpretation of Confederation as an opposition to the American approach of "the melting pot concept of national unity." Instead, Pearson saw Canada as a place where "national political unity would be achieved and maintained without the imposition of racial, cultural or linguistic uniformity" (Canada 1962, 2723). Many MPs agreed with Pearson, and to solve the crisis they called for open public dialogue. Their demand was realized when Diefenbaker's government was defeated and Pearson's Liberal Party of Canada received a mandate to govern following the 8 April 1963 election, forming a minority government that was dependent on the support of the social democratic New Democratic Party in order to pass legislation. The 16 May 1963 Speech from the Throne announced the

---

8. Jean Burnet (1975) has pointed out that the strongest advocates for multicultural-ism were not immigrants but in fact the predominantly Canadian-born ethnic groups that had been receiving few immigrants for many years.

launching of a royal commission to study "how the fundamentally bicultural character of Canada may be best ensured and the contribution of other cultures recognized." The government declared that "the character and strength of our nation are drawn from the diverse cultures of people who came from many lands" and "the greater Canada that is in our power to make will be built not on uniformity but on continuing diversity, and particularly on the basic partnership of English speaking and French speaking people" (Canada 1963, 6).

The word *multiculturalism* was not used in these House of Commons speeches. Rather, these statements reveal a belief that dualism had fundamental priority. Pearson's insistence on the "fundamentally bicultural" character of Canada and "the basic partnership" of anglophones and francophones has led some commentators to characterize multiculturalism as simply an "afterthought" (Granatstein 1986, 248). This stubborn adherence to dualism also permeated the RCBB, which tried to restrict its focus to the specific equilibrium between Canadians of French and British origins. The co-chairmen themselves endorsed this dualist focus, defending the RCBB's terms of reference and rejecting specifically the word *multiculturalism*. For example, in an interview broadcast on CBC television on 20 August 1963, journalist Norman DePoe asked the newly appointed co-chairmen, André Laurendeau and Davidson Dunton, "is this then a commission on biculturalism or is it a commission on multiculturalism?" While acknowledging the importance of other ethnic groups, both chairmen were adamant about the RCBB's dualist terms of reference and mandate. DePoe replied: "So it's a bicultural commission with some multicultural aspects?" Laurendeau demurred. "It's a bicultural commission because the country as a whole is bicultural but at the same time takes into account the fact that many groups are here which bring with them their own culture which is something ... we must not put aside" (CBC 2019a). In a 1964 diary entry written during the RCBB's deliberations, Laurendeau confessed similar sentiments. While recognizing that multiculturalism was an "undeniable fact" that "must be taken into account," he placed clear priority on biculturalism: "over and above," he wrote, "it is the great problem of French-English relations in Canada." He lamented further: "How can we get across that an ethnic group," he asks, "is not at all the same thing as an organized society like Quebec?" (Laurendeau 1991, 38).

Despite the insistence on biculturalism, activists from the other ethnic groups vehemently repudiated such narrow terms of debate (Burnet 1976, 202). They were joined by at least two of the 10 RCBB commissioners (J. B. Rudnyckyj and Paul Wyczynski) and by some federal MPs who recognized the importance of these groups.[9] The most politically significant challenge to

---

9. For example, in his 23 May address to Parliament respecting the Speech from the Throne, Toronto-Spadina MP Sylvester Perry Ryan said that without "the

dualism was delivered by Canadians of Ukrainian ancestry and their most prominent spokesperson, Senator Paul Yuzyk (Lupul 2005). The Senator was the first to employ the word *multiculturalism* in parliamentary debate, and amongst the first to acknowledge publicly the changes that were already occurring in Canada.[10]

In these parliamentary debates, many policy-makers recognized the importance of a polyethnic society, and they embraced non-uniform principles of national unity, of unity in diversity. And they launched an open public dialogue, the goal of which was to learn from one another and to become a little like one another, and thereby become better citizens. It was in this context of a popular public dialogue that the word *multiculturalism* was introduced and then adopted into widespread public use. Multicultural recognition was promoted on the grounds that it was a valuable and indispensable way of life that would contribute to the flourishing and enrichment of the country, strengthen the bonds of civic solidarity, bolster citizenship, and build loyalty to Canada.[11]

The RCBB's purpose was to convince Canadians to talk and listen to one another. Accordingly, the hearings were described as "a great dialogue"; at the Preliminary Hearing on 7 and 8 November 1963, Laurendeau defined the RCBB as a "dialogue" in which "the discussions between the Commission and the public will have to be continuous, intimate and free" (RCBB 1965, 26, 178). So, in addition to the conventional approach adopted by such commissions of inquiry, which was to invite expert research, one of the RCBB's significant innovations was that it sought to "encourage discussion" and "active participation by as many citizens as possible" by means of an unprecedented

---

recognition of the stimulating contribution of other cultures, this nation cannot flourish as it should." The following day in his address, Vancouver-Burrard MP Ron Basford urged his colleagues "not to forget in our consideration of biculturalism" the thousands of people "who have come to Canada to build new homes and new lives" (Canada 1963, 180, 271).

10. Yuzyk was appointed to the Senate on 4 February 1963 on the eve of Diefenbaker's defeat. In his maiden speech on 3 March 1964, he cited the 1961 census data to deliver a survey of population statistics and trends, a history of immigration, and the cultural contribution of the British, the French and "all other ethnic groups," particularly Ukrainians. Yuzyk dismissed the very idea of biculturalism as a "misnomer." He said: "In reality Canada never was bicultural … Canada has become multicultural," a principle that meant "continuing diversity" and "unity in diversity" and "unity with variety." Yuzyk then defended "the Canadian system of multiculturalism," which marked perhaps the first occasion in which this word was used in the Parliament of Canada. He went on to argue that Canada's "system of multiculturalism" was an aspect of the Canadian identity that had "obvious advantages over the American melting-pot concept" (Canada 1965, 50–58).

11. For a more detailed historical account of this civic idea of multiculturalism, see Temelini (2007).

number of regional public hearings.[12] From 18 March to 16 June 1964, 23 meetings were held across Canada with more than 11,800 participants (RCBB 1965, 29, 158–159). Addressing the Empire Club of Canada on 9 April 1964, Laurendeau and Dunton outlined the significance of the regional meetings, which Dunton described as an attempt to try something "quite new for Federal Royal Commissions." The aim of the meetings was to attract "a considerable number of people from many different occupations and backgrounds." The participants were asked to "discuss the problems as they see them—and we listen." Dunton described these discussions as "highly successful," offering the Commission "frank spontaneous views from ordinary Canadians" and "vivid, contrasting impressions" (Laurendeau and Dunton 1964). An indication how popular these hearings turned out to be is evident in a 6 May 1964 report on CBC television, which described the participation as "surprising." Audiences ranged in size from 100 to 700 people and "a measure of the interest shown" according to the report was "the fact that a Vancouver crowd demanded more time for discussion when the RCBB tried to adjourn its evening meeting" (CBC 2019b).

Throughout the RCBB's "continuous, intimate and free" discussions the participants defended at least four contested images of the Canadian identity: dualistic (bicultural and bilingual), unitary ("melting pot"), Indigenous, and multicultural. These disputed images were rooted in "widely differing conceptions of the Canadian state and society" as well as contested interpretations of history (RCBB 1965, 45 §29). Francophones, for example, endorsed the dualism expressed in the RCBB's terms of reference on the basis of a conception of Canada as a compact of two founding nations. Others defended this as a bulwark against "union or dependence" on the USA (RCBB 1965, 45–48 §§30–33, 56–57 §§43–44). Alternatively, many rejected the compact theory of Confederation. They fell into three categories. Some defended assimilation and the unitary conception of statehood—"the necessity of unity of language and culture within one country." In this category, the RCBB noticed a "coincidence

---

12. A preliminary hearing held in Ottawa consisted of five meetings on 7 and 8 November 1963, when the Commission heard "the opinions of 76 associations and individuals from seven provinces" representing "a wide range of institutions and groups, provincial governments ethnic groups, the mass media, the Civil Service, universities, management and labour unions, political parties, artists, patriotic groups, etc." The Commission finished its preliminary work in January 1964 and began the next phase of its work. The premiers of the ten provinces were consulted in addition to provincial cabinet ministers and provincial representatives of business, education, journalism, urban and rural organizations. "Thus they came into contact with over 500 outstanding Canadians from many backgrounds, cultures, beliefs and occupations. This was followed by regional meetings" (RCBB 1965, 23 §4, 24–27 §§9–15).

of opposites": anglophone conformists promoting the example of cultural uniformity of the USA and francophones promoting either "a new and distinct political status for Quebec" or "the idea of a fully independent Quebec" (RCBB 1965, 48–49 §34, 56–59 §§43–47). Other participants rejecting duality were Indigenous peoples and their supporters who protested the lack of representation on the RCBB and who demanded their own recognition. The RCBB refused to study the question of Canada's Indigenous population "since the terms of reference contain no mention of Indians and Eskimos" (RCBB 1965, 49–50 §35; RCBB 1970, 4, n1).

The most influential opponents of biculturalism were members of what the RCBB terms of reference called "the other ethnic groups" and their supporters. The RCBB reported that dualism "aroused fears" among these groups that "in the developing dialogue" and "power-play" between Canadians of French and of British origins they would be forgotten or considered "second-class citizens" or "their place in Canadian society might be endangered" (RCBB 1965, 50 §36, 51 §37, 59 §48). So they lodged "the strongest possible protest," promoting instead "a multiplicity of cultures" and "unity in diversity: the harmonious co-operation of all ethnic groups in the Canadian country as a whole" (RCBB 1965, 52 §38, 59 §47). In its *Preliminary Report* completed 1 February 1965, the RCBB documented this protest as follows:

> What image of Canada would do justice to the presence of these varied ethnic groups? This question preoccupied western participants especially, and the answer they often gave was "multiculturalism", or, more elaborately, "the Canadian mosaic." They asked: if two cultures are accepted, why not many? Why should Canada not be a country in which a multitude of cultural groups live side by side and yet distinct from one another, all contributing to a richly varied society? Certainly, it was stated, the mosaic idea was infinitely preferable to the "melting pot." (RCBB 1965, 51 §37)

Despite the widespread grassroots opposition to biculturalism, the growing political movement for multiculturalism did not sway the RCBB. In Volume 1 of its *Final Report*, completed on 8 October 1967, the majority of commissioners steadfastly defended "the basically bicultural character" of Canada. The report declared that there are "many reasons, the first moral, against considering ethnic difference, either by group or by origin, as a basic principle for shaping society." It then rejected legislation "based on ethnic origin or ethnic group" because it would be a "direct denial of the principle" of equality before the law (RCBB 1967, xxiii §9). Instead, it gave "more importance to language than to ethnic origin" (RCBB 1967, xxiv §11). In contrast, biculturalism was recognized due to "the undisputed role played by Canadians of French and British origin" (RCBB 1967, xxii §5) and on the premise that "the two dominant cultures in Canada are embodied in distinct societies." This was recognition of "a distinct French-speaking society in Quebec" and also "elements of an autonomous society" found elsewhere such as in New Brunswick (RCBB 1967, xxx–xxxiv §§35–47).

Purpose of 1968 Conference: "The First of Its Kind"

So, the context of the Thinkers' Conference was a growing consensus, particularly among steadfast elites, to promote the fundamental or essential biculturalism of Canada. It was in response to this obstinate lack of recognition that the conference, "the first of its kind in the history of Canada" (Yuzyk 1969, 13), was organized to influence public opinion and public policy. Held in English and French, it brought together a broad section of journalists, professors, politicians, and activist citizens comprising some 150 registered delegates and 50 observers representing 20 linguistic backgrounds and various ethnic and cultural groups to discuss presentations by prominent Canadians.

The conference was jointly organized by two groups: a five-member Senate Committee of Patrons, led by Yuzyk (the chairman of the conference), together with Maurice Lamontagne, David Croll, Norman A. M. MacKenzie, and James Gladstone; and an association of interested citizens called the Canadian Cultural Rights Committee comprised of Leon Kossar (conference coordinator, journalist of the *Toronto Telegram*, and Executive Director of the Canadian Folk Arts Council), Bruno K. J. Bragoli, John W.V. Stephen, Ted Glista, and Myer Scharzer (CCRC 1969). Money and other assistance was provided by two levels of government and four non-governmental organizations: the Canadian Citizenship Branch of the Department of Secretary of State, the Citizenship Branch (Province of Ontario), the Canadian Folk Arts Council (which had been active for many years in multicultural programs), the Canadian Citizenship Council, the Canadian Council of Christians and Jews, and the Canadian Ethnic Press Association (CCRC 1969; Jaworsky 1979, 54–55; Blanding 2013, 195). Furthermore, Ontario Premier John Robarts brought greetings to the delegates. So did one of Prime Minister Trudeau's closest friends, most trusted advisors, and his first secretary of state, the Montreal-Hochelaga Member of Parliament Gérard Pelletier (CCRC 1969).

The stated fourfold goals of the conference all aimed to promote and recognize multiculturalism, and put pressure on policy-makers to do the same: to discuss "with a wide variety of ethnic, religious, social and community organizations" the "multi-cultural aspect of Canadian life"; to discuss "the responsibilities and rights of cultural groups in Canada with respect to current constitutional dialogue between federal and provincial governments"; to recommend how governments can preserve Canada's "multi-cultural tradition"; and to establish a government advisory body representing "Canada's cultural minorities" (CCRC 1969).

Twelve prominent speakers were invited to present position papers: journalists such as Radio-Canada's Rotislav Choulguine and *Le Devoir* editor and eventual Quebec Liberal Party leader Claude Ryan; university professors such as Windsor's Dean of Law, Professor Walter Tarnopolsky, as well as University of Ottawa Professor of Psychiatry and Psychotherapy Dr. Victor Szyrynski, and Dr. Clive Cardinal, University of Calgary Germanic and Slavic Studies professor and Director of the Centre for Canadian Ethnic Studies. High-ranking provincial politicians were invited, such as Ontario Education Minister (and future Premier) Bill Davis, and his cabinet colleague, Ontario Minister of Social and Family Services John Yaremko. There were also senators, such as Yuzyk and his colleagues Andrew Thompson and Norman MacKenzie. Representing Indigenous Canadians was Omer Peters, President of the Indian-Eskimo Association. And, finally, the Director of the Royal Ontario Museum, Peter Swann, was invited.

Commencing on the evening of Friday, 13 December, the conference began each day with a plenary session, and it ended on Sunday, 15 December, with a closing general plenary session where delegates voted on resolutions (CCRC 1969). Following each day's opening plenary, invited speakers presented 20-minute position papers, and on Saturday, 14 December, four guests participated in a panel discussion. These in turn were followed by workshops organized into groups of five, which allowed delegates to discuss issues raised in each paper and the panel.

The conference began in the King Edward Sheraton Hotel at 8:00 pm on 13 December with the presentation of three position papers on the "Rights and Responsibilities of Cultural Groups in Canadian Life." The keynote address was delivered on the topic of "Historical Résumé and Current Position" by Yuzyk in English and by Choulguine in French, followed by papers from Peters and Tarnopolsky. On the Saturday morning, delegates moved to St. Lawrence Hall at 157 King Street East, where they heard three papers on the "Preservation of Cultural Traditions in Canada," from speakers Szyrynski, Davis, and Thompson. At 1:30 pm on the topic of "Striking a Balance in the Canadian Cultural Pattern," Dr. Cardinal gave a presentation that was followed by a panel discussion comprised of RCBB commissioner Royce Frith, York University Department of Sociology chairman Frederick Elkin, and Dr. Cardinal. On the same day, two other guests spoke during conference meals: at 12:30 pm, Peter Swann was the guest speaker for the luncheon, and at night Senator MacKenzie was the guest speaker for dinner, which took place at the Toronto-Dominion Centre on Wellington and Bay Streets. Back at the King Edward Sheraton

Hotel on the closing day, Claude Ryan presented his paper followed by a general plenary session and discussion of resolutions. The Government of Ontario sponsored the closing luncheon, featuring guest speaker John Yaremko, and to end the final day from 2:30 to 4:00 pm a closing plenary session was held in which delegates had an opportunity to vote on the resolutions.

Among the most frequently discussed topics raised in the papers and workshop discussions, the speakers and delegates focused on the status of ethnic and cultural minorities, the need for recognition and a public policy on multiculturalism, and how to reconcile these ideas with the more robust policy of bilingualism that the newly elected Trudeau federal government signalled it would pursue. The participants were also unequivocal in their rejection of biculturalism, with the notable exception of Claude Ryan, whose address received considerable media attention. Ryan struggled to reconcile multiculturalism, biculturalism, and bilingualism. On the one hand, he appeared to echo Laurendeau's diary entry: "Canada is principally and primarily," he argued "a bilingual and bicultural society," which was widely quoted in newspapers such as the *Calgary Herald*, Regina's *Leader-Post*, the *Toronto Daily Star*, the *Globe and Mail*, *Le Droit*, the *Windsor Star*, and the *Quebec Chronicle-Telegraph*. Therefore, Ryan urged others to "adapt themselves to the reality" of the French and English cultures, and particularly to bilingualism, which he defended as one of the non-negotiable "essential cornerstones upon which the future of this country rests." But Canada, he added, "is also a multicultural society." He accepted multiculturalism as "a fact of Canadian life" and "a formidable asset" that is "worthy of our most serious consideration even in the formulation of public policy," a point reported in the *Telegram*, as well as on CBC television news (Ryan 1969, 126–127; *Toronto Telegram* 1968b, 9; CBC 1968). The public policy Ryan was trying to articulate was multiculturalism within a bilingual framework. Remarkably, he went on to propose a number of recommendations to bolster multiculturalism, basically endorsing and elaborating on the draft resolutions presented to delegates, some of which were reiterated in the recommendations of the RCBB report Volume 4, namely: supporting voluntary ethnic organizations (including the ethnic press), promoting the teaching of languages other than English and French, and incorporating the artistic and cultural contribution of other ethnic groups in the curricula of schools, in national institutions, and in public broadcasting.

Claude Ryan's paper is just one of many examples in which participants tried to find a compromise among the contested and seemingly incompatible demands of biculturalism, multiculturalism, and bilingualism. Several speakers and workshop discussions promoted what was at the time the quite novel idea that bilingualism and multiculturalism were complementary values worthy of public policy, and they too received media coverage. For example, in his keynote address reported in the *Montreal Star,* Yuzyk argued that "English and French should continue to be the official languages as defined in the B.N.A. Act" but "That is the only privilege that the British and the French are entitled to." Nevertheless, he conceded that "The concept of a 'bilingual, multicultural Canadian nation' is realistic and the very essence of a dynamic Canadianism" (Yuzyk 1969, 5–6; Greer 1968, 29). Rotislav Choulguine described bilingualism as an excellent way to enrich the entire country ("une excellente mesure, une source d'enrichissement pour le pays tout entier") and at the same time he expressed support for Canadian citizens descended from immigrants who formed communities who also have the right to be respected and listened to ("ont droit elles aussi à être respectées et écoutées") (Choulguine 1969, 28). Likewise, Victor Szyrynski talked about Canada as a "bilingual and multicultural nation" in his position paper (Szyrynski 1969, 57). And the *Globe and Mail* reported that conference presenter Walter Tarnopolsky criticized provincial leaders "who balk at legislating French language rights on the grounds that they have larger populations of other ethnic origin." Tarnopolsky was quoted as saying that "ethnic groups should be in the forefront in urging greater recognition to French-language demands," and "other ethnic groups would profit by the strengthening of French rights" (*Globe and Mail* 1968b, 5).

Like the guest speakers, delegates participating in the workshop group discussions on 13 and 14 December "totally" rejected biculturalism and the very notion of two founding races, and they demanded the preservation, development, and greater public awareness of multiculturalism, and "the need for recognition" (CCRC 1969, 52–53, 91–93, 117–118). They likewise wrestled with the question of how to accommodate these demands within a context of bilingualism. For example, in one of the workshops on 13 December, in response to Yuzyk and Choulguine, some delegates agreed that the "historical resumé" explained in their presentations was "a valid basis in accepting the status of the two major languages." Others in that same workshop were not so sure, arguing that bilingualism "appears to be an accepted fact in eastern Canada whereas western Canada rejects this concept" and so "it is unfair to impose by law rather than by choice a second language foreign to the vast majority of the inhabitants." Whereas learning "either of the official languages … should not entail imposition," the delegates grudgingly conceded that bilingualism "should be limited to providing an opportunity to communicate in government levels" (CCRC 1969, 52).

On the afternoon of 14 December, following Swann's luncheon speech, Cardinal's presentation, and the panel discussion, a summary of one workshop group reported: "Our group can expect the fact that Canada will become bilingual, but how in justice can we be compelled to accept the overt pressure for biculturalism[?] Surely, this is contrary to the spirit of equal citizenship for all groups other than French and English." In another workshop group that same afternoon, delegates reacted strongly to statements by RCBB commissioner Royce Frith (one of the three panellists), in which he allegedly denied the existence of "Canadian citizens of origins other than British and French." The delegates replied: "In spite of Mr. Frith's statements during the panel discussion, [we] do exist, are part of Canada, and are continuing to contribute to the development and progress of Canadian nationhood" (CCRC 1969, 114, 117).

In the end, the conference delegates adopted six of the resolutions that had been presented for discussion: the conference commended the work of the Canadian Folk Arts Council and recommended that its work be expanded and publicly funded; it recommended establishing an advisory body to cooperate with the federal government on the needs and interests of Canada's ethnic groups; it proposed that publicly funded media organizations such as the CBC and National Film Board of Canada should take into account in their programming "the multicultural composition of Canadian society"; it strongly urged all levels of government to expand existing programs of language teaching and recognizing them as credit subjects; and it recommended changing school textbooks to more accurately present "the backgrounds and contributions of all Canadians" (CCRC 1969, Appendix 1, "Resolutions"). The most important resolution adopted, the one that grabbed headlines and ran as lead stories in several major newspapers of the day, was that the conference "unequivocally rejects the concept of biculturalism" and "seeks official recognition of the multicultural character of Canada" from federal and provincial governments in the Canadian constitution. Of the 200 delegates, only one voted against this resolution (Greer 1968, 29).

These speeches and workshop discussions reveal compelling evidence about the innovation that emerged from the conference, and this points to its importance and influence. Contrary to some historical accounts, the concept of multiculturalism within a bilingual framework—the policy announced in 1971—was not the brainchild of Trudeau or his bureaucrats in the federal civil service because an embryonic version was articulated during the debates of the Thinkers' Conference. This idea had emerged earlier than believed and earlier than had been reported in the news across Canada.[13]

Media Attention
The conference received considerable and favourable coverage in print media across Canada, albeit with some notable exceptions: other than the Ottawa

---

13. In this respect, one can question Blanding's assertions that the multicultural movement "played a small role in influencing the policy process," and "was unsuccessful in advancing its aims," and "had only limited success during the ... 1960s" (Blanding 2013, 28–29, 325).

daily *Le Droit*, the leading francophone newspapers ignored it, including, most conspicuously, both *Le Devoir* and *La Presse*, the influential and popular Montreal-based dailies. On the other hand, many of Canada's leading anglophone newspapers ran stories, including the *Montreal Star*, the *Globe and Mail*, the *Toronto Telegram*, the *Toronto Daily Star*, the *Calgary Herald*, the *Leader-Post* (Regina), the *Winnipeg Free Press*, the *Ottawa Citizen*, the *Quebec Chronicle-Telegraph*, and smaller, regional organs such as the *Windsor Star*, the *Brandon Sun*, and the *Welland-Port Colborne Evening Tribune* (hereafter *Tribune*). Three papers, the *Globe and Mail*, the *Leader-Post*, and the *Brandon Sun*, deemed the conference important enough to feature on the front page. And at least three others, the *Ottawa Citizen*, the *Telegram*, and the *Tribune* ran favourable editorials in support of the conference and its demand for multiculturalism.

What these papers found particularly newsworthy, and to which they devoted almost exclusive coverage, were the final resolutions adopted by the delegates rejecting biculturalism, demanding multiculturalism, and conceding bilingualism. On 16 December 1968, in its cover story on the conference the *Globe and Mail* headline announced, "Ethnic groups reject biculturalism concept but back bilingualism," and likewise in its front-page story, Regina's *Leader-Post* declared, "Ethnic aim bilingual, multicultural nation." In both papers, the lead paragraphs explained that conference delegates rejected biculturalism and favoured instead "the recognition of a multicultural society in this country." Both papers quoted conference chairman Leon Kossar who said that the delegates were "in favour of official bilingualism, but against official biculturalism." Kossar explained that "two official languages is one thing, but to say there are only two cultures in Canada is a complete negation of the Canadian fact." He added that there are "at least 50 viable language communities in the country with their own organizations, churches and so on, and at least 50 more languages are spoken here" (*Globe and Mail* 1968a, 1–2; *Regina Leader-Post* 1968, 1). Similarly, the *Toronto Telegram* headline declared, "'50 Language Communities': Ethnic Groups Attack Biculturalism" (1968a, 2). The corresponding article cited conference officials who said the resolutions adopted were not "a rejection of the existence of two official languages" but instead "an attack on the growing belief that only two cultures exist in Canada," and the article quoted Kossar about language communities. Likewise, in the *Calgary Herald* (1968, 2), *Le Droit* (1968), the *Quebec Chronicle-Telegraph* (1968, 2), the *Windsor Star* (1968, 20), and the *Winnipeg Free Press* (1968, 10), lead paragraphs reported that delegates favoured bilingualism but were against official biculturalism, and they all included the same quote from Kossar about biculturalism being a "complete negation." Reporting on the resolutions adopted by the conference delegates, the lead in a 16 December article in the *Montreal Star* announced: "The concept of biculturalism was overwhelmingly rejected in favour of a multicultural

Canada." Reporter Harold Greer described the "fairly unanimous opinion that Canada should be bilingual in some form, that our country is not bicultural but in reality multicultural." Greer explained: "the conference unequivocally rejects the concept of biculturalism and seeks the official recognition of the multicultural character of Canada" (Greer 1968, 29).

The generally positive news coverage of the conference was also reflected in the editorial pages. In its editorial, the *Telegram* acknowledged that "the great debate on bilingualism and biculturalism has caused Canada's ethnic groups to feel left out," and the contribution of immigrants "gets little attention." It was this impetus, the editors explained, that representatives of these groups met in Toronto "to remind the nation that one-third of its citizens are neither French nor English in origin." Rejecting the idea that it was the federal government's responsibility to promote multiculturalism, the editors questioned "how far Government subsidy" and tax money should go in promoting it. But they concluded that "in the final analysis Canada owes ethnic groups free opportunity to sustain and perpetuate their respective cultures," even though this cultural survival depends for the most part on voluntary effort" (*Toronto Telegram* 1968b). An editorial in the *Ottawa Citizen* expressed "a great deal of sympathy with the case put to Prime Minster Trudeau" by the "20 national ethnic organizations meeting in Toronto at the weekend… The problem … of all ethnic minorities in Canada," it explained, was "to sustain their own culture when the tendency to drift into the main cultural stream becomes increasingly strong with each successive generation" (*Ottawa Citizen* 1968).

The most favourable editorial was perhaps the one in the *Tribune,* which is not surprising given the "large segments of people of Hungarian, Italian, Ukrainian, Polish, Czechoslovakian, Croatian, Dutch and German descent" throughout the Niagara peninsula. Recognizing that "those whose origin is other than British and French" are being ignored in the attempts to promote bilingualism and biculturalism, it acknowledged that "understandably, these other ethnic groups are suspicious of attempts … which seek to force them willy nilly into one or other of these mainstreams." Citing Canadian census statistics, and the growth of immigration, the editorial went on to reject the dualistic idea of Canada. There would be "insurmountable obstacles" to creating "two cultural melting pots," it argued. Instead, the commentary offered something "far more preferable than the melting pot theory." It concluded: "There is no valid reason" why the cultural contributions of immigrants should not "form part of the Canadian mosaic" (*Welland Port-Colborne Evening Tribune* 1968).

Political Impact and Significance: Attention from Public Officials

Conference chairman Kossar emphasized that its purpose was not to create a "political force," but it was rather "the expression of a serious concern" (Kossar 1969). This is a curious statement considering all the high-ranking political actors involved, and its obvious political goals and implications, not the least of which was the demand for equal rights and dignity. The position papers submitted for discussion addressed profoundly political values of freedom, participatory democracy, justice, equality, and the denunciation of racism, ethnocentrism, assimilation, second-class citizenship, and economic insecurity. The concerns these delegates were expressing were political, and the conference was political in another sense: it was organized out of frustration with the lack of any official response to the growing opposition to biculturalism (Jaworsky 1979, 54).

There are many reasons why the political importance of this conference cannot be underestimated. Its goals were to put the importance of multiculturalism front and centre in public debate and thereby shape public opinion, to get the attention of policy-makers and persuade them to recognize multiculturalism in law and the constitution. In these respects, there is no denying its success. We have seen how it received favourable coverage in print media (and in some non-print media as well), thereby creating considerable awareness among the wider public. Furthermore, in addition to the participation of Canadian senators, a host of members of Parliament and provincial premiers acknowledged the political significance of the conference. This recognition was in part due to the activism of the conference organizers who continued their government relations campaign soon after the meeting was adjourned.

Following up on the 1968 conference, on 30 January 1969, Yuzyk began an intensive lobbying campaign to promote its goals. He sent letters with documents from the conference, including its resolutions, to Canadian heads of government and ministers of the Crown. Yuzyk received many very favourable replies congratulating him and acknowledging the importance of the conference, with assurances that the documents would be studied in detail. Official replies were forthcoming from Alberta Premier Harry Strom on 4 February 1969, New Brunswick Premier Louis-J. Robichaud on 5 February 1969, Ontario Premier Robarts on 19 February 1969, and Secretary of State Pelletier on 10 March 1969. Pelletier promised that the conference report would receive "the same careful consideration" as the impending release of the RCBB's Volume 4. Robarts indicated that the resolutions of the conference would be "circulated widely throughout" his government. And Strom said they would be "borne in mind" by his government's delegation prior to their attendance of the February 1969 constitutional conference (CCRC 1969). Two of these respondents are worthy of special mention for their particular roles in shaping multiculturalism policy in Canada. Strom, as mentioned earlier, ushered in Canada's first multiculturalism policy in Alberta in July 1971. Pelletier is recognized as one of the principal architects of the federal 1971 policy, together with his Parliamentary Secretary to the Secretary of State, York-Scarborough MP Robert Stanbury, and his Assistant Under-Secretary of State, Bernard Ostry (Jaworsky 1979; Blanding 2013).

Another favourable response to Yuzyk came in a letter sent by Trudeau on 4 February 1969. "I am directing that these reports should be studied," the Prime Minister replied, "so that the views there presented may be appropriately taken in to account both in the area of constitutional review and of cultural development." In fact, Trudeau had already publicly acknowledged the importance of the Thinkers' Conference. On 17 December 1968, during Question Period in the House of Commons, Saskatchewan Progressive Conservative MP Stanley Korchinski asked Trudeau whether he would give recognition to "the recent Thinkers' Conference at Toronto which dealt with the multicultural aspects of Canada." In reply to this and a further question, Trudeau said that he would give consideration to the Conference's final report, and that his government would study it (Canada 1968, 4030).

Did the Conference Have a Role in Shaping Public Policy?

Scholars of multiculturalism in Canada have long debated why the 1971 policy was adopted and how it gained widespread public support. Some studies focus on the role of elites, as well as government inquiries and the state bureaucracy, while others point to Canada's fortunate geopolitics.[14] What these perspectives share is a tendency to devalue, minimize, or dismiss the role and political significance of multiculturalism as a grassroots, popular movement or struggle for recognition.[15] Historian Franca Iacovetta offers a notable exception to these

---

14. The pioneering work here is Jaworsky's 1979 MA thesis. A more recent example of this type of scholarship is Blanding's 2013 doctoral dissertation. Kymlicka (2007) insists that the emergence and success of multiculturalism is explained by luck (timing and geography).

15. Jaworsky (1979, 57) argues that the most important influence in the formulation of the policy, the reason Trudeau embraced it, was the "atmosphere of change and innovation" in Ottawa in the late 1960s until 1971, particularly in government agencies such as the Department of Secretary of State, and Citizenship Branch, in promoting innovative policies such as ethnocultural pluralism. This was the primary impetus for the policy rather than the "piece-meal lobbying efforts by ethnic organizations." Likewise, Breton (1986, 45–47) rejects the idea that the multiculturalism policy was the outcome of either a popular or organized grassroots political mobilization at all, but that it came "primarily from ethnic organizational elites and their supporters, from government agencies and their officers, and from political authorities." Echoing Jaworsky and Breton, Blanding (2013, 28–29) argues

perspectives. Lamenting this preoccupation with government inquiries and formal politics, she provides an alternative "bottom-up perspective to a Canadian multiculturalism scholarship" (Iacovetta 2011, 35). In contrast, I suggest that there is room in the explanation for all of these aspects: We must examine the role of policy-makers, public administration, and the arcane inner workings of the government agencies to understand the bureaucratic logic underlying the adoption of specific public policies. And we must take into consideration the role of organized and active citizens who demanded the policy and who, as Iacovetta explains, lived every day a way of life embracing unity in diversity. Privileging one of these aspects only results in a partial understanding. A richer and fuller account of the emergence of the 1971 policy is not possible by neglecting or downplaying the impact of activist citizens demanding a policy change, or what we could call the multicultural movement, even if it was frequently spontaneous and sometimes disorganized. A more accurate explanation requires taking into consideration how the policy came to be seen as a public good, and demanded by a wider public who saw it as something valuable and worth promoting. In the case of multiculturalism there is considerable evidence, particularly from the wildly popular public hearings of the RCBB, that the idea was not simply elite driven or invented by bureaucrats. The Thinkers' Conference was a moment when the movement was well organized and effective in capturing the attention of policy-makers who were hitherto refusing to listen.

It is also instructive to examine how elites attempted to use or manipulate political vocabulary. Even if multiculturalism was embraced by certain elites for cynical or self-serving political reasons, we still need an explanation as to why the politicians saw this as politically expedient in the first place, worthy of manipulation. As the British intellectual historian Quentin Skinner masterfully explains in numerous essays, even if political elites opportunistically take advantage of public demands, or attempt to manipulate prevailing political vocabulary for their own nefarious purposes, the demands are not therefore automatically rendered invalid.[16] The attempt to manipulate contested political vocabulary does not render that vocabulary illegitimate, but on the contrary illustrates how that vocabulary constitutes a legitimate political language in the first place. The question Skinner asks is, how is political vocabulary rendered legitimate? In the case of multiculturalism, there is clear historical evidence that a citizens' movement played an important role.

that the federal civil service was "the most important factor" behind the adoption of a federal multiculturalism policy in Canada, while the multiculturalism movement was divided, leaderless, and "had limited success in advancing its aims." Furthermore, the leaders of the movement "played a small role in influencing the policy process."

16. On Skinner's innovative approach, see Temelini (2015).

The purpose of examining government inquiries, formal politics, and state bureaucracy is that they point to a moment when social movements and public opinion influenced the shaping of public policy. In this particular case, government inquiries and reports, such as the RCBB publications, offer an official public record identifying a political climate in which the adoption of a multiculturalism policy was seen as something good, as a favourable or positive thing worth pursuing. Therefore the reports explain why policy-makers would be motivated to pursue such a policy in the first place, and this has to do in part with non-governmental activism. The Canadian public's acceptance of multiculturalism, and its demand for this policy, created a political will such that the policy was something that policy-makers willingly wanted to adopt. In this respect, the 1968 conference is critically important because it shows the pressure that was put on policy-makers when they were ignoring a growing demand for multicultural recognition.

While there is no direct evidence expressly linking the Thinkers' Conference to the 1971 policy (no policy-maker directly pointed to it as the policy's source), nevertheless many policy-makers did publicly acknowledge its importance in shaping the policy. The conference was the first occasion in which there was a public dialogue not simply to reject biculturalism and the traditional idea of dualism associated with it, but to detach bilingualism from biculturalism, and connect it instead to multiculturalism. Canadian ethnic groups demanded a multiculturalism policy, and they conceded the fact of bilingualism, and key policy-makers heard this message loud and clear. In short, there is compelling evidence pointing to the importance of this conference.

There is also a puzzling historical discrepancy in the official statements that invites further discussion. Trudeau admitted to studying the reports of the conference (as did his secretary of state, Gérard Pelletier, who was in attendance) so we can reasonably assume that Trudeau understood its demands. What Trudeau told Korchinski in the Commons that day in 1968 was that before his government would commit to any policy recommended by the Thinkers' Conference, he would wait until the impending publication of the RCBB Volume 4 report on the role of cultural minorities, which was due to be released sometime in 1969. Trudeau also mentioned that he had just met in Winnipeg with Ukrainian-Canadian organizations, who were well-known as the most vocal proponents of multiculturalism.

No one can deny that the RCBB's Volume 4 played a decisive role in shaping the 1971 policy. Indeed it did, because when Trudeau announced the policy that day he did so by specifically mentioning the recommendations of that report, and he tabled a detailed reply to every recommendation. What is puzzling is that RCBB Volume 4 did not recognize, endorse, or recommend any policy of multiculturalism. Volume 4 of the *Final Report*, entitled *The*

Cultural Contribution of Other Ethnic Groups, was completed 23 October 1969.[17] In it, the RCBB commissioners completely ignored months of hearings where citizens demanded multiculturalism and rejected biculturalism. Instead, the RCBB commissioners simply reiterated their defence of biculturalism as origi- nally stated in Volume 1, expressly rejecting the claim that Canada was "officially bilingual but fundamentally multi-cultural" (RCBB 1970, 12 §26). They declared that other ethnic groups did not exist "in any political sense" and that they were "more or less integrated with the Francophone and Anglophone communities." To be clear, the *Report rejected the outdated idea of assimilation of ethnic groups.*[18] But it was "within one of these two communities" that their cultural distinctiveness "should find a climate of respect and encouragement to survive" (RCBB 1970, 10 §21, 86–87 §§231–232). This explains why the 16 recommendations in Volume 4 focus on the fair accommodation of cultural groups other than British and French (RCBB 1970, 228–230).

Notwithstanding its support for cultural diversity, not one of the 16 recom- mendations in Volume 4 mentions the word *multiculturalism*. So it is puzzling that on 8 October 1971 Trudeau announced that his government "accepted those recommendations of the Royal Commission on Bilingualism and Biculturalism which are contained in Volume 4 of its reports." Trudeau's gov- ernment did accept, endorse, or recognize all 16 recommendations to foster cultural groups other than British and French. But his government rejected the RCBB's claims in Volumes 1 and 4 that Canada was "basically bicultural." The Appendix document Trudeau submitted to the House that day declared: "The very name of the royal commission whose recommendations we now seek to implement tends to indicate that bilingualism and biculturalism are indivisible. But, biculturalism does not properly describe our society; multicul- turalism is more accurate" (Canada 1971, 8581).

---

17. This publication is entitled "Volume 4" and sometimes cited as "Book IV" and "Book 4."

18. While avoiding any endorsement of multiculturalism, Volume 4 was ground break- ing in supporting its underlying ideal: "... in adopting fully the Canadian way of life ... those whose origin is neither French nor British do not have to cast off or hide their own culture. It may happen that in their determination to express their desire to live fully in this mode, their culture may conflict with the customs of their adopted society. But Canadian society, open and modern, should be able to integrate heterogeneous elements into a harmonious system, to achieve 'unity in diversity'" (RCBB 1970, 6–7 §12). Furthermore, the RCBB declared that the "presence in Canada of many people whose language and culture are distinctive by reason of their birth or ancestry represents an inestimable enrichment that Canadians cannot afford to lose." And then it endorsed "the right—a basic human one" of other cultural groups "to safeguard their languages and cultures" (RCBB 1970, 13–14 §§30–31).

If "multiculturalism within a bilingual framework" was not one of the 16 RCBB recommendations, then where did it come from, and why was it adopted? One of the principal reasons the policy was adopted was that ethnic groups and their supporters demanded it, and in the end they were successful in their organized struggle for recognition.[19] The policy was implemented to satisfy demands from the political movement that mobilized at the hearings of the RCBB and whose demand for recognition was explicitly articulated in those hearings. These same demands were expressed in the resolutions of the 1968 Thinkers' Conference, particularly Resolution 3, which states: "the Conference unequivocally rejects the concept of biculturalism and seeks official recognition of the multicultural character of Canada" (see Figure 6.2, below). It is a remarkable fact that at least three of the six resolutions discussed at the 1968 Thinkers' Conference (Resolutions 2, 4, and 5) were reiterated throughout the RCBB Volume 4 recommendations, particularly the demands that the CBC and National Film Board take into account in their programming the cultural variety of Canada and that educational authorities at all levels of government expand existing programs of language teaching. Even more remarkable is that before the 1971 announcement, the governments of Alberta and Ontario moved toward adopting the official recognition demanded by the Conference in Resolution 3.

In effect, the RCBB was simply wrong in reporting that other ethnic groups did not exist "in any political sense." One reason why the policy was adopted was precisely because of the successful political pressure from organized ethnic groups, particularly Ukrainians in western Canada. Another reason is the fact that federal parliamentarians, such as Senator Yuzyk, were among its most active and prominent members. The political success of this movement is also partly due to the fact that it attracted the support of the governments of several provinces. And the movement's political success is also attributable to the fact that its goals complemented those of Pierre Trudeau, who became its most famous champion. Trudeau mobilized an individualist interpretation of multiculturalism[20] in his political campaign against both Quebec nationalism and asymmetrical federalism, and against the RCBB's recognition of Quebec as a distinct society as well as the two-nations concept of Confederation

---

19. It is no coincidence that on 9 October 1971, the day after announcing the policy, Trudeau addressed the tenth congress of the Ukrainian Canadian Committee (Lupul 1982, 98).

20. Trudeau argued that "National unity if it is to mean anything in the deeply personal sense, must be founded on confidence in one's own individual identity; out of this can grow respect for others and a willingness to share ideas, attitudes and assumptions. A vigorous policy of multiculturalism will help create this initial confidence" (Canada 1971, 8545). For more on the clash between multiculturalism and the principles expressed in the RCBB, see Lapointe-Gagnon (2018).

sanctioned by its various reports. Trudeau also shrewdly embraced multiculturalism to appease western Canadians in their lingering resentment over the *Official Languages Act* and the perception of special treatment for Quebec.

Perhaps one of the clearest indications regarding the effectiveness of this conference in shaping the policy was an acknowledgement from Mark MacGuigan, the former justice minister and former parliamentary secretary to the minister responsible for multiculturalism, in a speech he delivered on 19 February 1975. In an address entitled "Multiculturalism in Canada," presented to an international conference in Gaithersburg, Maryland, MacGuigan listed several factors which he claimed contributed to the genesis of a multicultural policy: "The principal single factor" according to MacGuigan was setting up the RCBB, and the categorical rejection of biculturalism by representatives of ethnic minorities. The second was the establishment of the Canadian Folk Arts Council in November 1964 because it raised awareness regarding the "cultural, social, community, and political aspects of multiculturalism." Third was the celebration of Canada's Centennial in 1967, including Expo 67 in Montreal, which "gave Canadians a new perspective of other [and each other's] cultures." Fourth, according to MacGuigan, was the 1968 Thinkers' Conference on Cultural Rights, and he mentioned several reasons why it "contributed significantly towards the development and ultimate formulation of a multiculturalism policy." One was that the conference "unequivocally rejected the concept of biculturalism" as incompatible with the ideal (and Trudeau campaign slogan) of a Just Society, and called instead for the government's "official recognition of the multicultural character of Canada." The other reason he gave was that the conference succeeded in the "reorientation of the media and of public funding of culture and education" (Bociurkiw 1978, 103–104).

Conclusion

There are a number of connected reasons why the 1968 Thinkers' Conference is an important moment in the history of Canadian multiculturalism. It illustrates how a political movement, an example of non-governmental activism, raised public awareness, shaped public opinion, and influenced public policy. With this, it provides important insights into the motivations for the policy: why citizens wanted it in the first place. And because the multiculturalism policy was eventually implemented, the conference helps explain its genesis as something not merely elite-driven or concocted behind the scenes by well-connected bureaucrats or strategically minded parliamentarians. Rather, it emerged out of a conversation among citizens and was implemented in response to a popular struggle over recognition—a multicultural movement for hearts and minds. The mere fact that this multicultural movement was sometimes spontaneous and haphazard, does not minimize its importance. In this case, the

THINKERS' CONFERENCE ON CULTURAL RIGHTS

Report of the Resolutions
Committee

Dec. 15, 1968
Toronto

PREAMBLE:

The delegates to the Thinkers' Conference on Cultural Rights express their appreciation to Senator Yuzyk, the organizing committee, and the sponsoring organizations
for their efforts in convening this conference. They wish to state clearly that the
Conference should in no way be considered a formation of a third political force --
but rather the expression of a serious concern by those citizens making up the third
element of Canada's population in the cultural development of our country.

RESOLUTIONS

First draft

1.   The Conference recommends that the work of the Canadian Cultural Rights
Committee be continued with a view to cooperating with the federal government in
establishing a meaningful representative advisory body that would make recommendations and assist in assessing the general needs and interests of Canada's ethnic
groups to ensure their full participation in the cultural development of Canada.

2.   The Conference confirms and commends the splendid work of the Canadian
Folk Arts Council in the multicultural field and recommends not only that this work
be continued, but expanded, and that this program should receive the full moral and
financial support of all levels of government.

3.   Whereas the Conference supports the efforts of the Federal and Provincial
governments in formulating a viable Canadian constitution and the Conference unequivocally rejects the concept of biculturalism and seeks official recognition of the
multicultural character of Canada.

4.   The Conference is of the opinion that communication media supported by
public funds, such as the CBC and the National Film Board, should take into account,
in programming, the multicultural composition of Canadian society and should reflect
in its work the cultural variety of the Canadian people.

5.   The Conference strongly urges the educational authorities at all levels
of Government to expand existing programs of language teaching, and that language
courses of all cultural groups should be recognized as credit subjects to the matriculation level.

6.   The Conference recommends that the Canada Council and other grant-giving
institutions in Canada be encouraged to support the research and development of
standardized history texts for the schools by the responsible authorities in this
field, and that these texts make a factual presentation of the backgrounds and contributions of all Canadians to the development of our country and subsidize creative
efforts in this direction.

Figure 6.2. Resolutions from the Thinkers' Conference. *Source:* Canadian Cultural Rights Committee, *Concern: A Conference to Study Canada's Multicultural Patterns in the Sixties December 13, 14, 15, 1968* – Toronto, Ottawa: Canadian Cultural Rights Committee, 1969.

movement was very organized, and the conference offers insight into its particular organizational and communications tactics.

Being the first of its kind, the conference garnered significant and favourable media coverage, capturing the attention of federal and provincial politicians
and the wider public in the midst of a highly politically charged moment: when

the RCBB was about to release its report on other ethnic groups, when federal and provincial governments were in constitutional negotiations, and when the federal government was rethinking its cultural policy. Unlike the RCBB, the conference explicitly recommended the recognition of multiculturalism with bilingualism. Dozens of high-ranking parliamentarians, advisers, and policy-makers either participated in the conference, acknowledged its importance, or admitted to having studied its reports, and were openly sympathetic to the movement demanding multicultural recognition. One of the best ways to explain why the 1971 policy was adopted is to see it as a response to this popular and organized struggle over recognition. And a pivotal moment of this struggle for hearts and minds was the 1968 Thinkers' Conference. Because it played a key role in the development of the iconic Canadian public policy, it is among the most important contributions to the birth of Canadian multiculturalism.

In short, there are several reasons why the 1968 Thinkers' Conference is important. Its immediate impact was to successfully put the issue of multiculturalism back into the public spotlight at a time when it was being ignored or downplayed. Its long-term legacy is in the articulation of the idea that multiculturalism and bilingualism are complementary and compatible as a single public policy. This was the first time that Canadian citizens of various ethnic origins came together to talk about the idea and endorse it publicly. This innovation of combining bilingualism and multiculturalism became the official government policy in 1971, a constitutional principle in 1982, an Act of Parliament in 1988, one of Canada's most important public policies in a generation, one of the defining aspects of the Canadian identity, and one of the most enduring ways Canadians collectively understand their society.

Acknowledgment

The author would like to thank Library Technician Carolyne Le Sieur Daigneau at the University of Ottawa's Annex Library for her generous assistance in obtaining copies of all the newspaper articles cited in this chapter.

References

Alcantara, Christopher, Renan Levine, and James C. Walz. 2014. "Canadian First Ministers' Conferences and Heresthetic Strategies: Explaining Alberta's Position on Multiculturalism at the 1971 Victoria Conference." *Journal of Canadian Studies/ Revue d'études canadiennes* 48 (2): 99–121.

Blanding, Lee. 2013. "Re-branding Canada: The Origins of Canadian Multiculturalism Policy, 1945–1974." PhD diss., University of Victoria.

Bociurkiw, Bohdan. 1978. "The Federal Policy of Multiculturalism and the Ukrainian-Canadian Community." In *Ukrainian Canadians, Multiculturalism, and Separatism: An*

Assessment, edited by Manoly R. Lupul, 98–128. Edmonton: The Canadian Institute of Ukrainian Studies and University of Alberta Press.

Breton, Raymond. 1986. "Multiculturalism and Canadian Nation-Building." In *The Politics of Gender, Ethnicity and Language in Canada*, edited by Alain Cairns and Cynthia Williams, 27–66. Toronto: University of Toronto Press.

Burnet, Jean. 1976. "Ethnicity: Canadian Experience and Policy." *Sociological Focus* 9, no. 2 (April): 199–207.

———. 1975. "Multiculturalism, Immigration, and Racism: A Comment on the Canadian Immigration and Population Study." *Canadian Ethnic Studies/Études ethniques au Canada* 7 (1): 35–39.

Calgary Herald. 1968. "Thinkers for Multiculture." 16 December.

Canada. 1971. *House of Commons Debates Official Report*. "Announcement of Implementation of Policy of Multiculturalism within a Bilingual Framework." Third Session, 28th Parliament, Vol. VIII, 8 October. Ottawa: Queen's Printer for Canada, 8545–8548, Appendix 8580–8585.

———. 1968. *House of Commons Debates Official Report*. First Session, 28th Parliament, Vol IV, December 3, 1968-January 20, 1969. Ottawa: The Queen's Printer.

———. 1965. *Debates of the Senate Official Report (Hansard)*. Second Session, 26th Parliament, Vol. I, February 18, 1964–April 3, 1965. Ottawa: Queen's Printer and Controller of Stationery.

———. 1963. *House of Commons Debates Official Report*. First Session, 26th Parliament, Vol. I, May 16, 1963–June 12, 1963. Ottawa: Queen's Printer and Controller of Stationery.

———. 1962. *House of Commons Debates Official Report*. First Session, 25th Parliament, Vol. III., December 3, 1962-February 5, 1963. Ottawa: Queen's Printer and Controller of Stationery.

CBC (Canadian Broadcasting Corporation). 2019a. "Laurendeau and Dunton Chair Bilingualism Commission." CBC Digital Archives: *The Road to Bilingualism*. https://www.cbc.ca/archives/entry/bilingualism-laurendeau-and-dunton.

———. 2019b. "A Thousand and One Opinions on Bilingualism." CBC Digital Archives: *The Road to Bilingualism*. https://www.cbc.ca/archives/entry/bilingualism-a-thousand-and-one-opinions.

———. 1968. "Ryan Speech." CBC Television, Toronto: 16 December.

CCRC (Canadian Cultural Rights Committee). 1969. *Concern: A Conference to Study Canada's Multicultural Patterns in the Sixties December 13, 14, 15, 1968 - Toronto*. Ottawa: Canadian Cultural Rights Committee.

Choulguine, Rotislav. 1969. "Les minoritiés ethniques du Canada en face des deux groupes linguistiques prépondérants." In *Concern: A Conference to Study Canada's Multicultural Patterns in the Sixties December 13, 14, 15, 1968 - Toronto*, 17–31. Ottawa: Canadian Cultural Rights Committee.

Fleras, Augie, and Jean Leonard Elliott. 2002. *Engaging Diversity: Multiculturalism in Canada*, 2nd ed. Toronto: Nelson Thomson Learning.

Globe and Mail. 1968a. "Ethnic Groups Reject Biculturalism Concept but Back Bilingualism." 16 December: 1–2.

————. 1968b. "French-Canadian Issue: Time to Call Bluff on Language Rights: Dean." 14 December: 5.

Granatstein, J. L. 1986. *Canada 1957–1967: The Years of Uncertainty and Innovation.* Toronto: McClelland & Stewart.

Greer, Harold. 1968. "Human Rights Conference: Third Force Bucks Bicultural Concept." *Montreal Star,* 16 December.

Iacovetta, Franca. 2011. "Immigrant Gifts, Canadian Treasures, and Spectacles of Pluralism: The International Institute of Toronto in North American Context, 1950s–1970s." *Journal of American Ethnic History* 31, no. 1 (Fall): 34–73.

Jaworsky J. S. 1979. "A Case Study of the Federal Government's Multiculturalism Policy." MA thesis, Carleton University.

Kossar, Leon. 1969. "Introduction—Leon Kossar, Conference Coordinator." In *Concern: A Conference to Study Canada's Multicultural Patterns in the Sixties December 13, 14, 15, 1968 - Toronto.* Ottawa: Canadian Cultural Rights Committee.

Kymlicka, Will. 2007. "The Canadian Model of Multiculturalism in a Comparative Perspective." In *Multiculturalism and the Canadian Constitution,* edited by Stephen Tierney, 61–90. Vancouver: University of British Columbia Press.

Lapointe-Gagnon, Valérie. 2018. *Panser le Canada : une histoire intellectuelle de la commission Laurendeau-Dunton.* Montréal: Boréal.

Laurendeau, André. 1991. *The Diary of André Laurendeau Written during the Royal Commission on Bilingualism and Biculturalism, 1964–1967,* selected and with an introduction by Patricia Smart, translated by Patricia Smart and Dorothy Howard. Toronto: Lorimer.

Laurendeau, André, and Davidson Dunton. 1964. "The Work of the Royal Commission on Bilingualism and Biculturalism." In *The Empire Club of Canada Addresses 1963–1964,* edited by C. C. Goldring, 328–338. Toronto: T. H. Best Printing.

Le Droit. 1968. "Opposés au bilinguisme, ils proposent le développement multiculturel du pays." 16 December.

Lupul, Manoly R. 2005. *The Politics of Multiculturalism: A Ukrainian-Canadian Memoir.* Toronto/Edmonton: Canadian Institute of Ukrainian Studies Press.

————. 1982. "The Political Implementation of Multiculturalism." *Journal of Canadian Studies/Revue d'études Canadiennes* 17, no. 1 (Spring): 93–102.

McRoberts, Kenneth. 2003. "Conceiving Diversity: Dualism, Multiculturalism, and Multinationalism." In *New Trends in Canadian Federalism,* 2nd ed., edited by François Rocher and Miriam Smith, 85–109. Toronto: Broadview.

Ottawa Citizen. 1968. "Unity's Price, for Some It's Trilingualism." 17 December: 6.

Palmer, Howard. 1976. "Mosaic versus Melting Pot: Immigration and Ethnicity in Canada and the United States." *International Journal* 31 (3): 488–528.

Quebec Chronicle-Telegraph. 1968. "Multicultural Society Favored by Delegates." 16 December.

RCBB (Royal Commission on Bilingualism and Biculturalism). 1970. *Report of the Royal Commission on Bilingualism and Biculturalism, Volume 4, The Cultural Contribution of the Other Ethnic Groups.* Ottawa: Queen's Printer for Canada.

————. 1967. *Report of the Royal Commission on Bilingualism and Biculturalism, Volume 1.* Ottawa: Queen's Printer, 8 October.

———.1965. *A Preliminary Report of the Royal Commission on Bilingualism and Biculturalism*. Ottawa: Crown Copyrights, 1 February.

Regina Leader-Post. 1968. "Ethnic Aim Bilingual, Multicultural Nation." 16 December.

Ryan, Claude. 1969. "Public Policy and the Preservation of Multicultural Traditions." In *Concern: A Conference to Study Canada's Multicultural Patterns in the Sixties December 13, 14, 15, 1968 - Toronto*, 121–130. Ottawa: Canadian Cultural Rights Committee.

Szyrynski, Victor. 1969. "Motivation for Self-Expression of Cultural Groups: The Need for a Distinctive Identity." In *Concern: A Conference to Study Canada's Multicultural Patterns in the Sixties December 13, 14, 15, 1968 - Toronto*, 54–63. Ottawa: Canadian Cultural Rights Committee.

Taylor, Charles. 1994. *The Politics of Recognition*. Princeton, NJ: Princeton University Press.

———. 1989. *Sources of the Self: The Making of the Modern Identity*. New York: Cambridge University Press.

Temelini, Michael. 2015. *Wittgenstein and the Study of Politics*. Toronto: University of Toronto Press.

———. 2012. "The Ideological Foundations of Multiculturalism and Interculturalism." In "Multiculturalism, Interculturalism and Cross Cultural Understanding: Communities and Stakeholders," special issue, *Canadian Diversity* 9 (2): 57–60.

———. 2007. "Multicultural Rights, Multicultural Virtues: A History of Multiculturalism in Canada." In *Multiculturalism and the Canadian Constitution*, edited by Stephen Tierney, 43–60. Vancouver: University of British Columbia Press.

Toronto Telegram. 1968a. "'50 Language Communities': Ethnic Groups Attack Biculturalism." 16 December.

———. 1968b. "The Ethnic Community." 17 December.

Troper, Harold. 1979. "An Uncertain Past: Reflections on the History of Multiculturalism." *TESL Talk: Quarterly for Teachers of English as a Second Language* 10, no. 3 (Summer): 7–15.

Tully, James. 2008. *Public Philosophy in a New Key: Volume 1, Democracy and Civic Freedom*. Cambridge, UK: Cambridge University Press.

———. 2000. "Struggles over Recognition and Distribution." *Constellations* 7 (4): 469–482.

Welland Port-Colborne Evening Tribune. 1968. "Third Canadian Force Just Can't Be Ignored." 23 December.

Windsor Star. 1968. "Thinkers Favor Multiculturalism: English-French Canada Vetoed." 16 December.

Winnipeg Free Press. 1968. "Multicultural Society Favored." 16 December.

Yuzyk, Paul. 1969. "The Emerging New Force in This Emerging New Canada." In *Concern: A Conference to Study Canada's Multicultural Patterns in the Sixties December 13, 14, 15, 1968 - Toronto*, 1–16. Ottawa: Canadian Cultural Rights Committee.

Chapter 7
Defending Indigenous Rights against the Just Society

Andrew Gemmell

Abstract

This chapter traces the historical importance of, and interrelations between, developments in federal "Indian policy" and investments in fossil fuel extraction, and Indigenous activism and organizations, as they emerged in 1968. Part of this importance concerns the lead-up to the disastrous *Statement of the Government of Canada on Indian Policy, 1969,* aka "the White Paper," and its contemporary repercussions. On the federal side, special attention is given to P. E. Trudeau's controversial administrative changes reflecting his ultimately contradictory approach to Indian Affairs, which led to tensions within the "Indian portfolio" between Jean Chrétien and Robert Andras and to frustrations experienced by an important but largely overlooked bureaucrat named John A. MacDonald. On the Indigenous side, Kahn-Tineta Horn is centred as an important independent actor, alongside major organization-affiliated figures such as George Manuel and Harold Cardinal, each of whom had their own nuanced and brilliant, but widely misunderstood, relationship to federal policy.

I

For many, the year 1968 seemed charged with possibility. The incoming prime minister announced electoral victory to cheering delegates: "Canada must be Unified, Canada must be One, Canada must be Progressive, Canada must be a Just Society" (Litt 2016, 239). Pierre Trudeau's pledge of wide-ranging, reason-guided reform held great promise and many sensed change in the air, but for Kahn-Tineta Horn, the 28-year-old Kanawá:ke Kanien'kehá:ka fluent in Kanien'kéha, 1968 stank of scandal. At the Caughnawaga garbage dump, owned and operated on Kanawá:ke land by those she considered the "first invading race" (RCBB 1965, 4321), both the stench and the scandal were literal. Horn resolved to do something about it.

Encompassing 60 distinct Indigenous languages and 634 federally recognized First Nations as of 2019 (Assembly of First Nations, n.d.), Indigenous

Figure 7.1. Kahn-Tineta Horn engages the Hon. Robert Andras, 28 September 1968. *Source: Toronto Star.* Courtesy of Getty Images.

politics in the Canadian context represents "outstandingly heterogeneous" (Abele 1996, 120) political traditions originating from before the colonial state (Abele 1996, 129). This chapter sketches this diversity as it relates to Indigenous–federal relations in 1968, ranging from integrationist to segregationist perspectives. On the federal side, Canadian "Indian policy" in 1968 was the purview of the Indian Affairs Branch of the Department of Indian Affairs and Northern Development (DIAND), acting under the authority of a problematic piece of legislation called the *Indian Act, 1876* (which is still presently in force). This code and its nearly annual amendments enacted federal control of Indigenous people, families, and societies. With its roots in pre-Confederation imperial-commissioned investigations and numerous colonial acts intended to "civilize," "modernize," "assimilate," or "protect" Indigenous peoples (Leslie 1985), the *Indian Act* represents the government's violent control and disruptive social planning. And yet, it was precisely this legislation and its administration that enshrined the special status of Indigenous peoples in Canada. Faced with the termination of this special status and the abolishment of the Indian Affairs Branch as later proposed by the 1969 White Paper, many Indigenous political actors and organizations fought to maintain the *Indian Act* and its related

Branch, as its legislative terms and institutional practices promised at least some protection for Indigenous and treaty rights. The idea that Indigenous advocates must defend racist legislation in order to maintain special status was the embarrassing dilemma that was exhibited in spectacular fashion in 1968.

In the 1960s, Indian Affairs policy-makers described their portfolio as the "Indian question" or the "Indian problem" (Weaver 1981, 12). This followed a colonial tradition running from pre-Confederation commentators such as Herman Merivale (Leslie 1985, 39) through those in the Duncan Campbell Scott era (1913–1932; Titley 1986, 50) and mid-twentieth-century anthropologists such as Diamond Jenness (Jenness 1941). Although this racist language continued as a new era of federal policy-making began in 1968, instead of answering questions and solving problems, Indian Affairs became the site of a struggle between contradictory approaches.

The immediate result was 1969's failed policy paper, but the dynamics established in 1968 carry on today. For the first time, in 1968, a national landscape of federally funded Indigenous political organizations took shape. Concurrently, 1968 saw more radical Indigenous voices emerge, such as those in the American Indian Movement (AIM), *Akwesasne Notes*, and the Caughnawaga Defence Committee. Technocratic Liberal integrationists took the federal policy-making reins in 1968, and their conviction that Aboriginal title and treaty rights prevented egalitarian citizenship still dominates thinking in the federal establishment (Diabo 2017). Simultaneously, Panarctic Oils' operations began in 1968, inaugurating the Canadian government's direct investment in petroleum extraction and subordinating "Indian policy" to fossil fuel industry concerns.[1] Following the 1969 policy proposal, Indigenous activists mobilized with unparalleled force and efficiency to defend Aboriginal title and the treaties against termination and assimilation. A precedent to movements such as 1981's Constitution Express and today's Idle No More, this defence made possible all subsequent legal decisions concerning Aboriginal title and Indigenous rights. In 1968, Indian status was poised to be terminated. All Indigenous politics in Canada today is downstream of the hard-fought battles that began that year. These events are foundational to contemporary Aboriginal politics in Canada and set the parameters for federal–Indigenous policy discourse in the present day.

---

1. Representing 75 companies and individuals eager to speculate in Canada's high Arctic for crude oil, Panarctic Oils Ltd. was the government's entry into the oil and gas industry, as it held 45 percent of Panarctic's equity. Panarctic operated approximately 75 percent of the 175 high Arctic wells, and in 1969 initiated a series of discoveries that includes Canada's largest gas reserves, totalling more than 17.5 trillion cubic feet (500 square km) of natural gas. Having played a major role in the development of Canada's petroleum industry, Panarctic ceased operations in 1986 (Masterson 2013).

II

In the decades before 1968, it was servicemen who were awarded key bureau-cratic positions in Indian Affairs. The result was militaristic and isolationist, and there was an exceptionally strong and unrivalled continuity among senior civil servants (Weaver 1981, 45–46). This continuity notwithstanding, by 1968 the Branch was in crisis. Scholars often trace this crisis to the early 1940s (according to policy experts such as John F. Leslie [1985; 1999] and Laurie Meijer Drees [2002]) or 1963 (according to Sally Weaver [1981]), but serious concerns about the viability of the project of Indigenous relations had been harboured since at least the *Bagot Commission Report* in 1844. Regardless, by the end of the Second World War, fuelled by media reports of exemplary Indigenous wartime service, a surging Native population, and deplorable living conditions, reform of the *Indian Act* was broadly supported.

Between 1956 and 1968, the Branch's total expenditures had increased seven-fold from $23.7 million to $165.8 million (Weaver 1981, 25). However, political instability (1962–1968 saw minority governments) and bureaucratic ineffectiveness compounded fiscal bloat resulting in significant departmental dysfunction. The decade preceding the White Paper saw eight ministers hold the Indian Affairs portfolio, with six holding terms of a year or less (Weaver 1981, 44). In a letter dated 15 February 1965, Kahn-Tineta Horn told John Nicholson, Minister of Citizenship and Immigration (the ministry which, at the time, was responsible for Indian Affairs), that "During the past few years in which I have been engaged in arousing Indians to the problems surrounding them, and at the same time endeavouring to communicate truth to the 99% non-Indian population, it has been my privilege to communicate with no less than five ministers of your department" (LAC, n.d., 1:326). Contrasting with this leadership churn was the old guard's remarkable bureaucratic consistency. Come 1968, they had been gripping the reins for more than two decades and had crafted and implemented Indian policy largely unimpeded by external oversight and unconcerned by Indigenous voices.[2]

In many ways, Branch Deputy Superintendent Duncan Campbell Scott, whose era spanned 1913 to 1932, was emblematic of the department's isolation-ist culture and its profound insensitivity to Indigenous living conditions. In 1920, Scott supervised the implementation of legislation mandating the com-pulsory attendance of Indigenous children at residential schools. When Dr. Peter Bryce first reported the schools' abysmal living conditions and high mortality rates in 1907, Scott had been dismissive. According to Scott, the suffering and deaths of Indigenous children was simply part of solving the "Indian problem. I do not think as a matter of fact, that this country ought to

---

2.   One notable exception was Walter Rudnicki's 1964 Indian Affairs Community Development Program (Weaver 1981, 46).

continuously protect a class of people who are able to stand alone. ... Our objective is to continue until there is not a single Indian in Canada that has not been absorbed into the body politic, and there is no Indian question, and no Indian Department" (Titley 1986, 50). The separation of Indigenous children from their families reached new heights in the 1960s. The Sixties Scoop saw "10,000 Aboriginal children attending Canadian residential schools in 1966, fully 75 per cent [of whom] had been 'placed' because their parents were judged by white social service workers and other officials as somehow inadequate" (Palmer 2009, 382).[3] In 1968, Horn had to fight to keep her brother Joseph from being scooped (LAC, n.d., 1:272).

While several Indigenous political actors and organizations were important in the politics of 1968, perhaps none was more prominent than activist Kahn-Tineta Horn. Her 1965 submission to the Royal Commission on Bilingualism and Biculturalism made her position clear: "I am not a citizen of Canada. I am a private citizen of the six nations Iroquois Confederacy" (RCBB 1965, 4316). Although not representative of Indigenous politics *in toto*, Horn's profound aesthetic sensibilities, strength of character, and deeply held principles combined in 1968 to cement her place as an important character in this historical moment—and she seemed to know that. In a letter to the Indian Affairs Branch dated 19 September 1968, Horn described her experience that year as "a comedy to some but [a] dark tragedy to me" (LAC, n.d., 1:180).

An evocative presence, Horn gave an inaugural address at her "First Indian Film Festival" held in Ottawa on 29 and 30 November 1968, in which she labelled the Branch "the Siberia of the Civil Service" (LAC, n.d., 1:44). Even with its characteristic insensitivity and isolationism, the old guard was frustrated by the intractability of the "dilemma that had plagued Indian policy since Confederation," namely the question of "special rights versus equality" (Weaver 1981, 47). Pierre Trudeau, newly elected as prime minister in 1968, inserted himself into this impasse promising decisive and wide-ranging reform. Unfortunately, while the cerebral Trudeau championed a Just Society of rational policy and participatory democracy, that concept confounded the Indian Affairs Branch.

III

Trudeau's own inconsistencies were not limited to the tension between his liberal individualism and his consultative "platformities" (Litt 2016, chap. 8). Rather, his liberal ideology was itself contradictory. As Weaver put it, liberalism "fails to detect that choices are possible only under certain social conditions"

---

3. In British Columbia from 1955 to 1966, "the representation of Native children in [the province's] child welfare system [jumped] from almost nil to a third[. It] was a pattern being repeated in other parts of Canada as well" (Johnston 1983, 23).

and thus "'blames the victim' for any failure to use the opportunities which society is said to offer" (Weaver 1981, 55). Trudeau, whose dictum was "reason over passion" (Litt 2016, 365n31), wished to be known as the prime minister of the "transitional period, ushering us into the electronic age, the age of reason" (*The Canadian Magazine* 1968). Ironically, he was unable to rationalize the contradiction between the liberal fiction of ahistorical autonomous individualism and the reality of daily life.[4]

As prime minister, Trudeau made immediate structural changes to the federal policy-making apparatus, the most controversial being the politicization of the Office of the Prime Minister (PMO)[5] and the empowerment of the Office of the Privy Council (PCO).[6] This Cabinet reform replaced the PMO's staff of civil servants with Trudeau's 1968 campaign strategists, serving on several small permanent committees. Trudeau's new Cabinet Committee on Social Policy handled Indian policy, and had among its members Marc Lalonde and Jim Davey.[7] One of the new Canadian "scientific planning technocrats" (Cunningham 1999, 58), Davey had degrees in physics and computer science. He approached government policy and programs according to a systems approach that "comprehensively planned and coordinated across departments" (Weaver 1981, 56). Davey's scientific worldview and putatively objective methods, which "borrowed from the Kennedy administration of system analysis and management by objectives (MBO)" (Cunningham 1999, 55), worked to get Trudeau elected but proved, according to Trudeau's own diagnosis, disastrously "naive" (Weaver 1981, 185) when drafting Indigenous policy. Davey's systems theory implemented "Trudeau's ahistorical approach to policies and his stand against special status for cultural groups" (Weaver 1981, 56). Intended to revolutionize policy-making discourse, these changes instead rehearsed more than a century of problematic policy errors in a new register.

Curiously, Weaver points to one innovative dimension in the 1969 proposals: "The White Paper's only innovation was termination, a policy designed to eradicate all special Indian rights in the immediate future" (Weaver 1981, 197).

---

4. To borrow Mohawk scholar Audra Simpson's phrase from *Mohawk Interruptus*, ideological contradictions as "concepts have teeth, and teeth that bite through time" (Simpson 2014, 100).

5. This made the PMO "into a partisan Liberal party nerve centre within government" (Weaver 1981, 56).

6. He transformed the PCO "from a passive to a more active influence in policy making, and it was staffed by some of the most powerful civil servants in Ottawa." Weaver identifies two of these, protecting one with anonymity: "Jordan (pseudonym) and [Walter] Rudnicki," the latter having "played a major role in shaping the course of Indian policy" (Weaver 1981, 57).

7. Weaver describes Davey as "the most influential PMO figure in terms of Indian policy" (Weaver 1981, 56).

However, 1969's proposed abolishment of Indian Affairs and the termination of Indian status had been explored previously by the Colonial Office in its pursuit of imperial devolution in the decades prior to 1860. Jim Miller lists similar termination attempts had been attempted "in 1876, 1880, 1884, 1895, 1911, 1920, 1922, 1927, 1933, and 1951" (Anderson and Robertson 2011, 157).

While termination itself was not new policy, there were other truly new policies that combined in 1968 to present an unavoidable dilemma. One innovative dimension was the pursuit of universal enfranchisement in the modern liberal context of technocratic administration and human rights policy—1968 being the International Year for Human Rights and the twentieth anniversary of the UN Declaration. Here was Trudeau's principled stand against "minority rights." Another innovative dimension was the effort to elevate and centre Indigenous perspectives in recorded, transcribed, and widely disseminated national consultations with the promise to include Indigenous voices in policy decisions. This was evidence of Trudeau's avowed support of participatory democracy in the Just Society. However, since those consulted in the latter did not want the former, something had to give.

The push to include Indigenous voices was built on recent attempts to implement Pearson's "consultative federalism" (Weaver 1981, 27) following recommendations by multiple committees and reports. The Special Committee on the *Indian Act*, 1948, proposed forming an Indian Claims Commission (Leslie 1999, 394), which was subsequently endorsed by the 1959–1961 Joint Committee on Indian Administration as a forum for adjudicating Indigenous concerns (Leslie 1999, 16). The Commission never materialized, but in 1964 Walter Rudnicki organized nation-wide community development meetings under the auspices of the Department's Social Programs Division. The Branch then established National and Regional Indian Advisory Boards in 1965 (Leslie 1999, 12) to further consult Indigenous leaders on its programming. The 1024-page *Hawthorn Report, 1966* similarly recommended that the Branch reorient itself from being preoccupied with managing Indian lands, assets, and resources toward being an organization that aimed to facilitate, advise, and educate (Leslie 1999, 278). Undermining these consultative efforts, however, were practices such as the Sixties Scoop and the forcible relocation of entire communities from traditional lands to barely habitable spaces. As Rudnicki's "community development" meetings were underway, elsewhere in the same department bureaucrats were busy relocating, among others, the Ojibwa of Grassy Narrows reserve from "a wide expanse of territory into a narrow and claustrophobic cluster of residences" (Palmer 2009, 383) located in an area poisoned by mercury effluent. Beginning in 1963, this relocation proved disastrous to the health and welfare of the community, and had been undertaken without any consultation. Cree activist Harold Cardinal did not mince words. He described Branch bureaucrats as "faceless," "gutless" "mandarins" of "endless ignorance" who maintain power by subjecting "durable Indian leaders to endless exercises in futility, to repeated, pointless re-organizations, to endless barrages of verbal diarrhea promising never-coming changes" (Cardinal 1969, 6–7).

By early 1967, Arthur Laing, the Minister of Indian Affairs in the Pearson government, was under considerable pressure. Public opinion held the government responsible for the plight of Indigenous people (Weaver 1981, 52). Three western provincial premiers concluded their 1967 Prairie Economic Council with a letter to the Prime Minister urging a complete revision of Indian policy and programming. Throughout 1967, the PCO consistently championed the idea of a task force tackling Indian policy reform. As a result, Laing announced a series of 18 consultation meetings with Indigenous representatives across the country. They were to discuss revisions to the *Indian Act* and run from April or May 1968 through autumn. In preparation, Laing and newly appointed Deputy Minister John A. MacDonald distributed a booklet in March to every Indigenous household in Canada, entitled *Choosing a Path* (DIAND 1968). This booklet of 36 questions asked Indigenous peoples how they hoped to determine their own future. Laing's policy-makers anticipated an expansion of the Indian Affairs bureaucracy, an amplification of special rights, and the founding of the long-sought Indian Claims Commission (Weaver 1981, 190). On 1 May, however, Laing postponed consultation until after the 25 June federal election. Once elected, Trudeau agreed to honour Laing's commitments, but reassigned him to Public Works. The consultations began without Laing on 25 July in Yellowknife, two weeks after Jean Chrétien was appointed Minister of Indian Affairs (Weaver 1981, 60). These 1968–1969 consultations on Indigenous policy resulted in the White Paper. While initiating a new pan-Indigenous nativism, these meetings also revealed the paradoxical nature of the government's discourse. The consultations resonated with Trudeau's campaign platform but revealed contradictions within the liberal positions on special rights, positions on which he had built his career.

Before Trudeau arrived in Ottawa, he made a name in the 1950s as a law professor critical of Québécois nationalism. He admonished the Duplessis regime for its antimodern, exploitative, and retrograde national ideology. According to historian Paul Litt, Trudeau feared such nationalism "blocked his compatriots from full participation in modern society and full enjoyment of its benefits" (Litt 2016, 129). Trudeau rode this position to Parliament, becoming Minister of Justice in 1967. His national profile was elevated in early February 1968 when he defended federalism in a "Constitutional showdown" with Quebec Premier Daniel Johnson. Soon thereafter, 1968 became an election year, and Trudeau adopted what Litt terms his liberal "platformities," which expressed a tolerant and peaceable "optimistic humanism" (Litt 2016, 114). While the 1967 Centennial Commission chief John Fisher announced that the

Centennial Exposition was "our never-to-be-seen-again chance to achieve unity-in-diversity" (Litt 2016, 105), Trudeau may have felt that the same idea was true about his own election.

Leading up to the 1968 federal election, this vision of unity and tolerance, one critical of minority rights, was distilled as Trudeau's Just Society. Trudeau described his project as the legislative "freeing of the individual so he will be rid of his shackles" and equality of opportunity "in which all of our people will have the means and the motivation to participate." Although this vision of a unified Canadian Just Society arose from Trudeau's hard-won positions against Quebec nationalism, he also applied his rhetoric to Indigenous peoples: "The Just Society will be one in which our Indian and Inuit population will be encouraged to assume the full rights of citizenship through policies which will give them both greater responsibility for their own future and more meaningful equality of opportunity" (Litt 2016, 240–241). According to Litt's analysis, "This was garden-variety twentieth-century liberalism" (378) and "in 1968 the rights of Indigenous peoples did not figure prominently in the federal election campaign" (379). Nevertheless, from 25 July 1968 until the National Conference on the *Indian Act* held in Ottawa from 28 April to 2 May 1969, Chrétien went through the motions in nationwide consultations with Indigenous peoples regarding their special rights. Behind the scenes, however, the Liberals were approaching Indigenous issues in the same way they approached Quebec: "equal rights for all rather than collective rights for minorities" (379).

Tensions were palpable at the time, even in Trudeau's Cabinet. A public fight erupted in October between Jean Chrétien, the newly appointed 34-year-old Minister of Indian Affairs and Northern Development, and Robert K. Andras, the older minister without portfolio assigned to accompany him. Behind the scenes, the technocrats in the PMO, with their systems analysis and management-by-objectives approach, jostled with the liberal activists in the PCO and the Indian Affairs old guard for control of policy. Indigenous peoples throughout Canada were soon caught in Trudeau's constitutive irony, caught between optimistic political rhetoric about progressive participatory democracy and a Just Society and entrenched ideological positions.

These tensions produced the *Statement of the Government of Canada on Indian Policy, 1969* (Canada 1969). Presented to Parliament on 25 June 1969, one year to the day after Trudeau's election win, it has been known since as the White Paper.[8] This six-point plan[9] applied Trudeau's critique of Quebec nationalism

---

8. Chrétien tried to avoid this title and "misleadingly presented the policy statement as a 'green paper.' In fact, the copy mailed out to Indian bands across the country did have a green cover. The steps failed" (Tennant 1990, 149–150).

9. The points were: 1) Repeal the *Indian Act* and special rights; 2) Devolve federal responsibilities to the provinces; 3) Encourage integration over assimilation or the

to the "Indian problem." In it, Indigenous peoples would become Canadian citizens with no special status, the *Indian Act* would be abolished, and Indian Affairs and the reserve system would be disbanded. The Indigenous response was, first, disappointment, then hostility (Cunningham 1999, 64). It caught the Liberals completely off guard.

After a year of intensive consultation and repeated commitments to participatory democracy, how could Trudeau's Liberals get it so wrong? In the weeks that followed, unprecedented Indigenous mobilization against the White Paper forced its withdrawal. Trudeau addressed the Indian Association of Alberta (IAA) and the National Indian Brotherhood (NIB) in Ottawa on 4 June 1970 to admit that "we were very naive in some of the statements we made in the paper. We had perhaps the prejudices of small 'l' liberals and White men who thought that equality meant the same law for everyone. ... But we have learned in the process that perhaps we were a bit too theoretical, we were a bit too abstract" (Weaver 1981, 185). But Trudeau seemed hardly to have learned any lessons at all. As he withdrew the White Paper in 1971, Trudeau reportedly said: "We'll keep them in the ghetto as long as they want" (Lagace and Sinclair 2015).

As Weaver points out, while the summer of 1968 began with radical promise and the dazzling political rhetoric of a new age, Trudeau's administrative reforms "underestimated the competitiveness of politicians and their personal advisors" (74). When Chrétien was named Minister of Indian Affairs and Northern Development,[10] Trudeau assigned Robert Andras, a retired infantry major, to accompany Chrétien as minister without portfolio. Trudeau did not anticipate the profound and public antagonism that grew between the two of them. Chrétien and Andras split along opposite alignments within Trudeau's liberal ideology: Chrétien with the old guard and Deputy Minister John A. MacDonald;[11] Andras with PCO activists like Rudnicki who were advocating substantive consultation with Indigenous peoples (Weaver 1981, 194).

Their differences were soon apparent. Consultations positioned microphones in front of DIAND representatives, prominent Indigenous delegates, translators, and local band members, producing verbatim transcripts distributed nationally to the press and public. The conversations were wide-ranging and informal, and while Weaver describes profound dissatisfaction on behalf of Indigenous participants (61), Paul Tennant points out that for Indigenous

---

reserve system; 4) Interim funding; 5) Terminate any remaining treaty obligations with Commission oversight; 6) Transfer reserves to Indigenous band councils, removing protections against taxation and sale.

10. It was an appointment that some saw as a gesture towards national bi-cultural unity (*Ottawa Journal* 1968).

11. Harold Cardinal referred to the White Paper as the "MacDonald-Chrétien doctrine" (Cardinal 1969, 1).

peoples in British Columbia, they were seen as "a worthwhile endeavour" (Tennant 1990, 146) because they spurred political organization and offered a way for them to hear what other Indigenous peoples thought. The more formal Chrétien cautiously avoided making commitments. Carefully managing participants' expectations, he repeated that Cabinet held all decision-making powers. Portentously, in the first meeting in Yellowknife, Chrétien equated the "Indian problem" with the "Quebec question": "Being from a minority group in this country, I understand what it is to be a member of such a group" (Weaver 1981, 62). Andras, on the other hand, was friendly and easy-going and devoted more time to consultation.[12] According to Weaver, "it was obvious from the earliest meetings that Indians preferred Andras's activist approach" (65). Harold Cardinal agreed, calling Andras a "notable exception" to the "gutless" politicians who "stall," "procrastinate," and "produce injustice" (1969, 7). Kahn-Tineta Horn, however, was not impressed with Andras, who blocked Horn from presenting in Quebec City. On 1 October 1968, she wrote in a letter to Prime Minister Trudeau that "A very kind and good man, Hon. Robert K. Andras, is going around the country like a Judas goat. He is holding hearings of Indians but only the Indians appearing before him are the ones cunningly selected to say what the higher ups want" (LAC, n.d., 1:149). Moreover, Horn wanted nothing of Chrétien's minority comparisons. In a 9 February 1968 letter to the Branch, she wrote: "I am not a minority" (LAC, n.d., 1:275). Not only was Andras' style contradictory to Chrétien's but it was also misleading, contributing, Weaver suggests, "to Indian expectations not only that Andras was sympathetic to their views, but also that Ottawa might heed his recommendations" (1981, 63). A fuse was lit between Chrétien and Andras months before the PMO, the PCO, and the Department had even begun talking policy. It exploded in the press in October 1968 when Andras went public with his displeasure at Chrétien's sudden and secret reorganization of DIAND. According to Weaver, Andras' repeated suggestion "that past injustices to Indians would be rectified, possibly in the way they desired" (63) contributed to the shock.

At the end of the year-long consultation process, it was clear that Ottawa had not been listening. The White Paper generated a number of responses, including the IAA's *Citizens Plus* (1970; a.k.a. *The Red Paper*), the Manitoba Indian Brotherhood's *Wahbung: Our Tomorrows* (1971), and the Union of British Columbia Indian Chiefs' *A Declaration of Indian Rights: The B.C. Indian Position Paper* (1970).[13] The majority of those involved expressed shock at how badly the federal government had misread Indigenous politics in 1968. A notable

---

12. Chrétien attended nine of the 18 meetings; Andras attended "nearly all" (Weaver 1981, 62).

13. Also known as *The Brown Paper*, partly drafted by George Manuel in collaboration with Charlie Rose and the Indian Homemakers Association of B.C.

outlier was Kahn-Tineta Horn, who anticipated 1969's proposed devolution and termination years in advance in her letters to Prime Minister Pearson. On 17 August 1965, Horn wrote that she anticipated a "long painful lingering death by torture by transferring" the portfolio to the provinces (LAC, n.d., 1:312). By the end of 1968, she was already describing the upcoming federal policy as "the theft of our lands set for 1969" (Horn 1968a).

IV

The structural irony within Trudeau's Indian Affairs administration caused headaches all around, but while its pretensions toward participatory and collaborative reform ultimately proved false, the government's failed efforts catalyzed new pan-Indigenous advocacy efforts. Organizations that emerged in 1968 are foundational to those active today. Nineteen sixty-eight was the founding year for a large number of regional and national Indigenous associations. The proliferation of Indigenous organizations and activism correlated with a surging Indigenous population and growing public awareness about their often abysmal living conditions under DIAND wardship. As Weaver notes, although a "politically unorganized minority," during "1968 the question of whether a more coherent Indian movement would develop was being asked by both native spokesmen and government officials" (41). Indigenous activism had been disorganized largely because of the 1927 federal proscription against Indigenous peoples pursuing legal counsel, political organization, or fundraising (though it was lifted with the 1951 amendments to the *Indian Act*). In 1960, Indigenous peoples regained the right to vote in federal elections without the enfranchisement that had accompanied voting privileges since 1880. The result was a new generation in the 1960s of politically engaged Indigenous actors and organizations making waves on the national scene.

In 1968, regional and provincial Indigenous organizations proliferated. As Paul Tennant underlines with respect to this flourishing of Indigenous political bodies in 1968, "Their creation and early growth had been almost entirely dependent upon government funding ... a crucial new factor [affecting] virtually every aspect of aboriginal political activity" (1990, 164). Laurie Meijer Drees, in her important study of the IAA, notes that funding may well have been a government attempt to co-opt a threat. Nineteen sixty-eight marked the first year that Indian Affairs began offering per-capita grants to Indigenous political organizations, completely bureaucratizing and integrating federal–Indigenous relations into the federal budget (Drees 2002, 163). Many were critical of this development. In a rare moment of agreement, both Kahn-Tineta Horn and her adversary, William Wuttunee, disapproved.[14] Horn's 4 December

---

14. During this period, Horn was broadly critical of Indigenous cooptation, "the well-bought Indian" (LAC, n.d., 1:274), and often took care to note her own

1968 letter to the *Ottawa Journal* editor began with: "How sublime is folly! How sad are the bought! How tragic are those untrue to their destiny and the whispers of 3000 generations of their ancestors" (Horn 1968a). Some, such as Métis leaders Adrian Hope and Maria Campbell, were prompted to step away from national Indigenous politics altogether (Drees 2002, 165).

The National Indian Council (NIC), one of the few high-profile national organizations at the time, dissolved and splintered into factions in 1968. New Indigenous political actors arose, partly due to their roles as directors of new associations, and partly in response to federal preparations for the upcoming White Paper. Sucker Creek Cree wunderkind, 23-year-old Harold Cardinal, took control of the powerful and longstanding IAA in 1968, and veteran Secwépemc political organizer George Manuel moved his family to Edmonton to work with Cardinal and the IAA executive.

Concurrently, Manuel's 35-year-old Okanagan protégé and the first Indigenous university graduate from BC's interior, Len Marchand, was breaking ground in Ottawa. Faced with ongoing pressure from the Nisga'a Tribal Council's land claim and unable to parse the complexities of Indigenous politics in the interior of BC, the Ministry hired Marchand as the first Indigenous person on a federal minister's staff in 1965, working with Vancouver MP and Minister of Indian Affairs J. R. Nicholson. Marchand retained the post when another Vancouver MP, Arthur Laing, became minister in 1966 (Tennant 1990, 133). Marchand was elected to Parliament as a Liberal in 1968, and so he was no longer in the minister's office when the White Paper came out.[15]

That same year, Sagneenk Ojibwa Dave Courchene helped form the Manitoba Indian Brotherhood (MIB), and Ermineskin Cree Chief Apitchitchiw, also known as Chief Johnny Robert Smallboy, led an autonomy movement in the foothills of Alberta (so had his grandfather, Chief Mistahi Maska, also known as Chief Big Bear). In 1968, Calgary-based Red Pheasant Plains Cree lawyer William Wuttunee, an outspoken integrationist, co-founder of the NIC, and one of the few staunch Indigenous supporters of the White Paper, stepped off the national stage to lick his wounds, many of which had been inflicted by the enigmatic, controversial, and brilliant 28-year-old Kanien'kehá:ka power-house Kahn-Tineta Horn. As the first Indigenous lawyer to appear before the

---

independence. Wuttunee took aim at the federal funding of Indigenous leaders and organizations of 1968–1970 in his book *Ruffled Feathers* (Wuttunee 1971, 7). Horn would no doubt have pointed out the hypocrisy of Wuttunee, who misappropriated federal funding intended for the NIC.

15. MacFarlane writes, "[a]s it turned out, Marchand would end up being 'the first of everything,' the first Indian MP in 1968 and the first Indian cabinet minister in the mid-1970s" (MacFarlane 1993, 70). In 1984, Marchand was the second Indigenous person appointed to the Canadian Senate (the first being former IAA head James Gladstone under John Diefenbaker's tenure).

Supreme Court, an early defender of LGBT rights and an advocate for the Indigenous people's right to vote, Wuttunee was no slouch. Horn was a formidable opponent, however, and when she accused him of corruption it tarred his reputation (Horn, n.d.).

In 1968, Horn established her status as one of the most important figures in modern Indigenous politics in Canada. Her activism and voluminous correspondence from that year demonstrate that she was one of few not shocked by the White Paper's proposals. In fact, in 1965 she had warned of "the forthcoming crisis" (LAC, n.d., 1:319). Her early positions calling for a National Assembly of Chiefs that might act as an Indian Claims Court, her worries dating to the Pearson administration regarding the devolution of Indian issues to the provinces, and her profound dissatisfaction with Wuttunee's NIC all proved percipient (LAC, n.d., 1:312, 340).[16]

Kahn-Tineta Horn's 1968 closed with her arrest alongside dozens of Kanien'kehá:ka blockading the Seaway International Bridge at Akwesasne. The 18 December protest against violations of the *Jay Treaty, 1794* won important concessions (LAC, n.d., 2:534), and Horn followed up with a hand-delivered petition to the Queen. Her 1968 collaboration with the Ahkwesáhsne Kanien'kehá:ka was one aspect of that community's impact on 1968 Aboriginal politics. Parallel to the late 1968 bridge blockade was the founding of *Akwesasne Notes*, perhaps the most important Indigenous activist journal of the twentieth century (George-Kanentiio [1993] 2011). Akwesasne activist Richard Oakes moved to San Francisco in 1968, where his organizing converged with the American Indian Movement[17] to occupy Alcatraz the following year. Michael Kanentarekon Mitchell documented the Akwesasne bridge blockade in his National Film Board cinéma-vérité masterpiece *You Are On Indian Land* (Mitchell 1969), which opens with: "There's been many wrongs done in the past. And today we don't even trust the white man coming onto this reservation. You cannot blame us for that. We don't want to be a Canadian citizen."

In a confidential 4 September 1968 memo to Minister Chrétien, Deputy Minister MacDonald warned that "During the past five years Miss Horn has carried on a voluminous correspondence with the Department on a wide variety of subjects." MacDonald cautioned that "Despite her antagonisms with many of the Indian people, her public statements, which are often bitter and extreme, unfortunately command widespread attention and credibility across the country" (LAC, n.d., 1:199). Little did he know what Horn had in store.

Kahn-Tineta Horn's correspondence with the Indian Affairs Branch began in 1963 (LAC 1963–1964), but the frequency increased dramatically mid-1968.

---

16. Horn proposed an "Indian Exhibit" at the 1967 World Fair as early as 28 May 1962 (LAC, n.d., 1:359).

17. Founded in Minneapolis, July 1968.

A brief archived by Indian Affairs on 4 August 1963 lists five letters sent by Horn to the Ministry between May and August 1963. In these, Horn apprised officials of her activities, research, opinions, and media appearances,[18] regularly requesting information, statistics, and official legal positions. Horn's communications in 1963 were straightforward. By 1968, however, her intentions became more difficult to discern; she became more strategic and adept at playing to departmental expectations. R. F. Battle, Assistant Deputy Minister of Indian Affairs, wrote in an internal memo dated 26 August 1965, that "there is nothing to be gained by continuing correspondence with Miss Horn" (LAC, n.d., 1:307). But Horn's persistence and rising public profile made her impossible to ignore.

In the spring of 1964, as Peter Gzowski profiled Horn for the national magazine *Maclean's* (Gzowski 1964a; 1964b), Horn began informing the Ministry of an upcoming three-year speaking tour of the United States, Canada, and Europe, undertaken at her own expense. She returned with a splash in early February 1968, calling out Minister Laing for his inaction regarding the trafficking of "Indian girls" by powerful white men, which she had witnessed in Laing's own constituency. Her brother, Taiotenake Horn, had undertaken "six months of fact finding travel among Indians in the West" and Kahn-Tineta followed up "at my own expense to study conditions on Vancouver's Skid Row." What she found there appalled her, writing to Laing on 28 January 1968, that "there are around 400 Indian girls who are engaged in full time or part time prostitution. … Some have 20 customers a day" (LAC, n.d., 1:277). Ms. Horn asserted that their procurers and pimps were protected by police and politicians, and she requested a meeting with Laing for 2 February 1968 to discuss the prostitution scandal as well as the Caughnawaga dump and Kanawaki Golf Club leases. Newspapers reported that the "beauty contest winner" had "failed to impress" Laing, who retorted that Horn used "'bitter language' in letters she wrote to him about these and other matters" (*Edmonton Journal* 1968). Laing said Horn wrote "'ridiculous and dangerous' letters and failed to give a shred of evidence backing her charges" (LAC, n.d., 1:151). The *Toronto Daily Star* reported that this infuriated "[t]he beautiful Indian princess" who, "wearing a purple miniskirt and silver shoes," addressed students at York University on 6 February 1968, telling them that Laing was "misguided and mean" (LAC, n.d., 1:277). Obnoxiously, the *Toronto Daily Star* gave her the teen magazine treatment. The short article detailing Horn's allegations of racketeering, her criticisms of residential schools, and her demands for better education and health care for Indigenous peoples was overshadowed by a glamorous half-page series of close-up paparazzo portraits with a subtitle reading "It's Kahn-tineta

---

18. See, for example, Deputy Minister Isbister's thank you note to Horn for sending him a newspaper clipping of her article "I Speak for My People" (Horn 1963).

again... and her No. 1 target." Laing dismissed her as "only a model" who was "spouting fatuous nonsense" (Dunford 1968).

Subsequently, Horn wrote Laing a letter dated 9 February 1968 that should be classed among the most important in Canadian history. Changing tack, Horn wrote that despite knowing "from looking closely into your face that you are a good and kind man" who seemed "to have such potential," he was obviously being duped by his assistants:

> ... your information is tragically wrong. ... What a grim tragedy that I should be a curse upon you to awaken you to the truth when you have been lulled by falsehood into believing something that is not so. How tragic it is that truth said gently, as I always speak, should be rejected with personal insults. [And yet,] I bear no grudge. I have no resentment. (LAC, n.d., 1:275)[19]

To Horn, the least of Laing's falsehoods were his "directing personal insults" via the press, which made him "look like a foolish old gentleman." Horn was more concerned with "terrible scandal" (Dunford 1968). Government and police officials were complicit in a "$100,000 racket per week" of a "filthy, evil prostitution ring in your riding" and of "those beauteous 16-year-old Indian girls being depraved, debauched and destroyed" on Vancouver's Skid Row.

Horn sent Laing an ultimatum. The on-reserve "multimillionaire garbage dump contracts" and the whites-only Kanawaki Golf Club with its absurdly cheap lease and its lucrative alcohol sales were held by "millionaires and haughty people" and "Indian despisers." Kanawá:ke Kanien'kehá:ka saw a paltry two-cents-a-day per capita in proceeds from the dump's license, while the Golf Club enjoyed an illegal free-of-charge alcohol license and illicitly paid off the "government controlled" tribal council, which Horn described as a "Mohawk syndicate [with] champagne appetites." By Horn's estimation, Laing was caught in contradiction. He was either "ignorant or condoned illegal activities." So she gave him an option:[20] "open up the garbage dump files and the golf club files and look into this" (LAC, n.d., 1:184).

The departmental response, delivered on 12 February, was muted, claiming that the position of the Department had already been outlined in previous correspondence (LAC, n.d., 1:266). Kahn-Tineta Horn was, as always, quick

---

19. Compounding the letter's importance, Horn also defended her younger brother Joseph from being scooped 650 km to the Mohawk Institute Residential School in Brantford. Joseph had recently been "arrested and jailed for the terrible crime of going to Westmount High School" (LAC, n.d., 1:272).
20. She later accused Jean Chrétien of the same thing (LAC, n.d., 1:210).

to reply as she did in a letter to Laing dated 21 February: "It is with interest that I have heard of the vote of confidence being lost in the House of Commons. It would appear that this will mean that the regime of the Liberal government is drawing to a close. It is with deep regret that I feel very little was accomplished under you when a bold, courageous and enlightened mind could have done so very much" (LAC, n.d., v1:259). While Horn was incorrect to think that the Liberal regime was about to end, Trudeau's bold mind did indeed take centre stage.

Laing was reassigned from Indian Affairs to Public Works on 6 July. But Horn's "awakening curse" was not dispelled. Instead, it befell a new DIAND Deputy Minister, the aptronymic bureaucrat and oil executive John A. MacDonald. For MacDonald, the 1968 Indian Affairs portfolio was biblically cursed. In a 26 September 1968 letter to Horn, he wrote that "we are caught between two conflicting forces": reform on the one hand and avoiding paternalism on the other (LAC, n.d., 1:171). He later described it as "a snake's nest" (Weaver 1981, 82) complete with a rodent pestilence, courtesy of Miss Horn.

When Horn wrote to Laing's successor, Chrétien, on 7 August, she asked whether he believed "in the so called 'just society'" and whether he was "what the papers say ... courageous, fearless, honest?" (LAC, n.d., 1:211). If he was, would he address the problem of the Golf Club lease and the festering garbage dump on the reserve? The Department's response was dismissive (LAC, n.d., 1:208), so Kahn-Tineta Horn formulated a plan. Writing to Branch Director Churchman on 13 August, she asked, "How would the Indian Affairs Branch executives like to be entertained by an Indian? ... I would like to come and show some of the National Film Board films on Indians and Eskimos, to speak what is going to be my 'standard' address on tour and answer some questions" (LAC, n.d., 1:205).[21] Associate Deputy Minister R.F. Battle asked Deputy Minister MacDonald, in a memo dated 21 August, "Do you approve?" MacDonald's scrawled response was blunt: "Refusal could create untold problems. Acceptance might give us a chance to tamper some excuses. I would recommend approved" (LAC, n.d., 1:204).

It was a fateful decision. MacDonald described the 18 September screening in a 17 October letter to Brigadier-General Louis-Frémont Trudeau, Assistant Secretary to the Governor General:

> Our conference room and projection facilities were placed at the disposal of Miss Horn. During the course of a talk about Indian problems Miss Horn produced cartons containing a dead rat and a live rat, which she held aloft for all to see. Then, apparently by accident, she kicked a carton

---

21. This tour was Horn's "First Indian Film Festival," inaugurated in Ottawa in November 1968.

and let a live rat loose into the room, as well as two mice. This action was designed to bring to the attention of all those present the purported unsanitary condition of a garbage dump on the Caughnawaga Reserve. Miss Horn stated that the rats and mice were caught in her home, and left her audience to infer that they had come there from the dump. ... At the meeting Miss Horn was accompanied by staff members of a local TV station and she apparently made her own arrangements to have both personnel and TV equipment available. (LAC, n.d., 1:137)[22]

When Horn expressed her intention to show the films to the Governor General and hopefully also send them to the Queen, MacDonald scrawled on the letter: "God save the Queen!" (LAC, n.d., 1:175).

V

A veteran of the Second World War, John A. MacDonald returned to Canada in 1942 ("MacDonald, John A." 1968). Joining the Industrial Development Bank in 1947, he was transferred to the Economic Policy Division of the Department of Finance in 1949, and then to the Treasury Board in 1955. Appointed Assistant Deputy Minister to the Department of Northern Affairs and Natural Resources in 1964, he became Senior Assistant Deputy Minister in 1966. To this point, MacDonald's expertise was in finance and natural resource extraction. On 27 May 1966, MacDonald helped incorporate Panarctic Oils Ltd., and was appointed Director when it began operations in 1968, a post he held simultaneously to being Chairman of the Northern Canada Power Commission, a Crown agency. When the Prudhoe Bay oil field was discovered in June 1968, the department's response was the formation of a Task Force on Northern Development which, according to Rianne Mahon, "included no representative from the Indian Affairs Branch: the department saw no need to consult with native peoples" (1977, 190).

How was it, then, that oil executive MacDonald became responsible for drafting the most important policy proposal in the history of modern Aboriginal politics in Canada? The Department of Indian Affairs, formed in 1880, was reduced to a branch within the Department of Mines and Resources in 1936, and then transferred to the Ministry of Citizenship and Immigration in 1950. But with the *Government Organization Act, 1966*, the Indian Affairs Branch and the Northern Development portfolio were amalgamated into the

---

22. Horn followed up with an obsequious letter to MacDonald, to tell him "how much I admired your courage and impeccable conduct during my recent visit. ... I hope in the near future to have an opportunity to pay tribute publicly to your poise, courtesy, and good judgment in a matter that might seem to be comedy to some but is a dark tragedy to me" (LAC, n.d., 1:180).

Department of Indian Affairs and Northern Development. MacDonald, up to this point a Senior Assistant Deputy Minister overseeing an extractive portfolio, was made Deputy Minister of DIAND in March of 1968. MacDonald is representative of how, as Rianne Mahon put it, "[t]he Northern Development Branch, with its mandate to encourage large corporations engaged in resource exploitation to develop the North, has held primacy over Indian Affairs" and "reflected the emerging alliance of the federal government and the large corporations with actual (or potential) interests in northern resource development" (1977, 190).

This subsumed "Indian policy" under a development discourse that was "established by the central resource and pipeline decisions worked out in confidence between private executives and senior officials in Ottawa" (Dosman 1975, 169). It put the Indian Affairs portfolio in the hands of an assertive and secretive oil executive (Weaver 1981, 107) at precisely the moment when policy-makers were suddenly expected to emerge from behind their desks and engage in public discourse. The results were disastrous. MacDonald was thrust into the spotlight at a three-day forum sponsored by Glendon College at York University in Toronto in late October 1968. He lectured to a "free-wheeling expression of hostility" (Weaver 1981, 81) during which, as the *Toronto Telegram* reported, he was "called a 'liar' and 'the house N****r' by a band of heavy hecklers" (1968).

This experience, along with Flora Elk's death, precipitated MacDonald's road to Damascus moment. On 1 December 1968, 22-year-old Flora Elk was released from Pine Grove correctional facility in Prince Albert, Saskatchewan, with a total of $2.00 for fare to make the 650-kilometre trip to her home on the Oak River Reserve[23] near Griswold, Manitoba. Fifteen hours after her release, her body was found in a snow bank alongside the highway. Her shocking death became a national news story (Fairbairn 1968). New Democratic Party MP Frank Howard submitted a case to the House of Commons on 16 December 1968, demanding a full report. Trudeau promised a prompt reply, but since Chrétien was vacationing in Mexico at the time, the case fell squarely on MacDonald's shoulders. Freshly traumatized by the Glendon College Forum, and deeply concerned that the "public reaction to Flora Elk's death had all the features of 'excessive emotionalism,'" MacDonald became convinced in mid-December that whatever came next, it had to be disruptive towards a new direction in Indian policy (Weaver 1981, 100, 103). It was. Quoting Weaver: "When MacDonald's belief in the destructiveness of emotionalism, compatible with Trudeau's views on reason as the proper basis for public action, combined with the old guard's frustrations with the Elk incident, departmental thinking 'turned right around' as one official described it" (100). The result was the

---

23. It is now called the Sioux Valley Dakota Nation.

disastrous White Paper—the proposed "theft of Indian lands" (Horn 1968a)— produced by a department that gave priority to its responsibility for resource extraction over its responsibility for Indian Affairs.

VI

Settler historians should be careful not to subsume Indigenous politics during Canada's 1960s within Eurocentric epistemological paradigms. Parallels with 1968 Québécois struggles for decolonization, civil rights, and modernization are tempting, as is the idea of some confluence between Indigenous activism, the New Left, and Black Power movements in the United Stated. Nineteen-sixties Indigenous politics were not analogous, however. Indigenous activism during Canada's 1960s was more concerned with community self-direction in health, education, and economic development, and with the assertion of treaty rights than it was with socialism or civil rights.

Bryan Palmer's 2009 book *Canada's 1960s: The Ironies of Identity in a Rebellious Era* errs on this point. His chapter on Indigenous political activism in the 1960s is couched within a broader narrative of youth, rebelliousness, and the New Left. Palmer argues that in the 1960s, "Native peoples across Canada began to align with their counterparts in the United States in a Red Power movement" (367) that was "loosely connected" to the New Left and to "the Black Power mobilizations" that were "increasingly influential in young Native activist circles" (368). The chapter begins with a full-page portrait of Kahn-Tineta Horn, arms crossed and gazing sardonically into the camera, suggesting that Horn was somehow emblematic of the movement. Palmer contrasts his narrative of widespread left-leaning young Indigenous militant radicalism with a co-opted Indigenous leadership of "conservative, pro-capitalist, and corrupt Native 'politicians' … whose purpose it has been to eradicate the radical political potential of 1960s Native organizing" (410). Though a reasonable and intuitive account on the surface, it does not hold up under scrutiny. Palmer describes the prominent Secwépemc political organizer George Manuel as a 1960s "militant" (397). Undoubtedly a "powerful regional voice" (397) advocating Indigenous unification, by 1968 Manuel was a seasoned 47-year-old political operator with decades of experience on the federal payroll as a community development worker under Rudnicki's 1964 social development program, organizer of the 1967 Centennial's Indian Pavilion, and, later, a delegate during the Chrétien–Andras consultation meetings. Although critical of the Department and one of the first Indigenous activists in BC to advocate Indigenous self-determination and independence,[24] lumping

---

24. "In 1968," MacFarlane writes, Manuel went further and "spoke the forbidden word in Canada by calling for 'independence' for First Nations with the DIA budget being turned over to the various communities" (1993, 91).

pre-1970s Manuel in with the left-leaning and militant Red Power movement is incorrect.[25] At the time, he held "a Conservative party membership card, which he was rather pleased to receive. The 'Marxist' was thus, in fact, a Conservative party cardholder" (Tennant 1990, 126–127). As Peter MacFarlane points out, Manuel's interest in socialism began in the early 1970s, when his travels accompanying Chrétien to Tanzania exposed him to a new sort of leftist politics (1993, 193). In 1968, Manuel moved his family to Edmonton to join the IAA executive. By that time, it was a profoundly "conventionalist" and pro-capitalist organization committed to working "through established government channels, to lobby behind the scenes, and to not challenge the supremacy of the DIA" (Drees 2002, 93, 99).

Harold Cardinal, who was 24 years old and head of the IAA in 1968, provides another interesting example. Although Palmer describes Cardinal as a being to the right of most Red Power advocates (Palmer 2009, 405), he claims that Cardinal's book *The Unjust Society* shared the perspective of Red Power advocates such as Kahn-Tineta Horn, the "Akwesasne militants" (403), and the non-reserve-based Trotskyist and Maoist Native Alliance of Red Power (NARP), a "small but committed cadre" that Palmer thinks modelled itself after the Black Panther Party (405). In 1968, Cardinal became head of the conventionalist IAA, making him lead author of the *Red Paper*,[26] which has come to represent Red Power's answer to the White Paper.[27] Palmer describes Cardinal's drafting of the *Red Paper* as "motivated by a belief that the late 1960s represented a final moment of reform possibility, one that needed desperately an infusion of state funds." But does the *Red Paper* champion "government-assisted development of Indian business, or 'red' capitalism" (405) in the manner Palmer suggests? Consider Drees' authoritative summary:

> Following the discussion of treaty rights and the critique of Indian policy in Canada, the *Red Paper* moved into concrete proposals for reserve educational programs and strategies for economic development. Significantly, the section related to economic development promoted a model based on profit and non-profit corporations that would serve reserve communities. Taking a step away from its socialist roots, the IAA had embraced a

---

25. "According to some observers," Palmer writes, "George Manuel was the first interior Indian to challenge the Indian agent's authority directly and around the Agency it sparked rumours that he was a 'Marxist,' a serious charge in the Cold War paranoia of the 1950s" (2009, 46).

26. It is also known as *Citizens Plus*. At the time, Cardinal said of the *Red Paper*: "Politically, this was our high point; our greatest success, our political equivalent to Little Big Horn" (Drees 2002, 169).

27. During a convention at Carleton University in June 1970, the *Red Paper* was adopted by the NIB as the official "Indian response" to the White Paper.

research company to prepare the *Red Paper*—a company whose broad goal was "defending capitalism from the socialist threat." (2002, 169)

According to Drees, Cardinal and the IAA "employed M and M Systems Research, a research firm established by the former Social Credit premier of Alberta and his son, Preston Manning, for a reputed fee of $25,000" (169). Several sources agree on this point: William Wuttunee and Maria Campbell both knew of the Mannings helping draft the IAA response to the White Paper. Its emphatically proto-neoliberal proposals led Wuttunee to suggest that "the Red Paper should probably have been called the 'Socred Paper'" (Wuttunee 1971, 58). As Drees wrote: "The Mannings, who ran M and M Systems Research, believed that supplanting government by private enterprise in as many areas of social life as possible was a good thing, and it appears they felt Indian peoples in Canada would benefit from such a change as well" (2002, 169–170).

Curiously, no mention is made of this consultation in Preston Manning's autobiographies or biographies, and in a 2018 email he denied any involvement with the *Red Paper*.[28] There is some suggestion in the literature, however, that an early collaboration between the Mannings and the IAA may have soured by the mid-1970s after crude oil was found in the Alberta tar sands. Syncrude Canada Ltd., a privately-owned joint venture formed in 1964 in Fort McMurray, Alberta, began construction at Mildred Lake in 1973, but production was delayed because the IAA kept filing caveats to prevent the process from going forward without Indigenous consultation. Syncrude hired Preston Manning to resolve the problem, which doubtless led to bad blood with the IAA. As Murray Dobbin writes in his book *Preston Manning and the Reform Party*:

> There is a disturbing aspect to Preston Manning's steadfast commitment to free-market principles and strategies: it seemed to permit him to separate his personal morality and conduct from his public actions. Every individual who knows Preston Manning well testifies to his great honesty and his personal integrity. Yet in his dealings with aboriginal people and their democratic organizations, he proved willing to use deception and back-room maneuvering in the interests of the oil companies he worked for. (1991, 62)

Dobbin refers to a "clandestine mentality" shared by father and son "which grew out of the convictions that there was a communist/socialist conspiracy which threatened the foundations of the country." This conspiracy played an

---

28. Confidential source, personal email communication with Preston Manning, 30 September 2018.

important role in his political thinking (62). What led to Manning's subsequent denial of prior involvement with the IAA, or if he had ever in fact collaborated with it, are unresolved questions. That so many see Manning's fingerprints on the *Red Paper*, however, demonstrates sufficiently that it was not the left-leaning Red Power manifesto Palmer takes it to be.

Finally, Palmer misinterprets Kahn-Tineta Horn. He asserts that during the 1960s, "Native peoples across Canada began to align with their counterparts in the United States in a Red Power movement" that was "loosely connected" the New Left and to "the Black Power mobilizations" that were "increasingly influential in young Native activist circles" (2009, 367, 368, 400). Palmer prominently displays Horn's image, suggesting that she is emblematic of a "brief but important" (368) 1960s New Left, Black Power, and Red Power synergy. But Horn's own words emphatically deny this claim. For example, Horn wrote to John Munro, Minister of Health, on 22 November 1968, that

> I do not believe for one minute that there will be any movement similar to Black Power and I really do not think these threats should be made unless you are sure of what you say. … Your suggestion that there ever would be such a thing as "native power" serves to encourage idiots. … I respectfully advise you to avoid inaccurate comment on such things as "native power." (LAC, n.d., 1:65)

When African American civil rights leaders organized a Poor People's Campaign (12 May to 24 June 1968), Horn attended to articulate displeasure at their having co-opted Indigenous struggles. Writing to Ralph Abernathy on 10 June 1968, Horn said that "[t]he motivations of Negroes and those of Whites are identical—ambition, effort, discipline, acquisition, possession, competition and destruction. The motivations of Indians are the opposite and are not related and there is no common ground or motivation" (Horn 1968b, 3). Strangely, the one prominent 1960s Indigenous political figure associated with American Black Power radicals was the ostensibly integrationist William Wuttunee, who Horn exposed as having sought an alliance with "the Black Muslims [,] a hate organization that preaches violence against whites," a charge Wuttunee denied (Palmer 1964; see also *Globe and Mail* 1964).

With respect to white leftists, Horn responded to a student conference invitation on 11 November 1968, by lamenting the "shocking manner" by which the Red Power activists "abused" MacDonald at Glendon College (LAC, n.d., 1:91). Horn was disgusted "with these ridiculous gatherings involving Indians with beatniks, bleeding hearts, negro civil rights, Viet Nam and Biafra idiots." Rather than participate in the conference, Horn told the organizer that "Indians are not interested in the morality of the dissenters, or for that matter of white society[,] we do not want any part of those Longhair, bleeding heart, civil rights confusions so many of your students seem to suffer from." For years, Horn made explicit her repulsion at collaborating with young New Left activists (Stevens 1965).

Palmer describes these important Indigenous activists as part of a collaborative and left-leaning Indigenous militancy in the 1960s in Canada. In some instances, they were more conventional and in other instances more radical than Palmer understands. The point is not to reposition them according to Eurocentric political epistemologies, however. Instead, they were not easily commensurate with Western paradigms because their first-order concerns were not to champion the free-market or socialist organizing or human rights. Indigenous activists in the 1960s were predominantly concerned with treaty rights, land claims, and Aboriginal title, and their staunch defence made possible subsequent court decisions supporting special rights, beginning with the 1973 Calder Supreme Court decision on the Nisga'a land claim. In 1968, Indigenous activists were not defending a current state of affairs, nor were they demanding wholesale change. Their struggle was for the possibilities implied by special rights.

This is one major repercussion from 1968 felt in the present day. All subsequent court decisions supporting Indigenous rights and Aboriginal title are downstream of this defence of special rights undertaken by Indigenous organizations (without forgetting independents such as Horn), many of which were formed in 1968. Their arguments resulted in the withdrawal of the White Paper, which proposed termination of Indigenous rights and title. Trudeau intended to eliminate what he called "a weak hot-house culture" (Trudeau 1968, 23), "a ghetto mentality," and "a wig-wam complex" (42). He obviously mistook the stakes. The importance of Indigenous rights and title became apparent with the decision handed down by the Supreme Court of Canada in December of 1973, in *Calder v Regina, 1971*, to which Trudeau is reported to have responded: "perhaps you have more rights than we thought you did" (Manuel 2017, 101).

In the decades following the 1960s, Indigenous activism in the Canadian context was transformed in many ways. In *Red Skin, White Masks* (2014) Yellowknives Dene scholar Glen Coulthard describes how, following the 1975 Dene Declaration, "our communities were greeted with an enormous display of support by progressive political organizations from across the country" (69). Coulthard himself is a prominent anti-capitalist critical Indigenous theorist, and in a 2016 collaboration with Miichi Saagig Nishnaabeg scholar Leanne Betasamosake Simpson entitled "Grounded Normativity/Place-Based Solidarity," they underline the importance of "subaltern solidarity" and the "difficulties and tensions" of "transformative alliances within and across nation, race, and class" (Coulthard and Simpson 2016, 250). These considerations, at the forefront of Indigenous theory and activism across the Canadian context today, should not be retrospectively applied to Indigenous politics in the 1960s. And yet, like so much else in Indigenous politics during Canada's 1960s, germinal anti-capitalist, environmental, and subaltern solidarity discourse, peripheral rather than dominant at the time, would later grow in importance. The opposition concretized in 1968 between Trudeau's Liberals maneuvering to abolish Indigenous special status and those defending Indigenous rights against their Just Society continues to this day. So, too, does the landscape of federally funded Indigenous organizations and the primacy of fossil-fuel extraction over federal–Indigenous relations, dynamics instantiated in 1968. The error against which scholars should be vigilant, however, is of retrospectively mapping subsequent developments onto the actors and organizations active in these early days of modern Indigenous politics in the Canadian context.

References

Abele, Frances. 1996. "Understanding What Happened Here: The Political Economy of Indigenous Peoples." In *Understanding Canada: Building on the New Canadian Political Economy*, edited by Wallace Clement, 127–149. Montreal: McGill-Queen's University Press.

Anderson, Mark Cronlund, and Carmen L. Robertson. 2011. *Seeing Red: A History of Natives in Canadian Newspapers*. Winnipeg: University of Manitoba Press.

Assembly of First Nations. n.d. "Description of the AFN." https://www.afn.ca/description-of-the-afn/. Accessed 2 April 2019.

Canada, Department of Indian Affairs and Northern Development. 1969. *Statement of the Government of Canada on Indian Policy* (White Paper). Ottawa: Queen's Printer.

Canadian Magazine, The. 1968. "Trudeau and Stanfield on Movies, Luck, Women… Things Like That." 22 June: 7.

Cardinal, Harold. 1969. *The Unjust Society.* Vancouver: McIntyre.

Coulthard, Glen. 2014. *Red Skins, White Masks.* Minneapolis: University of Minnesota.

Coulthard, Glen, and Leanne Betasamosake Simpson. 2016. "Grounded Normativity/ Place-Based Solidarity." *American Quarterly* 68, no. 2 (June): 249–255.

Cunningham, Alain. 1999. *Canadian Indian Policy and Development Planning Theory.* New York: Routledge.

Diabo, Russell. 2017. "When Moving Past the *Indian Act* Means Something Worse." *Policy Options* (22 September). Institute for Research on Public Policy. http:// policyoptions.irpp.org/magazines/september-2017/when-moving-past-the-indian-act-means-something-worse/.

DIAND (Department of Indian Affairs and Northern Development). 1968. *Choosing a Path: A Discussion Handbook for the Indian People.* Ottawa: Queen's Printer.

Dobbin, Murray. 1991. *Preston Manning and the Reform Party.* Toronto: Lorimer.

Dosman, Edgar. 1975. *The National Interest: The Politics of Northern Development 1968–75.* Toronto: McClelland & Stewart.

Drees, Laurie Meijer. 2002. *The Indian Association of Alberta.* Vancouver: UBC Press.

Dunford, Gary. 1968. "Laing Doesn't Answer Our Letters." *Toronto Daily Star*, 7 February: 43.

Edmonton Journal. 1968. "Indian Beauty Fails to Move Laing." 3 February: 10.

Fairbairn, Joyce. 1968. "PM Wants Details on Road Death: Indian Affairs Dept. Blamed in Fatality Near Griswold." *Winnipeg Free Press*, 17 December: 1, 9.

George-Kanentiio, Doug. (1993) 2011. "Akwesasne Notes: How the Mohawk Nation Created a Newspaper and Shaped Contemporary Native America." In *Insider Histories of the Vietnam Era Underground Press, Part 1*, edited by Ken Wachsberger, 109–137. East Lansing: Michigan State University Press.

Globe and Mail. 1964. "Kahn-Tineta Appears as Uninvited Guest." 15 June: 15.

Gzowski, Peter. 1964a. "Portrait of a Beautiful Segregationist." *Maclean's*, 2 May: 12.

———. 1964b. "How Kahn-Tineta Horn Became an Indian." *Maclean's*, 16 May: 12.

Horn, Kahn-Tineta. n.d. "Statement Submitted to the National Indian Council of Canada, Point of Order: The Constitution," 1. Walter Rudnicki fonds, box 147, folder 1, University of Manitoba Archives, Winnipeg.

———. 1968a. "Letter to the Editor." *Ottawa Journal*, 4 December.

———. 1968b. Letter to Ralph Abernathy, 10 June. Reies Tijerina Papers, box 31, folder 20, Center for Southwest Research, University of New Mexico.

———. 1963. "I Speak for My People." *Montreal Gazette* (Canadian Weekly Issue), 11–17 April: 347.

Indian Association of Alberta. 1970. *Citizens Plus: A Presentation*. Calgary: Indian Association of Alberta.

Jenness, Diamond. 1941. "Canada's Indian Problem." *America Indigena* 1 (2): 29–38.

Johnston, Patrick. 1983. *Native Children and the Child Welfare System*. Toronto: Lorimer.

LAC (Library and Archives Canada). 1963–1964. "Complaints and Petitions Received on Behalf of the Indian People of Canada from Miss Kahn Tineta Horn." RG 10, vol. 7143, file 1/3-8-2.

———. n.d. "(Miss) Kahn-Tineta Horn, Miscellaneous Correspondence re: Indian Affairs." RG 22, 6-10-3, vols. 1 and 2.

Lagace, Nathan, and Niigaanwewidam James Sinclair. 2015. "The White Paper, 1969." *The Canadian Encyclopedia*. 11 September. https://www.thecanadianencyclopedia.ca/en/article/the-white-paper-1969/.

Leslie, John. 1999. "Assimilation, Integration or Termination? The Development of Canadian Indian Policy, 1943–1963." PhD diss., Carleton University.

———. 1985. *Commissions of Inquiry into Indian Affairs in the Canadas, 1828–1858: Evolving a Corporate Memory for the Indian Department*. Ottawa: Treaties and Historical Research Centre, Research Branch, Corporate Policy, Indian Affairs and Northern Development Canada.

Litt, Paul. 2016. *Trudeaumania*. Vancouver: University of British Columbia Press.

"MacDonald, John A." 1968. *The Canadian Who's Who: A Biographical Dictionary of Notable Living Men and Women, Vol. XI, 1967–1969*. Toronto: Who's Who Canadian Publications.

MacFarlane, Peter. 1993. *From Brotherhood to Nationhood*. Toronto: Between the Lines.

Mahon, Rianne. 1977. "Canadian Public Policy: The Unequal Structure of Representation." In *The Canadian State: Political Economy and Political Power,* edited by Leo Panitch, 165–198. Toronto: University of Toronto.

Manitoba Indian Brotherhood. 1971. *Wahbung: Our Tomorrows.* Winnipeg: Manitoba Indian Brotherhood.

Manuel, Arthur. 2017. *The Reconciliation Manifesto.* Toronto: Lorimer.

Masterson, D. M. 2013. "The Arctic Islands Adventure and Panarctic Oils, Ltd." *Cold Regions Science and Technology* 85, January: 1–14.

Mitchell, Mike Kanentakeron, dir. 1969. *You Are On Indian Land.* Montreal: National Film Board of Canada. https://www.nfb.ca/film/you_are_on_indian_land/.

Ottawa Journal. 1968. "Chrétien Living Proof on Point: French Can Get Top Portfolios." 3 September: 9.

Palmer, Al. 1964. "Princess Charges Wuttunee Seeking Black Muslim Tie." *Montreal Gazette,* 12 June: 3.

Palmer, Bryan. 2009. *Canada's 1960s: The Ironies of Identity in a Rebellious Era.* Toronto: University of Toronto.

RCBB (Royal Commission on Bilingualism and Biculturalism). 1965. "Submission of Miss Kahn-Tineta Horn," Transcripts of Public Hearings, 1 December: 4316–4345.

Simpson, Audra. 2014. *Mohawk Interruptus.* Durham, NC: Duke University Press.

Stevens, Geoffrey. 1965. "Students Told to Stay Away from Reserves." *Globe and Mail,* 29 November: 12.

Tennant, Paul. 1990. *Aboriginal Peoples and Politics.* Vancouver: UBC Press.

Titley, Brian. 1986. *Narrow Vision: Duncan Campbell Scott and the Administration of Indian Affairs in Canada.* Vancouver: UBC Press.

Toronto Telegram. 1968. "Red Power Whoops It Up." 11 October. Reprinted in Richard Bowles, *The Indian: Assimilation, Integration or Separation?* Toronto: Prentice-Hall of Canada, 1972.

Trudeau, Pierre Elliott. 1968. *Federalism and the French Canadians.* Toronto: MacMillan.

Union of British Columbia Indian Chiefs. 1970. *A Declaration of Indian Rights: The B.C. Indian Position Paper.* Vancouver: Union of British Columbia Indian Chiefs.

Weaver, Sally. 1981. *Making Canadian Indian Policy: The Hidden Agenda, 1968–1970.* Toronto: University of Toronto Press.

Wuttunee, William I. C. 1971. *Ruffled Feathers: Indian in Canadian Society.* Calgary: Bell Books, 1971.

Chapter 8
Between Canadians and Culture: The First Year of the CRTC

IRA WAGMAN

Abstract

This chapter considers the first year of the Canadian Radio-Television Commission, the country's broadcasting (and eventually, telecommunications) regulator. The establishment of the CRTC in 1968 from earlier incarnations of broadcast regulators marked a recognition that media were becoming a more complex and sophisticated feature of Canadian society requiring more sophisticated forms of oversight. This was due to several developments loosening the CBC's monopoly over television, the incorporation of private companies into the media landscape, and the development of new policy instruments aimed at supporting the development of film and television production as well as sound recording. In considering some of its early activities, this chapter shows the Commission's early attempts to unify a media landscape now conceived as a mixed "system" featuring private and public entities working in a national interest understood both in economic and cultural terms. This power affords the CRTC a considerable public profile—particularly that of its commissioner—that is evident in news coverage from the first year of its operation that helped to construct its public image. The combination of the Commission's decisions and media coverage during the first year of its operations are useful to foreshadow its long-standing role as both an institution that acts as a regulator of a complex media landscape and one that mediates diverse commercial, political, and social anxieties associated with the place of those technologies in Canadian life.

Nineteen sixty-eight marks an important moment during a period in which Canada experienced what Philip Resnick characterizes as an "eruption of nationalism" (Resnick 1977, 145). This year came amid an outpouring of national pride associated with the country's centennial and against a backdrop of rising concern about the Americanization of Canada's economy expressed by the country's social and political elite. As Bryan Palmer has noted, powerful

JUNEAU AND THE ART OF MAKING (AIR) WAVES

Figure 8.1. Pierre Juneau arrives as head of the CRTC, *Globe and Mail*, 9 November 1968. *Source:* Lewis Parker, courtesy of Matthew Parker.

voices of protest came from Indigenous peoples, students on university campuses, and within the province of Quebec (Palmer 2009). These groups argued that any attempts at national unification should come through a recognition of Canada's colonial past and the inequalities that have characterized its transition to modern nationhood. The sentiments emerging from federal institutions in the post-1968 period can be understood as attempts to produce a unifying character at a time of fracture, an attempt at rapprochement with disaffected populations while simultaneously charting out a path for Canada's continued development.

In this chapter, I argue that the establishment of the Canadian Radio-Television Commission (CRTC) in 1968 represented a particular institutional manifestation of those broader rapprochement efforts. As the regulator of Canadian radio, television and—eventually—telecommunications, the CRTC has been tasked with the management of the expansion of communication in Canada, an expansion that has navigated changing social, economic, and political tensions over the past 50 years. A review of its principal activities, its seminal figures in the early years (particularly its first commissioner, Pierre Juneau), and its key decisions in 1968 will demonstrate how the CRTC contributed significantly to the ways we understand the role of communication technologies in Canadian society.[1]

---

1. One can think of the considerable role played by Royal Commissions in various aspects of Canadian life—especially within culture, where everything from the nationalization of Canadian broadcasting to the creation of major cultural institutions like the Canadian Council, have taken place (Tippett 1991; Litt 1992). One

Canada's media landscape experienced a period of expansion and fragmentation at the end of the 1960s. The media institutions of the pre- and postwar era, namely the Canadian Broadcasting Corporation (CBC) and the National Film Board of Canada (NFB), were joined by a host of new actors, including private television outlets and radio stations, independent record companies, film producers, and services bringing these new media forms to Canadians. The emergence of early cable and satellite systems, and significant changes to the country's telecommunications infrastructure, also came into focus between the mid-1960s and 1970s. This raised questions about how best to manage relations between an existing system that was predominantly public and one that was to further incorporate private interests—all within an overarching framework that presented Canada's communication systems as an expression of the country's national identity.

This chapter is neither a legal nor political history of the agency nor a comprehensive assessment of its legacy.[2] Through a review of the CRTC's earliest and most important activities, the chapter argues that the inaugural year of the organization foreshadows a number of salient issues that would cement its place in the management of Canadian broadcasting and within the Canadian imagination. While the decisions differed and the names changed over the years, the CRTC's history can be understood as an effort to mitigate fragmentation of a Canadian population looking for expanded individual and collective rights, of a technologically expansive media landscape needing someone to make order out of the chaos, and of an agency seeking terms to justify its own existence. These efforts played out in media coverage of the CRTC as much as they were on display in the Commission's regulatory decisions. Against a legislative framework mixing economic protectionism and cultural nationalism, the CRTC has charted an effective—if contested—regulatory framework to cope with

---

can also think of the role played by formal inquiries and Truth and Reconciliation Commissions—most notably the recent inquiries pertaining to Canada's Indigenous peoples in the same regard. For the role of Truth and Reconciliation Commissions in Canada, see Henderson and Wakeham (2013).

2. In spite of this, it is surprising to note that while there exists a historical monograph on its predecessor, the Board of Broadcast Governors (Stewart, Null, and Null 1994), and also that we now have an impressive anthology providing a historical review of its decisions from a policy and legal perspective (Salter and Odartey-Wellington 2008), we remain without an institutional history of the CRTC as a cultural institution, one whose activities are more than just decisions shaping the media industries, but constitute a cultural industry of their own, producing prominent media figures—namely its commissioner—and playing a key role in the ways Canadians have experienced media technologies from telephones to television shows and influencing the prices they have to pay to access that material.

technological expansion and to channel forms of social protest present in other areas of Canadian society.

From Governors to Commissioners

The establishment of the CRTC was a decade in the making, the product of various features of an emerging Canadian broadcasting regulatory landscape. As the capabilities to deliver television and radio broadcasting improved during the postwar era, it became clear that a system entirely composed of public institutions would no longer be a feasible political option. This sentiment came from the discourse of private broadcasters, certainly, but it also was given voice in the pages of Canada's more influential newspapers and magazines. *Maclean's* magazine, for example, was particularly harsh on the subject of CBC's hold over television, publishing editorials asking, "Why can't we get our money's worth for CBC television?," along with a scathing critique by famed columnist Scott Young calling for an end to what he called "monopoly television" (Young 1954).

A Royal Commission, chaired by Robert Fowler, was created in 1955 to address the future regulation of Canadian broadcasting. The Commission's final report, published in 1957, struck a balance between these conflicting interests, simultaneously mixing the more traditional cultural nationalist discourse about broadcasting's unifying capabilities with critiques of state heavy-handedness. Among the report's conclusions were four main developments: First, the system of mixed ownership of private and public stations would be "here to stay." Second, the CBC should continue to develop but its functions were "not to be extended to do the whole job of providing radio and television services to Canadians." Third, private broadcasters should justify their "grant of a public franchise" by being subject to performance reviews but without worrying "about the bogey of nationalization" that has "filled them with suspicion and fear in the past." Finally, the Commission explained that for the foreseeable future "we will continue to have a single broadcasting system in which all Canadian radio and television stations, public and private, present and future, will be integral parts, regulated and controlled by an agency representing the public interest and responsible to Parliament" (*Report* 1957, 13).

These main recommendations assumed their shape in 1958 with the passage of a new Broadcasting Act by the Conservative government of John Diefenbaker. Further transformations followed shortly thereafter. A broadcasting license was given to CTV and Télé-Métropole in 1961. This was the first in a series of transformations to a newly mixed system that would take place through the 1960s and into the 1970s, beginning with early developments in cable television and initiatives aimed at specific audiences (such as educational television), as well as expanding the amount of coverage to the province of Quebec through the creation of Radio-Québec and the privately held TVA television network, and more assertive efforts by the province to exercise its jurisdiction into the federal territory of broadcasting (Raboy 1990).

While it might appear that a public system was effectively replaced with a new system benefiting private entities and governed at arm's length from the government, it is more accurate to consider the re-organization of Canadian broadcasting in the 1960s as part of a discursive shift away from seeing media in strictly cultural nationalist terms with public institutions as the primary instruments, to one that perceives radio and television through a more economically nationalist framework that situates the private sector as partners working to protect Canada's cultural distinctiveness.

The restructuring of Canadian broadcasting would eventually require new legislation to govern its activities and new means to ensure compliance among the various figures in the expanding media landscape. A follow-up report written by Fowler in 1965 placed greater emphasis on the idea of making broadcasting work to connect Canadians and on building up media and cultural industries as key sectors contributing to national economic activity. As Canada's media system appeared to be expanding, there was a corresponding belief that this expansion required regulatory oversight to make it an instrument of nation building.

An underappreciated figure in this transitional moment in the history of Canadian broadcasting is Judy LaMarsh. As Lester Pearson's Minister for Health and Welfare responsible for the development of medicare and the Canada Pension Plan, and later as Secretary of State responsible for coordinating Canada's centennial year activities, LaMarsh's role in the cultural field is less appreciated as part of the standard accounting of her storied political career—a career culminating in her involvement in the Federal Commission on the Status of Women. LaMarsh's contribution to the structure of Canadian broadcasting was, however, decidedly significant. In 1966, she managed the publication of the White Paper on Broadcasting. This report considered future regulatory measures within a language of technological expansion, pointing to revolutions in satellite technology that sped up information flows and offered the potential—and threat—for Canadians to receive more information from more places than before. Against this backdrop it asked, "How can the people of Canada retain a degree of collective control over the new techniques of electronic communication that will be sufficient to preserve and strengthen the political, social and economic fabric of Canada, which remains the most important objective of public policy?" (quoted in Bird 1988, 355). Many of the findings from that report served as the basis for the *Broadcasting Act* that came into force on 1 April 1968.

Among the new act's highlights were important statements that echoed the sentiments of the Fowler report linking the economic development of

Canada's media sector to the achievement of its nationalist objectives. An early section outlines that "the Canadian broadcasting system should be effectively owned and controlled by Canadians so as to safeguard, enrich, and strengthen the cultural, political, social and economic fabric of Canada." Another makes the case that the satisfaction of those objectives should make use of what it called "predominantly Canadian creative and other resources" (Canada 1967–1968, sec. 2). As Marc Raboy observes, the ostensible strength of the new act was also its biggest liability: no definitions were offered about what was meant by "national unity" and no benchmarks were provided to measure whether the objectives of the systems were being achieved (Raboy 1990, 178–181). The link between an increased role for the state in the regulation of broadcasting and an equation of public broadcasting with national unity could, however, be seen as an indirect expression of that argument, along with a more forceful remit to hold the CBC accountable for its contributing to the development of national unity.

A significant new component added to the *Broadcasting Act* was CATV (or community antenna television). A precursor to cable television, CATV emerged as a means for the distribution of television programming—including American programming—through more cable networks that were more reliable than "over the air" reception by means of TV antennas. The new providers of these services included American companies such as the film exhibition company Famous Players, but more significantly this technology set the stage for local entrepreneurs that would go on to be major players in Canada's media system, such as Ted Rogers. With an increased capacity to deliver consistent television service and as new "windows" for the dissemination of programming, CATV operators came under this new "single" system of Canadian broadcasting under the term "broadcasting receiving undertakings" (CRTC 1969, 21).

With a new act articulating a more ambitious regulatory agenda encompassing licensing, regulation, and research, it became evident that the existing regulator, the Board of Broadcast Governors, was no longer suited to the task. Created in 1958, the BBG emerged in an attempt by the government to provide some distance between itself and the CBC, to create an agency that was independent of the public broadcaster in order to regulate the media sector. During the decade of its operations, the Board performed a number of key roles, including granting the license to CTV to begin operations as well as creating "Canadian content" regulations for television that would be extended to radio by the CRTC in the 1970s. At the same time, though, the language of the 1958 *Broadcasting Act* limited the Board's powers to intervene in a number of key issues, and perceptions existed both within the industry and amongst the wider public that it was too close to industry, or too powerless to intervene in the CBC's activities. A new agency with even more independence was required: the Canadian Radio-Television Commission was created through an act of Parliament in 1968.

The range of people tasked with overseeing the Commission's activities reflected the CRTC's expanded mandate for its newly conceived single system of private and public broadcasting. On the CRTC's executive committee were Harry Boyle, a former supervisor of CBC network features and media industry veteran; influential *Montreal Star* television columnist Pat Pearce; the broadcasting consultant and engineer Réal Therrien; and Hal Dornan, a former publicist for Lester Pearson. Part-time members included writer Northrop Frye; Helen James, a social worker and former CBC employee; Gertrude Laing, a graduate of the Sorbonne, who would become the only female member of the Royal Commission on Bilingualism and Biculturalism; and Newfoundland physician Gordon Thomas. Finally, four part-time members came from the world of business: John Shanski from Manitoba, George McKeen from British Columbia, Armand Cormier from New Brunswick, and Colombe Cliche, an insurance broker from Quebec.

If the committee members and part-time officials represented a certain degree of regional and linguistic diversity (albeit lacking voices from student, Indigenous, and ethnic communities) and came from a cross-section of Canada's arts, business, and social sectors, its commissioner, Pierre Juneau, brought artistic and institutional experience. Born in Montreal and educated at the Sorbonne in Paris, Juneau came to the position from a series of positions in arts and cultural activities in Quebec through the 1950s and '60s. This included co-founding the federalist political magazine, *Cité Libre* with Pierre Trudeau, co-founding the Montreal International Film Festival in 1959, and working with the National Film Board in numerous roles (including serving as the Board's Director of French-language production), before moving briefly to the BBG and assuming the role as its first commissioner.

By 1968, Canada's regulatory framework for broadcasting had transformed from one that equated nationalism with public institutions to one that saw the national interest as something that could be served by a wider range of participants, including private enterprises. In this more systemic framework, private and public entities were now seen as nodes within a network of cultural production and distribution that could serve to bind the nation from coast to coast and contribute to a more diversified and fully functioning Canadian economy. These feelings were partly the result of extensive lobbying on behalf of the private sector, but they also reflected sentiments arising from anti-establishment protests directed against American imperialism and the Vietnam War—and in favour of more activist government intervention. The shift from the BBG to the CRTC signalled more than a name change; it served, as Bernard Ostry notes, as "the beginning of an activism on the part of this semi-judicial regulator authority into the relatively vacant field of policy-making" (Ostry 1978, 104). This combination of anti-establishment sentiment with economic and cultural nationalism created the conditions which would place the broadcasting system—and much of its content—in the middle of these powerful strains of thought.

The CRTC in the Media

Changes to the regulation of Canadian broadcasting received considerable coverage in Canada's newspapers and magazines. In one sense, media coverage about the CRTC reveals how the press framed the institution and its activities. This relationship was mutually beneficial, in that it was also in the public relations interests of the CRTC to achieve some coverage in the press as a way of assuaging any concerns people had about its operations and intentions. In another sense, this coverage can be understood through the prism of intra-industry competition. As print media was not subject to licensing and regula-tion, and as television and radio served as threats to its commercial business models, coverage of the CRTC in newspapers and magazines was also a power-ful form of surveillance on the activities and affairs of competing actors in Canada's media landscape. It is through this lens that articles about the CRTC—and especially about Juneau—are interesting windows to examine the new agency at its early beginnings and to see how media coverage helped to construct the public image of the agency by highlighting certain parts of its remit over others.

One way the print media framed the new CRTC was to champion Juneau himself, to construct the Commissioner as a semi-official celebrity. An early profile pointed to his appreciation of film from his previous work with the Montreal International Film Festival, while another article in the *Toronto Star* from 23 March 1968 identified Juneau as a "TV Addict" who "vaguely resem-bles [the American comedian and actor] Shelley Berman, goes home, switches on the TV and watches, hypnotized." The article presents Juneau as impressed with the quality of Canadian television, but also with an appreciation for American programming, particularly comedies. Still, the profile suggests that the new organization intends to "set the standards higher than the broadcasters meet" (Jones 1968, 9).

In a 29 June 1968 profile in the *Globe and Mail*, reporter Lewis Seale presents Juneau as a bridge figure, one that will be able to mediate between competing interests through the establishment of rules for different entities within the broadcasting industry. "Rules will not produce quality," Juneau is quoted in the article, with Seale noting that the new agency's job will be "to make broadcasting better by promoting the good things that are already there" (Seale 1968, A2). At the same time, the profile articulates Juneau's concern

This TV addict's new job -- boss of broadcasting

By FRANK JONES
Star staff writer

OTTAWA

Every evening Pierre Juneau, a small man who vaguely resembles Shelley Berman, goes home, switches on the TV, and watches, hypnotized.

Juneau, the man named this week to head the Board of Broadcast Governors, is a tube addict.

He admits he never had any problem disciplining his three children regarding the set; he is the only one who has to ration his viewing hours.

"I guess I'm a natural spectator," he says with a small, self-deprecatory smile.

Broadcasters who will have to live within the rules set by Juneau and the BBG—soon to become the Canadian Radio and Television Commission (CRTC)

under recently passed legislation—would laugh at Juneau's definition of himself. They see him as the inquisitive, interfering finger of Big Government in their business.

Juneau, working late hours in his first hectic week on the job he took over from Dr. Andrew Stewart, was doing everything he could to allay their fears.

His message: Creativity is the life blood of broadcasting and his new CRTC, when it goes into operation soon, will be willing to b e r e d r a t e and cajole until they're blue in the face to get it.

"Regulations won't produce a Wojeck, won't produce a Quentin Durgens," he said, referring to the outstanding CBC creative efforts of the past few seasons. "We must find a more positive role for the CBTG."

The main instrument the CRTC

has for doing this job is the right to set standards of program content for each station on an individual basis.

Juneau prefers to call them "goals for each station to aim for."

The CRTC will likely always set its standards a little higher than the broadcasters meet, he said.

The BBG has pursued Canadian content like the Holy Grail, but the new body is more likely to look at the quality of programs rather than the ethnic origins of the people who created them.

When he talks creative programming, Juneau, a 45-year-old native of Montreal, brings nearly 20 years of experience with the National Film Board to lend weight to his conviction.

He obtained his BA at the University of Montreal, studied phi-

losophy for two years in Paris, then joined the film board as its Montreal representative.

He scaled the executive ladder two rungs at a time and by 1964 he was senior assistant to the commissioner and director of French language production. He was a member of the federal government's task force on satellite communications, and says he also gained a knowledge of the electronic medium because about a third of the film board's production in recent years has been designed for TV.

He was appointed to the BBG in 1966 and was vice-chairman at the time of his latest appointment.

Since his BBG duties began, he finds it all the more difficult to switch off the set in the evening. Now he watches partly for pleas-

ure and partly from a sense of duty.

Other TV regulatory officials have been appalled at the flood of comedies produced in the Hollywood mills. Juneau is mostly amazed.

"The fact that a country can produce such an abundance of comic material week after week and even give it a sense of spontaneity is just amazing," he said.

On the Canadian scene, he admitted an admiration for great talkers like Lister Sinclair and Pierre Berton and, particularly, Patrick Watson.

Then, it being the need of the day, the small man in neat navy suit and plain red tie, went home to turn on the set. He's only got a black and white one now, but he's looking forward to getting a color one soon. That should be even harder to turn off.

PIERRE JUNEAU
"Natural spectator"

Figure 8.2. *Globe and Mail*, 23 March 1968. See p. 192 for a readable version.

about the power of border-hopping satellite technologies and their political impact on Canadian public life and the need for the new Commission to consider the effects of these technologies in CRTC decisions.

A similar futuristic theme was articulated in a speech that Juneau gave before the Canadian Association of Broadcasters (re-printed in *La Presse*), highlighting the potential for satellites to distribute educational television—and potential threats of new technologies in a range of activities from public life to the work of those in the cultural industries, including comedians, dancers, and others whose work is performed live. In the speech, Juneau referenced Marshall McLuhan and used John F. Kennedy's assassination as examples of how media now connect people globally and speed up flows of information that another time moved considerably slower. His address closed with a powerful characterization of the CRTC's role in a communication environment characterized by powerful new technologies: "Our role as stewards is equally clear: Preserve the liberty and the health of all communication channels between Earth and space, between nations, between cities, between cultural and social groups, and between individuals" (Juneau 1968).

This sample of news coverage allows us to make a few preliminary observations. First, little space is devoted to opportunities where the CRTC or Juneau articulate their positions in overtly nationalist terms. There is very little mention of broadcasting's nation-building and nation-binding capabilities, and problems of broadcasting regulation are rarely stated in anti-American terms. In fact, the overwhelming theme of these early articles presents the CRTC as a body of technicians, whose aim is to fine tune and ensure that Canada's broadcasting system is working efficiently to satisfy its basic purposes within the *Broadcasting Act*, and as oracles predicting the future direction of media technologies in development or on the horizon. Such a view reflects a sense of Cold War–era fascination with satellites and space-race enthusiasm for interplanetary travel. More importantly, however, these early profiles reflect a variation of technological humanism that combines elements of McLuhan's writings with ideas from the various exhibits and displays at Expo 67. Such an energy is further present across a range of areas of Canadian life, from investments in natural resources to the establishment of Distant Early Warning and NORAD systems (Wilson 1991, 165), to the construction of major architectural projects, ranging from the Ville-Marie highway in Montreal to the CN Tower.[3] As in previous instances, such as the establishment of the trans-Canadian railway, nation building, technological development, and a triumph over Canada's natural and environmental characteristics were brought very much together in these early CRTC profiles (Charland 1986). Given that a parallel rhetoric equating technology and nation were also being expressed in terms of the Quebecois national project, as Erin Hurley has convincingly argued (Hurley 2011), one can see the CRTC's articulation as part of a larger pan-Canadian initiative.

These early profiles and published remarks are also early fragments of the media-savviness we have come to associate with Trudeau-era politics of the 1960s and 1970s. Paul Litt has observed that Trudeau's political success was fuelled in part by consciously working the media as the means by which "the professional-managerial class made its way in the world ... operating the complex technologies and bureaucracies of modernity" (Litt 2016, 320). As Jennifer Bell notes, the period was also marked by an increase in the publication of "tell-all" memoirs from government ministers and other political figures, including, most notably, Judy LaMarsh (Bell 2016). From this perspective, Juneau's construction as a "with-it" bureaucrat is evidence of this type of activity. It also serves as a reminder that conceptions of political celebrity need to take into account the class of high-ranking officials—think of auditor generals, chief electoral officers, and CRTC commissioners—that operate in between elected politicians and the supposedly "faceless" bureaucracy.

In a less instrumental register, however, it is also the case that Juneau's co-constructed celebrity functionary also had the effect of marking the CRTC's entry into the field of discourse about popular culture in Canada—an agency that simultaneously regulates the activities of media industries, as well as the terms under which Canadians would receive their popular culture. At the same time, these developments also served to articulate an institutional disposition in line with the tenor of the day, which expressed the need for an articulation of a Canadian nationalism within the communication sphere—one that was being formalized in other areas of cultural activity. The CRTC would come to embody these tendencies in its behaviour and through its institutional construction in the pages of the Canadian press.

---

3. See Thibault and Hayward (2014) for an expanded discussion on technological humanism in 1960s Canadian arts and letters.

Paving the Way, One Decision at a Time

Over the course of 1968, the CRTC held a number of hearings and delivered a number of decisions, many of which are contained in its annual reports. Over the course of the 1968–1969 year, the Commission handled 379 applications, and approved new and renewed licenses for 240 radio stations, along with 17 new television station licenses and 89 CATV system operators (CRTC 1969). Many of these activities summarized in its annual report pertained to files or applications that had been in process while the BBG was in operation, while others arose out of the CRTC's expansive remit as a result of its new responsibilities under the *Broadcasting Act* (CRTC 1969).

From that activity, we can group the CRTC's initial moves into four general themes. The first thematic focus concerns efforts to make the broadcasting system more diverse and to expand the CBC's remit to serve Canadians. The second category of decisions could be considered reflections of the Commission's increased enforcement powers. The third reflects a series of decisions designed to delineate the contours of a marketplace in which the distribution of media content will take place. A fourth is informational: the agency clearly signalled that it would play an active role in the collection and dissemination of research about broadcasting through commissioning reports and studies of media systems across the country and soliciting expert feedback during its hearing process.

Among its first decisions was the granting of a radio broadcasting license in languages other than English and French to CHIN, the Toronto-based multilingual service started by Johnny Lombardi, a Canadian-born member of the Italian community. The station was the second devoted specifically to "new Canadians" as the primary audience. As Mark Hayward outlines, the decision to grant CHIN's license can be understood within a broader framework—part of a move to expand the representation of languages and cultures present on Canadian radio. Such a move can be understood in a sense as an extension of the cultural nationalism of Canada's new *Broadcasting Act* and as part of the creation of a system of Canadian media which is different from the monoculture of American broadcasting. As Hayward explains, however, the licensing of an ethnocultural radio station also reflected certain anxieties in Canadian life about the integration of non-English or French speaking Canadians into the broader elements of society (Hayward 2019). In his applications to the BBG, Lombardi specifically referenced the potential of a CHIN radio license as a valuable instrument for integrating immigrant communities into Canadian cultural and city life. As radio stations moved into "formats" by the end of the 1960s, CHIN's license can be viewed as part of the development of a style of "multicultural media" that would follow a commercial model and that would pave the way for the gradual centralization of ethnocultural media across different forms that would take place through the 1980s and 1990s and into the 2000s, even as the number of languages present on those media forms expanded over time. This period is also marked by the development of community broadcasting initiatives in both radio and television, including, most notably, the establishment of the provincially supported Radio-Québec and initiatives in Indigenous broadcasting that follow developments in cable and satellite technology (Roth 2005).

Another set of decisions concerned the licensing of broadcasting activities to serve Canada's Maritime provinces and its northern regions. An important component of this included the development of French-language television services, with directives to the CBC to establish a production centre in Moncton, a French-language radio station in the Fredericton–Saint John area, and a television service serving the southern area of Nova Scotia (CRTC 1969, 11–13). In addition, expanding the number of broadcasters to serve English-language audiences was also addressed in its first round of decisions, as a CTV affiliate in Moncton was also licensed and scheduled to go on air in 1970, making it the first private television outlet to serve New Brunswick. Applications to establish a CBC station in Churchill Falls, Newfoundland, as well as licenses for northern services for Whitehorse and Alma, Quebec, were also approved (CRTC 1969, 13–14). Such decisions reflected the CRTC's view that what it called "an extension of service" of broadcasting offerings to Atlantic Canada was one of its primary objectives, particularly to serve French-language populations. It also signalled an attempt to extend what were known as "alternative services"—private operations—to further areas of the country that had been historically underserved.

If this first grouping of decisions was thematically aimed at extension, the second group of decisions reflected the Commission's greater enforcement powers, particularly around broadcasters and their behaviour. Three examples are illustrative: In June 1968, the CRTC notified cable operators who carried U.S. television networks that it would be illegal for them to broadcast election results before the polls close in local coverage areas. In October, the Yarmouth, Nova Scotia, radio station CJLS, had its application for license renewal denied because of disreputable broadcasting practices, including suppressing news about members of the town council who operated businesses that advertised on the station. Montreal's *La Presse* then revealed that the Commission had been investigating the show "Hot Line," featuring controversial host Pat Burns on radio station CKGM, on the grounds that the program was denigrating French-speaking Canadians (CRTC 1969, 10). The Commission also rejected a number of applications asking for changes in the ownership structure of media companies based on concerns over potential consolidation within the media sector.

Many of these decisions also reveal a less-appreciated aspect of the CRTC's activities, namely their capacity to serve as collector and distributor on Canada's media sector. These powers were embedded in the language of the *Broadcasting Act*, which explicitly directed the Commission to "undertake, sponsor, promote or assist in research relating to any aspect of broadcasting" a charge facilitated by the establishment of a Research Branch within the Commission's organizational structure (Canada 1967–1968, sec. 18). Such powers were exercised heavily throughout its first year. First, the Commission undertook a study of FM stations in order to better determine future actions (CRTC 1969, 9). Consultations with officials from the Community Access television sector also took place during the year, as the Commission sought insights on whether to regulate this sector separately from the traditional broadcasting stations or to fold them together into one system. Second, the Commission imposed a mandatory reporting year for all radio and television stations. Third, before the end of the year, the CRTC undertook an investigation into "Air of Death," the CBC documentary about the health effects resulting from air pollution created by an Ontario fertilizer plant. The decision to investigate came after the broadcaster was criticized for unfairly hurting the reputation of the towns affected by the damage (Rutherford 1990, 424). Finally, it outlined that it was doing its own studies of the system: one on the question of media ownership, the other exploring policy options for newly developing satellite technology. This more robust "commissioning" component of the new Commission helped to articulate its place as a hub for cultural information, allowing it to intervene more directly in debates about the characteristics of Canada's broadcasting environment.

With these and other decisions behind the Commission, the *Globe and Mail* offered a portrait of the CRTC in its Business section, saying that "[p]laced alongside the old Board of Broadcast Governors the Canadian Radio-Television Commission looks like a zingy sports car beside a staid, slightly tired family sedan" (*Globe and Mail* 1969, B2). Atop another *Globe and Mail* article published toward the end of 1968, cartoonist Lewis Parker depicts Juneau as a religious figure dictating the enlightened views of the *Broadcasting Act*–as–New Testament to a group of frightened representatives from the broadcasting and film industries, along with a summary of its decisions undertaken over the first year of its operations (Millin 1968).

These decisions and their coverage in the press depict the CRTC as an ambitious new Canadian federal agency energetically navigating the discursive and regulatory terrain in which future arguments about the regulation of broadcasting in Canada would occur. This included concerns about how the organization itself understood the contours of a market that must be competitive and Canadian at the same time, about its attempts to delineate the territory of its regulatory activity, and about the complex dance between a desire to provide Canadians with their own service across a vast and expansive landmass with the simultaneous recognition of the importance of foreign content which is part of that enjoyment. What also becomes apparent is that, through its coverage of the CRTC and its commissioners, competing media forms such as newspapers and magazines played a role in framing the Commission's activities within a discourse of cultural defence rather than in the cooler, technocratic terms the Commission sought to imagine for itself.

There were bigger things on the horizon for the CRTC and for the regulation of Canada's media systems after 1968. A year to the day that the *Broadcasting Act* came into effect, Canada created a Department of Communications charged with developing a new technological infrastructure for telecommunication carriage, moving discussions of the role of the CBC, of private versus public ownership, and other regulatory matters to the CRTC. The Trudeau government also announced legislation creating Telesat, the institution responsible for developing satellite communication in Canada, and offering considerable opportunities for new participants in the broadcasting system, and further sought to tighten regulations for the cable television sector on the grounds that it was serving as a pipeline for the distribution of American television content. Jurisdiction for telecommunications would be passed formally to the CRTC by 1976. In addition, limits on the foreign ownership of media companies resulted in the slow but steady development of national media conglomerates. Near the end of 1968, the Commission announced it was studying the effectiveness of Canadian content regulations present in Canada since the early 1960s. What followed was the firming up of those regulations and their extension to radio in 1970. This is a fact that we acknowledge when we recognize achievements in Canada's music industry with "Juno awards" that are named in part after the CRTC's top bureaucrat and symbol of an era of Canadianization, Pierre Juneau.

Mediating Canadian Media

Some important themes emerge about the first year of the CRTC's operations. First, the more extensive political and social functions of the CRTC's original mandate are the result of the expansiveness of the Canadian broadcasting landscape, a push for greater participation from different sectors of Canadian society, and policies encouraging the involvement of the private sector. The Commission's early moves show that Canadian radio and television was more than a collection of individual broadcasters but an interconnected system of broadcasters, producers, and distributors working together in the service of a conception of the "national interest." This reconceptualization blended social cohesion objectives with forms of economic nationalism to produce particular forms of industrial development. While it was assuming its new position, the CRTC and its Commissioner were an object of fascination for Canada's print media who devoted articles to documenting its activities and profiling its various leaders, a move that served to legitimize its efforts and help to position its officials within discussions about the future of Canadian culture. These actions effectively positioned the CRTC as the medium through which Canadians communicate to understand the media and the ways in which various forms of cultural dissent, ranging from anti-Americanism to anti-consumerism, and from regional representation to linguistic and cultural diversity, have been organized and mapped onto the development of radio and television as distinctive media forms.

Over time, the CRTC's decisions have tended to produce complex and contradictory effects. In the name of ensuring a healthy Canadian broadcasting and telecommunications sector, media industries have been allowed to assume dominance within the marketplace, with ownership and control of a range of media properties, websites, and infrastructure. A review of the ownership and holdings of today's media giants, such as Bell and Rogers, are ideal cases of the historical circumstances of policies that have mixed cultural and economic nationalism and have tended towards industrial development and protection. As Christopher Ali has noted, in the name of seeing broadcasting in national terms, efforts to ensure healthy local broadcasting environments have suffered as a result (Ali 2012). The extensive formality of the CRTC hearings process has tended to privilege established players and industry voices over other kinds of representation, leading to charges of elitism and backroom dealing within the development of broadcasting regulation.

Such themes are particularly vivid in the contemporary media landscape. Today, the various platforms that mark the digital age enable forms of user participation that result in more individualistic and libertarian modes of engaging with and using media. Despite the presence of one key element in the nationalist discourse so prominent in public discourse around cultural issues in 1968—the arguably more powerful influence of American media companies—we have seen virtually little in the way of regulation of current American media giants, such as Google, Apple, Amazon, Facebook, and Netflix. This is in part due to the Commission's decision, issued in 1999, to steer clear of the direct regulation of the Internet. At the same time, this development is also part of a more consumer or user-friendly revolution taking place in the CRTC's offices aimed at pushing back against the protectionist demands of the industries the Commission once supported, while searching for grounds on which a regulator constructed to ensure Canadianness among sparse frequencies can operate in an environment of media abundance. As public pressures build on digital platforms and intermediaries to take greater accountability for their activity and the activity of their users, it will be interesting to see the terms under which the CRTC asserts its position in a realm they have historically avoided.

It is because of its position within Canadian life that a full accounting of the history of the CRTC as a *cultural institution*, as a key actor in the ways that Canadians understood the concept of culture, and of the ways ideas of culture often find themselves articulated and determined by government institutions, is in need of being written. Its absence within the literature may be a symptom of a larger problem, one linked to the broader absence of historical work in the area of radio and television broadcasting. The same could be said of the unwritten histories of the various institutions involved in the historical regulation of broadcasting, including the Departments of Communication and Canadian Heritage; lobbying groups such as the Friends of Canadian Broadcasting; or ACTRA, the union representing Canadian on-air talent; or ADISQ, the organization representing Quebec's sound recording industry. A slight shift away from thinking of the CRTC in straightforward policy analysis terms moves the discussion towards a more synthetic account which would see that advocacy as reflective of broader cultural trends, and as a contributor to public discourse about culture. It asks questions about the relationship between the CRTC's activities and the ways that Canadians think about, enjoy, and make sense of their own popular culture, rather than a simple concern about the policies they advanced.

Thinking about the CRTC as a *regulatory institution* that steers media systems and a cultural institution that contributes to how Canadians communicate about media would then point us in two interesting directions: one considers how federal institutions contribute to the formation and maintenance of the public sphere in Canada; the other raises questions about how these newer digital media challenge the role that broadcast media have played in Canadian society for the past 50 years.

References

Ali, Christopher. 2012. "A Broadcasting System in Whose Interest? Tracing the Origins of Broadcast Localism in Canadian and Australian Television Policy, 1950–1963," *International Communication Gazette* 74(3): 277–297.

Bell, Jennifer. 2016. "Canadian Political Celebrity: From Trudeau to Trudeau." In *Celebrity Culture in Canada,* edited by Katja Lee and Lorraine York, 73–92. Waterloo: Wilfrid Laurier University Press.

Bird, Roger. 1988. *Documents in Canadian Broadcasting.* Ottawa: Carleton University Press.

Canada. *Broadcasting Act,* S.C. 1967–1968. c.25.

Charland, Maurice. 1986. "Technological Nationalism." *Canadian Journal of Political and Social Theory* 10 (1–2): 196–220.

CRTC (Canadian Radio-Television Commission). 1969. *Annual Report.* Ottawa: Queen's Printer.

Globe and Mail. 1969. "Radio–TV Authority Has Teeth, Tastes Blood." 15 January: B2.

Hayward, Mark. 2019. *Identity and Industry: Making Media Multicultural in Canada.* Montreal and Kingston: McGill-Queen's University Press.

Henderson, Jennifer, and Pauline Wakeham, eds. 2013. *Reconciling Canada: Critical Perspectives on the Culture of Redress.* Toronto: University of Toronto Press.

Hurley, Erin. 2011. *National Performance: Representing Quebec from Expo'67 to Celine Dion.* Montreal: McGill-Queen's University Press.

Jones, Frank. 1968. "This TV Addict's New Job—Boss of Broadcasting." *Toronto Star,* 23 March: 9.

Juneau, Pierre. 1968. "L'avenir de la radio-télévision, vu par Pierre Juneau, président du CRTC." *La Presse,* 21 May: 7.

Litt, Paul. 2016. *Trudeaumania.* Vancouver: University of British Columbia Press.

———. 1992. *The Muses, the Masses and the Massey Commission.* Toronto: University of Toronto Press.

Millin, Leslie. 1968. "Juneau and the Art of Making (Air) Waves." *Globe and Mail,* 9 November: 23.

Ostry, Bernard. 1978. *The Cultural Connection: An Essay on Culture and Government Policy in Canada.* Toronto: McClelland & Stewart.

Palmer, Bryan. 2009. *Canada's 1960s: The Ironies of Identity in a Rebellious Era.* Toronto: University of Toronto Press.

Raboy, Marc. 1990. *Missed Opportunities: The Story of Canada's Broadcasting Policy.* Montreal and Kingston: McGill-Queen's University Press.

Report of the Royal Commission on Broadcasting (Chair Robert Fowler). 1957. Ottawa: Queen's Printer.

Resnick, Philip. 1977. *Land of Cain: Class and Nationalism in Canada, 1945–1975.* Vancouver: New Star Books.

Roth, Lorna. 2005. *Something New in the Air: The Story of First Peoples Television Broadcasting in Canada.* Montreal: McGill-Queen's University Press.

Rutherford, Paul. 1990. *When Television Was Young: Primetime Canada, 1952–1967.* Toronto: University of Toronto Press.

Salter, Liora, and Felix Odartey-Wellington. 2008. *The CRTC and Broadcasting Regulation.* Toronto: Thomson Carswell.

Seale, Lewis. 1968. "Ever More of the Good Things." *Globe and Mail,* 29 June: A2.

Stewart, Andrew, William H. N. Null, and William Null. 1994. *Canadian Television Policy and the Board of Broadcast Governors, 1958–1968.* Edmonton: University of Alberta Press.

Thibault, Ghislain, and Mark Hayward. 2014. "Jean Le Moyne's Itineraire Mechanologique: Machine Poetics, Reverie, and Technological Humanism." *Canadian Literature* 221:56–72.

Tippett, Maria. 1991. *Making Culture: English-Canadian Institutions and the Arts before the Massey Commission.* Toronto: University of Toronto Press.

Wilson, Alexander. 1991. *The Culture of Nature: North American Landscape from Disney to the Exxon Valdez.* Montreal: Between the Lines.

Young, Scott. 1954. "Let's Stop Monopoly Television." *Maclean's,* 1 May: 9, 75–78.

Text from figure 8.2

This TV addict's new job -- boss of broadcasting
By FRANK JONES
Star staff writer

OTTAWA

Every evening Pierre Juneau, a small man who vaguely resembles Shelley Berman, goes home, switches on the TV, and watches, hypnotized.

Juneau, the man named this week to head the Board of Broadcast Governors, is a tube addict.

He admits he never had any problem disciplining his three children regarding the set; he is the only one who has to ration his viewing hours.

"I guess I'm a natural spectator," he says with a small, self-deprecatory smile.

Broadcasters who will have to live within the rules set by Juneau and the BBG–soon to become the Canadian Radio and Television Commission (CRTC) under recently passes legislation–would laugh at Juneau's definition of himself. They see him as the inquisitive, interfering finger of Big Government in their business.

Juneau, working late hours in his first hectic week on the job he took over from Dr. Andrew Stewart, was doing everything he could to allay their fears.

His message: Creativity is the life blood of broadcasting and his new CRTC, when it goes into operation soon, will be willing to horse-trade and cajole until they're blue in the face to get it.

"Regulations won't produce a Wojeck, won't produce a Quentin Durgens," he said, referring to the outstanding CBC creative efforts of the past few seasons. "We must find a more positive role for the CRTC."

The main instrument the CRTC has for doing this job is the right to set standards of program content for each station on an individual basis.

Juneau prefers to call them "goals for each station to aim for."

The CRTC will likely always set its standards a little higher than the broadcasters meet, he said.

The BBG has pursued Canadian content like the Holy Grail, but the new body is more likely to look at the quality of programs rather than the ethnic origins of the people who created them.

When he talks creative programming, Juneau, a 45-year-old native of Montréal, brings nearly 20 years of experience with the National Firm Board to lend weight to his conviction.

He obtained his BA at the University of Montreal, studied philosophy for two years in Paris, then joined the film board as its Montréal representative.

He scaled the executive ladder two rungs at a time and by 1964 he was senior assistant to the commissioner and director of French language production. He was a member of the federal government's task force on satellite communications, and says he also gained a knowledge of the electronic medium because about a third of the film board's production in recent years has been designed for TV.

He was appointed to the BBG in 1966 and was vice-chairman at the time of his latest appointment.

Since his BBG duties began, he finds it all the more difficult to switch off the set in the evening. Now he watches partly for pleasure and partly from a sense of duty.

Other TV regulatory officials have been appalled at the flood of comedies produced in the Hollywood mills. Juneau is mostly amazed.

"The fact that a country can produce such an abundance of comic material week after week and even give it a sense of spontaneity is just amazing," he said.

On the Canadian scene, he admitted an admiration for great talkers like Lister Sinclair and Pierre Berton and, particularly, Patrick Watson.

Then, it being the need of the day, the small man in neat navy suit and plain red tie, went home to turn on the set. He's only got a black and white one now, but he's looking forward to getting a color one soon. That should be even harder to turn off.

Chapter 9
Portrait of a Publisher: Jack McClelland and McClelland & Stewart in 1968

LAURA K. DAVIS

Abstract

Nineteen sixty-eight was a tremendously eventful year for publisher Jack McClelland and his publishing house, McClelland & Stewart. On the one hand, spurred by funding opportunities initiated by the Massey Commission, his writers were burgeoning with success. On the other hand, however, the press was in financial crisis, and McClelland, an ardent nationalist, refused to sell to an American firm. In 1952, when McClelland was 30 years old, he took over the press from his father, John McClelland, and his business partner, John Stewart; but it was not until the spring of 1968, when his father died, that he would have sole control over the firm. This moment was particularly significant because unlike his father, Jack McClelland published only Canadian writers, a bold and risky move. This chapter articulates how and to what extent Jack McClelland shaped Canadian literature and culture in 1968 and beyond.

Nineteen sixty-eight was a tremendously eventful year for publisher Jack McClelland and his publishing house, McClelland & Stewart. On the one hand, spurred by funding opportunities initiated by the Massey Commission (1949),[1] that year saw an explosion of his writers making a mark on the Canadian literary scene: Margaret Laurence, Pierre Berton, Leonard Cohen, and Farley Mowat,[2] among others, were burgeoning with success. On the other hand, the press was in financial crisis, and McClelland, an ardent Canadian nationalist, refused to sell to an American firm. He was known for his flamboyant personality, and in response to rumours that year about the inefficiency of the

---

1. The Massey Commission, chaired by Vincent Massey, ultimately led to funding councils such as the Canada Council, which was established in 1957.
2. All of these important authors began their careers with McClelland & Stewart and published with the firm loyally throughout their careers.

Figure 9.1. A Jack McClelland publicity stunt: McClelland with author Aritha van Herk and a Scotiabank official. *Source:* William Ready Division of Archives and Research Collections, McMaster University.

press, McClelland famously said, "I'm surrounded by f*cking idiots" (King 1999, 163).

Certainly, that year was significant not only for McClelland & Stewart but for Canadian publishing as a whole. McClelland & Stewart was a rising success, and so too were smaller publishing houses, such as Anansi and Coach House,[3] which established themselves during the 1960s and 1970s. Some of the best-known authors in Canadian literature emerged in the 1960s, and yet the excitement surrounding Canadian arts and culture "wasn't just literary": "Canada awoke in the 1960s, shaken by the excitement leading up to the party in Montreal" (Mount 2017, 5). Expo 67 in Montreal kick-started the fervour, but it rose in 1968 on the heels of that party and Canada's centennial celebrations. Other significant factors that led to Canada's literary coup in 1968 included the efficacy of the Canada Council, whose mandate was to fund, assist, and

---

3. Stan Bevington founded Coach House Press in 1965, and Dennis Lee and David Godfrey founded House of Anansi Press in 1967. Initially, the two presses were situated only a few blocks from one another in Toronto. Both began as small literary presses but would publish some of Canada's most important authors, such as Michael Ondaatje, Margaret Atwood, and Erin Moure.

encourage Canadian writers and publishers; the creation of new universities and colleges in the 1960s, which fuelled the demand for books and the study of Canadian literature; and the influence of the paperback revolution in the United States. This was the dawn of an important era in Canadian literature, and Canadian publishing houses such as McClelland & Stewart were essential to its vibrancy and survival. Indeed, Jack McClelland and his publishing house were at the helm of Canada's literary revolution.

Anna Porter,[4] who worked for the press for many years before co-founding Key Porter Books, deemed McClelland "the prince of publishers" and "the most persistent and imaginative publisher to have erupted onto the world stage" (MacSkimming 2007, 118). Yet 1968 proved to be a year in which he needed to draw upon his persistence and imagination to overcome obstacles, both financial and personal. In 1952, when McClelland was 30 years old, he took over the press from his father, John McClelland, and his father's business partner, John Stewart, but it was not until the spring of 1968, when his father died, that he gained sole control over the firm (*Globe and Mail* 2004). This moment was particularly significant because, unlike his father, Jack McClelland published only Canadian writers, a move that many other publishers considered downright foolish. From 1952, when he took over the firm from his father, until 1985, when he sold it, McClelland completely transformed Canadian writing and publishing, not only inspiring the creation and development of smaller presses such as Anansi and Coach House, but also bringing Canadian writers and writing to the fore. Jack McClelland profoundly influenced the rise and shape of Canadian literature in 1968 and beyond.

Financial Crisis

If McClelland was known as such an innovative and imaginative publisher, then what might have caused the dire financial situation that the company was in during 1968? Archival letters and documents show that the firm was up against financial difficulty as early as 1964. In November of that year, McClelland wrote a letter to his colleague Hugh Kane, stating, "Financing is still an acute problem. … Budgeting has not been well done. Our projections have been far from accurate" (Kane 1968).[5] McClelland admitted that he cared more about books and authors than he did about money and felt that as long as he was able to

---

4. Anna Porter began working for McClelland & Stewart in 1969, when she was 26 years old. She became the editorial director in 1974 and then President of Seal Books, which was co-owned by McClelland & Stewart and the American company Bantam, before leaving the company and co-founding Key Porter Books in 1979.

5. Hugh Kane worked at McClelland & Stewart from 1937 to 1969, starting there as a salesperson and eventually becoming the vice president of the company. He left to work at Macmillan.

pay salaries and overhead, then the company was doing well (King 1999, 161). Yet the growing interest in Canadian literature amongst the general public and the burgeoning university system in Canada leading up to the centennial year of 1967 proved too much for the firm to handle. The firm took on major projects for the country's centennial and doubled its volume of output within 18 months. According to Kane, the firm expanded too fast and became a "victim of its own success" (King 1999, 162). Having focused on his books and authors, not his business per se, Jack McClelland could not secure bank loans or grants for the large amount of funds that the firm desperately needed in 1968.

In early 1968, McClelland almost struck a deal with Cemp Investments, a private investment firm, which, it was proposed, would become a silent partner in the ownership of the company. Yet when he met with the firm's representatives to sign the deal, he was informed that its conditions required that most of the publishing house's senior management be replaced. McClelland was willing to sell 50 percent of the company at below market value in order to gain financial security, but the deal, as it turned out, compromised McClelland's control over the company. "I got very emotional and dramatic," he said. "I told them to stuff it and walked out on the deal without knowing where the hell the money I needed would be coming from" (King 1999, 168). Cemp Investments returned to the bargaining table and McClelland eventually secured funds from bank loans and government support to keep his company afloat, but moments of financial crisis occurred regularly at the firm throughout his career.

One of the reasons for McClelland & Stewart's financial crisis in 1968 was, arguably, McClelland's insistence on expanding the titles on his list. In that year, Alfred Knopf, of Knopf publishing house, New York, wrote Jack a letter encouraging him to reduce the number of books he was publishing. He responded: "You are right. We can't keep track of the titles and authors. We'd be far better off with a much smaller list, except that my current philosophy is that we can't survive in the Canadian market without a lot of titles." James King suggests that this philosophy was McClelland's "Achilles heel" (1999, 169), a point well taken with regard to the firm's financial crisis in 1968. However, McClelland's insistence on increasing the firm's titles also led to its success. It was only by accumulating titles that he could establish his house's identity, and so he was strategic about discovering and publishing new Canadian authors and bringing them to acclaim. By building a base of excellent writers and expanding his list, he was able to create a stable yet dynamic identity for his house. As Elaine Dewar explains, "It took the canniest and most determined of Canadian trade publishers, Jack McClelland … to put aside the profitable educational publishing business and concentrate instead on finding and marketing Canadian authors of fiction and non-fiction" (2017, 24). This move involved significant risk, but enabled McClelland & Stewart to become the country's largest and most significant publisher of Canadian literature by 1968.

McClelland recognized the fleeting opportunity—following Canada's centennial year—to find, create, and publish Canadian writing. That year was an important historical moment in which the country valued arts, culture, literature, and scholarship; through these values, Canadians cultivated a sense of national pride within and beyond the country's borders. McClelland "became the darling of the writing community with the phrase 'I publish authors, not books'" (Lorimer 2012, 30), and his firm became "The Canadian Publisher," with an exclusive focus on new Canadian writing. The expansion of the titles on McClelland's list was a key to the house's success.

The Rise of Arts and Culture in Canada

Canada experienced a cultural awakening during the late 1960s. This awakening contributed to the quick expansion of McClelland & Stewart and the subsequent financial problems that became a crisis in 1968. In 1949, the federal government appointed the Royal Commission on the Development of Arts, Letters, and Sciences, headed by former governor general Vincent Massey (Gray 2016, 179). In 1951, the Commission released its report, which resulted in funding councils for scholars and writers. These councils included the Canada Council for the Arts and the Social Sciences and Humanities Research Council of Canada. CanLit scholar Nick Mount notes that "universities became an unexpectedly large part of the Massey Commission's work—no doubt partly because all five members held postgraduate degrees, three were professors, and one was a university president" (Mount 2017, 64). Moreover, university enrolments were exploding during this period; between 1963 and 1968 enrolments increased more than they had in the previous 50 years. Likewise, the number of universities in Canada quadrupled between 1960 and 1975. "More universities meant more university libraries and bookstores ... more literature departments ... [and] Canadians with more education" (Mount 2017, 64). Clearly, Jack McClelland's publishing firm was not the only beneficiary of the excitement about arts and education in the 1960s, nor would it have been prudent for his house to exclude itself from this unique historical moment by halting its own growth. The late 1960s was a time of flourishing for Canadian literature, and much of this activity began with and was made possible by the Massey Commission.

In 1968, writers benefitted from the establishment of funding councils that were initiated by the Commission. Yet the Aid to Scholarly Publishing Programme (ASPP), a fund that supports the publication of scholarly books in Canada, dates back to 1941, according to Robert A. Stebbins. In that year, the Rockefeller Foundation donated $5,000 to the Canadian Social Sciences

Research Council (CSSRC), which the federal government had created the year before (Stebbins 2001, 454). However, with the establishment of the Massey Commission in 1949, and then the initiation of the Canada Council in 1958, the ASPP could now operate with Canadian public money. It was no longer dependent on American philanthropy. Like the Canada Council, public support for the CSSRC and its counterpart, the Canadian Federation for the Humanities (which were consolidated in 1977 into the Social Sciences and Humanities Research Council of Canada [SSHRC]), was justified, in part, by the fact that Canadian academics could produce only a small number of scholarly books. These funding programs experienced substantial success during the years following their initiation, so much so that, by 1968, the ASPP, just one of the programs established, was a viable operation. In 1973–1974, the program distributed $115,000 for the publication of 41 books (Stebbins 2001, 455). The cultural and artistic environment in the late 1960s encouraged the proliferation of new Canadian scholarship and talent.

Such funding programs grew at the same time as did universities and their presses. University presses multiplied in the 1960s, and 1968 saw the peak of that growth. University presses were actually present in Canada as early as 1901, when the University of Toronto Press (UTP) was established, although there was little scholarly publishing in Canada prior to the 1950s (MacSkimming 2012, 89–90). The Université de Montréal's press was founded in 1962, the University of Manitoba's in 1967, the University of Alberta's in 1969, and the University of British Columbia's in 1971 (MacSkimming 2012, 113). Amidst such rapid growth, McClelland promoted even more of it. In an article that appeared in the *London Free Press* on 31 January 1967, he stated that "more libraries [were] needed in Canadian schools" and "warned that, unless children and their parents read more, the communicative gap between the generations will widen" (Taylor 1967).[6] He identified an increasing need and a desire for literacy and literature at a time when new universities were being established, interest in higher education was at its height, and the Canadian public valued arts and culture produced in Canada by Canadians.

The trade-book industry, like the scholarly one, also experienced unprecedented growth in the 1960s. In that decade, two chain bookstores became prominent in Canada, Classics and Coles. In 1968, there were more than 20 Classics Bookstores in Canada, almost all of them in Toronto and Montreal, and Coles Bookstore chains spanned Canada with about 50 stores (King 1999, 169). Coles on Bloor Street in Toronto was started by brothers Carl and Jack Cole; in the 1980s, it was purchased by K-Mart and became Waldenbooks; in 1995, it merged with W. H. Smith books and became Chapters; and in 2001,

---

6. A clipping of the Taylor article was found in box 23a, file 1, Jack McClelland fonds (n.d.).

the company merged again to become Chapters-Indigo (Davis and Morra 2018, 336). Out of necessity, McClelland worked closely with stores such as Classics and Coles, given their precedence and rapid growth in Canada during the 1960s and in the decades to follow. Yet problems between McClelland & Stewart and these chains were rife. As Davis and Morra point out, McClelland could not have anticipated the extent to which these Canadian companies would give way to corporate capitalism and American takeover (Davis and Morra 2018, 336).

McClelland did, though, live to see the early signs of American corporate capitalism in the book industry. Due in part, perhaps, to the large expansion of retail bookstores by 1968, Coles was selling remaindered U.S. copies of Canadian books in the 1970s (Davis and Morra 2018, lxiii), a situation that upset McClelland considerably. In so doing, Coles was undermining McClelland's sales and the royalties to which Canadian authors were entitled. In 1974, McClelland pursued a legal case against Coles for selling inexpensive remaindered American books in Canada, and urged federal politicians to change Canada's copyright law—but to no avail. The politicians with whom he corresponded on this subject included the Prime Minister, Pierre Trudeau, and Canada's Minister of Consumer and Corporate Affairs, André Ouellet (Davis and Morra 2018, 345–346).[7] Ironically, McClelland's business success was tied to these retail chains. Louis Melzac, the founder of Classics Bookstores, introduced McClelland to Leo Kolber, who managed Cemp Investments (King 1999, 166)—the company McClelland & Stewart had struck a deal with in 1968 that saved them from bankruptcy (Davis and Morra 2018, 336). Therefore, the growth of the book business and the field of Canadian literature created both success and hardship for McClelland and his firm. McClelland depended on major retail bookstores, but relations between his firm and them did not always lead to financial success, and resulted in antagonism that sometimes came to a head.

Canadian arts and culture in the year 1968 benefitted from the nationalist fervour that began during Canada's centennial year. In 1967, a number of initiatives were announced by the federal government to celebrate the Centennial, including a new medal of honour, the Order of Canada. In the *Toronto Star*, in April of 1967, reporter and writer Peter Newman[8] published a list of people whom he thought should receive the medal. His list included Jack McClelland,

---

7. Davis and Morra write, "Upon reading a letter by Ouellet that appeared in the *Globe & Mail*, McClelland wrote to [Margaret] Laurence in a fury about the ineffectual measures the government was taking in relation to the [copyright] issue" (2018, lix).

8. Peter C. Newman (b. 1926) became one of Canada's most prominent journalists.

whom Newman said should get the award for "imaginative and often uneconomic support of Canadian writers" (Newman 1967).[9] His list, which consisted mostly of men, included former governor general Vincent Massey, musician Glen Gould, historian W. L. Morton, and artist and book illustrator Harold Town. Although McClelland did not receive the Order of Canada until 2001, just a few years before his death, he received the Centennial Medal on 1 July 1967 for his contributions to the country in the publishing field.[10] He was on various committees to promote Canada's birthday on 1 July 1967, and he served as the chair of the Committee for an Independent Canada in 1971 (King 1999, 221).

McClelland & Stewart benefitted in 1968 from the nationalist fervour and explosion of work on the arts and culture scene that had taken place in the centennial year. Roy MacSkimming describes the last few years of the 1960s as a period when McClelland & Stewart was a hub of activity in Canadian arts and letters: "The place generated spontaneous staff parties; it attracted famous authors who arrived from out of town and were often billeted in employees' homes. Margaret Laurence dropped by [the publicist] Catherine Wilson's office with a poster from China for her wall. Margaret Atwood read her Tarot" (2012, 144). In 1968, the Canadian Radio-Television Commission (CRTC) was created, marking a key moment in the history of arts and culture in Canada (see Wagman, Chapter 8 in this volume). The Commission regulated Canadian broadcasting: it required that a certain percentage of programming was Canadian (Dewar 2017, 26). As part of a larger initiative to create and sustain arts and culture in Canada, the establishment of the CRTC set the stage for changes to book publishing as well. In 1971, the new premier of Ontario, William Davis, established a Royal Commission on Book Publishing. He did so in response "to concerns about foreign textbooks flooding Canadian schools and the sale of the original Canadian publisher, Ryerson Press, and Gage, to foreign interests" (Dewar 2017, 24).

In 1971, when McClelland & Stewart was unable to pay back the loan from Cemp Investments that the firm had received in 1968, the new Royal Commission on Book Publishing recommended that the government provide economic support for the firm, stating that the company was important to the nation and deserving of public funds (Dewar 2017, 25). Interestingly, while the Ontario government provided the financing McClelland & Stewart needed, McClelland's authors backed this up with emotional and ideological support. For example, Laurence wrote to McClelland, "if McClelland and Stewart is

---

9. A clipping of the article was found in box 23a, file 1, McClelland & Stewart fonds (n.d.).

10. A "Centennial Medal" file can be found in the Jack McClelland fonds (n.d.), box 24, file 5.

ever owned by an [American] firm, I won't want to be published by them … there is not one of your writers who does not, at heart, appreciate the fact that … you damn well have always cared about what you published. You have always read my manuscripts yourself—don't you think I know that?" (Davis and Morra 2018, 235). Not only the government but also writers and the public affirmed the centrality of arts and letters in Canada. They understood that McClelland & Stewart was a key part of Canada's artistic and literary culture.

The Canadian Publisher and His Authors

McClelland's relationships with his authors were what made him as successful as he was. His dedication to them was steadfast: he recognized their talents, predicted and created their successes. One of his authors was the writer and later famous singer-songwriter Leonard Cohen, and though they had a great mutual respect for one another, they also had some hefty disagreements and feisty moments of exchange, particularly in the 1960s, when Cohen had not yet acquired fame. The year 1968 marked a crucial moment for Cohen. His focus shifted from writing poetry to writing songs, and his debut album, *Songs of Leonard Cohen*, was released on 27 December 1967 by Columbia Records, just a few days before the new year. His real success, then, began in 1968, when that album gained traction in Canada and abroad: it was listed as number 83 in *Billboard 200* (Billboard Media, n.d.) and reached number 13 on the U.K. Albums chart (Official UK Charts Company, n.d.). The success of his debut album boosted the sales of his writing, which was beneficial for Cohen, for McClelland, and for Canadian arts and letters.

In the years leading up to the release of Cohen's first album, he and McClelland exchanged a number of letters. They would maintain a friendship throughout their lives, despite their frequent disagreements and stubbornness with one another. In one instance, Cohen sent McClelland the only copy of his manuscript for *The Spice Box of Earth* (1961), his first book of poetry, with the request that McClelland & Stewart publish it. He wrote to McClelland on 18 August 1960, "One scary thing. This is the only copy in the world" (McClelland & Stewart fonds, n.d., box 20, file 8). McClelland responded to Cohen on 7 September, "the manuscript arrived safely. But migod, what a bone-headed thing to do, that is to type only one copy of the manuscript. I am tempted to write to tell you that we have lost it already, just for the hell of it. But in case we do eventually lose it, I won't jest" (McClelland & Stewart fonds, n.d., box 20, file 8). McClelland's comment to Cohen about the possibility of losing his manuscript was in earnest, since he was known for disorganization and getting things done at the last minute. But his concern for the whereabouts of the manuscript also showed great faith in Cohen's work. As Margaret Laurence said in a letter to McClelland, "I know how many Canadian writers (Leonard Cohen and Irving Layton come to mind immediately, in addition to myself) owe their first books to the fact that you thought they had something and were willing to take a chance on them" (Davis and Morra 2018, 76). As difficult to work with as Cohen was, McClelland absolutely stood by and supported him.

Cohen was stubborn about the original form of his manuscripts and often refused to agree to any changes to his work. He also disliked the reviewing and editing process in general. In a 29 July 1963 letter to McClelland about the manuscript of his first novel, *The Favourite Game* (1963), Cohen wrote, "If you're waiting to gather a stack of vile readers' reports, then don't bother. Just send me a printed rejection slip and I'll gather the readers' reports for my biography when I'm in Canada" (McClelland & Stewart fonds, n.d., box 20, file 8). Yet by the time Cohen wrote this letter, McClelland had already written to him to tell him that he would publish the book, even before he sent it to readers for reports. He had written on 31 May 1963, "It is, as you so modestly say yourself, a beautiful book. There is no question about it. It sings. It has rhythm, and pace, and feeling. … I congratulate you, and at the same time, I reiterate that I hate your guts. … We'd like to do the book" (McClelland & Stewart fonds, n.d., box 20, file 8). McClelland's letter, which stated that he would accept the book, was written almost two months before Cohen's, which stated that he had not received a response. The delay was likely caused by a slow postal process and the fact that Cohen was in Greece at the time.

McClelland strongly disliked both the title and the cover art that Cohen insisted upon for his collection of poems *Flowers for Hitler* (1964). He reluctantly accepted the title, but when Cohen saw the cover art that McClelland had chosen for the book, he wrote on 8 September of that year, "It is clear that you want to punish me for insisting on my title" (McClelland & Stewart fonds, n.d., box 20, file 8). McClelland rebutted on 26 August: "To begin with Leonard, much against our judgment as publishers, we went along with your title. There is not a person in our shop that likes the title. There is not going to be anybody in the book trade that likes it very much. The public may like it. Who knows. That's unpredictable" (McClelland & Stewart fonds, n.d., box 20, file 8). Again, though, McClelland eventually succumbed to Cohen's insistence. "Anyone who writes a letter like your last one," McClelland stated on 11 September, "must have been pretty damn sure that we would back down, roll over, wag our tail, etc. Well, I have news for you my friend. Against my better judgment, that's exactly what we're going to do" (McClelland & Stewart fonds, n.d., box 20, file 8). This battle of egos between Cohen and McClelland subsided somewhat, especially as Cohen's work, in particular his controversial yet successful novel *Beautiful Losers* (1966), sold very well and resulted in great success for both the author and the publisher. During the year 1968, when Cohen's first album received so much attention, their friendship settled and their disagreements subsided. They would often turn to each other for advice, even as they sometimes continued to argue and often engaged in a battle of wills.

If McClelland joked about the possibility of losing Cohen's manuscript, then that jest became reality just a few years later, when he lost the manuscript for Margaret Atwood's first novel, *The Edible Woman*. The manuscript was finally found just before 1968, but Atwood had first sent it to him in 1965. Just as Cohen gained fame in 1968 because of the release of his debut album, so too did Margaret Atwood because of the release of her first novel. Atwood had, by this time, already gained some recognition as a poet: her book of poetry, *The Circle Game*, was published in 1966 and won the Governor General's Award that year. Both Cohen and Atwood essentially achieved fame in 1968. It is noteworthy, though, that both of them had also published successful works in 1966, two years prior to their respective breakthroughs: Cohen published *Beautiful Losers* with McClelland & Stewart, and Atwood published *The Circle Game* with Contact Press. Cohen and Atwood experienced frustration in their dealings with McClelland, and yet for both of them, he was integral to the launch of their careers.

Atwood published with House of Anansi as well as with McClelland & Stewart, and she worked as an in-house editor for Anansi from 1971 to 1973. Arguably, it was the fact that Contact Press published her first collection of poetry, *The Circle Game*, which led to the founding of Anansi. The book won the Governor's General's Award for poetry, but few copies of it were to be found, since the small Montreal press that published it could not keep up with the print demand. Dismayed by that situation, David Godfrey and Dennis Lee decided to start their own press, which became House of Anansi in 1967. McClelland said that the house "would be lucky to last 18 months," but it soon became one of Canada's leading publishers. Godfrey went on to found two more publishing houses, New Press in 1970 and Porcépic Press in 1973 (Adams 2015). That these presses were established and successful speaks to the literary coup of the late 1960s and early 1970s in Canada. McClelland & Stewart was not the only publishing house to benefit from the explosion of arts and culture in Canada during these decades.

McClelland had a disagreement with Atwood in 1971 about the publication of her book *Surfacing* (1972), which she had submitted to McClelland & Stewart for publication. In a letter dated 22 October, he stated, "I am told that we lost a manuscript of yours, for two years. Is this true? If it is, then it is the first time that it has ever been drawn to my attention. What manuscript, when, and to whom did you complain?" (McClelland & Stewart fonds, n.d., box 65, file 8). Three days later, Atwood responded,

The manuscript of mine you lost for two years was that of *The Edible Woman*, as you'll recall. I sent it in the Fall of '65, got an initial letter back, then silence. I wrote several letters in the Spring of '67 asking where it was; again, silence. It turns out the lady in charge had got pregnant and left the company, or something, and my manuscript was in a drawer somewhere along with those of my letters that had not been lost. I was about to request a return of the manuscript when I heard from you— you'd written me a long letter based on some newspaper interview, asking me whether I had an unpublished novel, then discovered you'd had the thing since '65. Surely you remember that. I complained, as I recall, to you, and you apologized. I'm not mad at you for that, though it does make a good story. (McClelland & Stewart fonds, n.d., box 65, file 8)

In this exchange, McClelland assured Atwood that he would publish *Surfacing*, though he was not a fan of the book. He wrote on 22 October 1971, "My personal reaction to the novel is somewhat less enthusiastic than that of our editors" (McClelland & Stewart fonds, n.d., box 65, file 8). Three days later, she responded to that point and to their tiff and general relationship as follows:

As for you and me, dear Jack, my major concern is that you be as stunning a publisher as possible. Far be it for me to wish to upset you except in ways conducive to that end. I know that my kind of thing is not exactly your favourite cup of tea but I don't care about that as long as it doesn't affect how well you publish the book. Compris? (McClelland & Stewart fonds, n.d., box 65, file 8)

Therefore, his professional relationship with Atwood, like that of Cohen, was full of prickly moments, and some distance, even as they each had a great respect for and trust of each other, as subsequent amicable letters between them throughout the 1970s show.

Perhaps in an attempt to make up for losing *The Edible Woman*, as well as the minimal promotional attention that McClelland gave the novel, he published and strongly promoted Atwood's second novel, *Surfacing*. He threw a party at his own home to launch the book on 12 September 1972 and created promotional events that included a canoe trip to celebrate the Canadian content of the book. Upon receiving a thank you note from Atwood, McClelland wrote on 21 September, "Thanks for your note. I am glad you liked the party. You are, as they say, a good draw" (McClelland & Stewart fonds, n.d., box 65, file 8). In response to his question to Atwood about whether she was bitter about the lost manuscript and the company's lack of promotion of her first novel, Atwood wrote in a 25 October letter, "I'm not 'bitter' about M & S. No one in Canada is bitter about them, because they have been a major publishing force and I'm in favour of seeing that continue." But, she added, they are "notorious in certain areas," and "one discusses their failings as one discusses the failings of an eccentric aunt to whom one is, inevitably, related & committed" (McClelland & Stewart fonds, n.d., box 65, file 8).

Just as Atwood expressed her simultaneous vexation and respect for McClelland, so too did Margaret Laurence, who was one of McClelland's favourite authors. Laurence wrote to McClelland in 1971 about the work he did for Canadian writers and for arts and letters in Canada:

> You and I have had our ups and downs, Jack, as you have had with all your writers. There is also not one of us who hasn't cursed your bloody-mindedness, your incredible ability to take umbrage, your Christly ego, and all the rest. But there also isn't one of your writers who does not, at heart, appreciate the fact that for about 2 decades you were the only original and interesting publisher in Canada. (Davis and Morra 2018, 235)

Laurence and McClelland had a particularly strong friendship, one that lasted 30 years—from when they first corresponded in the late 1950s until Laurence's death in 1987.

In March of 1968, when Laurence was writing *The Fire-Dwellers* (1969), she humbly expressed to McClelland her doubts about the manuscript: "First draft of novel now completed, thank God. I do not know what it is like. It may be positively lousy" (Davis and Morra 2018, 187). Laurence's hesitation about her work stands in direct contrast to Cohen's statements about his own work: Cohen often pointed out (as he did in a 31 May 1962 letter) to McClelland the strength of his own work (McClelland & Stewart fonds, n.d., box 20, file 8). McClelland's immediate response to Laurence, however, showed his absolute faith in her:

> Wonderful news and a typical Margaret Laurence reaction on completion of a manuscript. Some day, the historical record is going to indicate that every time you finish a script, you think it's lousy. I'm betting on the fact that historical record will also continue to show that every time you finish a script, it's actually superb. (Davis and Morra 2018, 188)

They exchanged a number of letters from March through June of 1968 about the publication of her novel, in which the theme of Laurence's self-disparagement and McClelland's faith in her continued. When McClelland was about to read the full manuscript, Laurence said, "Give [your criticism of] it straight; if you hate the damn thing, don't try to soften the blow" (Davis and Morra

2018, 189). But McClelland of course loved the book: "*The Fire-Dwellers* is superb. I have said to you several times before, and I can say it again in all sincerity, that you are the only writer I know that improves with each successive manuscript and you are still doing it" (Davis and Morra 2018, 193).

When he found out that Margaret Laurence had terminal cancer, he said to her that doctors have about a .500 batting average. "They are right as often as they are wrong. They are like book publishers. My batting average is about the same" (Davis and Morra 2018, 578). McClelland had a talent for spotting and publishing talented Canadian writing. Though he might have missed the mark in a few instances, he came in at far better than 50 percent.

The canoeing trip that McClelland organized to launch Margaret Atwood's *Surfacing* was apropos to his style. As MacSkimming notes, during the period of the 1960s and 1970s, "M & S became renowned for one-of-a-kind publishing gambits." "Some of the schemes," he notes, "are the stuff of publishing legend":

> McClelland in a billowing toga and snow boots, the novelist Sylvia Fraser in an off-the-shoulder silver gown, her blond locks crowned with laurels, launching *The Emperor's Virgin* in a March blizzard; McClelland climbing a rickety scaffold with Aritha Van Herk to present the young author with a giant "cheque" for winning the $50 000.00 Seal Book Award; shoeboxes delivered to the media to promote *The Snakes of Canada*, each supposedly containing a live reptile that had escaped through a ragged hole in the side. (MacSkimming 2012, 151)

As these promotional stunts demonstrate, "McClelland would do anything, no matter how outlandish, to sell M & S books" (MacSkimming 2012, 152). He ceaselessly promoted Canadian authors and literature. It is no accident that in 1968 he helped to launch Cohen's and Atwood's success, and to promulgate Laurence's. These writers possessed remarkable talent, and in all instances, McClelland recognized it. In terms of their early careers, and certainly throughout Laurence's, he was there at the helm.

His dedication to his authors, moreover, contributed to the proliferation of Canadian writing talent that occurred at this time. Pierre Berton's *The National Dream* and *The Last Spike* were published in 1971 and 1972 respectively, and he won the Order of Canada in 1974. Farley Mowat's *Never Cry Wolf* was published in 1963 to great acclaim, and he won the Canadian Centennial Medal in 1967 and the Order of Canada in 1981. Margaret Laurence was at the height of her writing in 1968, and in that year she was working on her novel *The Fire-Dwellers* (1969), a collection of stories, *A Bird in the House* (1970), and a children's book, *Jason's Quest* (1970). She became one of Canada's most beloved writers. McClelland tirelessly worked with, encouraged, and promoted all of these authors, urging them toward success. With the help of Jack McClelland, the 1960s and 1970s produced Canadian literature that became legacy in the years that followed.

The Personal and the Professional
Nineteen sixty-eight was a difficult year for Jack McClelland, not only for professional reasons but personal ones. His father, John McClelland, passed away on 7 May 1968 at the age of 93. Along with Frederick Goodchild, John McClelland founded the publishing company in 1906. When George Stewart joined the firm in 1914 and Goodchild left, the firm changed its name from McClelland & Goodchild to McClelland & Stewart. John McClelland had worked in the publishing industry for 79 years according to his obituary in *Publisher's Weekly*. He began his career at age 14 with the Methodist Book Room, which later became Ryerson Press, and he became the head of that company's trade department before leaving it in 1906 to begin his own company. That his obituary mentions the English writer A. A. Milne and the English Prime Minister Winston Churchill as two authors with whom he worked demonstrates the extent to which the press changed during the years when Jack McClelland ran it. When John McClelland ran the company, the literary landscape in Canada was one that valued authors from the United Kingdom and the United States over new writers from Canada, hence the firm's "close association with many major publishers in New York, Boston, and London."[11] By contrast, when Jack McClelland ran the company, he took a great risk in shifting its focus from international authors from the U.K. and the U.S. to writers at home. Canadian arts and culture at this time was ready for this change, and that readiness was indicated by funding initiatives such as the Canada Council for the Arts and commissions such as the Book Publishing Commission of Ontario. Yet the country also needed someone to foster that readiness and turn Canada's desire to create and sustain its own literature into reality. Through McClelland & Stewart, Jack McClelland was the person who did just that.

In 1959, Jack McClelland set up a pension plan for his parents, which was to be approved by the Board at the press. In a letter to his parents that outlines his establishment of the plan, he indicated that his father was "still rendering a considerable service to the company" (Jack McClelland fonds, n.d., box 24, file 21). Yet after his father's death in 1968, McClelland faced challenges with regard to the estate. "Ever since Dad's death last spring—and indeed before that," he wrote in a letter to his lawyer, John Desbrisay, in March 1969, "I've been caught in a web that has been impossible to escape from" (Jack McClelland

---

11. The obituary of John McClelland in *Publisher's Weekly* can be found in box 24, file 21, Jack McClelland fonds (n.d.).

fonds, n.d., box 11, file 4). The complexities of his father's estate, as he summarized them for his lawyer, included tax issues related to common shares in the firm. Nineteen sixty-eight was thus a stressful year for McClelland both on professional and personal counts. Professionally, he was simultaneously facing potential bankruptcy and an explosion of new writers on the Canadian literary scene. Personally, he was dealing with familial loss, grief, and his father's will.

In other instances, too, McClelland's personal life erupted into his professional one, making the two inseparable. For medical reasons, he sometimes took leave from work. In May of 1973, for example, when Margaret Laurence wrote to him, his secretary, Marge Hodgeman, responded to her. She said that McClelland was away from the office, since the doctor had demanded that he take a vacation so that he would not have "a nervous breakdown." "But don't tell him I told you," she added (Davis and Morra 2018, 274). McClelland carefully balanced his professional and personal lives throughout his career, as he worked tirelessly to produce new Canadian literature, a passion that was both personal and professional.

Jack McClelland and the Legacy of 1968

The excitement about and growth of Canadian literature specifically, and the arts in Canada generally, did not last indefinitely. Canadian publishers benefitted from laws in the 1960s and 1970s that protected them from foreign multinationals, but the literary landscape in Canada changed significantly in subsequent decades. In the 1980s, many small presses entered the scene, competing with those such as Anansi (MacSkimming 2012, 351). Jack Stoddart's company, Stoddart Publishing, rose to prominence.[12] In the 1980s, large American houses expressed interest in publishing Canadian trade books (MacSkimming 2012, 367)—the tip of the iceberg in terms of American involvement in the Canadian book business. In the 1990s, the federal government under Prime Minister Jean Chrétien did little to seek benefits for Canadian writers and readers when the country's presses merged with American ones (MacSkimming 2012, 368). By the new millennium, many Canadian publishing companies began to fold. In 2002, Stoddart's publishing company went bankrupt (Martin 2002). In 2012, eight years after Jack McClelland's death, McClelland & Stewart was sold to Penguin Random House, an American firm (Davis and Morra 2018, lx). As Elaine Dewar put it in 2017, "Canadian-owned and controlled publishing

---

12. Jack Stoddart was the head of Stoddart Publishing, and later General Publishing Co. Ltd., and its book distribution arm, General Distribution Services Ltd. He was president of the Association of Canadian Publishers (ACP) for three terms, and his company was voted publisher of the year in 1994 and 1996, and distributer of the year in 1998 by Canadian booksellers. The company filed for bankruptcy in 2002 (Martin 2002).

companies are the endangered coral reefs in what federal servants call the publishing eco-system" (15).

McClelland might not have anticipated the extent to which American and multinational companies would take over Canadian publishing, despite the fact that he struck a partnership in 1977 with the U.S.-owned publisher, Bantam, to create Seal Books—with an eye to expanding the paperback business (Woodcock 1977).[13] He did, though, foresee the future of the digital age with regard to the publishing business. In 1967 and 1968, McClelland predicted that the form of books and the book business would change. "In the future," he said, "sooner than we think, book forms will change ... books will be on tiny rolls of microfilm that can be projected onto a screen ... when you go away for a weekend and you can't make up your mind what to read, you can take a few thousand with you" (Taylor 1967). He believed that this change was "inevitable" (*Globe and Mail* 1967).[14] In his letters to Margaret Laurence in the early 1980s, he spoke with excitement and delight about the new Apple Macintosh computer, which was being supplied to his authors. Laurence expressed reservation about accepting the computer and wondered whether she would be expected to pose in a picture to promote it. "Hell, I don't know, but it's not a bad idea," McClelland responded. "They just may and I will urge them to do it." He accepted "$260,000 worth of Apple Macintosh computers for his writers. This move was an example not only of large changes in globalized publishing, but also of corporate influence on arts and culture in Canada, a kind of influence which was not yet common but was soon to come (Davis and Morra 2018, lxi).

Since 1968, Canadian publishing has changed drastically. In an increasingly global market, Canadian presses presently struggle to maintain their independence from large American and multinational firms. However, Canada has also produced a plethora of English- and French-language writers who have made a mark on the world stage. In 2013, for example, Alice Munro won the Nobel Prize for literature, the thirteenth woman and the first Canadian woman to do so. McClelland had much to do with inspiring Canadian writers and promoting them within and beyond the country—a legacy that continues today. He was a legendary publisher who strongly contributed to the legacy of writers and the shape of Canadian literature. He ran a company that was at once unique, disorganized, and brilliant. From the time that he took over the firm from his father in 1959, to the time that he handed it over to others to run in the 1980s, he built a publishing house like no other in Canada. Willing to take risks on

---

13. A clipping of the Woodcock piece can be found in the Margaret Laurence fonds, 1980-001/014, file 27, item 1688, Clara Thomas Archives and Special Collections, York University, Toronto.

14. A clipping of the article was found in box 23a, file 1, Jack McClelland fonds (n.d.).

new Canadian writing and to focus on literary talent at home rather than abroad, McClelland was instrumental in changing the face of Canadian writing and publishing in the country.

Jack McClelland and McClelland & Stewart were instrumental to the establishment and growth of Canadian literature. His influence was particularly significant throughout the 1960s and 1970s. Within those two decades, 1968 was a stand-out year for McClelland and his publishing company for a variety of reasons: the company almost went bankrupt that year, but was spared that fate with the involvement of Cemp Investments and eventually the Ontario Government; the CRTC was established that year, which promulgated the book business; spurred by the Massey Commission and new funding councils such as the Canada Council for the Arts—not to mention McClelland's own work of finding and promoting Canadian writers—1968 also saw an explosion of new Canadian writing; and the firm itself was bursting with new work and energy, with the likes of Leonard Cohen, Margaret Laurence, and Margaret Atwood entering the literary scene. McClelland & Stewart in 1968 was a tour de force, even as, incredibly, it was on the brink of bankruptcy. McClelland himself was a major personality behind the company, and masterminded a firm that brought so many important, canonical Canadian writers success. Looking back at McClelland & Stewart in 1968, we see a publishing house that both created and promoted arts and letters. It would come to define the country and its literary history within and well beyond that moment in time.

Acknowledgements

I would like to express my sincere thanks to the archivists at the William Ready Division of Archives and Special Collections at McMaster University, Hamilton, Ontario, where the McClelland & Stewart fonds and the Jack McClelland fonds reside. In particular, Myron Groover, Bridget Whittle, Renu Barrett, and Rick Stapleton were instrumental to my work there and to my research for this chapter. I would like to thank Suzanne McClelland Drinkwater and the William Ready Division of Archives and Special Collections for permission to publish the photograph in this chapter. Thank you also to Aritha Van Herk for providing informative details about the photograph.

References

Adams, James. 2015. "Writer Created Three Publishing Houses." *Globe and Mail*, 4 July: S11.

Billboard Media, LLC. n.d. "Leonard Cohen." https://www.billboard.com/music/leonard-cohen. Accessed 20 March 2019.

Davis, Laura K., and Linda M. Morra, eds. 2018. *Margaret Laurence and Jack McClelland, Letters*. Edmonton: University of Alberta Press.

Dewar, Elaine. 2017. *The Handover: How Bigwigs and Bureaucrats Transferred Canada's Best Publisher and the Best Part of Our Literary Heritage to a Foreign Multinational.* Windsor: Biblioasis.

Globe and Mail. 2004. "Jack McClelland Dead at 81." 15 June: A9.

———. 1967. "One Little Package of 500 Books Predicted for Students of Future." 20 January: 10.

Gray, Charlotte. 2016. *The Promise of Canada: People and Ideas That Have Shaped Our Country.* Toronto: Simon and Schuster Canada.

Jack McClelland fonds. n.d. William Ready Division of Archives and Special Collections, McMaster University, Hamilton.

Kane, Hugh. 1968. Memo to Jack McClelland, 4 November. McClelland & Stewart fonds, box 11, file 4, William Ready Division of Archives and Special Collections, McMaster University, Hamilton.

King, James. 1999. *Jack, A Life with Writers: The Story of Jack McClelland.* Toronto: Knopf Canada.

Lorimer, Rowland. 2012. *Ultra Libris: Policy, Technology, and the Creative Economy of Book Publishing in Canada.* Toronto: ECW Press.

MacSkimming, Roy. 2012. *The Perilous Trade: Book Publishing in Canada, 1946–2006.* Toronto: McClelland & Stewart.

Martin, Sandra. 2002. "Fall of the House of Stoddart." *Globe and Mail,* 31 August: R1.

McClelland & Stewart fonds. n.d. William Ready Division of Archives and Special Collections, McMaster University, Hamilton.

Mount, Nick. 2017. *Arrival: The Story of CanLit.* Toronto: Anansi.

Newman, Peter C. 1967. "Canadian Companions All—from B-W: Peter Newman's Own List of 50 Canadians for That New Medal." *Toronto Star,* 19 April: 7.

Official UK Charts Company, The. n.d. "Leonard Cohen." https://www.officialcharts.com/artist/2600/leonard-cohen. Accessed 19 March 2019.

Stebbins, Robert A. 2001. "The Aid to Scholarly Publications Programme: Contributions to Canadian Sociology." *Canadian Journal of Sociology* 26 (3): 453–468.

Taylor, Jim. 1967. "Publisher Flips Another Page in Stronach's Library Row." *London Free Press,* 31 January: 7.

Woodcock, Connie. 1977. "Canadian Jack Finds US Jill." *Toronto Sun,* 8 February: 15.

Chapter 10
Immigration and "Medical Manpower": 1968 and the Awkward Introduction of Medicare in Canada

DAVID WRIGHT AND SASHA MULLALLY

Abstract

The year 1968 witnessed the launch of medicare, a public program so important that 50 years later many Canadians identify universal health insurance as a defining feature of our national identity. At the time, the Pearson government sought to frame the passage of the *Medical Care Act* (1966) as one of a series of nation-building exercises that would culminate in the Centenary celebrations. Nevertheless, the advent of medicare was accompanied by uncertainty, resistance, and large doses of criticism from many fronts. Fiscal and constitutional considerations loomed large, of course. However, the principal challenge was that there was not enough medical staff to accommodate the demand for services that a new single-payer system would inevitably unleash. This chapter examines the awkward launching of medicare in a fiscal, political, and medical context that made its success anything but inevitable.

July 1, 1968 witnessed the official launch of medicare, a social policy that became so deeply ingrained in Canadian society that it is now a signature of national identity. Indeed, the putative founder of medicare, Saskatchewan premier Tommy Douglas, was voted the "Greatest Canadian" of all time by a popular CBC contest, easily beating out hockey legend Wayne Gretzky and inventor of the telephone, Alexander Graham Bell (CBC 2004). The viability of universal health insurance, however, was far from assured at the outset. Far from being universally acclaimed and financially sustainable, it proved to be unpopular in many circles, particularly with political leaders who held passionately to the belief that health care was uniquely a provincial constitutional responsibility. However, there were also practical anxieties on the ground:

Canada simply did not have enough doctors or nurses on hand to respond to the extension of health care to all Canadian residents free at the point of delivery. As this chapter illustrates, the experiment of medicare only survived through the concurrent influx of foreign-trained health-care practitioners willing to leave their countries of origin and take advantage of Canada's new immigration regulations. It constitutes one of the great ironies in the contemporary history of Canada that a cardinal event of social justice—the implementation of medicare—was enabled only by the influx of thousands of non-Canadian professionals, inadvertently exacerbating health inequalities on an international scale (Mullally and Wright 2020).

The political and policy history of medicare has been well documented by social scientists and by those who were involved in the charged debates of the time (Taylor 2009; Vayda and Deber 1992). Borrowing the ideas of the British Health Service and left-leaning American medical activists (Jones 2018), Canada's two layers of government bickered over jurisdictional and funding issues. Ultimately, Saskatchewan struck out on its own, led by Douglas's Co-operative Commonwealth Federation (CCF) party, which repeatedly invoked universal health care as a rallying cry. Piece by piece, Saskatchewan extended medical services to the elderly and indigent, pioneered community psychiatric care, and engaged in comprehensive hospitalization insurance from the 1940s onwards (Houston 2003). Other provinces acted more cautiously, introducing their own versions of subsidized

THERE IS OPPORTUNITY FOR YOU IN YOUNG DYNAMIC CANADA

If you have a skill, trade or profession, the time is right, the mood is right for you and Canada to get together. Industrial production in Canada has more than doubled in the last 15 years and is still forging ahead. For years to come Canada will be a country of growth.

You will enjoy life in this young land of opportunity. Wages and salaries are high. Canadians enjoy one of the highest standards of living in the world.

Your children will have the best possible start in life—free secondary and primary education and every chance of going on to University or to a modern Technical Institute. You and your family will be protected too, by a social welfare programme : family allowances, hospital insurance, unemployment insurance and retirement pension.

Canadians are friendly, down-to-earth people—and remember—emigrating to Canada is not like going to the far corners of the globe, you are only six hours away by air, six days by sea.

Go and grow with CANADA the land of opportunity

CANADA
Needs Doctors

Expansion in Canada creates many opportunities for medical personnel—Physicians, Surgeons, Pathologists, also Laboratory Technicians and Radiographers.

Write today for further information about Canada to:

CANADIAN GOVERNMENT Immigration Service, Dept. 6 B.M.J.17/2, 38 Grosvenor Street, London W.1.

(16503)

Figure 10.1. Canadian Department of Immigration advertisement in the *British Medical Journal*, January 1968.

medical services for the poor and for specific medical emergencies (Marchildon 2012). By the 1950s, however, the popularity of provincially run health services combined with the dramatic economic success of postwar Canada emboldened the federal government to introduce co-funding for hospitalization insurance (in 1957) and, later, a Royal Commission on Health Services (the Hall Commission, 1961–1964) to examine the feasibility of extending federal co-funding to all "medically necessary" services (Naylor 1986). The recommendations of the Royal Commission were taken up in the *Medical Care Act* of 1966, which provided the national framework enabling the extension of hospitalization coverage to extra-mural medical services. In this way, medicare reflected a "parting at the crossroads" of Canada and the United States in the domain of public health care (Maioni 1998).

Although medicare is now widely supported by the Canadian public, it was deeply divisive in the 1960s. Provincial and national medical associations were wary of their members becoming glorified civil servants and having their scope of practice determined by government bureaucrats; hospital boards were resistant to losing their independence and the endowments of their respective medical institutions, many of which (both within and without Quebec) were run by Catholic orders; private insurance companies inevitably feared becoming rendered redundant by so-called socialist medicine; and prosperous Canadian families worried that they would lose long-cherished relationships with individual practitioners of their choice (Naylor 1986). Despite these multiple concerns, the winds of change appeared to be blowing in the direction of a National Health Service (NHS)–style system in Canada. However, the situation was complicated by the constitutional provision that the provinces run medical institutions and health services. When the multi-volume Hall Commission report was tabled in 1964, recommending universal health insurance co-funded by Ottawa (Canada 1964), the debate shifted to a scramble over funds and the operationalization of the plan, even though the two largest provinces—Ontario and Quebec—remained deeply ambivalent about, even hostile towards, the new system (see below). Nevertheless, the Pearson government moved forward, convinced that it had added a popular plank to its electoral platform, and an answer to the sniping of the emergent New Democratic Party (NDP) on the political left. The federal Liberals adopted the recommendations of the Hall Commission. They engaged in lengthy talks during 1965 with provincial ministers of health over the allocation of $500 million of a new Health Research Infrastructure Fund for new medical, dental, and nursing schools across the country. The date for the launch of medicare was not supposed to be 1968; rather, it was initially timed to coincide with the Centenary celebrations in 1967. This was far more than coincidence: medicare was to be a cornerstone of a new Canada for a new century. Following the gains of the NDP in the federal election of 1965, that party began "pressing for action literally every week" in the House of Commons launching a Health Charter Campaign and linking it to the upcoming Centenary celebrations (Maioni 1998, 130).

The Pearson cabinet, however, failed to anticipate the degree of pushback from certain quarters, and, as the Centenary celebrations approached, uncertainty about the ultimate cost of the national medicare initiative. Citing "administrative" reasons, the federal Liberals delayed the launch of medicare by one year. Even this postponement was subject to debate by the autumn of 1967. Walter Gordon, the former Finance Minister, rose in the House of Commons to quash rumours that the federal Liberal Party was considering a delay of a further year, putting in question its commitment to universal health care across the nation. "We in the Liberal Party are for medicare," he reassured the House, "to rousing back-bench cheers" (*Globe and Mail* 1967). Similarly, Pearson himself felt the need to re-state 1 July 1968 as the firm date for the beginning of medicare. According to newspaper reports, however, there was pressure "within and outside the Cabinet" to delay the implementation yet again. The *Toronto Star* reported, in January of 1968, that the issue had divided the cabinet in the months leading up to the federal Liberal leadership convention, with Health Minister Allan MacEachen and External Affairs Minister Paul Martin defending the medicare plan, while Trade Minister Robert Winters and Transport Minister Paul Hellyer claimed that the government ought not to bring in new, expensive programs while it was running a deficit (Gray 1968; Hazlitt 1968). Indeed, the fiscal year 1967–1968 ushered in a budget deficit of nearly $700 million, nearly double that of the previous year. The Prime Minister, however, found some comfort in the support of David Lewis (NDP), who stated confidently that economic production in the country would be enhanced by the proper medical care given to all its people, which would (conveniently) compensate for any financial shortfall (Seale 1968).

Despite these reassurances, after several years of economic boom the Canadian economy was heading into strong headwinds in the winter of 1967–1968, enough to give some Liberal ministers pause. Rumours began to circulate that medicare would be delayed again or scaled back. Pearson, however, was quietly confident about the financial impact for both tactical and political reasons. Because the program was scheduled to start in July of 1968, the financial cost to the federal government for the fiscal year 1968–1969 would not include a full year's reimbursement to the participating provinces. Perhaps more importantly, it was clear by the beginning of 1968 that only one or two provinces would likely join at the outset. Paradoxically, Pearson reassured MPs of the viability of the new national plan by insisting that there would not be a *nation-wide* program in 1968 because many provinces either were not ready or not supportive. He suggested that medicare would be years in the making: "[W]hen the act comes into effect," Pearson observed, "there will not be anything approaching a universal medicare program in Canada provided jointly by the federal-provincial action" (Seale 1968).

This awkward introduction of medicare in 1968 was reflected in the reporting in national newspapers. In contrast to the euphoria and hyperbole surrounding the success of Expo 67, Canada's broadsheets appeared to take comparatively little interest in the official launch of universal health insurance on 1 July 1968. The *Globe and Mail*, sensing its readers' priorities, reported that the travel time to cottage country had eased considerably, following terrible traffic jams on the way to Muskoka the previous Friday. The Bank of Canada had also stolen the headlines by deciding to cut its prime interest rate to 7 percent in response to a strong Canadian dollar. Medicare was relegated to a small article on page two (*Globe and Mail* 1968a). Neither the *Globe* nor the *Toronto Daily Star* bothered to mention it on its cover page. In the United States, where there had emerged a similar debate over the role of their federal government in subsidizing national health care, the *New York Times* covered the launch of Canadian medicare with a minor, page 4 piece about the "controversial national plan" of "free medical services" north of the border, pointing out snidely that only 10 percent of the Canadian population (meaning only those resident in Saskatchewan and British Columbia) were likely to benefit (Walz 1968).

Members of these two provinces might have been surprised to read about the "free medical services" alluded to in the *New York Times*. In fact, the British Columbia Ministry of Health ran notices in local newspapers alerting all residents of the coming premiums to be paid for a range of services under the new system, including the $5/month premium for regular subscribers with no dependents (*Quesnel Cariboo Observer* 1968). In the other qualifying province, Saskatchewan's Ross Thatcher (then Liberal premier) complained of the "cries of anguish" that had accompanied his province-wide "deterrent fees" for unnecessary hospital visits that were also to be part of the new medicare system. Those living in the provincial birthplace of medicare were to be charged $1.50 for each visit to a doctor ($2.00 for a house call) and $2.50 for every day in the hospital. Thatcher insisted that these "deterrent measures" were necessary because of the long history of the indiscriminate use of medical services unleashed by the Saskatchewan provincial plan of universal health care, which had been in place since 1962 (Jones 2018). New Brunswick and Nova Scotia had both postponed participation on the grounds that they could not afford their share of the predicted rise in health-care costs (*Globe and Mail* 1968b).

The lukewarm reception to the launch of medicare reflected the long, bureaucratic, and political process whereby most provinces had to pass companion legislation fulfilling the four principles of federal funding (comprehensiveness, universality, portability, and public administration) as well as the opposition of Canada's two largest provinces. Early in 1968, John Robarts, the premier of Ontario, "condemned" the medicare plan as "rigid" and "excessively expensive." He announced that there was no way Ontario would join at the launch in 1968 since it was not consistent with the "priorities" of the people of Ontario (*Toronto Star* 1968, C1). In Quebec, the Liberal government of Jean Lesage had been surprisingly replaced by the Union Nationale in 1966. Quebec, which had rejected the federal Canada Pension Plan in 1963, was ambivalent about a national medicare proposal arising from the Hall Commission in the following year. Like some other provinces (Kealey and Molyneaux 2007), Quebec had launched its own provincial commission. The Castonguay-Nepveu commission, established by the Lesage government, but ultimately reporting to Premier Daniel Johnson in 1967, had advocated a form of universal health insurance, but one "made in Quebec" that placed greater emphasis on local health centres or CLSCs (Centre local de services communautaires). However, a surprising opinion poll taken in 1968 indicated that popular support of provincially run universal health insurance was not only strong in the entire country, it was strongest in La Belle Province. Nevertheless, 1968 was a volatile year in Quebec (see the chapters in this volume by Létourneau [Chapter 3] and Turgeon [Chapter 13]). And Quebec's leadership was placed in crisis by the death of Johnson in September of 1968, the third Union Nationale premier to die in office in ten years.

In keeping with many postwar cost-sharing programs, as more and more provinces joined the medicare program, those staying outside would be, in effect, subsidizing health services for residents in other provinces (through their general taxation). This irked John Robarts, the Ontario provincial premier, who complained bitterly about the coercive nature of the new legislation. By the autumn of 1968, however, he acknowledged that, despite his opposition, he felt that the province had no choice but to ultimately join the program. "After all," he declared frustratedly, "we can't expect the people of Ontario to pay the health costs of the rest of the country" (Cahill 1968, 1). He bowed to what he considered inevitable and agreed to participate the following year. With the return of the Quebec Liberals under Robert Bourassa in the spring of 1970, Claude Castonguay, the co-author of the provincial commission's report on universal health insurance, was appointed Minister of Health, Family and Social Welfare. One of his first initiatives was to introduce Quebec's enabling legislation to the 1966 *Medical Care Act*, legislation which (unlike the other provinces) outlawed extra billing. The move prompted a specialists' strike in October of 1970, the timing of which could have been better. In what was probably the most forgotten moment in the national drama of the October Crisis, the Quebec government passed legislation forcing medical specialists back to work. One by one, the rest of the provinces joined, with New Brunswick being the last to enter medicare in 1971 (Marchildon and O'Byrne 2013).

"Medical Manpower"

In many respects, the launch of medicare—as a national policy initiative—was at least a decade in the making and had as much to do with immigration reform as political disputes over constitutional responsibilities or the self-interested posturing of professional health-care organizations. The year 1958 had witnessed the implementation of the now long-forgotten *Hospital Insurance and Diagnostic Services Act (HIDSA)*, which provided matching federal government funding for acute hospital care and diagnostic services (*HIDSA* 1957). This federal benevolence came with strings attached—provisos that signalled the federal government's desire to ensure a national plan through universality and full coverage. Provinces that elected to participate were required to pass legislation that made hospital services available to all residents "upon uniform terms and conditions," which included a comprehensive slate of services for standard in-patient services and amenities. One notable clause, presaging constitutional debates later in the century, was that the federal plan was only to be operationalized when at least six provinces, containing at least one half of the population of Canada, passed enabling legislation pursuant to the federal provisions. However, with Ontario dragging its feet, and in the face of the dogged resistance of Quebec and Alberta, this stipulation was quietly withdrawn. By 1961, however, all provinces (many reluctantly) had passed enabling legislation pursuant to the national hospitalization program (Maioni 1998). Hospitalization insurance proved immensely popular throughout the country, owing in no small part to the reality that, despite the postwar economic boom, a sizeable minority of Canadians lacked proper medical care and hospitalization insurance. The Royal Commission on Health Services (1961–1964), for example, estimated that 40 percent of Canadians had no, or inadequate, health care for medical services (in general) at the time of their inquiry (Canada 1964, 1:727). As a consequence, the advent of public hospitalization and diagnostic services led to a significant increase in demand for these new clinical services that were free at the point of delivery.

The Royal Commission on Health Services (Hall Commission 1961–1964) recognized that if access to nurses and physicians was tight in many parts of the country in the pre-medicare era, it would become much more problematic with the establishment of universal health insurance. The commissioners predicted as much as a doubling of the number of persons seeking health services if universal health insurance were to be introduced. Commissioners worried about, amongst other things, "the capacity of medical schools in Canada to graduate a sufficient supply of well-qualified physicians" (Canada 1964, 1:69–73) particularly in the light of the fact that Canada was losing approximately 200 doctors to the United States every year. Although the Royal Commission spoke much less to the challenges of nursing personnel, its statistics estimated that the nation had also lost more than 10,000 Canadian-trained nurses to the United States in the seven-year period leading up to 1960 (Canada 1964, 1:270). Central to the success of any new system of universal health insurance, therefore, was a dramatic ramping up of the physician and nurse workforce in the country lest any new system collapse under the weight of the pent-up demand. In the short term, the country turned to more and more foreign-trained medical practitioners.

The *Report of the Royal Commission* (1964) acknowledged that "a significant characteristic of the composition of Canadian medical manpower is the large proportion of immigrant physicians in the post-war years" (Canada 1964, 1:241–242). This was a bit of an understatement. Canada's loss of some 2,000 doctors to the United States in the 1950s had only been compensated for by the arrival of 2,000 doctors fleeing the British National Health Service (Wright, Mullally, and Cordukes 2010). A similar substitution effect had also occurred for nurses. The 10,000 nurses leaving for the United States in the 1950s had themselves been "replaced" by British and Caribbean nurses who had trained and worked in Britain, as Karen Flynn has illustrated (Flynn 2003, 2011). Implicit in the discourse, however, was a sense that relying on foreign-trained doctors and nurses was inherently risky. Indeed, the 1964 Royal Commission report, assuming that immigrants would always predominantly come from Britain, Ireland, and the United States, predicted gloomily that immigration from these counties would likely decline after 1970, throwing the country into a potential health-care personnel crisis (Canada 1964, 1:521–528).

It is in this context that the *Final Report* of the Royal Commission on Health Services was submitted in July 1964. The *Report* recommended federally co-funded, provincially administered universal health insurance throughout the country. Provinces that passed enabling legislation pursuant to four principles of medicare would receive 50 percent of insured services in a health transfer at the end of the year. Emphasizing the pan-Canadian nature of the program, the government insisted on portability among provinces and that all residents be covered. With regard to the anticipated physician shortage, the *Report* recommended at least four new medical schools and the expansion of existing ones. Nursing education proved to be more complicated, since the national nursing associations were concurrently pushing for an end to hospital-based nurse training and the movement of professional education into community colleges and universities (McPherson 2003). As a consequence, funding for new research-oriented, multi-disciplinary health sciences centres was also part of the larger, decade-long plan that involved the transformation of nursing education.

The problem with this approach was that new medical and nursing schools took years to become fully functioning—it took time to have the physical infrastructure built, time to recruit teaching faculty and scientists, and, after that, time to train cohorts of undergraduate medical students and nurses for whom the undergraduate degrees were three to four years. Of the four new medical schools that were constructed (Sherbrooke, McMaster, Memorial, and Calgary), only Sherbrooke would graduate students in the late 1960s. Thus, by 1966, Canada had committed to universal health insurance, even though the architects of the new system knew full well that the domestic capacity of health-care practitioners was likely insufficient to meet the demand for medical services for about ten years. Fortunately for advocates of the new system, the decline of new immigrants at the end of the decade did not materialize. Quite the contrary: changes in immigration regulations saved the new medicare system from collapsing while dramatically expanding the scope and range of the countries from which doctors and nurses arrived.

"A Young, Progressive Country"

The Diefenbaker government (1957–1963), which came to power in the same year that *HIDSA* was passed, attempted to establish a more consistent and bureaucratic approach to the selection of new Canadians. It was Ellen Fairclough, the first woman federal cabinet minister in Canadian history, who was given the sensitive portfolio of Minister of Immigration a year later. Fairclough introduced in the House of Commons a change to immigration regulations, which forbade the discrimination of landed immigrant candidates on the basis of race, colour, or nation of origin. Now known as the Fairclough Guidelines, this 1962 ministerial directive followed naturally from Diefenbaker's much-cherished Bill of Rights, which had been passed by Parliament in 1960. With this statement of principles, Canada, at least on paper, became the first major industrialized, immigrant-receiving country to eliminate race as a basis for immigration (Immigration Regulations 1962). Of course, individual immigration officers continued to be influenced by their own judgment as to the "suitability" of particular candidates and sponsorship of family members was restricted to specific "preferred countries." Nonetheless, the Fairclough Guidelines foreshadowed further changes during the next decade that affected health services across the country.

Fairclough became accustomed to the complaint that foreign workers were arriving in a haphazard manner, taking jobs from ordinary Canadians. In response, the Minister of Immigration attempted to reframe federal immigration as the pursuit of *highly skilled* immigrants filling positions desperately needed by the country and that no native-born Canadian could fill. Her gambit was largely successful. The resulting Parliamentary debates of the early 1960s reflected a flip-flopping of immigration positions in the country. The Liberal Party, formerly the party more sympathetic to immigration, increasingly criticized the Progressive Conservative government for the arrival of professionals from "Third World" countries. Taking a suspiciously convenient stand on the moral high ground, the Liberal Immigration critic complained in 1962 that Canada was welcoming too much talent from poor countries. The *Globe and Mail* weighed in, quoting a trade union leader, Charles Millard, complaining that Canada was engaged in "poaching" skilled labour from Asia, Africa, and the Middle East. The editors opined that Canada should only accept foreign trainees if it intended to provide them with enhanced skills which they could then take back with them to their home countries (*Globe and Mail* 1962a; 1962b). However, the sanctimony of the federal Liberals faded with their return to power in 1963.

Building on Fairclough's initiatives, the federal Liberals under Pearson sought to make immigration selection less capricious and more "scientific." Gone were the days where immigrant candidates' suitability lay at the discretion of individual immigration officers. In its place, senior civil servants hatched a new, seemingly objective, plan that scored potential immigrants on a points scale, as outlined in the *White Paper on Immigration* (Canada 1966). Under the new system, candidates were to complete a pro forma sheet of qualifications. They earned points for language skills (English and/or French), education level, age, a letter of employment, and having relatives already in the country. Candidates whose intended occupation was in high demand (a status that could be changed annually by the Department of Manpower, which, not by chance, was part of the same Ministry) were given special bonus points. The new points system assigned each aspiring immigrant to Canada a mark out of 100, and accepted those who "passed" with a score of 50 and higher (Triadafilopoulos 2013). It is little surprise that English- or French-speaking medical practitioners, due to their high level of education, their training, and their demand in the mid-1960s, were virtually guaranteed to rank high enough for admission. The new system was enshrined in the 1967 *Immigration (Appeals Board) Act*, which drew its name from the new appeal protocols that had also been introduced in the wake of deportation of so-called "illegal immigrants" (*Immigration Act* 1967). Its first full year of implementation of the new regulations overlapped with the launch of medicare—that is, in 1968.

It should be remembered that the points system put in place had not been intended as a mechanism to encourage the acceptance of immigrants from non-traditional countries. As Deputy Minister of Manpower and Immigration Tom Kent later acknowledged, it was a social scientific attempt to "identify and define the various factors affecting a person's ability to settle successfully in Canada, and attach relative weights to them [so that] immigration officers would have a consistent basis on which to assess potential immigrants" (Kent 1988, 408). Ultimately, the 1967 *Immigration (Appeals Board) Act* had proved enormously successful and did, on one level, facilitate the arrival of the tens of thousands of foreign professionals to staff the rapidly expanding public sector—engineers, university professors, and health-care practitioners. But it was not just the absolute number, or even the professional qualifications, that increasingly attracted public attention. Canada became the destination for an ever-increasing number of non-white immigrants.

The demographic impact of these discrete, but cumulative, immigration changes was dramatic. Total immigration under Diefenbaker's government had dropped to a postwar low of only 72,000 and continued to be relatively low during the economic malaise of 1957–1960 (Knowles 1992, 139–141). A decade later, the absolute number of immigrants entering the country had trebled, reaching nearly 200,000 in 1968, one of the few postwar years in which Canada almost achieved the mystical immigration target of 1 percent of the existing general population (Canada, Department of Manpower and Immigration 1969). Noticeable amongst the tens of thousands of arrivals were families from countries that had hitherto not figured prominently as sources of landed immigrants, such as India, the Philippines, China, and the English- and French-speaking islands of the Caribbean. During this time, a contemporary report observed that the percentage of "visible minorities"—a rather vague and problematic term generally referring to non-white, non-European immigrants—more than doubled to greater than 30 percent (Richmond and Rao 1976, 188). The importance of these new source countries was not only a function of the new points system in immigration regulations. There were physical and practical changes that had happened abroad. By 1968, Canada had opened new immigration offices in Egypt, Japan, Lebanon, the Philippines, the West Indies, and Pakistan, tripling the number of immigration offices outside of Europe from the era before the 1962 Fairclough Directive (Troper 1993, 267).

Historians have rightly identified the new immigration regulations as an important turning point towards a multi-ethnic society that became formalized in government policy as official multiculturalism. As this chapter demonstrates, however, the immigration changes that occurred in the 1960s intersected with the urgent need for health-care personnel, paving the way for an extraordinary surge of foreign-trained doctors and nurses entering the country. Hospitals, health science centres, medical schools, and even the Department of Immigration advertised in British and American medical journals to fill vacant or new positions in Canada. Of course, hundreds of British-born and British-trained doctors and nurses continued to enter the country, as they did in the 1950s. But Britain was also home to thousands of non-British-born doctors and nurses who had returned to the metropole for graduate training and employment. Due to the reciprocity between most Canadian provinces and the British General Medical Council (Haynes 2017), immediate accreditation of doctors was assured almost everywhere. Table 10.2 reflects Citizenship and Immigration data on the number of landed immigrants stating "physician or surgeon" or "nurses" as their intended occupation, and illustrates how dramatic the uptick had been. The annual number of doctors among landed immigrants rose dramatically by the end of the decade—from 400 in 1960 to 1,277 in 1968 (Canada, Department of Manpower and Immigration 1969).

It is difficult to categorize, in any simple manner, the decision-making of doctors and nurses who migrated to Canada immediately following the Centenary. The year 1968 was a particularly troubled year in international politics, and some health-care practitioners were fleeing domestic unrest in their home countries, such as the doctors escaping Czechoslovakia following the Prague Spring, the research scientists from Haiti eager to avoid the worsening oppression of the Duvalier regime, or the Taiwanese doctors suffering under martial law on that island state. Other health-care practitioners were re-migrating, such as hundreds of Jamaican nurses and Indian doctors who were sensing their racial marginalization in British society (in general) and in the British National Health Service in particular. The year 1968, of course, was the year in which the British Conservative politician Enoch Powell unleashed his ominous "rivers of blood" speech, predicting a future of racial violence in British cities. For many non-white health-care practitioners, it seemed like a good time to leave (Bivins 2015). Immigration officials positioned Canada as a "friendly" and "progressive" country eager to welcome health-care practitioners. Advertisements emphasized the proximity of Canada (in comparison, presumably, to Australia and New Zealand) as well as the safety of the country. The last theme was presumably a not-so-subtle contrast to the violence erupting in the United States, replete as it was in 1968 with race riots, political assassinations, and the furore that was growing over American casualties in Vietnam (Wright, Ketchum, and Marks 2016).

Nurses immigrated to Canada in even larger numbers than doctors. From a steady state in the 1950s of a loss of 1,500 nurses annually to the United States (balanced by a gain of 1,500 nurses from elsewhere), Canada began to accept significantly more nurses on an annual basis and from a more diverse array of countries. Indeed, by the late 1960s, Canada was granting landed immigrant status to well over 3,000 foreign-trained nurses per year (see Table 10.2). The transition to practice for nurses was less straightforward than

Table 10.2. Country of Former Residence and Intended Occupation of Immigrants seeking employment in the Health Sector, Calendar Year 1968 (principal countries, in descending order)

	All Countries	Great Britain	Philippines	United States	China	Australia
Health Professions						
Physicians and Surgeons	1,277	378	78	79	123	32
Dentists	99	22	4	14	8	4
Nurses (graduate)	3,375	1,120	727	231	198	245
Therapists	198	92	3	32	1	19
Pharmacists	132	22	6	15	12	5
Medical and Dental Technicians	1,169	204	263	105	34	19
Other	405	135	10	53	7	46
Total	6,655	1,973	1,091	529	383	370

	West Indies	Germany	India	Ireland	France	Egypt
Health Professions						
Physicians and Surgeons	48	40	93	38	36	29
Dentists	3	1	1	0	6	2
Nurses (graduate)	104	116	81	99	32	1
Therapists	5	8	2	8	2	1
Pharmacists	9	2	4	0	4	8
Medical and Dental Technicians	43	37	13	4	17	17
Other	22	17	10	7	8	0
Total	234	221	204	156	105	58

Source: Department of Manpower and Immigration (Canada Immigration Division), *1968 Immigration Statistics* (Ottawa: The Queen's Printer, 1969), adapted from Table 11: "Country of Former Residence and Intended Occupation of Immigrants: Calendar Year 1968."

for doctors since some Canadian provinces had eliminated independent mid-wifery practice, thereby limiting the scope of practice among nurse-midwives who had trained or practiced in Britain (Bourgeault 2006). Nevertheless, despite these restrictions, international research ranked Canada third (behind

Britain and the United States) in terms of the absolute number of nurse immigrants and first in terms of per capita immigration of nurses amongst major industrialized countries in the late 1960s (Van Hoek 1970, 73). Notwithstanding the excellent monograph by Karen Flynn (2011), the multiple waves of nursing immigration to Canada during the early years of medicare is an area ripe for further investigation.

Conclusion

Medicare constituted a watershed moment in Canadian history, an ambitious, even audacious policy gamble that affected all Canadians in profound and intimate ways, providing an important component of their identity as a nation over the past two generations. As Antonia Maioni has argued, although Canadian and American policy-makers had been discussing similar opportunities for state-run, or state-subsidized, health care, Canada ultimately adopted a national system on uniform terms and conditions. At the same time, the Americans opted for more targeted assistance to the elderly and indigent. Maioni attributes this "parting of the ways" of the two countries to multiple factors, the most important of which were the flexibility of the Canadian parliamentary system as well as the lack of a third national party in the United States (Maioni 1998). It seems undeniable that the organization of a national social-democratic party in Canada, from 1960 onwards, proved important in pushing the Pearson Liberals into introducing universal health insurance as part of a broader mandate of constructing the postwar welfare state. In this way, the year 1968 was a turning point for the medical history of Canada and, indirectly, its sense of identity as a "progressive" country that could stand apart from, and in contrast to, its southern neighbour.

The Royal Commission on Health Services, however, was under no illusion that medicare constituted a huge undertaking requiring an enormous financial investment by the federal government. But it was an investment that, in the heady days of the 1960s, seemed affordable. Under the *Medical Care Act* of 1966, the federal government agreed to provide annual health transfers to provinces which had passed enabling legislation that abided by the guiding principles. Concurrently, the Health Research Infrastructure Grant program (started in 1966) pumped a staggering $500 million to provinces to assist in the construction of new medical, dental, and nursing schools. The year 1968 thus also witnessed four new medical schools at different stages of completion (Sherbrooke, McMaster, Memorial, and Calgary). However, the time taken to identify teaching faculty, to construct programs, to build new infrastructure, to recruit students, and to teach the students both at the undergraduate and the postgraduate levels, resulted in a decade-long delay before the complete flow of doctors and university-trained nurses reached communities. As a consequence, there would be a multi-year gap of health-care personnel at the very moment of the inception of medicare, one that, as this chapter illustrates, was filled by foreign-trained health-care practitioners.

The success of medicare was thus inextricably linked to changes in immigration regulations. When the federal Liberals returned to power in 1963, they quietly formulated a new White Paper on Immigration in 1966, which ushered in a new act the following year. Although entitled the *Immigration (Appeals Board) Act of 1967*, more profound than an appeals mechanism for the history of immigration to Canada was its introduction of a new, purportedly objective and transparent system of ranking candidates, known to this day as the "points system." Within a few short years, immigration from traditional countries— Britain, the United States, France, Ireland—became complemented by immigration from India, Pakistan, China, and the Philippines. Leading this surge of immigrants were highly skilled, English-speaking "medical manpower"—doctors, nurses, and medical scientists. They had a transformative effect on the rolling out of medicare in this country. For a remarkable four years, beginning with the implementation of medicare in 1968 and concluding with the last province signing on in 1971, Canada admitted more than 5,000 foreign-trained doctors and 12,000 foreign nursing graduates, greater numbers than it graduated domestically during the same time period. In the history of modern Canadian medicine, it was an era without precedent.

Acknowledgments

The authors would like to acknowledge the organizers of the conference 1968: A Year in Canadian History and the Canadian Museum of History. We would also like to thank René Saucier for her excellent research assistance in various stages of the paper. Funding for the larger project from which this chapter was drawn came from Canada Research Chairs program, from the University of New Brunswick, and from McGill University.

References

Bivins, Roberta. 2015. *Contagious Communities: Medicine, Migration and the NHS in Post War Britain*. Oxford: Oxford University Press.

Bourgeault, Ivy. 2006. *Push! The Struggle for Midwifery in Ontario*. Montreal and Kingston: McGill-Queen's University Press.

Cahill, Jack. 1968. "We'll Have to Join Medicare—Robarts." *Toronto Daily Star*, 14 September: 1.

Canada, Department of Manpower and Immigration, Canada Immigration Division. 1969. *Immigration Statistics for 1968*. Ottawa: The Queen's Printer.

———. 1966. *White Paper on Immigration*. Digital History - Histoire Numérique. http://biblio.uottawa.ca/omeka2/jmccutcheon/items/show/24. Accessed 1 December 2020.

———. 1964. *Royal Commission on Health Services for Canada Report (Hall Report)*. Ottawa: Queen's Printer.

CBC (Canadian Broadcasting Company). 2004. "The Greatest Canadian." http://www. cbc.ca/archives/entry/and-the-greatest-canadian-of-all-time-is.

Flynn, Karen. 2011. *Moving Beyond Borders: A History of Black Canadian and Caribbean Women in the Diaspora*. Toronto: University of Toronto Press.

———. 2003. "Race, the State, and Caribbean Immigrant Nurses, 1950–1962." In *Women, Health, and Nation: Canada and the United States since 1945*, edited by Georgina Feldberg, Molly Ladd-Taylor, Alison Li, and Kathryn McPherson, 247–263. Montreal and Kingston: McGill-Queen's University Press.

Globe and Mail. 1968a. "Traffic from Cottage Country Makes Orderly Return to City." 2 July: 1.

———. 1968b. "BC Starts Medicare Plan on Monday." 29 June: 4.

———. 1967. "Gordon Sees 1968 Rosier Than Critics Suggest: Vows Medicare to Be Implemented." 7 October: 11.

———. 1962a. "Labor Leader Assails Immigration Policy." 12 March: 4.

———. 1962b. "Selective Immigration." 13 March: 6.

Gray, Walter. 1968. "Cabinet Splits over Pledge to Launch Medicare." *Toronto Star*, 13 January: A1.

Haynes, Douglas M. 2017. *Fit to Practice: Empire, Race, Gender, and the Making of British Medicine, 1850–1980*. Rochester, NY: University of Rochester Press.

Hazlitt, Tom. 1968. "MacEachen Fights for Leadership—and Medicare—on 1 July." *Toronto Daily Star*, 13 January: A1.

HIDSA. 1957. *Hospital Insurance and Diagnostic Services Act, formally titled An Act to Authorize Contributions by Canada in respect of Programmes Administered by the Provinces, Providing Hospital Insurance and Laboratory and Other Services in Aid of Diagnosis*. 12 April.

Houston, C. Stuart. 2003. *Steps on the Road to Medicare: Why Saskatchewan Led the Way*. Montreal and Kingston: McGill-Queen's University Press.

Immigration Act. 1967. *Immigration Act, Immigration Regulations*, Part 1, Amended, RG2-A-1-a, volume 2380, PC1967–1616, 16 August.

Immigration Regulations. 1962. Order in Council, PC 1962–1986, 18 January.

Jones, Esyllt. 2018. *Radical Medicine: The International Origins of Socialized Health Care in Canada*. Winnipeg: ARP Books.

Kealey, Linda, and Heather Molyneaux. 2007. "On the Road to Medicare: Newfoundland in the 1960s." *Journal of Canadian Studies* 41:90–111.

Kent, Tom. 1988. *A Public Purpose: An Experience of Liberal Opposition and Canadian Government*. Montreal and Kingston: McGill-Queen's University Press.

Knowles, Valerie. 1992. *Strangers at Our Gates: Canadian Immigration and Immigration Policy, 1540–2006*. Hamilton, ON: Dundurn.

Maioni, Antonia. 1998. *Parting at the Crossroads: The Emergence of Health Insurance in the United States and Canada*. Princeton, NJ: Princeton University Press.

Marchildon, Gregory, ed. 2012. *Making Medicare: New Perspectives on the History of Medicare in Canada*. Toronto: University of Toronto Press.

Marchildon, Gregory P., and Nicole O'Byrne. 2013. "Last Province Aboard: New Brunswick and National Medicare." *Acadiensis* 47 (Winter/Spring): 150–167.

McPherson, Kathryn. 2003. *Bedside Matters: The Transformation of Canadian Nursing, 1900–1990.* Toronto: University of Toronto Press.

Mullally, Sasha, and David Wright. 2020. *Doctors in a Strange Land: The Immigration of Foreign-Trained Doctors and the Advent of Medicare, 1957–1984.* Montreal and Kingston: McGill-Queen's University Press.

Naylor, C. David. 1986. *Private Practice, Public Payment: Canadian Medicine and the Politics of Health Insurance, 1911–1966.* Montreal and Kingston: McGill-Queen's University Press.

Quesnel Cariboo Observer. 1968. 13 June: 4.

Richmond, Anthony, and G. Lakshmana Rao. 1976. "Recent Developments in Immigration to Canada and Australia: A Comparative Analysis." *International Journal of Comparative Sociology* 17 (Fall): 183–205.

Seale, Lewis. 1968. "PM Retains July 1 Start for Medicare." *Globe and Mail*, 13 February: 1.

Taylor, Malcolm. 2009. *Health Insurance and Canadian Public Policy*, 3rd ed. Montreal and Kingston: McGill-Queen's University Press.

Toronto Star. 1968. "Robarts Rejects Medicare, at Least for '68." 25 January: C1, C3.

Triadafilopoulos, Triadafilos. 2013. "Dismantling White Canada: Race, Rights and the Origins of the Points System." In *Wanted and Welcome? Policies for Highly Skilled Immigrants in Comparative Perspective*, edited by Triadafilos Triadafilopoulos, 86–119. New York: Springer.

Troper, Harold. 1993. "Canada's Immigration Policy Since 1945." *International Journal* 48:255–281.

Van Hoek, F. J. 1970. *The Migration of High Level Manpower from Developing to Developed Countries.* The Hague/Paris: Mouton.

Vayda, Eugene, and Raisa Deber. 1992. "The Canadian Health Care System: A Developmental Overview." In *Canadian Health Care and the State: A Century of Evolution*, edited by David Naylor, 125–140. Montreal and Kingston: McGill-Queen's University Press.

Walz, Jay. 1968. "Only 2 Provinces in Canada Ready as Medicare Opens." *New York Times*, 1 July: 4.

Wright, David, Alexandra Ketchum, and Gregory Marks. 2016. "Draft Doctors: The Impact of the Vietnam War on the Migration of Foreign Doctors to Canada." In *Doctors Beyond Borders: The Transnational Migration of Physicians in the Twentieth Century*, edited by Laurence Monnais and David Wright, 166–184. Toronto: University of Toronto Press.

Wright, David, Sasha Mullally, and Colleen Cordukes. 2010. "'Worse Than Being Married': The Exodus of British Doctors from the National Health Service to Canada, c. 1955–1975." *Journal of the History of Medicine and Allied Sciences* 65:546–575.

Chapter 11
1968: A Turning Point for Language in Canada and Quebec

GRAHAM FRASER

Abstract

One of the many ways that 1968 was a crucial moment in Canadian history is in the area of language policy. In January 1968, René Lévesque published his manifesto *Option Québec*; a month later, Pierre Elliott Trudeau announced that he was a candidate for the leadership of the Liberal Party of Canada. In October, Lévesque became the first leader of the Parti Québécois. Their competing visions would shape Canadian politics—and Canadian language policy—for decades to come. On 1 June, André Laurendeau, co-chair of the Royal Commission on Bilingualism and Biculturalism, which had recommended the creation of an Official Languages Act, died from a stroke. He had called for recognition of Quebec as a distinct society, a concept that re-emerged years later with the Meech Lake Accord, and which Trudeau opposed. The year 1968 also saw the eruption of the St. Léonard school crisis which provoked the debate that led to a series of language laws, culminating with Bill 101 in 1977—legislation which is still debated today. The events of 1968—the election of Pierre Trudeau, the tabling of the *Official Languages Act*, the crisis in St. Léonard, the creation of the Parti Québécois with René Lévesque, as its first leader—set the stage for the next half-century of political and constitutional debate in Canada.

One of the many ways that 1968 was a crucial moment in Canadian history is in the area of language policy. Language has been a defining element in Canadian life throughout the country's history. It has always been, and remains, at the heart of the Canadian experience. The fact that there is a thriving French-speaking society in Canada, and the tensions that have resulted from this fact, is as central to Canadian politics and society as race is to the United States and as class is to Great Britain. From the discussions that led to Confederation in the 1860s, through the crisis created by the hanging of Louis Riel and the conscription crises of the two world wars, the referendums of

Figure 11.1. "Two-Way Street." *Source:* John Collins, c.1968. McCord Museum, Montreal M965.199.6666.

1980 and 1995, the constitutional struggles that led to the patriation of the Constitution and its amendment with a Charter of Rights in 1982 and the failures of the Meech Lake and Charlottetown accords in 1990 and 1992—not to mention the fact that Quebec has provided the backbone of almost every majority government in Canadian parliamentary history—the unspoken subtext to each of these events has been the relationship between French speakers and English speakers in Canada. In the 1960s, those rules changed under the pressure to deal with the explosion—sometimes literally—of nationalism in Quebec. Those who changed the rules changed the country. And 1968 was a critical moment in those changes. During that year, major figures emerged and collided while others disappeared. Their convergences shaped the way the country saw itself, and the conflicts that would play out in the decades that followed.

Competing Visions for Language Policy: Lévesque and Trudeau

In January 1968, future Parti Québécois leader René Lévesque published a slim volume, *Option Québec*, which was translated and published in English as *An Option for Quebec*. He had burst into public consciousness as a Quebec nationalist ten years earlier when, as a Radio-Canada broadcaster concentrating on international affairs, he had become a leading spokesman during the producers' strike. His encounter with the Diefenbaker government's indifference to French-speaking Quebec had transformed him into an activist; his decision to run for the Quebec Liberals in 1960 made him the best-known and most progressive member of Jean Lesage's new government, and he spearheaded the campaign to nationalize the private hydroelectric companies, transforming Hydro-Quebec into a powerful economic and industrial force in the province.

When the Lesage government was defeated in 1966, Lévesque had the time to reflect, and concluded that, in order to progress, Quebec needed to become politically independent with an economic association with the rest of Canada: a formula he called sovereignty-association. The concept was political, but the underlying definition of the society he wanted to develop was linguistic. He began the book with a simple statement: "We are Québécois."

> What that means, first and foremost—and if need be all that it means —is that we are attached to this one corner of the earth where we can be completely ourselves: this Quebec, the only place where we have the unmistakeable feeling that "here we can be really at home." Being ourselves is essentially a matter of keeping and developing a personality that has survived for three and a half centuries. At the core of this personality is the fact that we speak French. Everything else depends on this one essential element and follows from or leads us infallibly back to it. (Lévesque 1968, 14)

Lévesque's vision of an independent Quebec was of a society that was generous to its English-speaking minority; he would stake his leadership on the issue in defiance of more militant members of the Party.

As a minister, he had brought together a group that he would use as a sounding-board for ideas: André Laurendeau, the editor-in-chief of *Le Devoir*; Gérard Pelletier, the editor of *La Presse*; Jean Marchand, the head of the Confédération des syndicats nationaux; and Pierre Trudeau, a law professor at the Université de Montréal. "I would give them a backstage view of public life, telling them how the government was getting through its day-to-day, and they in turn would give me their unbridled comments, and plenty of blunt advice, too, that was often very useful," Lévesque recalled in his memoirs. "As keen observers they shared a strong sense that the awakening of our people was an important step in our development that should be marked by multiple, concrete achievements, among which the plan to nationalize hydro met the requirements perfectly. All seemed to agree on this point—all but one, that is. The very mention of the word 'nationalization' was enough to make Trudeau's hair stand on end" (Lévesque 1986, 173).

It was neither the first nor the last disagreement that Lévesque had with Trudeau. And yet, there was a kind of intimacy to their rivalry that few other political figures could match. They were both closer to Marchand and Pelletier than to each other; Trudeau had teased Lévesque when they first met, at the Radio-Canada cafeteria in the 1950s, when there was a possibility of Lévesque writing for *Cité Libre*, a small independent magazine that was a forum for liberals and progressives, implying that Lévesque, a television host, might find writing a challenge. Lévesque never forgot the insult, which he found arrogant and condescending.

And yet, when Marchand was considering running for the Liberals in 1965, it was Lévesque who told him not to go to Ottawa alone, but to go with Pelletier and Trudeau. (Two years earlier, when he had been offered the opportunity to co-chair the Royal Commission on Bilingualism and Biculturalism, Laurendeau sounded out Lévesque for advice. Lévesque told him to take it—saying that if he quit, it would have a powerful impact.)

Lévesque's and Trudeau's views of language were different. They were both flawlessly bilingual, but Lévesque, who had spent his childhood as part of a French-speaking minority in New Carlisle, in Quebec's Gaspé peninsula, saw it as a critical element in a collective identity, while Trudeau, the son of an English-speaking mother and a French-speaking father, saw it as part of an individual right.

Pierre Trudeau had been one of the first witnesses at the first public hearing of the Royal Commission on Bilingualism and Biculturalism in the fall of 1963, and his focus was on finding legal remedies to discrimination and eliminating the barriers to power that existed for different ethnic groups. "There is an area, I say, where it is essential to do an inquiry ... it is to find out how to ensure the equality in law of Canada's two languages," he said. "I don't mean that in

changing laws we will succeed in changing the sociological or political reality—
I don't think that's possible—but I think that the very source of French-
Canadian nationalism is a defensive attitude towards an English-Canadian
nationalist interpretation of the laws, of the judicial formulas." As far as other
things were concerned, he seemed to shrug. "For the rest, my God, let the
economic and social forces decide once the laws are just. Let the consumer
decide and let the investor decide what he is going to do within the framework
of those laws." He added that the economic and human costs of bilingualism
had to be established. "When we have established that, we will really know if
the country can live, if it should continue to operate as a country" (quoted in
G. Fraser 2006, 87).

F. R. Scott, a law professor at McGill, a poet, civil libertarian, and social
democrat, was a friend and mentor to Trudeau and a member of the Royal
Commission on Bilingualism and Biculturalism. But he was unimpressed, and
felt Trudeau had lost touch with what was happening in Quebec. Two years
later, in 1965, Trudeau was elected to Parliament with Marchand and Pelletier,
and in 1967, became Minister of Justice. In January 1968, Trudeau published
a document entitled *A Canadian Charter of Human Rights*—an idea that Scott
had written about and encouraged for at least two decades. And, in the document, Trudeau laid out his idea for the implementation of the recommendations
of the Royal Commission: the incorporation of language rights into a constitutional bill of rights. "The rights fall into two categories," he wrote:

> (a) *Communication with governmental institutions*—guaranteeing the right of
> the individual to deal with agencies of government in either official lan-
> guage. It would be necessary to decide whether this should apply to all
> agencies—legislative, executive, and judicial—and to all governments—
> federal, provincial and municipal.
> (b) *Education*—guaranteeing the right of the individual to education in
> institutions using as a medium of instruction the official language of his
> choice.

Those two rights—the right to use French or English in communication with
government and the right to learn—would become the pillars of Canadian
language policy. And Trudeau clearly defined them as individual rights rather
than collective rights. Lévesque, in contrast, saw them as critical elements in
Quebec's collective identity.

In February 1968, Pierre Trudeau announced that he was running for the
Liberal Party leadership. He was, in the terminology of Canadian philosopher
and media theorist Marshall McLuhan, "cool." He was completely comfortable
in both English and French, intellectual, combative, sexy, Jesuitically logical,

flirtatious … and highly critical of Quebec nationalism. He was running against men who seemed old (Paul Martin was 64), establishment (Bob Winters had been a successful businessman), conventional (Paul Hellyer was six years younger, but stodgier and, with 19 years' experience in the House of Commons, seemed years older), and square (John Turner). And yet, in some ways he was the establishment candidate. His predecessor, Lester Pearson, quietly supported him. Publicly, so did his Finance Minister, Mitchell Sharp, who had pulled out of the race and thrown his support to Trudeau. Those who opposed him, like Paul Hellyer, Joe Greene, and Judy LaMarsh, saw themselves as challenging the elite. On 5 April, Trudeau was elected Liberal leader, and became prime minister.

Later in the month, at a convention of the Mouvement Souveraineté-Association (MSA), former Quebec Liberal François Aquin, proposed doing away with English-language schools in Quebec: "Tax-supported English schools are a privilege, not a right," he told the delegates. "We should not be afraid to change this situation, and have at last a truly French state." "His opponents in debate fared badly," wrote *Maclean's* Ottawa editor Blair Fraser. "Most of them were booed, even those who were among the founders of the movement last autumn. The one outstanding exception was the founder René Lévesque" (B. Fraser 1968, 135–136).

To Fraser, Lévesque looked "like a small and weary Canute [who] commanded the tide to turn." He won the vote, not because of his argument—"A nation is judged by its fairness to minorities. A free Quebec must be a just society, a people serene and self-confident. The arguments in favour of this amendment are based on an inferiority complex"—but because of his implicit threat: "I ask you for 30 seconds of reflection. After all, my name is attached to this movement." As Fraser observed, "He didn't quite say, but he quite clearly meant, that he could not remain in a party that adopted a posture of injustice. Lévesque is still the M.S.A.'s strongest asset, and whatever their own views may be the members know it. So they backed him—at least for now" (B. Fraser 1968, 135–136).

Laurendeau and the Mission of the B and B Commission

On 15 May 1968, André Laurendeau suffered a stroke, and on 1 June, he died. He was 56. It was the end of a remarkable life: nationalist, activist, politician, editor, and Royal Commissioner, he was exquisitely sensitive, remarkably articulate, and deeply concerned about the future of French in Canada. His death silenced a passionate voice for more powers for Quebec in order to better protect the French language and culture. It was Laurendeau's editorial in *Le Devoir* in 1962, where he was editor-in-chief, that called for the creation of a Royal Commission to examine language use in Canada and recommend policy for the future.

Born in 1912, André Laurendeau was the son of Arthur Laurendeau, a musician and conductor and the editor of *l'Action nationale*, a nationalist journal. His mother, Blanche, was a music teacher; he grew up immersed in music and, at 14, was determined to pursue a musical career. In the 1930s, he became involved in the nationalist movement Jeune-Canada and engaged in anti-Semitic rhetoric that he later regretted and apologized for—recalling with shame that at the time when Jews were being rounded up and murdered in Europe, and there was a protest demonstration in Montreal, he organized and spoke at a counter-demonstration. "Nous avons prononcé d'affreux discours"—"Our speeches were dreadful,"—he wrote in 1963, deeply embarrassed that they had claimed that the suffering of French Canadians was real, in comparison with the so-called persecution and claimed persecution of the Jews (Laurendeau 1963, 275–278).

In 1935, he and his wife went to Paris where he studied under the French scholar André Siegfried and discovered that he knew very little about Canada:

> I felt humiliated in France when I was asked about English Canada, given my almost complete ignorance of the subject. The clearest elements of my meagre knowledge of the subject I had acquired at the Collège de France, in André Siegfried's course. So a young French Canadian was giving his French acquaintances a reply that a French intellectual had given him—when it concerned his own country. It was pathetic. I resolved to have a dialogue with English Canada after I returned. Once I was back in Montreal, I realized that in my own city, where there were several hundred thousand Anglo Canadians, it was difficult since the two groups lived apart. I resolved the problem in registering in a course in sociology at McGill. Thus I was able to establish contacts with several students and professors. (Laurendeau 1962, 22)[1]

Similarly, he decided in Paris that separatism was not the answer—a position he never abandoned. He was also repulsed by the rise of fascism and was one

---

1. "Je m'étais senti humilié en France, lorsqu'on m'interrogeait sur le Canada anglais, de mon ignorance à peu près complète sur le sujet. Le plus clair de mes maigres connaissances, je l'avais acquis au Collège de France, dans un cours d'André Siegfried. Ainsi, un jeune Canadien Français servait-il à ses interlocuteurs français des réponses que venait de lui souffler un intellectuel français, alors qu'il s'agissait de son propre pays: c'était pitoyable. Je résolus d'entrer, dès le retour, en dialogue avec le Canada anglais. Une fois revenu je constatai que dans ma propre ville, où les Anglo-Canadiens étaient pourtant plusieurs centaines de milliers, c'était difficile tant les deux groupes vivaient à l'écart l'un de l'autre: je résolus le problème en m'inscrivant en sociologie à McGill. Je pus ainsi établir des contacts avec plusieurs étudiants et professeurs."

of the few French-Canadian nationalists to oppose the Spanish dictator Francisco Franco. When he returned to Canada, he assumed the editorship of *l'Action nationale*, and became part of a discussion group with Frank Scott.

However, just as World War I had shattered the Bonne Entente group,[2] World War II had the effect of driving English-speaking and French-speaking Canadians apart. Laurendeau became deeply involved in the campaign against conscription in the referendum of 1942, and in 1944 became the leader of the Bloc Populaire and was elected a member of the legislature in Quebec City. In 1947, the Bloc decided to focus on federal politics. Laurendeau, who disagreed with this approach, feeling it would be a federal voice of the Union Nationale, left politics to become editor-in-chief of *Le Devoir*. "He was disappointed by his parliamentary experience," wrote Denis Monière. "He no longer believed in the effectiveness of political action. He no longer managed to be passionate about the role and give himself to it completely" (Monière 1983).[3]

Laurendeau was 35. He had been a passionate nationalist for 15 years. For the next 15 years, as an editorial writer, he became Maurice Duplessis' most pungent critic. He remained a nationalist, but was curious, open, and engaged with those with whom he disagreed. In the early 1940s, he had advised Pierre Trudeau to study economics—and, while he disagreed with Trudeau's attacks on nationalism in *Cité Libre*, he took them seriously and argued with them respectfully in the pages of *Le Devoir*. When René Lévesque, appointed Minister of Natural Resources in Lesage's Liberal cabinet in 1960, wanted a sounding board, it was only natural that he would include Laurendeau in the group with Marchand, Pelletier, and Trudeau.

There was a deep sensitivity to Laurendeau, a sense of nuance. He had lost his religious faith, which he kept a secret so as not to lose his connection with the Catholic community of which he was a part. He wrote a moving piece in 1964 about a small-town *marguillier* (church warden) who still went to church but, at the end of a long evening of erudite conversation, asked "Can you even begin to imagine what it's like to live in a place like this when you've lost your faith?" (Laurendeau 1964, 265). The anecdote was likely autobiographical.

---

2. In 1916, during World War I, a group of English Canadians, including W. H. Moore, Arthur Hawkes, P. F. Morley, and Lorne Pierce established a group known as the Bonne Entente, an attempt to reconcile the growing rift between Ottawa and Quebec. It resulted in a group of Ontario professionals visiting Quebec and a Quebec delegation visiting Ontario. However, it fell apart over conflicting expectations: some of the Ontario members hoped to see united support for conscription, while their Quebec counterparts wanted to see united opposition to Regulation 17, the Ontario law banning French-language instruction.

3. "Il avait été déçu par son expérience parlementaire. ... Il ne croyait plus à l'efficacité de l'action politique. Il n'arrivait plus à se passionner pour ce rôle et à se donner entièrement."

This was the man whom Maurice Lamontagne, a former Laval University economist who was a senior advisor to Lester Pearson, sought out to be the co-chair of the Royal Commission. They had crossed paths on election night, in a television studio, in April 1963, and Lamontagne said that they had to talk, "you know about what." It was a month-long courtship. Laurendeau had written an editorial citing Trudeau's attack on Pearson as the defrocked priest of peace for accepting nuclear weapons, so Laurendeau had assumed that he would be *persona non grata* in Ottawa. Later, during a lunch meeting with Liberal veteran Lionel Chevrier, Laurendeau and Pelletier learned that two names were under consideration: Vincent Massey, the former governor general, and Renaud St. Laurent, son of the former prime minister. "As for Vincent Massey, whom we all respect, I point out that his name is still associated with the inquiry into the arts, literature and sciences in Canada (1949–1951), that he's since been Governor-General, and that nothing very new could be expected from such a noble old man," Laurendeau wrote in his diary. "Mr. Chevrier seems very surprised" (Laurendeau 1991, 22).

In June, Prime Minister Pearson called him, said that he wanted him to be part of the Royal Commission since he was "in a certain way the father of the commission," and asked him to discuss it with Lamontagne. Laurendeau asked for a week to think it over—and began to consult quite widely. René Lévesque thought it was a good idea—because if Laurendeau ever had to resign, it would have a major impact. Others were skeptical. Finally, he agreed to accept the appointment after meeting with Pearson in Ottawa.

The mandate itself was food for thought and debate: it was set up to "inquire into and report on the existing state of bilingualism in Canada and to recommend what steps should be taken to develop the Canadian Confederation on the basis of an equal partnership between the two founding races, taking into account the contribution made by the other ethnic groups to the cultural enrichment of Canada and the measures that should be taken to safeguard that contribution." The mandate letter went on to refer to "the situation and practice of bilingualism within all agencies and branches of the federal government" and "the role of public and private organizations, including the mass communications media, in promoting bilingualism," and directed the commissioners "to discuss with the provincial governments the opportunities available to Canadians to learn the English and French languages and to recommend what could be done to enable Canadians to become bilingual" (RCBB 1965, Appendix 1, 151–152).

Laurendeau's co-chair was Davidson Dunton, a former chair of the Canadian Broadcasting Corporation and president of Carleton University. A calm, erudite former journalist, he was the only member of the Commission from Ottawa with connections to the senior ranks of the government.

The Commission's first assignment was to address the question of the mandate. What, exactly, did bilingualism and biculturalism mean? They quickly concluded that it did not mean that everyone in the country should learn both languages. Laurendeau and Dunton opened every public meeting with the questions: "Can English-speaking and French-speaking Canadians live together, and do they want to? Under what new conditions? And are they prepared to accept those conditions?" The public meetings were extensive, and sometimes raucous. In 1964, there were 23 public sessions, each one with a meeting during the day and another at night, across the country, in every province except Prince Edward Island. The most dramatic meeting was in Quebec City on 16 June, where 600 people came to the evening meeting. As Robert McKenzie of the *Montreal Gazette* reported, "Separatists completely took over the last informal public meeting of the Royal Commission on Bilingualism and Biculturalism here last night. For more than two hours, they drew applause and cheers—and some jeers for the members of the commission as they rose one after another to outline the arguments to favour Quebec seceding from the nation" (McKenzie 1964). Laurendeau wrote in his diary: "What struck me is that there were more than a hundred separatists in the room. ... As a result, they dominated the meeting, despite the relatively numerous anti-separatists perfectly capable of expressing themselves, of whom only three or four did— and extremely poorly" (Laurendeau 1990, 242).[4]

The commissioners were shaken. And this led to the decision to publish a *Preliminary Report* summarizing what they had heard.

> The members of the Commission feel the need to share with their fellow citizens the experience they have been through, and the lessons they have taken from it. This experience may be summarized very simply. The Commissioners, like all Canadians who read newspapers, fully expected to find themselves confronted by tensions and conflicts. They knew that there have been strains throughout the history of Confederation; and that difficulties can be expected in a country where cultures exist side by side. What the Commissioners have discovered little by little, however, is very different: they have been driven to the conclusion that Canada, without being fully conscious of the fact, is passing through the greatest crisis in its history. (RCBB 1965, 13)

---

4. "Ce qui m'a frappé, c'est qu'il y avait au plus une centaine de séparatistes dans la salle. ... Or, ils ont dominé l'assemblée, malgré la présence relativement nombreuse d'anti-séparatistes parfaitement capables de s'exprimer, et dont trois ou quatre seulement ont pris la parole, d'ailleurs fort mal."

That phrase became the best-known of the report, indeed, perhaps of the Royal Commission. The reaction: Quebec commentators thought it was self-evident; a number of comments in English suggested that it was too sympathetic to Quebec and French-Canadians.

Bi and Bi: The Aftermath

The commissioners agreed easily enough on what they had seen and heard; the challenge was to reach a consensus on what they should recommend. The Commission itself became vulnerable after the Liberals failed to win a majority in 1965. In November, the minutes of the Commission record the opening of the meeting on 15 November 1965:

> Mr. Dunton began the discussion by suggesting that events will not be as favourable to the Commission as before. The election results have shown that too much was done for Quebec. The Commission will be more in danger of Opposition attacks because it is a nice way of getting at Quebec, and, likely, the Government's defence of the Commission at this time will be even less vigorous. He advised the Commission to be ready for the real possibility of nasty things in the House, the submission of estimates being a case in point. (Lapointe-Gagnon 2018, 215)

The result was a growing sense of unease on the Commission, and a feeling of pressure to produce reports.

In 1967, they did. The first report began with André Laurendeau's "blue pages." He began by addressing the term in the mandate of "two founding races," which had caused the commissioners some problems at the public meetings. He acknowledged that this had been a source of misunderstanding, and that some people "pictured a kind of hereditary aristocracy composed of two founding peoples, perpetuating itself from father to son, and a lower order of other ethnic groups, forever excluded from spheres of influence." This was not the way in which they understood their terms of reference, which they saw as referring to language and culture rather than race (RCBB 1967, 1:xxii).

There was a missing piece in this puzzle, and Laurendeau admitted it, right near the beginning. The terms of reference made no allusion to Indigenous peoples.

> 22. The integration of the native populations into Canadian society raises very complex problems. The process of integration calls into question the very nature of the traditions and customs of native society. The Commission realizes that it was not the Government's intention—and the terms of

reference are a proof of this—to have the Commission undertake long studies on the rightful status of the Indians and the Eskimos within the Canadian Confederation; other bodies, whether official or private in nature—and most of the private organizations are financially assisted by the Department of Indian Affairs and Northern Development—have been entrusted with the research required for the making of government policy.

23. However, the Commission considers it a duty to remind the proper authorities that everything possible must be done to help the native populations preserve their cultural heritage, which is an essential part of the patrimony of all Canadians. The Commission also feels that the Canadian government, in close co-operation with the provinces concerned, should take the necessary steps to assist the survival of the Eskimo language and the most common Indian dialects. (RCBB 1967, 1:xxvi–xxvii)

And that was it, as far as Indigenous peoples were concerned. It is worth noting that the federal government has only now, more than 50 years later, tabled Bill C-91, *An Act respecting Indigenous Languages*. It is a response to recommendations outlined in the *Final Report* of the Truth and Reconciliation Commission.

Laurendeau went on to discuss what he called "the strong bond between a language and a culture."

Language is the most evident expression of a culture the one which most readily distinguishes cultural groups even for the most superficial observer. … (C)ulture is a way of being, thinking, and feeling. It is a driving force animating a significant group of individuals united by a common tongue, and sharing the same customs, habits, and experiences. Clearly, the two cultures designated in our terms of reference are those associated with the English and French languages in Canada. But as there are two dominant languages, there are two principal cultures, and their influence extends, in varying degrees, to the whole country. (RCBB 1967, 1:xxx–xxxi)

Laurendeau described what the Commission had recognized as "the main elements of a distinct society in Quebec" adding "On the French side there is not only the distinct society in Quebec; elements of an autonomous society are taking shape elsewhere" (RCBB 1967, 1:xxxiii). The phrase "distinct society" would emerge as a point of disagreement and discord during the discussions of the Meech Lake Accord, two decades later. In addressing the issue of "the equal partnership between the two founding races" ("Le principe d'égalité entre les deux peuples"), Laurendeau wrote that this equality

... should be the equal partnership not only of the two peoples who founded Confederation, but also of each of their respective languages and cultures. What we are aiming for, then is the equal partnership of all who speak either language and participate in either country, whatever their ethnic origin. For us the principle of equal partnership takes priority over all historical and legal considerations, regardless of how interesting and important such considerations may be. (RCBB 1967, 1:xxxix)

There was pragmatism in Laurendeau's collective view of language rights: "A milieu is not transformed for one individual; a university is not built for a single family. But," he went on to say, "languages and cultures are essentially collective phenomena" (RCBB 1967, 1:xliii).

And, in discussing the political dimension, he raised the issue of self-determination: "the power of decision of each group to act, not only in its cultural life but in all aspects of its collective life." Laurendeau made the point that historian Valérie Lapointe-Gagnon underlines in her book *Panser le Canada*: "the principle of equality requires that the minority receive generous treatment." He asked, "How can we integrate the new Quebec into present-day Canada, without curbing Quebec's forward drive and, at the same time, without risking the breaking up of the country?" He added: "All of these facts combine to give Quebec a leading role in promoting the French language and culture in Canada, whatever may be the political solution finally adopted" (RCBB 1967, 1:xlvi–xlvii).

That introduction was printed on blue pages, widely known as "les *Pages Bleues*," and has also been called Laurendeau's last will and testament. In the body of the *Report*—the first of four—the commissioners looked at international examples, such as South Africa, Switzerland, Belgium, and Finland: models of individual bilingualism, territorial bilingualism, and a compromise model between the two. The key to success, the report argued, was collaboration. "To guarantee survival and equality for the minority language may thus become one of the duties of the majority," they wrote, saying this required acceptance, quality assurance, and a certain amount of linguistic self-determination. "All this is basically a question of attitudes and understanding on the part of the majority. But the minority also has certain duties, mainly to participate in the national or federal government of the country and to agree to work with the majority group" (RCBB 1967, 1:14).

In the recommendations, the Commissioners called for the formal declaration that English and French are official languages, that New Brunswick and Ontario recognize English and French as official languages, that bilingual districts be created where the minority represented 10 percent of the population, that the federal capital be fully bilingual, that Canadian parents have the right to have their children educated in the official language of their choice, and that the position of Commissioner of Official Languages be created as "the active conscience—actually the protector—of the Canadian public where the official languages are concerned" (RCBB 1967, 1:340).

Throughout the first volume of the *Report*, it is possible to see some of the strains of Laurendeau's sensibility and some of the threads of Scott's viewpoint. Laurendeau wanted Quebec's French-speaking characteristics as a distinct society to be protected and those protections to be extended to French-language minority communities across Canada. Scott argued that constitutionally, historically, politically, and socially, Quebec was a bilingual society—and that bilingualism should be extended across Canada. They both felt they had lost: Laurendeau because there was no recommendation for greater constitutional powers for Quebec, and Scott because of the creeping acceptance—most explicitly in Book III: The Work World—of Quebec as a unilingual French-speaking society.

Popular reaction to Volume 1 was quite different from the reaction to the *Preliminary Report* in 1965. The *Globe and Mail* had called the *Preliminary Report* "unduly alarmist," but now conceded that "Perhaps the B and B Commission was right." Douglas Fisher and Harry Crowe, a former MP and an academic who jointly wrote a syndicated column, were more direct. "No-one can now say, as was common stuff at the time, that the B and B Commission overstated the dimensions of the emerging crisis in its much-criticized preliminary report. The Commission was right. The rest of us were wrong" (as quoted in G. Fraser 2006, 72).

A lot had happened in those two years. The Front de libération du Québec (FLQ) had continued to be active. Jean Lesage's Liberals were defeated in 1966. General Charles de Gaulle had attracted world-wide attention by proclaiming "Vive le Québec libre!" during his visit to Montreal in the summer of 1967. René Lévesque left the Liberal Party in the fall of 1967 to found the Mouvement Souveraineté-Association, precursor to the Parti Québécois. As a result, the reaction was quite different. As the *Prince Albert Herald* noted, "What was hypothetical nonsense four years ago is reality today. The separatist movement is for real; French Canada's aspirations within Confederation are for real; de Gaulle's plea for a sovereign Quebec is for real" (as quoted in G. Fraser 2006, 72).

At the same time, there were concerns that requiring public institutions to provide services in both languages would require employees able to speak both languages. It is worth remembering how dominant English was in the federal government in 1968, and how subordinate French was. As historian John English points out, "No English Canadian Prime Minister could speak French, including its greatest diplomat, Lester Pearson. External Affairs and

Defence were not bilingual departments. And nearly all French Canadians felt excluded from their inner ranks." Only 8 percent of Canadian public servants were francophones during the years of Louis St. Laurent's government (1948–1957), a time when 26 percent of the Canadian population was francophone. "Today," English wrote in 2011, "27% of Canadian soldiers are francophones, and all above the rank of Lieutenant-Colonel speak French. The Foreign Affairs department has a similar French presence. Our external face now reflects what we are—principally because of Pierre Trudeau" (English 2011). On 25 June 1968, Trudeau won the election, and one of his first acts was to name Gérard Pelletier, the former editor of *La Presse* with whom he had entered politics three years earlier, as secretary of state. Pelletier's first assignment was to supervise the draughting and the tabling of the *Official Languages Act* (1969). "No government in Canada had yet legislated on language, if it was not to restrict the use of French," Pelletier wrote in his memoirs. "So, for the first time, in the summer of 1968, a government prepared to legislate positively on the whole question" (Pelletier 1992, 62).

St-Léonard and the Gendron Commission: Language Rumblings in Quebec

In 1968, a language crisis erupted in St-Léonard, a suburb in northeast Montreal. In June, in the absence of a Quebec policy, the school board decided that French would be the only language of instruction. But in September, the Aimé-Renaud School was prepared to receive students from the Italian community and teach them in English. French-speaking students barricaded themselves in the school, vowing to stay until the government stopped the transfer of schools from French to English (Godin 1980, 366). The Italian community responded strongly, and there were violent demonstrations (Bouthillier and Meynaud 1972, 728).

Premier Daniel Johnson was furious. "School Commissioners in St-Léonard aren't going to tell me what to do," he told his Union Nationale caucus. He was convinced that it was not yet time to act. His caucus was largely indifferent to the issue, but pressure was increasing from nationalists. François-Albert Angers, the president of the Ligue d'action nationale, sent him a telegram urging him to take a strong position:

QUÉBEC DOIT DEVENIR UN ÉTAT FRANÇAIS DANS LE PLEIN RESPECT DES DROITS, DES PRIVILÈGES MINORITAIRES LÉGITIMES STOP TOUT COMPROMIS VERS BILINGUISME OFFICIEL POUR LE QUÉBEC EST DANGER DE MORT. (quoted in Godin 1980, 370)

But on 26 September 1968, Johnson died of a heart attack. His successor, Jean-Jacques Bertrand, responded to the language crisis with two initiatives: First, in December 1968, he created the Commission of Inquiry on the Position of the French Language and on Language Rights in Quebec—to be chaired by Jean-Denis Gendron and known as the Gendron Commission. Second, he introduced legislation establishing the rights of parents to choose the language of education for their children. As Kenneth McRoberts puts it, "The opposition among various Francophone groups was so intense that Bertrand temporarily yielded and the bill was shelved. (The surprise of Bertrand and other Union nationale leaders over the strength of the opposition betrayed their insensitivity to the character of linguistic conflict in Quebec)" (McRoberts 1988, 216). Then, in October 1969, Bertrand introduced Bill 63. It was framed as a bill to promote the teaching of the French language, but in fact it reversed the decision of the St-Léonard school commissioners and gave parents freedom of choice while stating that the program of study approved by the Minister of Education should ensure that students receiving an education in English would learn French.

The legislation, which provoked massive nationalist demonstrations in Montreal and Quebec City, was passed with the support of the Liberals, but opposed by René Lévesque; two Union Nationale members, Jérôme Proulx and Antonio Flamand; and Liberal Yves Michaud. All four later became members of the Parti Québécois. The legislation contributed to the defeat of the Union Nationale and the election of Robert Bourassa's Liberals in 1970.

The Gendron Commission reported in 1972, four years after it was appointed. The Commission consisted of Jean-Denis Gendron, Madeleine Doyon-Ferland, Edward McWhinney, Nicolas Matteo Matte, and Aimé Gagné. McWhinney was an interesting choice; he was a law professor but originally from Australia. Frank Scott wrote, "Neither the English business community nor the Quebec trade unions are represented, and the only anglophone, though a distinguished professor, was not a native Canadian and had lived only two years in Quebec when appointed. Whatever recommendations of the Gendron Commission may be, there will inevitably arise questions as to the authority with which it speaks" (Scott 1977, 388).

Certainly, Scott had questions. He had already dissented from the Royal Commission on Bilingualism and Biculturalism in its recommendations on language of work. The Commission had recommended as an objective that French must be "the principal language of work at all levels" in Quebec, in the private sector as well as the public sector. "I was obliged to differ with my colleagues on the Commission on this wording, not because I was opposed to the idea that French must become the principal language of work in Quebec, for I believe that to be the case, but because in the formulation of its recommendation the Commission did not, it seemed to me, sufficiently distinguish between the types of business to which this principle would apply," Scott said. "Business activities today are carried on in so many different kinds of institutions, with so many varieties of external and internal relationships, that it is impossible to impose a uniform rule on everyone" (Scott 1977, 386).

The Royal Commission did reveal that unilingual anglophones had higher incomes than bilingual francophones—a piece of information that, when leaked, added fuel to the fires of the nationalist cause in Quebec. But the recommendations of the Royal Commission were mild compared to those of the Gendron Commission. The Commission made 92 recommendations, beginning with the following:

> 1. We recommend that the Quebec Government set itself the general goal of making French the common language of Quebecers, that is, a language known by everyone which can thus serve as an instrument of communication in contact situations between French-speaking people and Quebecers of other language groups.
> 2. We recommend that—while maintaining section 133 of the B.N.A. Act—the Quebec Government pass a general law proclaiming French the official language of Quebec, and French and English the national languages of Quebec, and that English be maintained as the language of instruction in English protestant and English catholic schools and as one of the two languages of communication between individuals and government.
> 3. We recommend that the Quebec Government take the necessary steps to make French the language of internal communication in the Quebec work milieu.
> 4. We recommend that the Quebec Government move in stages to establish French as the internal language of communication within work milieus by negotiating each stage of the change with the business establishments. (Gendron Commission 1972, 291)

On it went for another 88 recommendations: a working knowledge of French would be required for admission to a trade or profession (recommendation 22); consumers' right to be served in French was established (recommendation 49); every private organization in Quebec would be required to use "either its French name or both its name and the French version of its name (recommendation 58); the use of French would be obligatory on all posters and signs in the public and parapublic sectors, and that no other language would take precedence over French (recommendation 73). The Bourassa government's response was Bill 22, which was tabled in 1974.

Conclusion

Events in 1968 marked a fork in the road in language policy. Laurendeau's death and Trudeau's election marked the beginning of the end of a constitutional special status for Quebec, although the argument would play out over the following decades. The *Official Languages Act* (1969) began the process of transforming the federal public service so that it would meet the requirements of institutional bilingualism and provide federal services to Canadians in the official language of their choice. However, institutional bilingualism did not result in widespread personal bilingualism.

But the language crisis in St-Léonard, and the Gendron Commission that was created in response, led Quebec in a different direction: toward institutional unilingualism in Quebec, and greater personal bilingualism. The political dynamic of language policy proved explosive; the Union Nationale language legislation in 1969 led to its defeat in 1970 just as the Liberals' language legislation in 1974 contributed to its defeat by the Parti Québécois in 1976.

The language criteria for admission to English school in Quebec—the language in which one parent was educated—developed for Bill 101 became the model used in the Charter of Rights and Freedoms. The language rights developed in the *Official Languages Act* became enshrined in the Charter. The tensions between André Laurendeau and F. R. Scott that marked the Royal Commission on Bilingualism and Biculturalism, and ended with Laurendeau's death in 1968, have echoed and re-echoed over the last five decades.

The year 1968 is also remembered, as the Introduction to this volume points out, for Mai 68, the student insurrection in Paris (also referred to by Litt in Chapter 1 of this volume as the "Paris Spring"). "In Canada, nothing so momentous unfolded," notes Bryan D. Palmer in his book on the 1960s in Canada. However, he added, "If we were to look for a locale of May '68 upheavals ... it would most certainly be Montreal." He quotes Charles Gagnon's call to arms from a jail cell in New York: "The people of Quebec are angry. ... All they need is the spark to start the fire. And that is precisely our role as the revolutionary vanguard—to set off that spark. We must start fires everywhere ... speak fiery words, do fiery deeds and repeat them over and over" (quoted in Palmer 2009, 348).

In retrospect, it becomes clear how the events of 1968—the election of Pierre Trudeau; the tabling of the *Official Languages Act*; the crisis in St-Léonard; the creation of the Parti Québécois; and the selection of its founder, René Lévesque, as its first leader—set the stage for the next half-century of political and constitutional debate in Canada. Those tensions, which have ebbed and flowed over the years, occasionally surge to the surface, as they did on 15 November 2018, when 14,000 Ontario residents demonstrated to protest the decision of the Ford government to abolish the position of French Language

Services Commissioner and shelve the plans for a French-language university. While the future of the country does not seem in jeopardy, as it did during some of the previous crises, the language question has not lost any of its potency or relevance to Canada's identity.

References

Bouthillier, Guy, and Jean Meynaud. 1972. *Le Choc des langues au Québec, 1760–1970.* Montréal: Les Presses de l'Université du Québec.

English, John. 2011. "Pierre Trudeau Saved Canada." *National Post*, 11 March. https://nationalpost.com/full-comment/john-english-pierre-trudeau-saved-canada. Accessed 28 November 2020.

Fraser, Blair. 1968. "René Lévesque, Separatist Moderate," *Maclean's*, July. Reprinted in *Blair Fraser Reports: Selections 1944–1968*, edited by John Fraser and Graham Fraser, 134–139. Toronto: Macmillan of Canada, 1969.

Fraser, Graham. 2006. *Sorry, I Don't Speak French*. Toronto: McClelland & Stewart.

Gendron Commission. 1972. *The Position of the French Language in Quebec*, Report of the Commission of Inquiry on the Position of the French Language and on Language Rights in Quebec. Vol. 1, Language of Work. Quebec: December.

Godin, Pierre. 1980. *Daniel Johnson Vol. II. 1963–1968*. Montréal: Les Éditions de L'Homme.

Lapointe-Gagnon, Valérie. 2018. *Panser le Canada : une histoire intellectuelle de la commission Laurendeau-Dunton*. Montréal: Boréal.

Laurendeau, André. 1991. *The Diary of André Laurendeau*, translated by Patricia Smart and Dorothy Howard. Toronto: James Lorimer and Company.

———. 1990. *Journal tenus pendant la Commission royale d'enquête sur le bilinguisme et le biculturalisme*. Montréal: VLB éditeur/Septentrion.

———. 1964. "The Churchwarden," *Maclean's*, May–June. Reprinted in *André Laurendeau: Witness for Quebec. Essays Selected and Translated by Philip Stratford*, 263–270. Toronto: Macmillan of Canada, 1973.

———. 1963. "Why Keep Reminding Us That He's a Jew?" *Maclean's*, February. Reprinted in *André Laurendeau: Witness for Quebec. Essays Selected and Translated by Philip Stratford*, 275–278. Toronto: Macmillan of Canada, 1973.

———. 1962. *La Crise de la conscription, 1942*. Montréal: Les Éditions du Jour.

Lévesque, René. 1986. *Memoirs*. Translated by Philip Stratford. Toronto: McClelland & Stewart.

———. 1968. *An Option for Quebec*. Toronto: McClelland & Stewart.

McKenzie, Robert. 1964. "Separatists Pack Quebec B-B Session." *Montreal Gazette*, 17 June: 4.

McRoberts, Kenneth. 1988. *Quebec: Social Change and Political Crisis*, 3rd ed. Toronto: McClelland & Stewart.

Monière, Denis. 1983. *André Laurendeau*. Montréal: Québec-Amérique.

Palmer, Bryan D. 2009. *Canada's 1960s: The Ironies of Identity in a Rebellious Era*. Toronto: University of Toronto Press.

Pelletier, Gérard. 1992. *L'Aventure du pouvoir, 1968–1975*. Montréal: Stanké.

RCBB (Royal Commission on Bilingualism and Biculturalism). 1967. *Report of the Royal Commission on Bilingualism and Biculturalism, Vol, 1.* 1967. Ottawa: Queen's Printer.

————. 1965. *A Preliminary Report of the Royal Commission on Bilingualism and Biculturalism.* Ottawa: Queen's Printer.

Scott, F. R. 1977. *Essays on the Constitution: Aspects of Canadian Law and Politics.* Toronto: University of Toronto Press.

Chapter 12
Standing on Guard for Our Waters: Ottawa's Response to the Transit of Alaskan Oil[1]

CHRISTOPHER KIRKEY

Abstract

The discovery of massive quantities of recoverable oil on the north slope of Alaska in July 1968 and competing shipping alternatives to transit the hydrocarbons south, through or adjacent to Canadian waters, prompted the government of Pierre Trudeau to pursue two strategies. Concerning the waters of the Canadian Arctic Archipelago, in 1969 Ottawa moved to monitor and challenge the maritime passage of the SS *Manhattan*, crafted progressive legislative initiatives in the form of the *1970 Arctic Waters Pollution Prevention Act* and amendments to the Territorial Sea and Fishing Zone Boundaries, and informed the International Court of Justice (ICJ) that it would reserve the right to accept the compulsory jurisdiction of the court, all in an effort to exert jurisdictional and regulatory control over Canada's northern waters. By 1971, when American oil industrialists' plans for transiting Alaskan crude through the Northwest Passage were abandoned (due to economic, technological, and climate concerns), they moved, with the full support of the administration of Richard Nixon, to pursue the option of a trans–Alaska pipeline system (TAPS). In light of this development, Ottawa actively promoted, from 1971 to 1973, an alternate *overland* route for the transportation of Prudhoe Bay oil, a southward corridor through Canada's Mackenzie Valley. This chapter examines these specific efforts by Ottawa to dissuade interested oil companies and the United States from embracing what the Trudeau government regarded as a profound ecological, economic, and human threat to Canadian waters.

---

1. Select sections included in this chapter previously appeared in Kirkey (1996) and Kirkey (1997). The author acknowledges and extends his gratitude to the Association for Canadian Studies in the United States and the International Council of Canadian Studies for permission to use this material.

Figure 12.1. Oil tanker in Prince William Sound. *Source:* Patrick Endres, AlaskaPhotoGraphics.

On 18 July 1968, Robert Anderson, chair of the Atlantic Richfield Company, announced that "one of the largest petroleum accumulations known to the world today" had been discovered on the north slope of Alaska (*New York Times* 1968; *Wall Street Journal* 1968b). According to Anderson, the Prudhoe Bay location would contain an estimated five to ten billion barrels of oil and soon undergo "commercial development," with "pipeline and transportation studies … begin[ning] immediately" (*World Oil* 1969). Within two weeks, Atlantic Richfield and Humble Oil and Refining Company had awarded a contract to Houston's Pipeline Technologies, Inc., "to study the feasibility of transporting … recently discovered Arctic oil to market by a pipeline to a port in southern Alaska" (*Wall Street Journal* 1968a).[2] By mid-February 1969, Atlantic Richfield, Humble, and British Petroleum jointly declared that they intended to proceed with the construction of a $900 million pipeline that would "run about 800 miles in a generally southern direction from the Prudhoe Bay area on the Arctic Ocean across Alaska's Brooks [mountain] Range to the Gulf of Alaska on the state's southern coastline."[3] The oil would then be transported

2. Humble, a subsidiary of Standard Oil, was Atlantic Richfield's partner in the exploration for and development of Prudhoe Bay hydrocarbons.
3. British Petroleum's participation in the planned building of the trans-Alaska pipeline system stemmed from the fact that it was involved in "drilling two wells close to one of the Atlantic-Humble discovery wells" and, therefore, anticipated discovering a major cache of recoverable oil—which would have to be transported to

by tanker to select refinery and distribution sites along the U.S. and Canadian Pacific coast.[4] The trio of oil corporations, while strongly indicating a preference for a trans-Alaska pipeline/tanker transportation scheme, nonetheless noted that "planning studies on alternate routes are continuing" (*Wall Street Journal* 1969; Cole 1969).[5]

One of these routes was announced in December 1968, when Atlantic Richfield, in conjunction with British Petroleum and the Standard Oil Company, declared its intention to determine the feasibility of using tankers to transport Prudhoe Bay oil through the waters of the Canadian Arctic archipelago to U.S. East Coast refineries.[6] The practicality of this option would be tested by sending a reinforced vessel, the SS *Manhattan*, through the Northwest Passage in June 1969. "If successful," the petroleum companies noted, "the test could result in the establishment of a new commercial shipping route through the Arctic region with broad implications for future Arctic development and international trade" (*Wall Street Journal* 1968c). A short time after that, the United States Coast Guard formally informed Canadian officials that one of its icebreakers, the USCGC *Northwind*, would be joining the *Manhattan* for the duration of its voyage.

The discovery of massive quantities of recoverable Alaskan oil and competing shipping alternatives to transit the hydrocarbons south, through or adjacent to Canadian waters, prompted the government of Pierre Trudeau to pursue two strategies successively. Concerning the waters of the Canadian Arctic archipelago, in 1969 Ottawa moved to monitor and challenge the maritime passage of the *Manhattan*, crafted progressive legislative initiatives, in the form

market. In short, the logic of sharing the financial costs of constructing an Alaskan pipeline, as opposed to independently delivering the oil to market, prevailed (*Wall Street Journal* 1969).

4. Although the port in southern Alaska was not specified at the time, it would later be identified as Valdez.

5. These alternatives would ultimately emerge to include an overland pipeline through Canada, reinforced oil tanker transits through the waters of the Canadian Arctic archipelago, a rail line from Alaska to the Northwest Territories, and, in perhaps the boldest proposals of all, the use of jumbo aircraft and nuclear-powered submarines. Atlantic Richfield, Humble, and BP (later to be joined by Mobil, Phillips, Jersey Standard, Amerada Hess, Union Oil, and Home Oil), under the corporate umbrella title Alyeska, filed right-of-way applications for the construction of the trans-Alaska pipeline with the U.S. Department of the Interior on 10 June 1969 (*Wall Street Journal* 1970).

6. The attractiveness of this option is explained by William Westermeyer: "Opening the Northwest Passage would enable oil companies to ship Prudhoe Bay oil directly to the East Coast of the United States avoiding the 780-mile crossing of Alaska by pipeline and the long southern journey through the Panama Canal" (Westermeyer 1984, 112).

of the 1970 *Arctic Waters Pollution Prevention Act* and amendments to the Territorial Sea and Fishing Zone Boundaries, and informed the International Court of Justice (ICJ) that it would reserve the right to accept the compulsory jurisdiction of the court to exert jurisdictional and regulatory control over Canada's northern waters. By 1971, when American oil industrialists' plans for transiting Alaskan oil through the Northwest Passage were abandoned (due to economic, technological, and climate concerns), they moved, with the support of the administration of Richard Nixon, to pursue the option of a trans-Alaska pipeline system (TAPS). In light of this development, Ottawa actively promoted, from 1971 to 1973, an alternate *overland* route for the transportation of Prudhoe Bay oil, a southward corridor through Canada's Mackenzie Valley. This chapter examines these specific efforts by Ottawa to dissuade interested oil companies and the United States from embracing what the Trudeau government regarded as a profound ecological, economic, and human threat to Canadian waters.

The Waters of the Canadian Arctic Archipelago

The prospect of the *Manhattan* and a U.S. Coast Guard icebreaker transiting through the disputed waters of the Canadian Arctic archipelago—particularly the Northwest Passage—was especially disconcerting to officials in Ottawa. In addition to raising complex questions about northern development, commercial shipping, and environmental regulation, the proposed voyage of the *Manhattan* and U.S.-commissioned *Northwind* dramatically underscored America's continued unwillingness to accept Canada's legal position on the status of the northern waters. The position of the United States, by contrast, was that all maritime waters beyond the three-mile territorial sea limit constituted "international waters"—including ice-bound Arctic waters such as the Northwest Passage—and therefore permission of coastal states to transit such "border waters" was not necessary. Canada, on the other hand, held the legal position that the entirety of the ice-laden waters of the Canadian Arctic archipelago, and in particular the Northwest Passage, were not international in character but rather sovereign Canadian waters.[7] By not requesting Ottawa's permission for the planned 1969 nautical transit, American authorities were implicitly challenging the validity of Canada's claim. The principal issue confronting Canadian officials was how best to protect the waters of the Canadian Arctic archipelago while simultaneously asserting national sovereignty in the North, in both the short and long term.

---

7. Several studies, in the immediate aftermath of the SS *Manhattan* passage, sought to comment on the respective Canadian and American jurisdictional claims and associated international legal principles. See, for example, Green (1970); Reinhard (1970); Konan (1970); Bilder (1970); Milsten (1972); Dellapenna (1972); and O'Brien and Chapelli (1973).

Canadian authorities decided to address the proposed voyage of the *Manhattan* and the *Northwind* pragmatically. Convinced that U.S. Coast Guard authorities would not seek Canadian permission for the upcoming transit, Ottawa moved to affirm de facto sovereignty over the waters of the Canadian Arctic archipelago by instituting two key measures purposely designed to simultaneously promote Canadian cooperative goodwill and foster Canada–U.S. northern maritime cooperation.[8] These measures, adopted at the December 1968 meeting of the Advisory Committee on Northern Development, called for the Canadian Coast Guard icebreaker CCGS *John A. Macdonald* to accompany the *Manhattan* on its voyage and made a formal proposal to U.S. authorities that icebreakers from both countries escort the *Manhattan* in northern Canadian and American waters (Dosman 1976, 39–40; Kirton and Munton 1987, 72). "Such joint arrangements involving the oil companies and the two governments," Edgar Dosman notes, "would make it difficult for the U.S. to refuse cooperation and might avoid a confrontation" (Dosman 1976, 40). These Canadian initiatives were subsequently agreed to by the sponsors of the Manhattan experiment and the U.S. government.

Apart from these actions related to the transit of the *Manhattan* and the *Northwind*, the Canadian government, in the spring of 1969, took further interim steps to bolster its sovereignty claim over the northern waters. The Governor General, it was announced on 27 March, would conduct an extensive 12-day tour of the Arctic. On 3 April, the newly revised responsibilities of Canada's Armed Forces were issued. The priority, according to a statement released by the Prime Minister's Office, would not be NATO or NORAD collective responsibilities, but would focus on "the surveillance of our own territory and coast lines, i.e., the protection of our sovereignty" (Canada, PMO 1969, 3). The most decisive expression of Canada's sovereign claims over the waters of the Canadian Arctic archipelago came on 15 May 1969 in a speech delivered by the Prime Minister before the House of Commons. In the course of reasserting Canadian maritime jurisdiction in the region, Trudeau moved to dispel concerns that the voyage of the American-sponsored *Manhattan* was a fundamental challenge to Canada's position on the northern waters. "I should point out," he claimed before Parliament,

> that the legal status of the waters of Canada's Arctic archipelago is not at issue in the proposed transit of the Northwest Passage by the ships involved in the *Manhattan* project. ... [T]he trials of the *Manhattan* may be of considerable significance for the development of Arctic navigation. Such development is consistent with both Canadian and international interests,

8. An early, informal suggestion by External Affairs representatives to State Department officials that the U.S. Coast Guard request Canadian permission received no reply.

and I do not see any conflict between Canada's national policy and international responsibilities in this connection. … [T]he Canadian government has welcomed the *Manhattan* exercise, has concurred in it and will participate in it. (Canada 1969, 8720–8721)

Satisfied that adequate short-term measures had been initiated in the wake of the upcoming *Manhattan/Northwind* transit, Canadian officials turned their attention to formulating legislative policy and exercising diplomatic options that would unambiguously assert Canada's national interests over the waters of the northern Arctic archipelago. In essence, Ottawa wanted to adopt an indirect approach that would implicitly reinforce Canada's territorial maritime claims over the waters of the Canadian Arctic archipelago while simultaneously addressing new concerns arising from increased levels of northern development—particularly environmental regulation.[9] Gordon Robertson, then Clerk of the Privy Council Office and Secretary to the Cabinet, explained:

> The ultimate objective was to establish and get international recognition for Canadian sovereignty over the waters of the Canadian Arctic archipelago. That was the overall objective. … There was also a legitimate concern about the consequences of oil spills or even just pollution from ships operating [in the area] and we did want to have some means for controlling those possibilities, but we also recognized that if we did something of that kind and if it was legitimate and if we carried out jurisdiction in a respectable and responsible way, that would over a period strengthen the claim that there was effective Canadian administration of these waters and therefore provide a better basis for an overall claim for sovereignty at some appropriate time. (Robertson 1991)

Canada's decision to fulfill its national interests by a combination of legislative and diplomatic means reflected Ottawa's desire to preserve the norm of Canadian–American cooperation. The Trudeau government could unilaterally act to meet sovereignty and pollution concerns regarding the waters of the Canadian Arctic archipelago, so long, Canadian authorities believed, as their chosen method would not jeopardize cooperative ties with the United States by inviting retaliation. "What we were anxious not to get ourselves caught up in," Ivan Head, special legislative assistant to the prime minister, acknowledged, "was a straightforward territorial struggle with the United States. … We wanted

---

9. The perceived need for environmental protection of northern waters was further reinforced by the disastrous 1967 *Torrey Canyon* oil spill, which caused widespread pollution of the United Kingdom coastline.

to act in a way that would protect our interests without upsetting our otherwise cooperative relationship with Washington" (Head 1991).

In early June 1969, the Department of External Affairs forwarded a diplomatic note to the U.S. Embassy in Ottawa formally outlining the position of the Canadian government on the issue of the Arctic waters. Taking its cue from the Prime Minister's statement of 15 May, the note underscored Canada's interpretation that the waters of the Canadian Arctic archipelago were territorial, and "that the status of Canadian jurisdiction over the waters of the Arctic Archipelago was not affected by the *Manhattan* project" (Dosman 1975, 53). This view was not received well at the Department of State. In reply to the Canadian note, American authorities rejected outright Canada's sovereign claim to the northern waters, insisting that Ottawa's jurisdiction was limited to the three-mile territorial sea limit. The waters of the Canadian Arctic archipelago were international, and "the United States would consider any unilateral extension of maritime jurisdiction as prejudicial to its interest" (Dosman 1975, 54).

These respective national positions were discussed at a Canada–U.S. ministerial gathering in late June. In addition to restating their position, Canadian officials informed their American counterparts that, if necessary, they were prepared to act alone, through the introduction of appropriate legislation, to reinforce Canada's northern maritime claim. American officials advised the Canadian delegation that it strongly preferred the idea of assembling a multilateral conference of shipping and coastal states to develop an international regime that might detail various rights and responsibilities for the use and environmental protection of northern waters beyond the three-mile limit. Canadian officials' response to the proposal was to take it under advisement. At the further suggestion of U.S. representatives, Canada agreed to hold bilateral talks before initiating any independent legislative action (Crane 1969; Cowan 1969).[10]

The first public indication that the Trudeau government was preparing to act unilaterally to strengthen its claim over the waters of the Canadian Arctic archipelago came on 18 September 1969. In an article published in the *Globe and Mail*, Secretary of State for External Affairs Mitchell Sharp indicated that the Canadian government was actively considering the introduction of legislative measures that would be consistent with existing international law and acceptable to the international community (Sharp 1969).[11] The first option,

---

10. The voyage of the SS *Manhattan* began on 24 August 1969. The reinforced tanker made its rendezvous with the icebreakers USCGC *Northwind* and CCGS *John A. Macdonald* off Frobisher Island and eventually completed passage of the northern waters on 14 September 1969. For further details of the transit, see Smith (1970); Keating (1970); and Storrs and Pullen (1970).

11. The government's aversion to a unilateral declaration of sovereignty over the northern waters was restated on 26 September by the Prime Minister. "We're not going to stand up and say flatly it [the Northwest Passage] is ours. We'd have to

one that the Trudeau government would eventually exercise, was highlighted three weeks later in a 6 October speech given by Jean Chrétien, the Minister of Indian Affairs and Northern Development. According to Chrétien, increasing pressures for expanded development in the North made it imperative that Canada act as quickly as possible to regulate the use and quality of Canadian Arctic waters.

> As yet, the waters of the North are relatively free of pollution. This situation is not likely to continue unless *a comprehensive water management program based on effective water rights and pollution control legislation is introduced in the near future.* … *Clearly we must start now to control pollution in the Arctic. Minimum standards of water quality must be established at this time. We cannot afford to wait.* (Chrétien 1969, 9; italics added)

This message—that Canada would unilaterally propose maritime environmental legislation—was given official sanction in the 23 October Speech from the Throne. It declared that "the Government will introduce legislation setting out the measures necessary to prevent pollution in the Arctic seas" (*Globe and Mail* 1969; Walz 1969). The statement further indicated that the government "is also considering other methods of protecting Canada's ocean coasts" (*Globe and Mail* 1969). In his discussion of this proposed legislative plan in the House of Commons, Prime Minister Trudeau repeatedly insisted that such an approach represented a progressive, responsible initiative by Ottawa in the face of a growing threat to northern maritime waters. Canada would be acting as the "steward" of these waters for the international community, and the proposed policy would "include standards for shipping on the waters of the archipelago, both in respect to the kinds of ships that can operate and the types of cargo they can carry" (Burns 1969b). The Prime Minister also pledged to solicit the support of the international community for an "international legal regime to safeguard the waters of the Canadian Arctic archipelago" (Canada 1969, 39).

Increasingly concerned that Ottawa would introduce pollution prevention legislation, the United States sent an aide-mémoire to the Canadian government on 6 November 1969. The diplomatic memorandum stressed four points. First, the U.S. commended the Prime Minister's suggestion that an international regime be established for the regulation of northern waters. The note specifically emphasized the American desire to convene an international conference of northern coastal states for this purpose. In keeping with this proposal, the

---

shoot at the *Manhattan* to back up the claim, and start a war with the world. There's no point in saying, it's ours, if people are going to say, 'It's not yours, and we're not going to fly your flag.' What are you going to do if they take that position? Shoot at them?" (Burns 1969a).

second part strongly objected to Canada's announcement of unilateral action on this issue. Such legislation would create a distasteful precedent by placing national territorial agendas above the common interests of the international community. Developing appropriate regulatory procedures for the waters of the Canadian Arctic archipelago was, according to U.S. authorities, an international task. Third, the United States reaffirmed its longstanding position on the legal status of the northern waters: namely, that all waters beyond the three-mile territorial sea limit were international waters. Finally, the American note repeated the call for bilateral talks between Canada and the U.S. that could eventually be extended to include other circumpolar states with similar maritime concerns.

Despite U.S. exhortations to postpone and abandon unilateral maritime pollution legislation in favour of an international regime, Canadian officials remained convinced that that course of action would best fulfill its national interests. The prospect of an international conference of states attempting to collectively develop and ultimately agree to a series of regulatory measures for northern waters was singularly unattractive. Increased economic development in the North posed significant challenges to Canadian sovereignty and environmental protection vis-à-vis the waters of the Canadian Arctic archipelago. Canadian authorities believed that it was necessary to act as promptly as possible to meet these challenges. An international conference might well involve years of protracted negotiations to reach an agreement, with no guarantee that Canadian interests would be reflected in the final statement. Given these imperatives and beliefs, Canadian officials politely ignored the thrust of the American position put forth in the 6 November memorandum.

Between December 1969 and February 1970, the Trudeau government carefully considered what options it could exercise to prevent pollution of the Arctic seas. By the end of February, the Cabinet had reached a decision and instructed the Department of External Affairs to brief U.S. officials about its upcoming legislation. Ottawa had decided to adopt three specific measures— two of which were legislative and a third diplomatic. The principal and most far-reaching option involved the creation of a 100-nautical-mile anti-pollution zone over the waters of the Canadian Arctic archipelago. The zone would apply to northern waters "adjacent to the mainland and islands of the Canadian Arctic within the area enclosed by the 60th parallel of north latitude, the 141st meridian of north longitude and a line measured seaward from the nearest Canadian land and a distance of 100 nautical miles" (*International Legal Materials* 1970, 544). Canada would exercise exclusive jurisdiction over this area, ensuring that economic development and, in particular, maritime shipping activities conformed to strict anti-pollution regulations. The second measure involved the extension of the outer territorial sea limit from three to 12 miles. Finally,

Ottawa moved to pre-empt any challenge to the legality of this legislative package by submitting a reservation to its acceptance of the compulsory jurisdiction of the ICJ.

Marcel Cadieux, Canada's ambassador to the United States, Ivan Head, and Alan Beesley (Chief of External Affairs' Legal Division) met with officials from the State Department on 11 March 1970 in Washington. "These discussions," according to the Secretary of State for External Affairs, "were very frank and friendly but they revealed, as expected, differences of views between our two governments on a number of questions, and it was agreed that a further round would be held after the United States government had had time to consider the matter further" (Canada 1970, 5952). On 16 March, Cadieux informed U. Alexis Johnson (U.S. Under Secretary of State for Political Affairs) that the Canadian "government was proceeding immediately to introduce the legislation necessary to implement these plans and saw no reason to discuss it further" (Johnson and McAllister 1984, 566). Johnson, in turn, "persuaded the President [Nixon] to call the Prime Minister right away to personally ask him to stall on the legislation" (Johnson 1991). In placing the telephone call on 17 March, Nixon exhorted Trudeau to postpone introducing legislative measures before the House of Commons, and suggested immediate Canada–U.S. talks on the issue (Canada 1970, 5953).

On 20 March, Johnson, accompanied by Joseph Scott (Director of Canadian Affairs at the State Department), the Under Secretary of the Navy, an Assistant Secretary of Transport, and other representatives from the departments of State, Defense, and the Interior travelled to Ottawa to meet with a Canadian delegation that included Mitchell Sharp, A. Edgar Ritchie (Under Secretary of State for External Affairs), Cadieux, Donald Macdonald (President of the Privy Council), Jean Chrétien, Ivan Head, and other senior officials (Johnson and McAllister 1984, 566; Crane 1970; Johnson 1991; Sharp 1991; Head 1991; Ritchie 1991). The U.S. objective at the meeting, according to Johnson, "was to prevent [Canada] from taking action. ... We wanted to take advantage of every opportunity or idea that would get things postponed" (Johnson 1991).

On 7 April, Yvon Beaulne, Canada's ambassador to the United Nations, presented a diplomatic letter to UN Secretary General U Thant declaring that Canada would not accept the compulsory jurisdiction of the International Court of Justice for disputes over questions which by international law fall exclusively within the jurisdiction of Canada or for "disputes arising out of or concerning jurisdiction or rights claimed or exercised by Canada in respect of the conservation, management or exploitation of the living resources of the sea, or in respect of the prevention or control of pollution or contamination of the marine environment in marine areas adjacent to the coast of Canada" (*International Legal Materials* 1970, 599). The following day, the Canadian government introduced Bills C-202 (the *Arctic Waters Pollution Prevention Act*) and C-203 (an *Act to amend the Territorial Sea and Fishing Zones Act*) in Parliament. Much to the dismay of U.S. officials, Bill C-203 received Royal Assent on 18 June 1970, as did Bill C-202 on 26 June 1970.[12] American efforts to prevent unilateral Canadian action and to develop an international regime for Arctic waters had failed.

The Coastal Waters of British Columbia and the Promotion of a Mackenzie Valley Oil Pipeline

Even as Ottawa worked in 1969 and 1970 to retard hydrocarbon tanker traffic through the waters of the Canadian Arctic archipelago, the Trudeau government was keenly aware that an assortment of oil companies, with the full support of the Nixon administration, strongly preferred a different option to transit Alaskan oil to market. Canadian authorities were mainly concerned over the passage of tankers through the environmentally delicate Juan de Fuca Strait and the Strait of Georgia en route to refineries in northwestern Washington State. According to Donald Macdonald, the minister responsible, the proposed transit through the straits involved "the consequent risk of disastrous oil spills to Vancouver Island and the British Columbia mainland" (Macdonald 1991). This possibility was compounded by two disconcerting realities then confronting the Trudeau government. First, the routing of tankers from Alaska to Washington State would be exclusively within American territorial and international waters. Not only would Ottawa be unable to subject these ships to Canadian maritime laws and regulations, but it would have no legal leverage to challenge the proposed routing. Second, there was no vessel management regulatory arrangement between Canada and the United States to oversee the safe passage of ships through the Juan de Fuca Strait and the Strait of Georgia. Fearful of the risks posed to the coastal waters and lands of British Columbia by a tanker accident and oil spill, Ottawa attempted to dissuade the United States from pursuing this option. The strategy and position taken by Ottawa focused, from

---

12. American officials continued to oppose Canada's legislative initiatives one month after bills C-202 and C-203 became law. In testimony before the Senate Subcommittee on Air and Water Pollution, Robert E. Neumann, the State Department's Assistant Legal Adviser for Politico-Military and Ocean Affairs, stated: "Canada has shown in many ways her opposition to international efforts to regulate coastal state legislation. … I don't see, for one thing … how that sort of action encourages international cooperation, nor do I see how that sort of action is enforceable. And the U.S. Government has firmly set the record straight on its opposition to the Canadian action. … In our view, Canada has no right to enact legislation on the high seas for any purpose, even for the purpose of pollution, purporting to control the navigation of vessels, dictating construction standards for vessels, and like matters" (USSSAW 1970, 11).

1971 to 1973, on working to convince American government and business officials that an overland pipeline through Canada's Mackenzie Valley region was a more attractive choice.

In order to convince Washington that the industry-favoured trans-Alaska plan should not be given regulatory approval (by the Department of the Interior) or government authorization (by Congress and the White House), Canada decided to pursue simultaneously two courses of action: first, to diplomatically protest, publicly and privately, the use of very large crude carriers for the shipment of Prudhoe Bay oil from Valdez to American West Coast terminals; and, second, to promote an alternative route for the transportation of Alaskan oil—a Mackenzie Valley pipeline. For Canadian officials, a Mackenzie Valley route would not only obviate the U.S. requirement for a trans-Alaska pipeline system—thereby eliminating unpalatable oil tanker transits along the British Columbia coast—but it would also offer numerous economic benefits to Canada. The Mackenzie Valley oil pipeline would originate at Prudhoe Bay, head east to the Mackenzie River Delta, follow the Mackenzie River Valley southward, and ultimately hook into the pre-existing interconnected pipeline network serving Canada and the United States. It would give Canada, should it find recoverable quantities of oil reserves in its North, ready access to a functional crude oil transportation system for southern markets.[13] By having a Mackenzie Valley pipeline in place that Canada could use jointly with the United States, the cost of transporting and marketing Canadian northern oil resources in the North American marketplace would be competitive, and Ottawa would also be spared the burden of independently financing and constructing a new pipeline. Second, the construction, operation, and maintenance of a Mackenzie Valley pipeline, the majority of which would be located in the Canadian North, offered enormous industrial and economic benefits to Canada. Hundreds of permanent and temporary jobs would be created in such fields as surveying, construction, and pipeline management. Ottawa would also stand

---

13. Extensive exploration for oil reserves in the Canadian North during the late 1960s and early 1970s, particularly in the Northwest Territories and in the area of the Mackenzie River Delta, was well established. A singular oil discovery by Imperial Oil at its Atkinson Point well 50 miles northeast of Tuktoyaktuk (and approximately 400 miles east of Prudhoe Bay) in January 1970 hinted at the possibility of large-scale Canadian oil deposits in the North (Canada, Department of Indian Affairs and Northern Development 1970; Cotter 1970; *New York Times* 1970). A subsequent discovery in September 1972 by Imperial Oil in the Mackenzie River Delta compounded this perception (*Financial Post* 1972). By March of 1973, though, that optimism had clearly waned. Evidence the following statement made by Robert Howland, Chairman of the National Energy Board: "No, I do not think we have any substantial quantities. ... The potential is there, but there are no established reserves of any significance" (Canada 1973a, 15).

to receive substantial tax revenues on American oil that would flow through the section of the pipeline housed on Canadian territory.

From 1969 to 1973, American business, political, and judicial authorities scrutinized the trans-Alaska pipeline/tanker plan. Despite widespread industry and government support, it took four years before a final decision on the proposal was made in Washington. A myriad of territorial compensation arrangements, bureaucratic regulatory overviews, congressional hearings and voting, presidential preferences, and, ultimately, judicial challenges, interpretations, and findings, would be required first.[14]

During this prolonged period of review in the United States, Canada repeatedly sought both to alert U.S. authorities to the hazards posed by tanker shipping along Canada's West Coast and to promote the Mackenzie Valley pipeline route for the transportation of Alaskan oil.[15] Three Cabinet members were particularly prominent in this effort: Mitchell Sharp, Secretary of State for External Affairs; J. J. Greene, Canadian Minister of Energy, Mines and Resources (later succeeded by Donald Macdonald); and Jean Chrétien, Minister of Indian Affairs and Northern Development. In various speeches, statements in the House of Commons, meetings, personal contacts, diplomatic aides-mémoires, and correspondence with American oil industry and government officials, they delivered a strong message.

Sharp was charged with leading Canada's opposition to West Coast oil tanker traffic. Time and again, the minister highlighted the hazards associated with the sea leg of the proposed TAPS plan. In a series of statements before the House of Commons, Sharp noted that Canada had "very serious concern about the dangers of pollution arising from the movement of oil by tanker down the Pacific coast. ... I am sure that the national interests of Canada and of the United States would be best served if a decision were made not to build the trans-Alaska pipeline system and then go down the Pacific coast to Bellingham [Washington]" (Canada 1971, 3379, 3946).

Discussions with U.S. authorities on 3 May 1971, initiated and authorized by Sharp, provided a forum in which Canada sought "to obtain maximum protection of Canadian interest[s] vis-a-vis the proposed Alaska oil movement ... by deflect[ing] all Alaska oil movements away from Puget Sound to

14. For a general, albeit incomplete and unsatisfactory account of these developments see Berry (1975). For a succinct chronicle of the major American political developments associated with the TAPS proposal, see Rogers Morton's statement (USHRSPL 1973, 1183–1185).

15. The government of British Columbia, headed by Premier Dave Barrett, was also a vocal opponent of the West Coast oil-shipping scheme. The vast bulk of its energies was spent on insuring that the Trudeau government incorporated the concerns of the province into federal policy.

California" (confidential government source, Ottawa, June 1991).[16] This message was followed up by a meeting between Sharp and Rogers Morton, U.S. Secretary of the Interior, on 10 June 1971, and two aides-mémoires, on 29 June and 20 August, from Ottawa to Washington. Both diplomatic documents stressed Canadian opposition to oil tanker traffic on the West Coast. The wording of the latter statement is particularly notable:

> The great concern of the Canadian government regarding proposals to transport oil by tanker from Alaska to the Puget Sound area has been made known to the United States government on a number of occasions during the course of this year. *This concern is based upon the certainty that any movement of oil by tanker on the scale which has been proposed will eventually result in oil spills.* … The Canadian government is convinced that if the full economic costs of the substantial environmental risks are taken into account it will be found desirable to avoid introducing large and hazardous tanker movements into the inner waters of the Pacific Coast. (Canada 1972, 3009; italics added)

In addition to voicing opposition to the tanker transport plan, Canada indicated that it was willing to examine the possibility of supplying the Puget Sound region with Canadian sources of oil. This suggestion, originally raised by U.S. authorities, would obviate the need for tankers in the waters of the Juan de Fuca Strait and the Strait of Georgia.[17]

The task of promoting the Mackenzie Valley alternative rested foremost with the Minister of Energy, Mines and Resources and, to a lesser extent, with the Minister of Indian Affairs and Northern Development. In addressing the

16. On the public announcement of these discussions see *Wall Street Journal* (1971f). At the conclusion of the talks, Canadian officials were not optimistic about the prospect of persuading the United States to abandon west coast oil tanker movements. As Sharp put it: "the Canadian government … [has] been making known to the United States government our concerns about the ecological dangers. So far we have not been satisfied with the replies we have received" (Canada 1971, 5473). The bilateral discussions, one confidential source stated, suggested "that the United States officials taking part in the consultations were convinced that the Alyeska Pipeline should and will be built and that Alaska North Slope oil will inevitably be shipped into the Puget Sound area and California. … The 'consultations' with Canada thus seemed to be a formality to be dispensed with as expeditiously as possible."

17. An internal study conducted by the National Energy Board had concluded "that the Western Sedimentary Basin of Canada would very likely be able to supply the entire oil market for the States of Washington and Oregon for a period of twenty years even without any 'further development' or additional tar sands assistance" (confidential government source, Ottawa, June 1991).

Vancouver Men's Canadian Club on 12 February 1971; J. J. Greene was the first official to express Ottawa's preference for the Mackenzie Valley route publicly:

> The Canadian Government is not opposed to the construction of oil and gas lines from Alaska through Canada to the continental United States. … To us it appears that an oil line from Alaska through Canadian territory would have the advantage of ruling out a vulnerable tanker link to markets and would provide more economic transportation of oil to the US. Midwest. (Greene 1971, 41895, 41896)

Speaking in Dallas before a meeting of the Society of Petroleum Engineers, Jean Chrétien announced that "if it is desirable to build an oil pipeline from Prudhoe Bay direct to the mid-continent market, then a right-of-way through Canada, I am sure, can and will be made available" (Crane 1971a). In a 12 March 1971 statement in the House of Commons, Greene went so far as to declare:

> I think we can assure the United States oil companies and the United States government … that there will be no unnecessary roadblocks at the Canadian end and Canadian governmental side. … [W]e are in a position to move with considerable expedition if it appears that the entrepreneurs, the oil companies, and the government of the United States are interested in having the Mackenzie valley line as the primary line. (Canada 1971, 4226)

This message was repeated to U.S. oil industry representatives at meetings held in Ottawa on 24 March (*Wall Street Journal* 1971e, 18; *New York Times* 1971d, 39). The Canadian delegation, headed by Greene, scheduled the discussions not only to promote the Mackenzie Valley pipeline option, but to determine the status of routing preferences held by the industry.[18]

----

18. The announcement of the meetings was made by Jean Chrétien in the House of Commons on 12 March 1971 (Canada 1971, 4238). On the content of the meetings, see Crane (1971b); *New York Times* (1971b). In addition to Greene, Canadian officials included Mitchell Sharp, Jean Chrétien, Jack Davis (Minister of Fisheries and Forestry), A. E. Ritchie, H. Basil Robinson, Peter Towe, R. F. Shaw (Deputy Minister, Department of Fisheries and Forestry), Jake Warren (Deputy Minister, Department of Industry, Trade and Commerce), O. G. Stoner (Deputy Minister, Department of Transport), Jack Austin (Deputy Minister, Department of Energy, Mines and Resources), Robert Howland, and D. H. W. Kirkwood (Assistant Secretary to the Cabinet). U.S. oil company representatives participating were Thornton Bradshaw (President, Atlantic Richfield), Robin Adam (President,

Upon assuming the Energy, Mines and Resources portfolio in January 1972, Donald Macdonald continued to stress Canada's preference for a Mackenzie Valley pipeline. Macdonald presented the case for the Mackenzie Valley pipeline to Morton on 30 March 1972. Macdonald used the occasion to inform U.S. officials "that Canada was prepared to supply additional quantities of oil to the [Puget Sound region of the] United States" for an extended period (Canada 1972, 1440). After the one-hour meeting in Washington, Macdonald believed it likely that the U.S. government would sanction the TAPS project. "Morton recognizes the Mackenzie as an alternative," Macdonald conceded, but "with so much effort and study invested in the Trans-Alaska pipeline ... it rather looks as though they would be giving that priority."[19] Macdonald informed reporters on 30 March 1972 that, as Minister, he was "not overly sanguine about the prospects of selling [the Mackenzie Valley option] at this point" (United States 1972, 12544).

U.S. domestic developments during 1971 and early 1972 had led Ottawa to conclude that the TAPS proposal would ultimately be approved by the United States, making oil tanker traffic adjacent to the coastal waters of British Columbia a near certainty and eliminating the Mackenzie Valley alternative. Among the first indications of this was a land claims settlement in Alaska, a U.S. administration plan to provide, among other things, 40 million acres and $962.5 million to 55,000 Native Alaskans, which had been endorsed by Congress and the Alaska Federation of Natives. The arrangement, signed into law by President Nixon on 19 December 1970, removed all domestic political and judicial encumbrances to the construction of the TAPS project.[20] Second, despite some jousting within the U.S. bureaucratic community, the trans-Alaska pipeline had gained momentum. A January 1971 Interior Department draft statement on the environmental impact of the TAPS proposal found that there

British Petroleum), Charles Spahr (Chairman, Standard Oil), William Tapoulareas (President, Mobil), and Thomas Barrow (President, Humble Oil and Refining). Oil company representatives were convinced to meet with Canadian decision-makers by Rogers Morton, U.S. Secretary of the Interior: "I got them to go collectively ... to Canada to explore the ramifications of a Canadian alternative" (USSCPW 1972, 537; Wills 1971).

19. In addition to Minister Macdonald, Canadian officials included Jack Austin, Robert Howland, Cadieux, Norman Chappell (Canadian Embassy, Washington), and J. Cullen (Parliamentary Secretary to Minister Macdonald). The U.S. delegation, in addition to Rogers Morton, included General Lincoln (Director, Office of Emergency Preparedness), William Pecora (Under Secretary, Department of the Interior), Hollis Dole (Assistant Secretary, Department of the Interior), and George Shultz (Director, Office of Management and Budget).

20. On the 19 December 1970 accord, see Blair (dates read: 1971a; 1971b; 1971c; 1971d; 1971e); *Wall Street Journal* (1971c); and *New York Times* (1971a; 1971c; and 1971e).

would be a "residue of unavoidable [environmental] effects" from the construction, operation, and maintenance of a trans-Alaska pipeline. Still, it concluded nevertheless that the pipeline should be constructed since Prudhoe Bay oil was "essential to the strength, growth and security of the United States" (Rosenbaum 1971; *Wall Street Journal* 1971b).[21] Support for the TAPS proposal was, nonetheless, particularly strong within Washington's bureaucratic corridors, evidenced by endorsements of the trans-Alaska pipeline by bodies such as the Office of Emergency Preparedness, the Department of Transportation, the Federal Power Commission, the Department of Commerce, the Treasury Department, and the Department of State (Blair 1971f; *Wall Street Journal* 1971a and 1971d).[22]

The final environmental impact statement of the Department of the Interior, delayed for several months, was finally released on 20 March 1972.[23] That report, along with the concomitant release of an economic and security analysis of the trans-Alaska proposal conducted by the Department of the Interior, advanced several conclusions. According to the six-volume environmental study, "no single oil delivery system would be free of environmental effects or of potential threats." A Canadian Mackenzie Valley route, however, was the least harmful to the environment as it offered the possibility of serving as a land corridor for both Alaskan oil and natural gas pipelines. The much-awaited report offered no recommendation as to whether the Alyeska consortium should be granted a permit to proceed with the TAPS project (USDI 1972; Blair 1972a; *Wall Street Journal* 1972c). The economic and security analysis, however, was far more precise in its findings: "From a national security point of view, it is important to get North Slope oil to the lower 48 states as soon as possible. … The Alaska pipeline gives promise of bringing in a significant quantity of North Slope oil to the lower 48 states by 1975. … Early completion of the Alaska pipeline must be considered an important national security objective" (USDI 1971, 5). With the intensive background research of the Interior

---

21. According to the terms of the 1969 *Environmental Policy Act*, each federal department/agency was required to prepare a statement on the environmental impact of any proposed action or legislation and to examine possible alternatives. In this case, the Department of the Interior was mandated to produce a final environmental impact study prior to issuing the necessary right-of-way permits for the construction of the trans-Alaska pipeline.

22. Not surprisingly, the Alaskan Congressional delegation, led by Senators Mike Gravel and Ted Stevens, and Alaskan state political leaders, led by Governor William Egan, fully supported the TAPS project.

23. Reasons for the delay, as identified by Rogers Morton, William Pecora, and other Department of Interior officials, included late submissions of technical data by Alyeska, the need to study various alternative pipeline and marine transportation routes (including the Mackenzie Valley), and the conclusion of an Alaskan Native land claims arrangement.

Department completed, all that remained was a decision by Secretary Morton to either authorize or cancel the trans-Alaska pipeline system.

Canadian officials soon learned of Morton's decision. On 11 May 1972, Morton announced—after consultations with President Nixon and senior administration officials—that he had decided to grant the necessary right-of-way permits for the trans-Alaska pipeline (Blair 1972b; *Wall Street Journal* 1972a).[24] The construction and operation of the TAPS project were, according to the Secretary, an overriding imperative for the United States. Macdonald, responding on behalf of the Canadian government, "expressed disappointment at the decision of the United States Government to announce its willingness to grant permits for construction of the Trans-Alaska pipeline," and reiterated the claim that "the government of Canada remains convinced that the alternative Canadian route through the Mackenzie Valley is the best from all aspects" (confidential government source, Ottawa, June 1991; *Wall Street Journal* 1972a).[25]

Ottawa, confronted with the growing prospect of West Coast oil tanker shipments and the rejection of the Mackenzie Valley pipeline route, sought a joint arrangement with the United States in 1972 and 1973 on oil-pollution controls in the Strait of Juan de Fuca–Georgia Strait–Puget Sound region. As well, it continued to indicate Canada's willingness to consider a Mackenzie Valley routing scheme. To achieve satisfaction on a bilateral plan for pollution

---

24. John Whitaker notes that "we [the United States] clearly were going to build the Alaska pipeline … that was never an issue in the Nixon administration from day one," and that the "official" Alaska pipeline decision meeting took place at the White House on 27 March 1972, from 4:00 to 4:30 p.m. In addition to President Nixon and John Whitaker, Rogers Morton, Alexander Haig, George Shultz, and Peter Flanigan (Assistant to the President for Economic Affairs) were present. Whitaker provides the following account of the meeting: "[Henry] Kissinger was out of town, so [Alexander] Haig was at the meeting. It was very short. Nixon said, in effect, we're going this way [that is, the trans-Alaska route] and we're going to get it done. He looked at Al [Haig] and asked 'Is there any Canadian global consequences if we tell the Canadians no we're not really interested in going that way' [that is, the Mackenzie Valley route]. Al just kind of nodded his head no, and that was it. [President] Nixon said 'Rog [Morton], keep going the way we're going.' And that was the end of it; this conversation couldn't have taken more than ten minutes. Those were our marching orders" (Whitaker 1991a). The author is deeply grateful to Mr. Whitaker for taking the time to review his appointment books to confirm the above dates, times, and attendees.

25. Whitaker suspects that Nixon informed Prime Minister Trudeau of the U.S. decision on TAPS during Nixon's visit to Ottawa, 13–15 April 1972—well in advance of Rogers Morton's statement of 11 May 1972 (Whitaker 1991b). Donald Macdonald prepared a reply letter to Rogers Morton, but decided on 15 June 1972 not to send it to the Secretary (confidential government source, Ottawa, June 1991).

regulation, Mitchell Sharp had proposed on 26 April to Rogers Morton that Canada and the United States use the International Joint Commission (IJC) to study the hazards of West Coast oil spills.[26] The absence of a quick reply from American authorities, coupled with a 12,000-gallon oil spill at Atlantic Richfield's Cherry Point, Washington, refinery in early June, prompted the House of Commons to unanimously adopt a resolution requesting that the IJC be charged with the responsibility of supervising the immediate environmental clean-up and examining the impact of regular oil movements in the area.[27] Despite various appeals from Ottawa, Washington turned down the Canadian IJC proposal.[28] In April 1973, the U.S. finally announced that it was willing to review the ecological environment of the Juan de Fuca Strait–Strait of Georgia–Puget Sound region. This preliminary step, the U.S. insisted, was necessary before the commencement of comprehensive pollution control planning, joint or otherwise.

Canada, despite marginal progress on the issue of environmental protection for British Columbia coastal waters, remained less than optimistic about the prospects for a Mackenzie Valley oil pipeline. The Trudeau government, immediately after the 11 May decision by Rogers Morton, officially withdrew from actively promoting the option except to indicate periodically that it would be willing to examine any application for a northern pipeline put before Canadian officials. The Nixon administration, determined to forge ahead as quickly as possible with the trans-Alaska project, secured congressional authorization for the trans-Alaska pipeline/tanker plan on 13 November 1973, claiming that it represented a vital step toward energy self-sufficiency for the United States. The Alaska pipeline bill was signed into law by President Nixon three days later.

Ottawa's repeated efforts from 1971 to 1973 to prevent tanker shipment of Alaskan oil in the coastal waters adjacent to British Columbia ultimately proved unsuccessful. In particular, the promotion by the Trudeau government

---

26. The International Joint Commission is a product of the 1909 Canada–United States Boundary Waters Treaty. The Commission's main purpose is to regulate and resolve outstanding transborder issues—principally involving water resources—between Canada and the United States.

27. For details on the oil spill and Canada's reaction to it, see *Wall Street Journal* (1972b); Russell (1972). The text of the resolution adopted by the House of Commons read: "That in the light of the damage in Canada and the United States of America arising from the recent oil spill at the Cherry Point refinery, this House supports the urgency of a reference to the International Joint Commission of the environmental consequences of the movement of oil in the narrow waters of the Straits of Juan de Fuca, Georgia Strait, and Puget Sound both now and in the future" (Canada 1972, 2995).

28. See Mitchell Sharp's public statement (Canada 1973b, 5987).

of a Canadian alternative pipeline transportation route through the Mackenzie River Valley failed because both American industry and U.S. government officials opposed it.[29] Simply put, unresolved political, regulatory, legal, financial, and ecological concerns ensured that a Mackenzie Valley overland route would not be chosen to deliver Prudhoe Bay oil to the lower 48 states.[30]

Canada, Alaskan Oil, and the Legacy of 1968

Confronted by the prospect of significant volumes of oil tanker traffic transiting in or adjacent to Canadian waters—first in the Canadian Arctic archipelago, and then along the coast of British Columbia—the government of Pierre Trudeau launched an ambitious, multi-year response. Ottawa's response, characterized by the use of political, diplomatic, legislative, legal, and economic levers, was designed to protect Canada's waterways from the introduction of unwelcome ecological pollutants and, in a worst-case scenario, a massive spill of Alaskan crude oil.

To address the threat posed by regularized oil tanker transits in the waters of the Canadian Arctic archipelago, Canada actively closely monitored the 1969 passage of the *Manhattan* and the *Northwind*. Repeated diplomatic exchanges with the United States were followed by legislative measures—the *Arctic Waters Pollution Prevention Act*, and an *Act to amend the Territorial Sea and Fishing Zones Act*—and legal action before the International Court of Justice.[31] Ultimately, transits of Prudhoe Bay oil in Canada's northern waters never materialized. Subsequent exploration for fossil fuels in the North, especially in the Beaufort Sea region, has continued to demand Ottawa's attention. Discussions and formal negotiations with the United States have to date proven unsuccessful in resolving competing maritime jurisdictional claims—specifically

29. The first significant shipment of Prudhoe Bay oil—transported by the trans-Alaska pipeline and tanker—to reach the lower 48 states arrived on 5 August 1977. The 824,803 barrels of crude were promptly unloaded at the Cherry Point, Washington, refinery facilities of Atlantic Richfield (*Washington Post* 1977).

30. On 4 July 1977, Canada's National Energy Board rejected the Canadian Arctic Gas Company's proposal to use the Mackenzie River Valley as a transportation corridor for the delivery of Alaskan natural gas to southern American markets. See Canada, National Energy Board (1977). The NEB report was preceded by the 9 May 1977 release of *Northern Frontier, Northern Homeland: The Report of the Mackenzie Valley Pipeline Inquiry* (Canada 1977). Commissioner Thomas Berger's principal recommendation to the Trudeau government was to postpone regulatory approval of a Mackenzie Valley pipeline for ten years.

31. On 11 January 1988, Canada and the United States signed the Arctic Cooperation Agreement to facilitate the transit of American military vessels conducting scientific research through the contested waters of the Canadian Arctic archipelago. See Kirkey (1995b).

the delineation of the offshore boundary. These unresolved claims in the Beaufort Sea leave a maritime area, viewed to contain sizable oil and gas reserves, of more than 21,000 square kilometres open to dispute (Kirkey 1995a).

In an effort to prevent oil tanker traffic along the coastal waters of British Columbia, Ottawa worked between 1971 and 1973 to convince oil companies and the United States government that an overland corridor transiting Canada's Mackenzie Valley was a preferable option for the movement of Prudhoe Bay crude. Despite regular political overtures from the Trudeau government, a trans-Alaska pipeline system, supplemented by the use of oil tankers to transit hydrocarbons from Valdez to the lower 48 states, was selected. Canada did receive a small modicum of satisfaction in April 1973 when the United States agreed to examine jointly with Canada the ecological health of the Juan de Fuca Strait–Strait of Georgia–Puget Sound region. This short-term initial bilateral effort did serve to assuage Canada's concerns over very large oil tanker transits. The results of the study were followed by joint contingency planning to minimize the threats posed by hydrocarbon spills, culminating in the 19 December 1979 Vessel Traffic Management Agreement, designed to facilitate the safe movement of oil tankers off the West Coast of Canada (Canada 1979; Kirkey 1997; McDorman 2009). Tragically, Canadian concerns about the prospect of an oil spill from West Coast tanker traffic were realized when, on 24 March 1989, the Exxon Valdez discharged several million gallons of crude oil into the Alaskan waters of Prince William Sound.

With the increased use of Canada's northern waters for military, scientific, and commercial purposes, coupled with the stark realities of rapid climate change, it seems that Ottawa has little choice but to continue to engage in efforts to protect the nation's maritime assets—especially given the likelihood of future industry plans for hydrocarbon development and related seaborne transit options.

References

Berry, Mary Clay. 1975. *The Politics of Oil and Native Land Claims.* Bloomington: Indiana University Press.

Bilder, Richard B. 1970. "The Canadian Arctic Waters Pollution Prevention Act: New Stresses on the Law of the Sea." *Michigan Law Review* 69, no. 1 (November): 1–54.

Blair, William M. 1972a. "Alaska Pipeline Called Vital Despite Risk." *New York Times,* 21 March: 1, 16.

———. 1972b. "Morton Approves Alaska Pipeline: Court Fight Seen." *New York Times,* 12 May: 1, 5.

———. 1971a. "Administration Drafts New Bill That Would Give More Land to Alaska Natives—A Fight Is Expected." *New York Times,* 28 March: 38.

———. 1971b. "Congress Votes Alaska Land Bill." *New York Times,* 15 December: 9.

———. 1971c. "House Vote Aids Alaskan Natives." *New York Times,* 21 October: 1, 15.

————. 1971d. "Nixon Offers Bill to Settle Claims of Alaskan Natives." *New York Times*, 7 April: 86.

————. 1971e. "Senate Sends Alaska Native Land Bill to Conference." *New York Times*, 2 November: 26.

————. 1971f. "Stans Urges Early Start on Trans-Alaska Pipeline." *New York Times*, 17 April: 58.

Burns, John. 1969a. "Northwest Passage Area to Be Termed Land in Canada's Bid for Sovereignty." *Globe and Mail*, 27 September: 10.

————. 1969b. "Trudeau Will Meet U Thant to Discuss Arctic Pollution." *Globe and Mail*, 25 October: 1.

Canada. 1979. "Exchange of Notes Between the Government of Canada and the Government of the United States of America Constituting an Agreement on Vessel Traffic Management for the Juan De Fuca Region." In Canada Treaty Series, E101698 - CTS 1979 no. 28. https://www.treaty-accord.gc.ca/text-texte.aspx?id=101698. Accessed 1 December 2020.

————. 1977. *Northern Frontier, Northern Homeland: The Report of the Mackenzie Valley Pipeline Inquiry, Volume 1*. Ottawa: Supply and Services Canada.

————. 1973a. "Minutes of Proceedings and Evidence of the Standing Committee on National Resources and Public Works," no. 3, 1 March.

————. 1973b. *House of Commons Debates*. VI.

————. 1972. *House of Commons Debates*. II, IV.

————. 1971. *House of Commons Debates*. IV, V.

————. 1970. *House of Commons Debates*. VI.

————. 1969. *House of Commons Debates*. I.

Canada, Department of Indian Affairs and Northern Development. 1970. "Minister Hails Arctic Oil Discovery." Press Release. January.

Canada, National Energy Board. 1977. *Reasons for Decision: Northern Pipelines*. Ottawa: Supply and Services Canada.

Canada, PMO (Prime Minister's Office). 1969. "Press Release." 3 April.

Chrétien, Jean. 1969. "A Speech to the Canadian Institute of Forestry." Prince George, British Columbia, 6 October.

Cole, Robert J. 1969. "Two Oil Projects Move Ahead." *New York Times*, 11 February: 41, 44.

Cotter. Nicholas. 1970. "Imperial Discovers Oil in Arctic." *Globe and Mail*, 16 January: B1.

Cowan, Edward. 1969. "Canadian Official Says the Arctic Route Is Open to All Countries." *New York Times*, 19 September: 3.

Crane, David. 1971a. "Chrétien Assures U.S. Oil, Gas Firms Capital Welcome." *Globe and Mail*, 10 March: B1.

————. 1971b. "Hopes Dim for Mackenzie Valley Oil Pipeline." *Globe and Mail*, 25 March: B1.

————. 1970. "Arctic Control Part of Agenda in Ottawa Talks." *Globe and Mail*, 21 March: 2.

————. 1969. "Ceding of Passage Rights Likely in Ottawa Claim to Arctic Waters." *Globe and Mail*, 3 September: B1.

Dellapenna, Joseph W. 1972. "Canadian Claims in Arctic Waters." *Land and Water Law Review* 7(2): 383–400.

Dosman, Edgar J. 1976. "The Northern Sovereignty Crisis 1968–1970." In *The Arctic in Question*, edited by Edgar J. Dosman, 34–57. Toronto: Oxford University Press.

———. 1975. *The National Interest: The Politics of Northern Development 1968–75*. Toronto: McClelland & Stewart.

Financial Post. 1972. "Imperial Finds Oil in Delta." 23 September: 2.

Globe and Mail. 1969. "Ottawa Pledges Control over Pollution in the Arctic." 24 October: 4.

Green, L. C. 1970. "Canada and Arctic Sovereignty." *Canadian Bar Review* 48(4): 740–775.

Greene, J. J. 1971. "National Resource Growth: By Plan or by Chance." 12 February. Reprinted in United States, *Congressional Record*, 117, Part 32.

Head, Ivan. 1991. Interview with author, Ottawa. 7 June.

International Legal Materials. 1970. "Canadian Legislation on Arctic Pollution and Territorial Sea and Fishing Zones." Vol. 9, no. 3 (May): 543–554.

Johnson, U. Alexis. 1991. Interview with author, Washington, DC. 31 May.

Johnson, U. Alexis, and Jef Olivarius McAllister. 1984. *The Right Hand of Power*. Englewood Cliffs, NJ: Prentice-Hall.

Keating, Bern. 1970. "North for Oil: Manhattan Makes the Historic Northwest Passage." *National Geographic* 137, no. 3 (March): 374–391.

Kirkey, Christopher. 1997. "Moving Alaskan Oil to Market: Canadian National Interests and the Trans-Alaska Pipeline, 1968–1973." *American Review of Canadian Studies* 27, no. 4 (Winter): 495–522.

———. 1996. "The Arctic Waters Pollution Prevention Initiatives: Canada's Response to an American Challenge." *International Journal of Canadian Studies* 13 (Spring): 41–59.

———. 1995a. "Delineating Maritime Boundaries: The 1977–1978 Canada–United States Beaufort Sea Continental Shelf Delimitation Boundary Negotiations." *Canadian Review of American Studies* 25, no. 2 (Spring): 49–66.

———. 1995b. "Smoothing Troubled Waters: The 1988 Canada–United States Arctic Co-operation Agreement." *International Journal* 50, no. 2 (Spring): 401–426.

Kirton, John, and Don Munton. 1987. "The Manhattan Voyages and Their Aftermath." In *Politics of the Northwest Passage*, edited by Franklyn Griffiths, 67–97. Montreal and Kingston: McGill-Queen's University Press.

Konan, Raymond W. 1970. "The Manhattan's Arctic Conquest and Canada's Response in Legal Diplomacy." *Cornell International Law Journal* 3, no. 2 (Spring): 189–204.

Macdonald, Donald. 1991. Personal correspondence with author, 19 July.

McDorman, Ted L. 2009. "Canada–U.S. International Ocean Law Relations in the North Pacific: Disputes, Agreements and Cooperation." In *Maritime Boundary Disputes, Settlement Processes, and the Law of the Sea*, edited by Seoung-Yong Hong and Jon M. Van Dyke, 176–197. Leiden: Martinus Nijhoff Publishers.

Milsten, Donald E. 1972. "Arctic Passage—Legal Heavy Weather." *Orbis* 15, no. 4 (Winter): 1173–1193.

New York Times. 1971a. "Alaskans Accept Land Claims Bill." 20 December: 9.

———. 1971b. "Canadian Hopes Dim for an Oil Pipeline." 25 March: 66.

———. 1971c. "House Panel Approves Bill on Land Claims in Alaska." 4 August: 7.

———. 1971d. "Oil Chiefs to Visit Ottawa." 20 March: 39.

———. 1971e. "Senate Panel Backs Alaska Land Claims." 16 September: 85.

———. 1970. "Canadian Official Lauds Oil Discovery in the Arctic." 17 January: 42.

———. 1968. "Big Oil Find Reported on Alaska's Arctic Slope." 19 July: 47.

O'Brien, William V., and Armando C. Chapelli. 1973. "The Law of the Sea in the 'Canadian' Arctic: The Pattern of Controversy." *McGill Law Journal* 19(3/4): 322–366.

Reinhard, W. G. 1970. "International Law: Implications of the Opening of the Northwest Passage." *Dickinson Law Review* 64:678–690.

Ritchie, A. Edgar. 1991. Interview with author, Ottawa. 7 June.

Robertson, Gordon. 1991. Interview with author, 12 June.

Rosenbaum, David E. 1971. "Alaska Pipeline Is Upheld by Interior Agency Study." *New York Times*, 14 January: 1, 74.

Russell, George. 1972. "Lewis Accuses U.S. of Unfriendly Move in Oil-Route Plans." *Globe and Mail,* 10 June: 10.

Sharp, Mitchell. 1991. Interview with author, Ottawa. 6 June.

———. 1969. "A Ship and Sovereignty in the North." *Globe and Mail*, 18 September: 7.

Smith, William D. 1970. *Northwest Passage.* New York: Heritage Press.

Storrs, A. H. G., and T. C. Pullen. 1970. "S.S. Manhattan in Arctic Waters." *Canadian Geographic* 80, no. 5 (May): 166–181.

United States. 1972. *Congressional Record.* 110, Part 10.

USDI (United States, Department of the Interior). 1972. *Final Environmental Impact Statement: Proposed Trans-Alaska Pipeline.* Volume 6.

———. 1971. *An Analysis of the Economic and Security Aspects of the Trans-Alaska Pipeline.*

USHRSPL (United States, House of Representatives Subcommittee on Public Lands of the Committee on Interior and Insular Affairs). 1973. *Hearings before the House of Representatives Subcommittee on Public Lands of the Committee on Interior and Insular Affairs: Oil and Natural Gas Pipeline Rights-of-way,* Part III. 15 June. Washington: Government Printing Office.

USSCPW (United States, Senate Committee on Public Works and the Committee on Interior and Insular Affairs). 1972. *Joint Hearings before the Senate Committee on Public Works and the Committee on Interior and Insular Affairs.* 1, 7, 8 and 9 March. Washington: Government Printing Office.

USSSAW (United States, Senate Subcommittee on Air and Water Pollution of the Committee on Public Works). 1970. IMCO Civil Liabilities Convention (Oil Pollution). 21 July. Washington: Government Printing Office.

Wall Street Journal. 1972a. "Alaska Oil Pipeline Is Approved by Nixon, but Injunction Blocks Issuing of Permits." 12 May: 3.

———. 1972b. "Canada Asks Oil-Spill Study." 10 June: 20.

———. 1972c. "Interior Agency's Paper on Alaska Pipeline Takes No Stand, but Nixon Backing Likely." 21 March: 2.

———. 1971a. "Commerce Agency Chief Endorses Alaskan Pipeline." 17 April: 22.

———. 1971b. "Interior Agency Urges Clearance for Alaska Line." 1971. 14 January: 2.

———. 1971c. "Plan to Settle Alaska Natives' Claims, End Pipeline Issue, Is Backed by Nixon." 7 April: 2.

———. 1971d. "Trans-Alaska Pipeline Gets Backing by FPC and Planning Agency." 22 March: 5.

———. 1971e. "Trans-Canada Pipeline Talks." 15 March: 18.

———. 1971f. "U.S., Canada Plan Talks." 8 March: 8.

———. 1969. "Big Oil Pipeline in Alaska Slated by 3 Companies." 11 February: 26.

———. 1968a. "Alaskan Pipeline Study." 1 August: 7.

———. 1968b. "Alaska Oil, Gas Find Is Potentially Vast, Consulting Firm Says." 19 July: 3.

———. 1968c. "Oil Concerns to Seek a Northwest Passage to Unlock the Arctic." 17 December: 8.

Walz, Jay. 1969. "Trudeau Reaffirms Canadian Sovereignty in Arctic as Parliament Opens." *New York Times*, 24 October: 4.

Washington Post. 1977. "Alaska Oil Tanker Reaches Waters Off Lower 48 States." 6 August: A3.

Westermeyer, William E. 1984. "The Transportation of Arctic Energy Resources." In *United States Arctic Interests: The 1980s and 1990s*, edited by William E. Westermeyer and Kurt M. Shusterich, 105–133. New York: Springer-Verlag.

Whitaker, John. 1991a. Interview with author, Washington, DC. 30 May.

———. 1991b. Personal correspondence with the author, 30 May.

Wills, Terrance. 1971. "Morton Sees Benefits in Canadian Corridor for Alaskan Oil, Gas." *Globe and Mail*, 12 March: B1.

World Oil. 1969. "Big Oil Find." Vol. 169 (August): 47.

Chapitre 13
L'Union nationale
à la croisée des chemins

ALEXANDRE TURGEON

Résumé

Après le décès de Maurice Duplessis et celui de Paul Sauvé, suivis de l'élection de Jean Lesage et de son « équipe du tonnerre », rien ne va plus pour l'Union nationale, qui semble condamnée à rester dans l'ombre de la Révolution tranquille. Contre toute attente, l'Union nationale revient au pouvoir en 1966, au plus fort de la Révolution tranquille. Dirigée par Daniel Johnson, l'Union nationale n'avait pas dit son dernier mot… mais le destin non plus. En 1968, Daniel Johnson est terrassé par une crise cardiaque. Tout est à refaire. Dans ce texte, je m'intéresse aux tentatives de l'Union nationale, à la croisée des chemins, de s'affirmer sur le plan mémoriel, entre 1959 et 1968. Alors que la reconfiguration mémorielle en cours durant la Révolution tranquille bat son plein, l'enjeu est de taille ; il en va de la survie de l'Union nationale, menacée qu'elle est sur tous les fronts.

Or, ce qui paraissait un rêve il y a neuf ans est devenu une splendide réalité, comme en témoigne ce barrage à voûtes multiples, le plus grand du genre au monde et sûrement l'une des plus belles réussites du génie humain. Derrière cette forteresse de béton seront emprisonnés cinq billions de pieds cubes d'eau, qui ne pourront désormais retrouver leur chemin vers la mer qu'en s'engouffrant dans les turbines, en entraînant les génératrices et en se mettant de tout leur poids au service de l'homme, de son industrie, de son travail, de ses loisirs, de son bien-être et de sa culture.

Daniel Johnson,
premier ministre du Québec, 1968

Figure 13.1. Daniel Johnson (aux côtés de René Lévesque et de Jean Lesage) la veille de son décès, le 25 septembre 1968. Source : *Hydro-Québec Archives, H01/fonds Hydro-Québec.*

Cette citation est tirée de l'un des plus célèbres discours de l'histoire du Québec (Perron, 2006, p. 174 ; S. Savard, 2009, p. 78-79). Il a été rédigé pour Daniel Johnson, alors chef de l'Union nationale et premier ministre du Québec, en vue de l'inauguration du barrage Manic-5 sur la rivière Manicouagan, le 26 septembre 1968. Mis en branle à l'origine par le gouvernement unioniste de Maurice Duplessis, en 1959 – Daniel Johnson était alors ministre des Ressources hydrauliques –, avant d'être repris par le gouvernement libéral de Jean Lesage après son élection, en 1960, le chantier de Manic-5 est l'un des plus importants du Québec dans les années 1960, le Québec de la Révolution tranquille. Bien qu'il se soit opposé bec et ongles à la nationalisation de l'hydroélectricité proposée par Jean Lesage en 1962, Daniel Johnson s'est rallié au projet et l'a appuyé entièrement à la suite de sa victoire électorale, en 1966, comme en fait foi l'extrait reproduit ci-dessus. Ce qui a toutefois consacré ce discours dans les annales politiques québécoises, ce n'est ni le propos ni le ton lyrique employé par le premier ministre, mais bien le fait que celui-ci n'ait jamais pu prononcer ce discours, en fin de compte.

Dans la nuit du 25 au 26 septembre 1968, Daniel Johnson est terrassé par une crise cardiaque pendant son sommeil. La nouvelle surprend tout autant qu'elle attriste ses partisans comme ses adversaires. La veille, Johnson affichait pourtant une forme splendide. Il avait d'ailleurs assisté à un banquet et donné une conférence de presse où il était en pleine possession de ses moyens, badinant avec les journalistes, les responsables politiques et les ouvriers (Nadeau, 2018). Aussi l'annonce de son décès plonge-t-elle le Québec dans le deuil, et l'Union nationale dans une crise sans précédent – du moins, serait-on porté à le croire, dans les circonstances, mais ce ne fut pas tout à fait le cas. En fait, il serait judicieux de mentionner ici que cette formation politique n'en était pas à son premier épisode douloureux. Rappelons brièvement de quoi il en retourne.

En effet, ce n'était pas la première fois que l'Union nationale perdait un chef en fonction. Le 7 septembre 1959, le premier ministre Maurice Duplessis décède des suites d'une attaque cérébrale à Schefferville, lors d'une tournée dans le Grand Nord québécois. Privée de son chef, qui était l'unique maître à bord, la formation politique avait ainsi été atteinte en son sein, peut-être même mortellement. À tout le moins, elle avait mis un genou à terre ; il ne restait plus qu'à finir le travail, l'achever une fois pour toutes… et Jean Lesage, le tout nouveau chef du Parti libéral du Québec (PLQ), était fin prêt à lui assener le coup fatal.

Mais si l'Union nationale avait mis un genou à terre, ce n'était que pour mieux se relever, semble-t-il. Quelques jours à peine après le décès de Duplessis, les membres de son cabinet ont désigné d'une seule et même voix leur collègue Paul Sauvé pour lui succéder. Fils d'Arthur Sauvé, qui fut chef du Parti conservateur du Québec durant l'entre-deux-guerres[1], Paul Sauvé a siégé presque sans interruption depuis 1930[2] à l'Assemblée législative aux côtés de Maurice Duplessis, dont il a tour à tour été orateur[3] (1936-1939) et ministre du Bien-être social et de la Jeunesse (1946-1959)[4].

Assermenté premier ministre le 11 septembre 1959, Sauvé ne perd pas une seconde pour agir : une foule de réformes sont lancées ; de nombreux projets de loi sont préparés ; d'importants dossiers, sujets de discorde avec le fédéral

---

1. L'Union nationale est issue d'une «union» entre le Parti conservateur du Québec, dirigé par Maurice Duplessis, et l'Action libérale nationale, dirigée par Paul Gouin, en 1935.
2. Défait aux élections de 1935, Paul Sauvé est réélu député de Deux-Montagnes en 1936.
3. C'est ainsi que s'appelait le «président» de l'Assemblée législative.
4. À compter du 15 janvier 1959, le ministère du Bien-être social et de la Jeunesse est scindé en deux : le ministère du Bien-être social et celui de la Jeunesse. Notons que Paul Sauvé est demeuré titulaire des deux ministères.

depuis des années, comme celui des subventions fédérales aux universités québécoises, sont rouverts. À cet effet, la première session du gouvernement Sauvé est certainement l'une des plus riches de l'histoire du Québec[5]. À un point tel que les premiers jours de son gouvernement seront appelés, par les journalistes d'abord et les historiens ensuite, la «révolution des cent jours». De Paul Sauvé, la mémoire collective ainsi que l'historiographie ont retenu le fameux «Désormais…» qu'il aurait prononcé, dit-on, après avoir succédé à Duplessis, marquant ainsi une rupture nette avec son prédécesseur[6]. Pour le dire autrement, tout semble sourire à Paul Sauvé, lui qui a le vent dans les voiles. Rien ne semble pouvoir l'arrêter, alors que Jean Lesage lui-même dira, des années plus tard, qu'il était alors persuadé que Sauvé était en voie de triompher aux prochaines élections provinciales prévues en 1960 (Cardinal, Lemieux et Sauvageau, 1978, p. 45)[7].

Mais le destin en voulut autrement. Cent dix-huit jours après le décès de Maurice Duplessis, Paul Sauvé meurt à son tour, frappé d'une crise cardiaque dans la nuit du 2 janvier 1960. L'élan de l'Union nationale est brisé, et ce, malgré les efforts soutenus de son successeur, Antonio Barrette, pour suivre la voie tracée par Sauvé. Antonio Barrette n'est pas Maurice Duplessis ni Paul Sauvé, dont il ne possède ni les qualités, ni les aptitudes, ni le talent, selon la littérature (Turgeon, 2017a, p. 795-796). Incapable de s'affirmer devant un Georges-Émile Lapalme déchaîné, qui le domine en Chambre[8], Barrette ne fait guère mieux durant la campagne électorale face à un Jean Lesage qui l'attend de pied ferme. C'est dans ce contexte bien particulier que le PLQ l'emporte, le 22 juin 1960, poussant son chef à déclarer que c'est «plus qu'un changement de gouvernement, c'est un changement de la vie!» (Bédard, 2013, p. 206).

Ce «changement de la vie» ne sera pas moindre: il s'agit de la Révolution tranquille, bien que certains auteurs la fassent plutôt débuter avec le «Désormais…» de Paul Sauvé (Ferretti, 2002, p. 133). Modernisation de l'État québécois, nationalisation de l'hydroélectricité et changement identitaire – de la figure du Canadien français à celle de Québécois – sont au rendez-vous. La réputation, si ce n'est la mémoire de la Révolution tranquille se construit déjà,

---

5. Pour en savoir plus sur le programme législatif de cette session, voir le chapitre portant sur cette session parlementaire dans l'ouvrage collectif *Histoire parlementaire du Québec, 1928-1962 : la crise, la guerre, le duplessisme, l'État providence* (Turgeon, 2015a).

6. C'est ce que retiendront la mémoire collective et l'historiographie, disons-nous, bien que Paul Sauvé n'ait jamais prononcé ce «Désormais…» (Turgeon, 2013a).

7. Le père Georges-Henri Lévesque, figure centrale des forces de l'opposition à l'administration duplessiste, en était lui aussi convaincu (Lapalme, 1970, p. 280), tout comme l'historien Lionel Groulx (s.a., 1967).

8. Georges-Émile Lapalme demeure alors le chef de l'Opposition officielle, puisque Jean Lesage n'a pas encore fait son entrée à l'Assemblée législative.

à ce moment, contre la mémoire de ce qu'il convient d'appeler la Grande Noirceur duplessiste. C'est ainsi que nombre d'acteurs, dès les années 1940 et 1950, commencent à nommer cette période qu'ils décrivent comme une sombre parenthèse dans l'histoire du Québec, à l'intérieur de laquelle tout aurait été figé, immobile et immuable à la fois, les forces de la tradition et de la réaction ayant le dessus sur celles du progrès grâce à une alliance tacite entre les pouvoirs temporel et spirituel, entre l'État québécois et l'Église catholique, placée sous la coupe de Maurice Duplessis[9], personnage terrible s'il en est dans l'imaginaire collectif des Québécois.

Dans ces jeux de mémoire où toutes nuances sont évacuées, il ne reste plus que du noir et du blanc, des ténèbres et de la lumière, de la noirceur et de la clarté. Les héros de l'histoire en marche sont ainsi clairement identifiés : il s'agit des libéraux de Jean Lesage avec son « équipe du tonnerre » ainsi que de tous ceux et celles qui l'ont appuyé ou qui ont participé, d'une façon ou d'une autre, à mettre à bas ce « régime » honni à leurs yeux. En retour, il est tout aussi facile de distinguer les perdants de cette histoire : il s'agit de l'Union nationale et de l'Église catholique, des milieux conservateurs de droite, discrédités, avec Maurice Duplessis cloué au pilori mémoriel, lui qui devient le symbole incontesté d'une époque qu'il faut rejeter, dépasser, pour enfin espérer être « maîtres chez nous ».

Aussi l'Union nationale semble-t-elle d'ores et déjà condamnée à écumer les oubliettes de l'Histoire, ou à tout le moins les banquettes de l'opposition, au tournant des années 1960 (Quinn, 1979, p. 200). Décapitée deux fois plutôt qu'une, elle reprend du mieux avec l'arrivée de Daniel Johnson à sa tête, le 23 septembre 1961, mais elle subit coup sur coup les audiences de la commission Salvas (1962 ; Lévesque, 2011), qui met en lumière la corruption et les sévices commis sous l'administration Duplessis, et le scrutin de 1962, qui voit le PLQ être plébiscité sur la question de la nationalisation de l'hydroélectricité, ce à quoi s'est opposée l'Union nationale. Or, contre toute attente, l'Union nationale revient au pouvoir en 1966, au plus fort de la Révolution tranquille.

Donnée pour morte au début des années 1960, l'Union nationale n'avait pas dit son dernier mot… mais le destin non plus, de toute évidence. À son tour, Daniel Johnson est emporté par une crise cardiaque, le 26 septembre 1968. Tout est à refaire. Face à l'émergence du Parti Québécois (PQ), dirigé par René Lévesque, prêt à lui couper l'herbe nationaliste sous les pieds, l'Union nationale est à la croisée des chemins. En 1968, deux voies possibles semblent se dessiner pour la formation politique. Si le décès de Daniel Johnson s'apparente un tant soit peu à celui de Maurice Duplessis, l'Union nationale pourrait fort bien se

---

9. Cette vision des relations entre l'Église catholique et l'État québécois sous Duplessis, qui a largement prévalu dans l'historiographie et dans l'imaginaire collectif, doit toutefois être nuancée. Voir Dumas (2019).

relever, plus forte encore, à moins que son décès ne soit davantage similaire à celui de Paul Sauvé, auquel cas la formation politique, incapable de se renouveler, pourrait au contraire s'effondrer devant l'adversité. Encore faudrait-il, pour cela, que le passé soit garant de l'avenir. Dans le Québec de la Révolution tranquille, où les fantômes du passé ne cessent de ressurgir, on serait parfois tenté de le croire.

Pour éclairer ce phénomène, je me propose dans ce texte d'étudier de plus près les tentatives de l'Union nationale de s'affirmer sur le plan mémoriel, entre 1959 et 1968. Alors que la reconfiguration mémorielle en cours durant la Révolution tranquille bat son plein, l'enjeu est de taille ; il en va de la survie même de la formation politique, au bord du gouffre, menacée qu'elle est sur tous les fronts. Pour les ténors de l'Union nationale, le défi est double. D'un côté, ils doivent composer avec l'héritage controversé de Maurice Duplessis, déjà associé de près au souvenir de la Grande Noirceur. De l'autre, ils doivent également se positionner face à Paul Sauvé, son dauphin, dont le célèbre « Désormais… », aussi faux soit-il, est vu comme un reniement du duplessisme tout autant qu'un prélude à la Révolution tranquille. D'autant plus que les libéraux, aux aguets, ne restent pas les bras croisés devant ce qui se trame. En d'autres termes : est-il possible pour l'Union nationale de réconcilier le duplessisme au « Désormais… » de Paul Sauvé, tout particulièrement en 1968 ? Et que reste-t-il, aujourd'hui, de ces tentatives de l'Union nationale de tirer son épingle de ces jeux mémoriels et politiques ? Voilà quelques-unes des questions abordées dans ce texte.

Les « cent jours » de Paul Sauvé

D'entrée de jeu, afin de bien comprendre ces jeux de mémoire et la façon dont l'Union nationale a su se démarquer dans ce contexte qui apparaissait des plus défavorables, du moins au premier regard, il importe de s'intéresser de plus près aux « cent jours » de Paul Sauvé. Aussi éphémère que fût son gouvernement, et bien qu'il ait été au pouvoir plus de six mois avant l'élection de Jean Lesage et l'avènement de la Révolution tranquille, tout semble porter à croire que Sauvé ait été à même de cerner les enjeux et les défis qui attendaient l'Union nationale, dans les années 1960, et de lui insuffler le souffle nécessaire pour les surmonter et s'affirmer face au Parti libéral du Québec.

Nous l'avons dit, une fois en poste, Sauvé s'empresse de mettre en branle une panoplie de réformes nécessaires qui, jusque-là, avaient été ignorées ou repoussées par son prédécesseur. Longtemps troubles sous Maurice Duplessis, pour culminer avec l'expulsion *manu militari* de Guy Lamarche, journaliste au *Devoir*, du bureau du premier ministre, les relations avec la presse sont normalisées ; le salaire des fonctionnaires est considérablement augmenté ; la loi sur l'énumérateur (recenseur) unique lors des scrutins, dénoncée avec virulence par Georges-Émile Lapalme durant des années, est abrogée. Voici quelques exemples des mesures et des réformes mises en place par Paul Sauvé, lesquelles étaient réclamées par l'opposition libérale depuis des années.

Appliquer ces réformes, aussi nécessaires soient-elles, requiert néanmoins un certain courage politique de la part de Paul Sauvé en ces temps où l'Union nationale est fragilisée, elle qui vient tout juste de perdre son « cheuf »[10]. Le nouveau premier ministre s'avance en effet sur un terrain glissant, où la frontière est mince entre la saine administration et le reniement, si ce n'est le désaveu de Maurice Duplessis, lui qui a obstinément refusé ces réformes jusqu'à son trépas. Cette question est d'autant plus sensible, à l'automne 1959, que les libéraux n'hésitent pas à alimenter les braises de la discorde à même d'enflammer l'Union nationale tout entière, aux prises avec ses contradictions internes.

Paul Sauvé en est toutefois bien conscient, lui qui sait à quel point la base électorale de l'Union nationale demeure fidèle à la mémoire de Duplessis. Aussi, nonobstant le fait que ses nombreuses réformes et mesures tranchent radicalement avec les façons de faire de celui qui fut son père politique, Sauvé n'hésite pas à affirmer, en Chambre et dans ses allocutions diffusées à la radio ou à la télévision, que rien n'a changé, au fond. Le 14 décembre 1959, il insiste sur le fait que la « voix de la province peut avoir changé et son ton peut avoir changé, mais la province n'a pas changé », depuis le départ de Maurice Duplessis, dont il poursuit « simplement le travail entrepris » (Assemblée nationale du Québec, 1959, p. 53). Une stratégie qui ne sourira pas à tous, cela dit. Mais nous y reviendrons.

Sauvé réalise en outre qu'il lui faut ménager la mémoire de Duplessis, laquelle est déjà, bien que toute récente, des plus controversées et la cible d'assauts répétés. Aussi lui consacre-t-il le tout premier projet de loi de son imposant programme législatif. Il s'agit du « bill 2 pour rendre hommage à la mémoire de l'honorable Maurice L. Duplessis », présenté le 19 novembre 1959 (Assemblée nationale du Québec, 1959, p. 11). La statue, façonnée par le sculpteur Émile Brunet, est complétée le 22 mai 1961. Le Québec est alors dirigé par Jean Lesage qui, n'osant l'exposer, la range plutôt dans un entrepôt, à l'abri des regards, où elle demeurera durant près de 16 ans. En fait, il faudra attendre l'arrivée au pouvoir du gouvernement du Parti Québécois de René Lévesque, le 9 septembre 1977, pour que cette statue voie enfin la lumière du jour et trouve sa place sur les pelouses de l'Assemblée nationale du Québec, en bordure de la Grande Allée. Lors de son inauguration, Lévesque tient d'ailleurs à expliquer sa décision. Selon le premier ministre péquiste, c'est « un très mauvais exercice pour une société que celui de prétendre effacer des morceaux de l'Histoire » (cité dans Leprince, 1979).

---

10. C'est ainsi que certains de ses partisans appelaient leur « chef », Maurice Duplessis. Voir Laporte (1960c, 65).

Cette habileté qu'a Paul Sauvé à ménager ainsi le chèvre et le chou, à se faire tout à la fois le héraut des réformes et le chantre de la continuité, soulève l'ire des libéraux, pris au dépourvu, eux qui ne savent plus à quels saints se vouer. Alors que Sauvé s'affaire à appliquer le programme des libéraux, à quelques détails près, leur coupant pour ainsi dire l'herbe sous le pied, celui-ci parvient du même souffle à honorer la mémoire de son père politique, marquant des points de tous bords, tous côtés.

Cela dit, les libéraux ne sont pas les seuls à ne pas savoir sur quel pied danser devant la contradiction inhérente chez Sauvé : il en est de même des observateurs et des analystes de la vie politique québécoise qui souhaitent en rendre compte dans leurs écrits. C'est le cas tout particulièrement des artisans du journal *Le Devoir*. Parmi les plus critiques de l'administration duplessiste depuis longtemps déjà, ils mènent une charge de tous les instants contre les travers et les vices de ce gouvernement dans une action concertée des journalistes, des éditorialistes et des caricaturistes. Que ce soit sous la plume de Pierre Laporte ou d'André Laurendeau, ou encore sous le coup de crayon de Robert La Palme ou de Normand Hudon, les attaques se font incisives et incessantes durant les années 1950. À partir de 1956, alors que s'intensifie la grogne contre le gouvernement de Maurice Duplessis et que s'organisent les forces d'opposition à l'Union nationale, qu'elles soient politiques ou civiles, *Le Devoir* s'impose comme un chef de file de ce mouvement (Turgeon, 2015b, p. 321-326).

À la mort de Maurice Duplessis, comme il est d'usage dans les circonstances, les artisans du *Devoir* se font plus circonspects, saluant la contribution de celui qui fut premier ministre de la province de 1936 à 1939, puis de 1944 à 1959, afin de lui rendre un hommage bien senti (s.a., 1959b). Lorsqu'il est annoncé que Paul Sauvé lui succédera, dans les jours qui suivent, les artisans du quotidien se montrent prudents, du moins dans un premier temps. Cette prudence ne sera toutefois que momentanée.

«Québec : l'atmosphère est complètement changée!» (Laporte, 1959b) titre *Le Devoir* en une le lendemain de l'assermentation de Paul Sauvé, sous la plume de Pierre Laporte. Il s'agit bien du même journaliste à qui l'on doit le scandale de la Corporation du gaz naturel, lequel a fait grand bruit en 1958 et tant nui au gouvernement Duplessis (Turgeon, 2013b, p. 380). En 24 heures seulement, au terme d'une seule conférence de presse, Sauvé parvient à subjuguer les journalistes rassemblés devant lui. La suite des événements ne fait que confirmer les dispositions favorables des artisans du *Devoir* à l'endroit du nouveau premier ministre[11].

---

11. À l'inverse, le caricaturiste Robert La Palme, qui se joint à *La Presse* en février 1959 après avoir travaillé au *Devoir* entre 1951 et 1959, demeure un critique féroce de Paul Sauvé. De toute évidence, il ne partage pas l'enthousiasme de ses anciens

Ils doivent toutefois composer, comme nous l'avons dit, avec la contradiction inhérente, et incontournable, entre les paroles et les actes de Sauvé. S'ils approuvent les gestes de rupture de l'administration Sauvé, ils sont toutefois plus dubitatifs devant les professions de foi inconditionnelles de celui-ci envers Duplessis. Aussi, lorsque vient le temps pour les observateurs et autres analystes d'expliquer ou de rationaliser le comportement de Sauvé, la tâche s'annonce pour le moins compliquée. C'est le cas d'André Laurendeau, qui ne sait trop sous quel angle l'aborder. Aussi en vient-il à user d'un subterfuge. Ne pouvant résoudre la contradiction entre les paroles et les gestes de Sauvé, Laurendeau passe outre en faisant prononcer au premier ministre un marqueur de rupture temporelle dans un encadré au titre sans équivoque : «Désormais, dit-il». Dans ce texte, signé de son pseudonyme Candide (1959), Laurendeau utilise le vocable à 15 reprises, ce qui est notable. Dès le départ, l'éditorialiste définit ce mythe tel qu'on le retrouvera par la suite dans la littérature : «Le mot éclate sans préparation. Il n'est précédé ni d'un *mais* ni d'un *cependant* avertisseur. Il se tient solidement sur ses trois pattes : dé-sor-mais. Il a comme une valeur propre. En lui se résorbent d'apparentes contradictions. C'est un jugement implicite et discret, et c'est en même temps une promesse formelle.»

Que ce soit sous la plume d'André Laurendeau (1959a) ou celle de Pierre Laporte (1959a), le «Désormais…» apparaît çà et là dans les pages du *Devoir* à l'automne 1959. Rapidement, il n'est plus seulement un mot qui serait prisé par le premier ministre ; il en vient à incarner ses politiques et ses réformes (s.a., 1959c ; 1959d). Grâce à ce terme, la contradiction entre les paroles et les gestes de Paul Sauvé n'est plus. Or, le «Désormais…» ne règle pas tout pour autant, en cela qu'il ne parvient pas à rendre justice à toute la complexité de l'époque. Il faut rappeler ici les propos d'André Laurendeau (1959b) du 28 novembre 1959. Dans ce texte, il constate que Sauvé «ne dit plus "désormais…"» ; «M. Sauvé, cette fois, n'a pas dit *désormais*. Là-dessus, le duplessisme continue.» Est-ce à dire que le «Désormais…», en quelques semaines à peine, aurait déjà épuisé toute sa charge symbolique ? Cela montre plutôt que pour André Laurendeau, la contradiction demeure entière chez Sauvé, jusqu'à sa mort, et ce, malgré la présence du «Désormais…», dont Laurendeau est non seulement l'auteur, mais aussi le premier promoteur.

Le bref intermède d'Antonio Barrette

Le pari tenté et remporté par Paul Sauvé, Antonio Barrette le tente à son tour, sans que ses efforts ne soient couronnés du même succès. Si Sauvé a été le choix unanime du cabinet à la mort de Maurice Duplessis, les discussions demeurant brèves du reste, Antonio Barrette, lui, a été le choix du compromis,

---

collègues du *Devoir* pour le nouveau premier ministre (Turgeon, 2015b, p. 395-401).

si ce n'est un choix par dépit ou par défaut pourrait-on dire, alors que les discussions s'éternisaient (Pelletier, 1989, p. 238). Une fois confirmé à titre de chef de l'Union nationale et assermenté premier ministre de la province de Québec, Barrette s'attelle lui aussi à la tâche avec une ardeur et une énergie dont il n'est pratiquement jamais fait mention dans la littérature, et qu'il faut lui reconnaître. Le nouveau premier ministre poursuit les réformes entamées par Sauvé, menant à terme le dossier des subventions fédérales aux universités québécoises, dans lequel il s'illustre.

Mais Antonio Barrette n'est pas Paul Sauvé. Au-delà du simple énoncé des faits, qui relève de l'évidence, cette distinction apparaît clairement dans la manière dont les libéraux le perçoivent et le considèrent. Le cas de Georges-Émile Lapalme est éloquent à cet effet. Modèle de politesse et homme politique raffiné, ce qui le desservait la plupart du temps lorsqu'il croisait le fer rhétorique et parlementaire avec Maurice Duplessis, Lapalme se révèle pugnace et cinglant envers Barrette, formulant des rappels au Règlement à tout propos, cherchant noise au nouveau premier ministre pour un rien. Il faut dire qu'une inimitié personnelle unit, ou désunit, les deux hommes, rivaux depuis longtemps et tous deux natifs du même patelin, Joliette. Lapalme méprise profondément Barrette. Dans ses mémoires, Lapalme (1970, p. 276) en profite d'ailleurs pour régler ses comptes avec l'ancien ministre du Travail de l'administration Duplessis, sur lequel il déverse son fiel : «Antonio Barrette croira, et croit peut-être encore, qu'il a été premier ministre.» Le coup porté à sa mémoire est fatal. Antonio Barrette sera dès lors relégué du côté des perdants de l'Histoire, au point de devenir, peut-être, le grand perdant de la Révolution tranquille[12].

Ce n'est pas faute d'essayer. Tout comme son prédécesseur, Barrette poursuit les réformes, assumant par là une certaine rupture, alors qu'il se réclame du même souffle de l'œuvre de Duplessis et de Sauvé. Il est vrai que Barrette ne pousse pas la note jusqu'à évoquer le «Désormais…» de Sauvé, d'une façon ou d'une autre, aussi faux le mot soit-il. À ce propos, il faut dire que Barrette n'est pas le seul à garder ses distances avec ce mythe ; à l'Assemblée législative, les membres de l'Union nationale et du Parti libéral ne se sont pas encore prononcés sur le «Désormais…» de Paul Sauvé, lequel demeure confiné, pour l'instant du moins, à la scène médiatique, pour ne pas dire à celle du *Devoir* exclusivement. Cela n'empêche pas un Pierre Laporte (1960b), justement, de reconnaître ou du moins d'entrevoir, dans les manières un peu plus rustres, un peu moins subtiles de Barrette, le «Désormais…» de Sauvé. Mais cette impression demeure fugace, évanescente. Le sentiment ne dure guère[13].

---

12. Pour un exemple récent de cet état de fait, voir le texte de Jonathan Livernois (2016) dans la revue *Argument*.

13. À l'inverse, durant la session parlementaire, Pierre Laporte (1960a) se montre pour le moins déçu d'Antonio Barrette : «André Laurendeau a créé une formule qui

Antonio Barrette est aussi capable de passer à l'offensive, de monter au front mémoriel afin de porter, chez les libéraux, le poids infâme et odieux de la Grande Noirceur. Le 4 mars 1960, il revient sur le gouvernement libéral d'Adélard Godbout, premier ministre de 1939 à 1944 après l'avoir été brièvement en 1936. C'est ainsi que ses propos sont rapportés dans les débats reconstitués de l'Assemblée législative : « Nous payons encore le prix du marché conclu alors entre libéraux provinciaux et fédéraux en mai 1939 et nous poursuivons l'œuvre de récupération des droits cédés. Ce fut la rupture avec la tradition autonomiste des libéraux. Il (l'honorable M. Barrette) compare le régime de M. Godbout à la grande noirceur. » (Assemblée nationale du Québec, 1960, p. 861). Pour Barrette, comme pour plusieurs nationalistes à l'époque, le crime d'Adélard Godbout est d'avoir sacrifié l'autonomie de la province sur l'autel de la coopération entre libéraux provinciaux et fédéraux durant la Seconde Guerre mondiale. C'est ce qui mérite, à ses yeux, l'anathème de la Grande Noirceur. Cette forme particulière de l'expression n'est toutefois pas restée, c'est-à-dire qu'elle ne fait pas partie des usages courants, alors que la Grande Noirceur continue, aujourd'hui encore, d'être associée au souvenir de Maurice Duplessis. Cela étant, cette tentative montre bien que les ténors de l'Union nationale étaient au courant des enjeux mémoriels de la période, eux qui tentaient de s'approprier, autant que possible, ces mythes en cours d'élaboration.

Durant la campagne électorale de 1960, Antonio Barrette aura beau se réclamer comme jamais auparavant de l'œuvre de ses prédécesseurs, poussant l'audace, si ce n'est la témérité, à se considérer leur égal[14] – les « trois grands », c'est ainsi que Duplessis, Sauvé et Barrette sont appelés dans les publicités électorales de l'Union nationale[15] –, ce n'est pas suffisant. Le stratagème de Paul

---

résume cela : "M. Barrette a fait voter (parfois) des lois de M. Sauvé avec des arguments de M. Duplessis." Il nous est arrivé d'avoir le goût de récrire le mot "désormais".»

14. Antonio Barrette voulait tant se montrer à la hauteur de son prédécesseur qu'il en vint à commettre des péchés d'orgueil. À titre d'exemple, la session parlementaire devait reprendre ses activités le 11 janvier 1960. C'était sans compter le décès de Paul Sauvé, survenu dans la nuit du 2 janvier 1960. Au terme d'âpres discussions menées au sein du cabinet, Barrette est désigné chef de l'Union nationale le 7 janvier, et assermenté premier ministre le lendemain. Or, la session reprend le cours de ses activités le 11 janvier, comme prévu. Alors que Sauvé avait eu plus de deux mois entre son assermentation (11 septembre) et l'ouverture de la session (18 novembre), Barrette ne bénéficie pour sa part que de quatre jours pour se préparer. Dans ses mémoires, Barrette (1966, p. 205) précise qu'il « [s]e faisai[t] un point d'honneur de siéger à la date désignée ».

15. Une telle publicité apparaît dans l'édition du journal *Le Devoir* du 14 mai 1960, à la page 5.

Sauvé, qui a tant souri au fils d'Arthur Sauvé, ne soustrait point Antonio Barrette aux foudres électorales[16]. Défait le 22 juin 1960, il ne demeure pas en poste comme chef du parti alors que s'amorce une période sombre pour l'Union nationale à l'heure, si ce n'est à l'ère, de la Révolution tranquille.

L'Union nationale sous Daniel Johnson

Arrivés au pouvoir, les libéraux ne perdent pas de temps pour appliquer leur programme, dont les grandes lignes se trouvent déjà dans le pamphlet *Pour une politique*, écrit à l'été 1959 par Georges-Émile Lapalme (1988; D. Savard, 1991, p. 177). Dans les faits, les libéraux se retrouvent eux aussi à emprunter le chemin tracé à l'origine par Paul Sauvé, à la suite d'Antonio Barrette, bien que le nom de ce dernier soit pratiquement effacé des mémoires. Dans la joute mémorielle qui s'annonce, à l'orée des années 1960, ce sera comme si Barrette n'avait jamais été premier ministre, ou presque. Là-dessus, force est d'admettre que Lapalme a vu juste – ou à tout le moins, que son interprétation a fait date (Lapalme, 1970, p. 276).

Les libéraux appliquent leur programme, mais ils ont également des comptes à régler avec leurs adversaires de l'Union nationale, et avec Maurice Duplessis en particulier. Seize années à ronger leur frein sur les banquettes de l'opposition et à subir railleries et moqueries de la part du «cheuf» ont laissé des traces, à n'en pas douter. Aussi s'attaquent-ils avec ferveur à la mémoire et à la réputation de Duplessis. Non pas qu'ils aient attendu d'être au pouvoir pour cela. Depuis le milieu des années 1940, le Parti libéral provincial s'est évertué à brosser un portrait fort peu reluisant du chef de l'Union nationale, s'assurant pour ce faire les services du caricaturiste Robert La Palme. Entre 1943 et 1951, au sein du journal *Le Canada*, organe officiel du Parti libéral, La Palme présente sa vision caustique et délurée du chef de l'Union nationale et de son «régime» (Turgeon, 2009). Ses caricatures sont également reprises dans des brochures électorales du Parti libéral, et ce, même après que La Palme ait mis un terme à son association avec *Le Canada* pour se joindre au *Devoir*, en 1951 (Turgeon, 2015b, p. 318-348). Dans ces images, élaborées de concert avec des apparatchiks libéraux dans le cadre d'une vaste entreprise de marketing politique (Turgeon, 2014), se trouvent quelques-unes des idées-forces de la Grande Noirceur duplessiste (Turgeon, 2013b).

Après 1960, si l'objectif des libéraux en la matière demeure le même, leurs moyens et les ressources à leur disposition sont tout autres. La Commission

---

16. Les critiques fusent également de son propre parti. Paul Ste-Marie, ancien substitut du procureur général, fait porter le poids de l'odieux de la défaite à Antonio Barrette, pour avoir «manqué de stratégie», mais aussi à Paul Sauvé, lui qui «a répudié la politique de son prédécesseur» avec ses «Désormais…» durant les «cent jours» (s.a., 1960).

d'enquête sur la vente du réseau de gaz de l'Hydro-Québec à la Corporation de gaz naturel, aussi connue sous le nom de commission Salvas, est mise en place le 5 octobre 1960, soit quelques mois à peine après la victoire libérale. Le monument à la mémoire de Maurice Duplessis commandé par Paul Sauvé, aussitôt reçu, est aussitôt rangé loin des regards, dans un entrepôt du gouvernement. En Chambre, les députés ministériels ne manquent pas une occasion de rappeler les liens des députés de l'opposition avec Duplessis pour leur faire ombrage. À ce sujet, le «Désormais…» de Paul Sauvé peut s'avérer une arme redoutable, pour qui sait bien l'utiliser.

Le premier député à évoquer de la sorte le «Désormais…» de Sauvé en Chambre est Pierre Laporte. L'ancien journaliste du *Devoir*, élu député libéral du comté de Chambly au terme d'une élection partielle, le 14 décembre 1961, se révèle un débatteur pugnace, à même de tirer son épingle du jeu dans l'arène parlementaire. Réagissant aux propos du nouveau chef de l'Union nationale, Daniel Johnson, qui dénonce le «gauchisme» dans le domaine de l'assurance édition au Québec, Pierre Laporte se fait cinglant dans son commentaire, le 3 avril 1962: «Au lieu de soutenir l'effort de la loi pour aider la culture, l'U.N. fait action négative et continue de traîner le gauchisme qu'elle moussa durant 15 ans. Mais le gauchisme est mort. Il est mort quand M. Sauvé, debout en face de moi, a dit: "Désormais!"» (Thivierge, 1962)

Mais de tels propos tenus à leur endroit n'empêchent pas les membres de l'Union nationale de tenter de récupérer le «Désormais…» de Paul Sauvé à leur profit, au tournant des années 1960. Dans les pages du journal *Notre Temps*, organe de l'Union nationale, le journaliste Léopold Richer prend avec humour et «gaieté» un éditorial d'André Laurendeau (1959a) intitulé «M. Sauvé déconcerte amis et adversaires». Dans son texte, s'il reconnaît d'emblée que les adversaires de l'Union nationale sont bel et bien déconcertés par les faits et gestes du nouveau premier ministre, Richer (1959) se défend bien de l'être, lui et «ceux qui le connaissent bien». Mais plus intéressant encore pour notre propos, Richer cite Laurendeau, alors que celui-ci mentionne justement le «Désormais…»:

> Voici, en tout cas, un paragraphe particulièrement comique de l'article de M. Laurendeau: «M. Sauvé a un tempérament très différent (de celui de M. Duplessis). Il s'est montré jusqu'ici sage et habile. En deux mois, il a complètement modifié le paysage. Ses "désormais", ses "à l'avenir" tombent comme des coups de hache sur ce qui reste de vieux embêtements duplessistes. Nous l'avons noté à diverses reprises: les partisans du gouvernement sont visiblement décontenancés, et ils parlent, faute de mieux, de la pluie et du beau temps.»

C'est gentil. Mais c'est faux. Les amis du gouvernement s'attendaient exactement à ce que M. Sauvé agisse comme il l'a fait. Et ils ne parlent pas, faute de mieux, de la pluie et du beau temps. Ils parlent, bien au contraire, d'innombrables innovations : le règlement du problème universitaire, la hausse des salaires des fonctionnaires, les amendements aux lois ouvrières. Et que sais-je encore ?

L'extrait est révélateur. Alors que Léopold Richer dément catégoriquement que les partisans du gouvernement soient décontenancés par les faits et gestes de Paul Sauvé, n'hésitant pas à clamer sans préambule que « c'est faux », il ne porte toutefois pas un jugement similaire et sans appel sur le « Désormais… ». Pour une raison ou pour une autre, le vocable n'est pas remis en question par le journaliste de *Notre Temps*, lui qui ne semble pas s'en préoccuper outre mesure.

Dans les pages du *Montréal-Matin*, un autre journal sous le contrôle de l'Union nationale, le « Désormais… » de Paul Sauvé n'est pas seulement toléré ou accepté, mais bien assumé cette fois-ci (s.a., 1959a). Tout comme pour *Notre Temps*, la rédaction du *Montréal-Matin* revient sur un texte du *Devoir*, signé cette fois par Pierre Laporte (1959a). Reprochant au correspondant parlementaire du *Devoir* de chercher noise pour un rien au nouveau premier ministre, usant du « Désormais… » pour mieux s'en moquer, la rédaction considère que « les "désormais" dont on cherche à se moquer ont valu et vaudront encore à la province le progrès et le bien-être ». Mais ce n'est pas tout, même si c'est déjà beaucoup. La rédaction du *Montréal-Matin* n'en reste pas là : « Il faut avouer, d'ailleurs, que ces "désormais", plus que par les années passées encore, sèment la déroute dans le camp libéral. » Non seulement le *Montréal-Matin* ne remet-il pas en question le « Désormais… », mais plus encore, celui-ci se retrouverait, ou du moins son esprit, au sein de l'Union nationale, et ce, depuis de nombreuses années déjà. C'est-à-dire que le « Désormais… », sous une forme ou sous une autre, serait en lui-même une partie intégrante du duplessisme. Le « Désormais… » de Paul Sauvé n'en est pas à sa première contradiction ; ce ne sera pas sa dernière non plus.

Non seulement les membres de l'Union nationale peuvent-ils se réclamer du « Désormais… » et l'assumer pleinement, mais ils peuvent s'en servir eux aussi comme une arme prête à être retournée contre les libéraux. C'est d'ailleurs ce qui se produira durant la campagne électorale de 1962. Une semaine avant la tenue du scrutin, le 14 novembre 1962, Jean Lesage y va d'une déclaration fracassante : il invite Jean-Jacques Bertrand à renier les siens pour se rallier au Parti libéral du Québec. Ce n'est pas un hasard si Lesage cible Bertrand. Aspirant malheureux à la direction du parti, en 1961, il était considéré comme le candidat des réformistes, dans la tradition de Paul Sauvé, tandis que Daniel Johnson aurait été, au contraire, dans celle de Maurice Duplessis, lui qui était associé à la vieille garde duplessiste de la formation politique. Lors du congrès au leadership de l'Union nationale, la veuve de Paul Sauvé, Luce Pelland, avait d'ailleurs appuyé symboliquement la candidature de Jean-Jacques Bertrand (Quinn, 1979, p. 202).

Sans surprise, Bertrand décline l'invitation de Jean Lesage. Loin d'accepter la main tendue par le premier ministre, celui qui fut ministre des Terres et Forêts dans le gouvernement Sauvé se rebiffe et dirige le tir contre le gouvernement libéral : « L'électorat nous donne l'occasion, à mes collègues et à moi-même, de poursuivre la politique de Paul Sauvé, de reprendre le fameux "Désormais" là où [les libéraux ont] échoué. » (Bertrand, 1962, p. 6) Mais l'appel de Bertrand est resté lettre morte. Non seulement l'électorat ne leur a pas donné l'occasion de poursuivre la politique de Sauvé, préférant reporter au pouvoir les libéraux pour un second mandat, mais aucun autre membre de l'Union nationale, y compris Daniel Johnson, n'a évoqué le « Désormais… » de Sauvé durant la campagne électorale de 1962. Quatre ans plus tard, la stratégie de l'Union nationale sur cet enjeu allait être tout autre.

Vers le retour de l'Union nationale au pouvoir

Pour la seconde fois en trois ans, l'Union nationale mord la poussière devant le Parti libéral du Québec. De toute évidence, les manières d'antan n'ont pas donné les résultats escomptés. Homme politique pragmatique et avisé, Daniel Johnson le voit bien. Aussi tire-t-il les leçons qui s'imposent de cette défaite électorale, en plus de mesurer l'écueil qui le sépare de l'aile réformiste de son parti, dont Jean-Jacques Bertrand est le leader officieux (Latouche, 2008). À ces fins, Johnson entreprend de revoir de fond en comble les structures du parti tout autant que son positionnement idéologique et sa stratégie électorale au cours d'un congrès qui se tient en mars 1965. Ce faisant, Johnson est appelé à statuer sur la place que Maurice Duplessis et Paul Sauvé peuvent occuper dans la rhétorique unioniste, si seulement encore il est possible de le faire alors que l'Union nationale se met au diapason des années 1960.

Le renouveau de l'Union nationale se déploie sur plus d'un front. Sensible aux critiques de Jean-Jacques Bertrand, qui reprochait depuis quelque temps déjà au parti de concentrer tous les pouvoirs entre les seules mains du chef, Daniel Johnson propose l'instauration d'un conseil national formé des membres du caucus, de trois délégués issus de chaque comté ainsi que du chef du parti. Les pouvoirs du conseil national sont tels qu'il peut remettre en question le leadership du chef, au besoin. Cette mesure, qui a pour effet de démocratiser grandement les instances de l'Union nationale, satisfait Bertrand, qui se rallie pour de bon à son chef (Quinn, 1979, p. 216).

Sur le plan idéologique, Daniel Johnson poursuit dans cette voie, éloignant l'Union nationale de ses tendances duplessistes pour la ramener au centre (Guay et Gaudreau, 2018, p. 330). Ce faisant, la formation politique est pour ainsi dire happée par l'esprit de la Révolution tranquille, dont elle était pourtant l'une des plus féroces critiques peu de temps auparavant. Les mesures adoptées lors du congrès de 1965 en témoignent : l'Union nationale propose notamment la création d'un ministère de l'Immigration et d'un ministère de la Planification économique, la gratuité pour tous à tous les niveaux d'éducation, un régime d'assurance maladie et une loi anti-briseurs de grève, autant de mesures qui s'inscrivent dans la mouvance de la Révolution tranquille (Quinn, 1979, p. 216).

Daniel Johnson positionne également son parti sur l'enjeu émergent de l'indépendance (Bélanger, 1999) en faisant paraître, tout juste avant la tenue du congrès, un essai au titre provocateur qui donne le ton en plus d'annoncer la politique à venir de l'Union nationale : Égalité ou indépendance (Johnson, 1965). Cet essai, qui se veut un pavé lancé dans la mare constitutionnelle canadienne, est bien reçu des milieux nationalistes québécois (Quinn, 1979, p. 212) et permet à sa formation politique de s'imposer favorablement sur ce terrain qu'occupent le Parti libéral du Québec et les partis indépendantistes, le Rassemblement pour l'indépendance nationale et le Ralliement national.

Enfin, l'Union nationale revoit sa stratégie en vue des prochaines élections. Au lieu de mener une campagne traditionnelle, à la grandeur de la province – ce qu'elle n'a plus les moyens de faire –, elle cible une soixantaine de comtés susceptibles d'être pris, « en concentrant [son] effort là où [ses] chances sont meilleures » (Francœur, 1966, p. 14), afin de pouvoir s'assurer une majorité parlementaire (Guay et Gaudreau, 2018, p. 331).

Sur le plan mémoriel, le déroulement de la campagne électorale témoigne de ce changement de ton. L'Union nationale fait alors le pari d'assumer pleinement la mémoire de ses deux premiers chefs. Alors que le « Désormais… » de Paul Sauvé est incompatible avec le duplessisme dans l'argumentaire libéral, il en est autrement dans la rhétorique unioniste. Pour les ténors de l'Union nationale, il ne semble y avoir là aucune contradiction. Par le fait même, la formation politique fait également le choix pour le moins judicieux d'oublier son troisième chef, Antonio Barrette, dont la parution des mémoires tout juste avant la tenue du scrutin, qui se voulait une bombe pour son ancien parti (Dufresne, 1966 ; s.a., 1966d), se révèle plutôt être un pétard mouillé.

Présidée par la veuve de Paul Sauvé, Luce Pelland, qui s'est ralliée elle aussi à Daniel Johnson, la dernière assemblée électorale de l'Union nationale se serait même tenue sous le thème du « Désormais… ». Selon Mario Cardinal (1966), journaliste au *Devoir*, « l'assemblée a fourni aux orateurs l'occasion de faire l'éloge de cet homme qui fut cent jours premier ministre de la province et dont M. Bertrand disait que l'Union nationale était prête à continuer le travail ». Or, aussi spontané qu'ait pu être ce choix, il est pour le moins curieux que ni *La Presse* (Turcotte, 1966), ni *Le Droit* (s.a., 1966c), ni le *Montréal-Matin* (Rioux,

1966), ni *Le Soleil* (Ladouceur, 1966), ni *The Gazette* (Pape, 1966), ni le *Montréal Star* (Cowan, 1966) n'aient cru bon de rapporter, dans leurs comptes rendus, que l'assemblée se serait tenue sous ce thème. Une fois de plus, *Le Devoir* fait cavalier seul lorsque vient le temps d'évoquer le «Désormais…» dans l'espace public québécois.

Ce qui est d'autant plus intéressant dans ces usages du passé, c'est que les membres de l'Union nationale se réclament de la sorte du «Désormais…» de Paul Sauvé sans pour autant renier l'héritage de Maurice Duplessis. Le député de Champlain, Maurice Bellemare, n'hésite pas à qualifier «la révolution tranquille du gouvernement Lesage de jargon de planificateur fait en faveur des amis partisans du pouvoir», reprochant du même souffle aux libéraux d'être des «démolisseurs des œuvres de feu Maurice Duplessis» (s.a., 1966a). À l'occasion d'une assemblée électorale qui se tient à Trois-Rivières, le fief de Maurice Duplessis, Daniel Johnson tient à rendre hommage lui aussi au fondateur de l'Union nationale. Il salue notamment l'«attitude autonomiste» de son ancien chef, lui qui devrait «être considéré comme l'inspirateur du nouveau nationalisme québécois» (s.a., 1966b).

En 1966, ce mariage de raison – ou de nécessité – entre le duplessisme et le «Désormais…» au sein de l'Union nationale semble plus fort que jamais. Sous le leadership renouvelé de Daniel Johnson, il est possible en effet de tenir une assemblée électorale sous le thème du «Désormais…» tout en se réclamant de Duplessis, de critiquer les fondements de la Révolution tranquille tout en s'inscrivant directement dans son sillage (Quinn, 1979, p. 219).

À terme, le positionnement idéologique et la stratégie de l'Union nationale portent fruit : après une campagne âprement disputée, l'Union nationale remporte la victoire, le 5 juin 1966, en faisant élire 56 députés contre 50 pour le Parti libéral du Québec sur 108 sièges. Or, au chapitre des votes, la domination libérale se poursuit : 1 099 435 électeurs ont voté pour un candidat libéral, contre seulement 948 928 pour un candidat unioniste. La situation est telle que Jean Lesage prend même quelques jours avant de concéder la défaite à Daniel Johnson (Lesage, 1966, p. 1).

Si certains analystes ont pu craindre que c'en était fini de la Révolution tranquille avec le retour au pouvoir de l'Union nationale (Guay et Gaudreau, 2018, p. 336), il n'en fut rien. Au contraire, elle en poursuivit l'œuvre (Quinn, 1979, p. 229). C'est le cas notamment dans le domaine de l'enseignement, où l'Union nationale a donné suite à certaines recommandations du rapport Parent. Ainsi, les premiers collèges d'enseignement général et professionnel – les cégeps – font leur apparition en 1967 tandis que le réseau de l'Université du Québec est lancé en 1968 afin de favoriser un accès plus large à l'enseignement supérieur au Québec, tout particulièrement en région. Des premières antennes sont fondées à Montréal, Trois-Rivières et Chicoutimi, puis d'autres s'ajouteront à Rimouski, Hull et Rouyn (Bilan du siècle, s.d.).

Le gouvernement Johnson se démarque également sur le plan culturel par la création de Radio-Québec en 1968, qui deviendra Télé-Québec en 1996. Institution majeure de la vie culturelle québécoise dès sa mise en place, l'influence de Radio-Québec est manifeste, pavant la voie à de nombreuses productions culturelles d'importance (Gaudreau et Dumais, 2018), comme *Passe-Partout*. L'action du gouvernement Johnson dans ce domaine se doit d'être soulignée. En fait, il est le premier à prendre acte de la *Loi autorisant la création d'un service provincial de radiodiffusion*, promulguée en 1945 à la suite d'un affrontement entre Québec et Ottawa, alors que le gouvernement Duplessis estimait qu'« il [était] juste et nécessaire de créer une organisation radiophonique conforme aux droits constitutionnels de la province et du pays sous la surveillance du gouvernement » (Simard, 1970, p. 89).

Cela dit, c'est l'inauguration du barrage Manic-5 sur la rivière Manicouagan, prévue pour le 26 septembre 1968, qui constitue le fait d'armes du gouvernement Johnson, si ce n'est sa réalisation la plus significative – à tout le moins, dans l'imaginaire collectif des Québécois.

Non seulement le barrage Manic-5 suscite-t-il l'admiration générale en plus de représenter, à bien des égards, la domination de la nature par l'homme – du moins, dans les discours véhiculés par l'État québécois et Hydro-Québec (Perron, 2006 ; Savard, 2009) –, il donne également l'occasion à Daniel Johnson d'asseoir son autorité sur la scène politique québécoise, et peut-être même sa place dans l'Histoire. Un cliché photographique en témoigne de manière éloquente. Selon l'ancien ministre péquiste Bernard Drainville (2015), alors leader parlementaire de l'Opposition officielle, il s'agit même de l'« une des grandes et [plus] célèbres photos de l'histoire politique du Québec ».

Fréquemment reprise dans la littérature et dans les articles de presse qui reviennent, des années plus tard, sur l'événement ou sur les suites de la Révolution tranquille, cette image présente un Daniel Johnson, tout sourire, réunissant dans une poignée de main les deux frères ennemis, Jean Lesage et son ancien ministre, René Lévesque, qui s'apprête alors à fonder le Parti Québécois.

D'une certaine manière, ce cliché photographique se veut une métaphore tout à la fois de la situation politique québécoise en 1968 et de la force d'attraction de Johnson. Aussi improbable qu'ait pu être sa victoire, en 1966, on ne saurait apparenter le retour au pouvoir de l'Union nationale à une simple aberration électorale, à un accident de parcours. Johnson est un politicien adroit, un rassembleur (Quinn, 1979, p. 210-217), ce que cette image est parvenue à capter dans son essence.

Cela n'est pas anodin. Avant d'accéder au pouvoir, Johnson a veillé à se réclamer tout à la fois de la mémoire de Maurice Duplessis et de celle de Paul

Sauvé. Ce faisant, il en est venu à incarner, en quelque sorte, une synthèse entre le duplessisme et le «Désormais…», pourtant donnés comme irréconciliables au premier abord. Une fois au pouvoir, il a toutefois sensiblement changé sa stratégie sur ces enjeux, faisant preuve de prudence sur le plan mémoriel. Ainsi, le monument à la mémoire de Duplessis, commandé par Paul Sauvé et entreposé par Jean Lesage, est-il laissé sagement dans son entrepôt par Johnson. Qui plus est, le «Désormais…» est évacué complètement de la rhétorique unioniste à partir de 1966.

En fait, en tant que premier ministre du Québec, Johnson a su ajuster le tir, se posant davantage comme l'homme de la synthèse, si ce n'est du compromis, non pas entre la mémoire de Duplessis et celle de Sauvé, mais entre les postures incarnées respectivement par Jean Lesage et René Lévesque. Dans ce contexte, l'Union nationale était à même de conserver toute sa pertinence tandis que son chef, par sa prestance, était au faîte de sa puissance, le 25 septembre 1968.

Daniel Johnson ne sera toutefois pas en mesure de poursuivre son œuvre. Dans la nuit du 25 au 26 septembre, le chef de l'Union nationale s'éteint dans son sommeil, quelques heures à peine avant l'inauguration de Manic-5[17]. Pour l'Union nationale, tout est alors à refaire. Entre les positions de Jean Lesage et celles de René Lévesque, entre la mémoire de Maurice Duplessis et celle de Paul Sauvé, entre le duplessisme et le «Désormais…», il lui faudra trancher ce nœud gordien si elle souhaite aller de l'avant.

Conclusion: et l'Union nationale après 1968?

Appelés à se donner un nouveau chef pour la troisième fois depuis 1959[18], les membres du cabinet désignent cette fois Jean-Jacques Bertrand pour succéder à Daniel Johnson, le 2 octobre 1968[19]. Devant un Parti libéral qui fourbit ses armes, bien qu'il soit dirigé par un Jean Lesage vieillissant[20], et les forces souverainistes, qui se rassembleront sous peu derrière le Parti Québécois du charismatique René Lévesque, fondé le 11 octobre 1968, le choix de l'Union

17. L'inauguration officielle du barrage Manic-5, qui recevra le nom Daniel-Johnson, est repoussée à l'année suivante, le 26 septembre 1969. L'honneur revient au premier ministre Jean-Jacques Bertrand. À cette occasion, il reprend de larges pans du discours que Daniel Johnson devait prononcer (S. Savard, 2009, p. 78).

18. Après la démission d'Antonio Barrette, Yves Prévost et Antonio Talbot assument tous deux l'intérim à la tête de l'Union nationale, le premier du 16 septembre 1960 au 11 janvier 1961, le second du 11 janvier au 23 septembre 1961.

19. Jean-Jacques Bertrand est officiellement confirmé à ce poste à l'issue d'un congrès de l'Union nationale, le 21 juin 1969.

20. Le 28 août 1969, Jean Lesage annonce qu'il quittera la vie politique au terme du mandat qu'il termine. Robert Bourassa lui succède à la tête du Parti libéral le 17 janvier 1970.

nationale semble être le bon. Jeune et dynamique, Jean-Jacques Bertrand est considéré depuis longtemps comme le chef de l'aile progressiste de l'Union nationale.

Rappelons à cet effet que Jean Lesage lui-même avait enjoint à Jean-Jacques Bertrand de quitter les rangs de son parti pour se joindre au PLQ, en novembre 1962. C'est le seul député de l'Opposition officielle à qui Lesage avait fait cette proposition. Qui plus est, Bertrand (1962), non content de refuser cette main tendue, avait profité de l'occasion pour évoquer le «Désormais…» de Sauvé, dont il se réclamait. De toute évidence, en 1968, Jean-Jacques Bertrand était le candidat idéal pour permettre à l'Union nationale, à la croisée des chemins, de poursuivre sa route.

Les premières semaines du nouveau gouvernement semblent donner raison au caucus de l'Union nationale. Alors que les forces souverainistes se rassemblent au sein du PQ, Jean-Jacques Bertrand s'attelle à la tâche (Gariépy, 1968), soucieux de mener à terme quelques-uns des projets annoncés dans le programme de son parti, en 1966 (Quinn, 1979, p. 219). Ce faisant, Bertrand laisse sa marque dans les affaires de la province, en plus de transformer comme peu l'ont fait avant lui le paysage politique québécois.

L'éducation est l'un des domaines dans lesquels il se démarque tout particulièrement. Brièvement ministre de l'Éducation dans le cabinet Johnson, Bertrand (1968) considère que «c'est l'évidence même que le Québec ne saurait céder une parcelle de sa compétence, quels que soient les moyens techniques employés, anciens, nouveaux ou futurs». Partisan des réformes des libéraux dans le domaine de l'éducation et de l'enseignement (Latouche, 2008), Bertrand poursuit le travail initié par son prédécesseur et veille à ce que le réseau de l'Université du Québec soit lancé comme prévu, le 14 décembre 1968.

On doit également à Jean-Jacques Bertrand le changement de nom de l'enceinte parlementaire québécoise qui devient, le 31 décembre 1968, l'Assemblée nationale du Québec dans un trait qui marque tout autant l'affirmation nationale du Québec, en phase avec l'esprit de la Révolution tranquille, qu'un certain attachement envers la France. Dans la foulée de cette réforme qui va bien au-delà du simple changement de nom (Bonsaint, 2012, p. 43-44), le Conseil législatif – la chambre haute de la province – est également aboli (Lesage, 1968, p. 1), cela dans l'indifférence la plus totale (Bélair-Cirino et Noël, 2018).

Malgré ces débuts prometteurs, Bertrand ne parvient pas à se dépêtrer de la crise linguistique, issue de Saint-Léonard, qui finit par l'emporter, lui et son parti[21]. Le 29 avril 1970, jour d'élections, l'Union nationale est écrasée. Fort

---

21. Alors que les Italo-Québécois envoient massivement leurs enfants à l'école anglaise, la décision est prise de «remplacer les classes dites "bilingues" (où les trois quarts

de 55 députés au déclenchement de la campagne (Lesage, 1970, p. 2), le caucus unioniste fond comme neige au soleil : ils ne sont plus que 17 à défendre les couleurs unionistes après le scrutin. Trois ans plus tard, rien ne va plus pour l'Union nationale, qui est carrément balayée lors des élections du 29 octobre 1973. En quelques années à peine, la formation politique s'est retrouvée dans un cul-de-sac. Pour le dire autrement, elle avait perdu sa place sur l'échiquier politique québécois, lequel était occupé dorénavant par le Parti libéral du Québec et le Parti Québécois. Il semblait bien lointain le temps où Daniel Johnson, à l'automne 1968, pouvait incarner une certaine synthèse entre Jean Lesage et René Lévesque, aux antipodes l'un de l'autre. Il se pourrait même que le temps de l'Union nationale était déjà compté, à ce moment-là (Quinn, 1979, p. 238-239).

Sur le plan mémoriel, le leadership de Jean-Jacques Bertrand fut semblable à celui de Daniel Johnson : la statue de Maurice Duplessis est restée cloîtrée dans un entrepôt gouvernemental, tandis que nul n'osait évoquer le « Désormais… » de Paul Sauvé dans les officines de l'Union nationale, en Chambre ou pendant la campagne électorale. Pour que celui-ci revienne enfin à l'ordre du jour à l'Assemblée nationale du Québec, il faudra attendre en fait la renaissance, en 1976, de l'Union nationale, dirigée par Rodrigue Biron (1980a ; 1980b). Mais c'est trop peu, trop tard pour l'Union nationale, qui est alors reléguée au rang de tiers parti, si ce n'est de parti marginal. Après avoir dissous ce qui restait de sa formation politique, son chef démissionnaire rejoignit d'ailleurs les rangs du Parti Québécois, le 11 novembre 1980, quelques mois à peine après le premier référendum sur la souveraineté du Québec, tenu le 20 mai.

C'en était définitivement fini de l'Union nationale. Mais le duplessisme, tout comme le « Désormais… » de Paul Sauvé, sont néanmoins demeurés d'actualité dans la province de Québec. En dépit de plusieurs tentatives infructueuses, aucun parti n'est toutefois parvenu à en faire la synthèse, ou à s'approprier la formule bienheureuse de Paul Sauvé (Turgeon, 2017b). À ce jour, du moins[22].

---

des cours sont en fait dispensés en anglais) par des classes unilingues françaises », au grand dam des Italo-Québécois de Saint-Léonard, qui « font alors valoir leur droit au libre choix de la langue d'enseignement devant les tribunaux et le gouvernement » (Marcil, 2002, p. 206). Alors que les manifestations tournent à l'émeute, le gouvernement Bertrand présente le projet de loi 63 qui, tout en soutenant faire la promotion du français, reconnaît néanmoins le libre choix de la langue d'enseignement, ce qui met le feu aux poudres et enflamme les esprits (Godin, 1990).

22. Ce n'est pas faute d'essayer. À titre d'exemple, certains ont cru reconnaître dans le slogan de la Coalition Avenir Québec en 2018, « Maintenant », le « Désormais… » de Paul Sauvé ou son équivalent (Baillargeon, 2018).

Références

Assemblée nationale du Québec (1959 et 1960). *Débats de l'Assemblée législative du Québec*, 4ᵉ session, 25ᵉ législature.

Baillargeon, Stéphane (2018). «La parenthèse souverainiste est-elle en train de se refermer?», *Le Devoir*, 25 août. [En ligne] http://www.ledevoir.com/politique/quebec/535287/la-parenthese-souverainiste-est-elle-en-train-de-se-refermer (page consultée le 22 mars 2019).

Barrette, Antonio (1966). *Mémoires*, Montréal, Beauchemin, 384 p.

Bédard, Éric (2013). «22 juin 1960 – L'élection de Jean Lesage : "un changement de la vie"?», dans Graveline, Pierre (dir.), *Dix journées qui ont fait le Québec*, Montréal, VLB éditeur, p. 187-207.

Bélair-Cirino, Marco et Dave Noël (2018). «Le Conseil législatif du Québec, rempart contre l'autoritarisme», *Le Devoir*, 14 décembre. [En ligne] http://www.ledevoir.com/politique/quebec/543499/le-conseil-legislatif-rempart-a-l-autoritarisme (page consultée le 6 avril 2019).

Bélanger, Éric (1999). «"Égalité ou indépendance". L'émergence de la menace de l'indépendance politique comme stratégie constitutionnelle du Québec», *Globe. Revue internationale d'études québécoises*, vol. 2, nᵒ 1, p. 117-138.

Bertrand, Jean-Jacques (1968). «La politique du Québec en matière de radio-télévision», *Le Devoir*, 27 novembre, p. 5.

_____ (1962). «"Je reste encore dans l'Union nationale"», *Le Devoir*, 8 novembre, p. 3 et 6.

Bilan du siècle (s.d.). «Création du réseau des Universités du Québec», Université de Sherbrooke. [En ligne] http://bilan.usherbrooke.ca/bilan/pages/evenements/1923.html (page consultée le 2 avril 2019).

Biron, Rodrigue (1980a). «Document – "Je me battrai donc pour le OUI…"», *Le Devoir*, 4 mars, p. 10.

_____. (1980b). «Oui, j'assume l'héritage», *Le Soleil*, 14 mars, p. A7.

Bonsaint, Michel (dir.) (2012). *La procédure parlementaire du Québec*, Québec, Assemblée nationale, 948 p.

Candide (1959). «Désormais, dit-il», *Le Devoir*, 5 novembre, p. 4.

Cardinal, Mario (1966). «10 000 personnes entendent M. Johnson faire l'éloge de l'équipe Drapeau-Saulnier et promettre le métro de St-Henri à Pont-Viau», *Le Devoir*, 3 juin, p. 1.

Cardinal, Mario, Vincent Lemieux et Florian Sauvageau (1978). *Si l'Union nationale m'était contée…*, Sillery, Boréal Express, 352 p.

Cowan, Peter (1966). «Johnson Promises Metro Aid», *Montreal Star*, 3 juin, p. 1 et 4.

Drainville, Bernard (@drainvillepm) (2015). «@PhotosHistos La veille du décès de Daniel Johnson. Une des grandes et + célèbres photos de l'histoire politique du Québec. Bravo :) #PolQc», 24 mars, 17 h 17. Gazouillis. [En ligne] http://twitter.com/drainvillepm/status/580478607933464576 (page consultée le 24 mars 2019).

Dufresne, Jean-Yves (1966). «La bombe redoutée par l'UN explosera demain à Montréal», *Le Devoir*, 25 mai, p. 1-2.

Dumas, Alexandre (2019). *L'Église et la politique québécoise, de Taschereau à Duplessis*, Montréal et Kingston, McGill-Queen's University Press, 352 p.

Ferretti, Lucia (2002). *Histoire des Dominicaines de Trois-Rivières : « C'est à moi que vous l'avez fait »*, Sillery, Éditions du Septentrion, 260 p.

Francœur, Jean (1966). « Johnson : trois raisons motivent le choix de Lesage », *Le Devoir*, 19 avril, p. 1 et 14.

Gariépy, Gilles (1968). « La rentrée parlementaire à Québec, mardi – Un important train de lois attend nos députés », *Le Devoir*, 21 octobre, p. 16.

Gaudreau, Amélie et Manon Dumais (2018). « Cinquante ans à penser le Québec », *Le Devoir*, 17 février. [En ligne] http://www.ledevoir.com/culture/ecrans/ 520380/grand-angle-cinquante-ans-a-penser-le-quebec (page consultée le 28 mars 2019).

Godin, Pierre (1990). *La poudrière linguistique*, Montréal, Boréal, 384 p.

Guay, Jean-Herman et Serge Gaudreau (2018). *Les élections au Québec : 150 ans d'une histoire mouvementée*, Québec, Presses de l'Université Laval, 508 p.

Johnson, Daniel (1965). *Égalité ou indépendance*, Montréal, Éditions Renaissance, 132 p.

Ladouceur, Antoine (1966). « Extension du métro de Montréal aux frais de l'État (Johnson) », *Le Soleil*, 3 juin, p. 1-2.

Lapalme, Georges-Émile (1988). *Pour une politique : le programme de la Révolution tranquille*, Montréal, VLB éditeur, 348 p.

———. (1970). *Mémoires*. Tome 2 : *Le vent de l'oubli*, Montréal, Leméac, 395 p.

Laporte, Pierre (1960a). « La session provinciale I – Deux périodes : celle de M. Paul Sauvé et celle de son successeur : M. Barrette », *Le Devoir*, 21 mars, p. 1.

———. (1960b). « L'élection provinciale – M. Antonio Barrette fait une campagne bien différente – en mieux – de celles de M. Duplessis », *Le Devoir*, 4 juin, p. 1.

———. (1960c). *Le vrai visage de Duplessis*, Montréal, Éditions de l'Homme.

———. (1959a). « "Désormais" l'Assemblée législative aura les documents prévus par les règlements », *Le Devoir*, 26 novembre, p. 1.

———. (1959b). « Québec : l'atmosphère est complètement changée ! », *Le Devoir*, 12 septembre, p. 1.

Latouche, Daniel (2008). « Jean-Jacques Bertrand », *L'Encyclopédie canadienne*, 18 février. [En ligne] http://www.thecanadianencyclopedia.ca/fr/article/jean-jacques-bertrand (page consultée le 19 avril 2019).

Laurendeau, André (1959a). « M. Sauvé déconcerte amis et adversaires », *Le Devoir*, 13 novembre, p. 4.

———. (1959b). « Où les "désormais" s'arrêtent », *Le Devoir*, 28 novembre, p. 4.

Leprince, Jean-Michel (1979). « Duplessis, mort et renié », archives de Radio-Canada, 7 septembre. [En ligne] http://archives.radio-canada.ca/sports/provincial_territo-rial/clips/7212/ (page consultée le 23 mars 2019).

Lesage, Gilles (1970). « Tout retard nuirait à "notre avenir collectif" – Bertrand – Québec aux urnes le 29 avril », *Le Devoir*, 13 mars, p. 1-2.

———. (1968). « Le discours du trône prévoit la réforme du Conseil législatif – La question de St-Michel sera étudiée en priorité », *Le Devoir*, 21 février, p. 1 et 14.

———. (1966). « M. Lesage ne croit pas nécessaire de nouvelles élections », *Le Devoir*, 6 juin, p. 1 et 6.

Lévesque, Michel (2011). «Il y a 50 ans, la commission Salvas – Une enquête sur le gouvernement de Duplessis», *Le Devoir*, 29 octobre, p. B5.

Livernois, Jonathan (2016). «Les leçons de "Tonio": surinterprétation des six premiers mois de l'année 1960 au Québec», *Argument*, vol. 18, n° 2 (printemps-été), p. 20-29.

Marcil, Olivier (2002). «La question linguistique dans la pensée de Claude Ryan au *Devoir* (1962-1978): la difficile conciliation de principes nationalistes et libéraux», *Mens: revue d'histoire intellectuelle de l'Amérique française*, vol. 2, n° 2 (printemps), p. 193-231.

Nadeau, Jean-François (2018). «Daniel Johnson, ni l'égalité ni l'indépendance», *Le Devoir*, 26 septembre. [En ligne] http://www.ledevoir.com/politique/quebec/537619/daniel-johson-ni-l-egalite-ni-l-independance (page consultée le 23 mars 2019).

Pape, Gordon (1966). «Johnson Pledges Metro Expansion», *The Gazette*, 3 juin, p. 1.

Pelletier, Réjean (1989). *Partis politiques et société québécoise: de Duplessis à Bourassa 1944-1970*, Montréal, Québec/Amérique, 397 p.

Perron, Dominique (2006). *Le nouveau roman de l'énergie nationale. Analyse des discours promotionnels d'Hydro-Québec de 1964 à 1997*, Calgary, University of Calgary Press, 316 p.

Quinn, Herbert (1979). *The Union Nationale: Québec Nationalism from Duplessis to Lévesque*, Toronto, University of Toronto Press, 360 p.

Richer, Léopold (1959). «Face au régime Sauvé, M. Laurendeau devient un auteur comique», *Notre Temps*, 21 novembre, p. 2.

Rioux, Roger (1966). «Daniel Johnson promet pour le Québec – Une nation LIBRE et responsable», *Montréal-Matin*, 3 juin, p. 2.

s.a. (1967). «Ses propos d'actualité», *La Presse*, 27 mai, p. 5.

————. (1966a). «Bellemare défend la mémoire de Duplessis», *Le Devoir*, 20 mai, p. 12.

————. (1966b). «Daniel Johnson a rendu hommage à la mémoire de Maurice Duplessis», *Le Bien Public*, 3 juin, p. 1.

————. (1966c). «Johnson reçoit un accueil triomphal à Montréal», *Le Droit*, 3 juin, p. 23.

————. (1966d). «La fille de M. Barrette affirme que la date de publication du livre de son père est un hasard», *Le Devoir*, 27 mai, p. 1.

————. (1960). «Potins politiques», *L'Avenir du Nord*, 27 juillet, p. 5.

————. (1959a). «Autour d'un adverbe», *Montréal-Matin*, 28 novembre, p. 4.

————. (1959b). «Avant les funérailles de M. Duplessis – Un dernier hommage de Trois-Rivières», *Le Devoir*, 10 septembre, p. 1.

————. (1959c). «Encore un heureux "désormais"… – M. Sauvé consulte ses collègues!», *Le Devoir*, 2 décembre, p. 1-2.

————. (1959d). «Un "désormais" de taille – Le bill 34: la clause relative à l'énumérateur unique est rayée!», *Le Devoir*, 19 décembre, p. 1.

Salvas, Élie (1962). *Rapport des commissaires sur la vente du réseau de gaz de l'Hydro-Québec à la Corporation de gaz naturel du Québec*, Montréal, La Commission.

Savard, Danielle (1991). «Compte rendu de *Pour une politique, le programme de la Révolution tranquille* de Georges-Émile Lapalme, préface de Claude Corbo,

Montréal, VLB éditeur et Maria Lapalme, 1988, 353 p.», *Politique*, n° 20 (automne), p. 177-179.

Savard, Stéphane (2009). « Quand l'histoire donne sens aux représentations collectives : l'Hydro-Québec, Manic-5 et la société québécoise », *Recherches sociographiques*, vol. 50, n° 1, p. 67-97.

Simard, Pierre (1970). « Loi sur l'Office de radio-télédiffusion du Québec. Loi du ministère des Communications », *Les Cahiers de droit*, vol. 11, n° 11, p. 89-91.

Thivierge, Marcel (1962). « L'assurance édition à l'Assemblée législative – Le projet de loi Lapalme reçoit l'appui de l'U. Nationale », *Le Devoir*, 4 avril, p. 2.

Turcotte, Claude (1966). « L'UN prendra des mesures précises pour éviter une récession en 1967 – Johnson », *La Presse*, 3 juin, p. 1-2.

Turgeon, Alexandre (2017a). « De la création à la commémoration : le "Désormais…" de Paul Sauvé dans l'histoire du Québec, 1959-2010 », *The Canadian Historical Review*, vol. 98, n° 4 (décembre), p. 765-797.

————. (2017b). «"When will we get her *désormais' ('From now on')?" A few thoughts about the rhetorical and strategic functions of Paul Sauvé's "From now on…" in Québec and in Canada, from the 1960s to the present day*», 24th Biennial Conference of the Association for Canadian Studies in the United States. *Celebrating Canada's Sesquicentennial Journey*, Las Vegas, 18-21 octobre. Inédit.

————. (2015a). « Entre la "grande noirceur" et la Révolution tranquille », dans Blais, Christian (dir.), *Histoire parlementaire du Québec, 1928-1962. La crise, la guerre, le duplessisme, l'État providence*, Québec, Éditions du Septentrion, p. 581-617.

————. (2015b). *Robert La Palme et les origines caricaturales de la Grande Noirceur duplessiste* : conception et diffusion d'un mythistoire au Québec, des années 1940 à nos jours, thèse de doctorat, Université Laval.

————. (2014). « La Palme présente *Displicuit Nasus Tuus* : quand la caricature sert de discours politique au Québec », *Journal of the Canadian Historical Association / Revue de la Société historique du Canada*, vol. 25, n° 1, p. 107-142.

————. (2013a). « Et si Paul Sauvé n'avait jamais prononcé le "Désormais…"? », *Revue d'histoire de l'Amérique française*, vol. 67, n° 1 (été), p. 33-56.

————. (2013b). «"Toé, tais-toé !" et la Grande Noirceur duplessiste. Genèse d'un mythistoire », *Histoire sociale / Social History*, vol. 46, n° 92 (novembre), p. 367-396.

————. (2009). *Le nez de Maurice Duplessis. Le Québec des années 1940 tel que vu, représenté et raconté par Robert La Palme : analyse d'un système figuratif*, mémoire de maîtrise, Université Laval.

Chapter 14
Canada and the Czechoslovak Crisis of 1968[1]

ANDREA CHANDLER

Abstract

In 1968, Czechoslovakia experienced its Prague Spring as a gradual political liberalization took place in this previously tightly controlled Communist nation. During the Prague Spring, political debate and artistic expression flourished under the relaxed leadership of the popular Alexander Dubček. Canada belonged to NATO, the military alliance that opposed the Soviet-dominated Warsaw Treaty Organization, of which Czechoslovakia was a member. Despite this divide, relations between Canada and Czechoslovakia had warmed prior to 1968, spurred by the Czechoslovaks' decision to host a pavilion at the 1967 World's Fair (Expo 67) in Montreal. Among the Warsaw Pact countries, Czechoslovakia had arguably the most fruitful relationship with Canada, owing in part to a growing cultural exchange between the two nations. When the Soviet Union and other members of the Warsaw Pact invaded Czechoslovakia in August 1968, it provided a major foreign policy test for the new government of Pierre Trudeau and his Secretary of State for External Affairs, Mitchell Sharp. How to respond to the Czechoslovak events: send a strong message against military intervention or take a softer line and hope to promote cooperation over the longer term? This was the first major international crisis the Trudeau government was faced with, and the case study analyzed in this chapter illustrates the balancing act that Canada had to perform as a middle power during the Cold War.

1. This research is part of a larger project with the working title *Canada and Eastern Europe during the Cold War, 1945–1989: Politics of Democracy Promotion*. I acknowledge the support of funding from Carleton University's Faculty of Public Affairs and, especially, from the German Academic Exchange Service (DAAD) through their program Research Stays for Academics and Scientists, which enabled me to do research in Berlin in fall 2017.

Figure 14.1. Demonstration against Soviet occupation of Czechoslovakia at Queen's Park in Toronto, 31 August 1968. *Source:* John McNeill / *The Globe and Mail.*

Nineteen sixty-eight marked a period of transition in Canada's international orientation, a time when the newly elected Liberal government of Pierre Trudeau sought to take stock by reviewing Canadian foreign-policy priorities and the country's overall engagement with the international community. By this time, Canada had achieved some major breakthroughs in constructing its international stature. Building on Canada's substantial contribution to the Allied war effort in the Second World War, the country gained attention for its substantial postwar roles in building international institutions, particularly in refugee resettlement in the 1940s and 1950s and peacekeeping from 1956 onwards. Canada's retiring prime minister, Lester B. Pearson, was known as one of the leading bridge builders of the Cold War era; his efforts to resolve the Suez crisis of 1956 won him the Nobel Peace Prize a year later ("Lester Bowles Pearson," n.d.). Pearson, along with skilled Canadian diplomats like George Ignatieff, enhanced Canada's reputation as a constructive actor in the international arena. The success of Expo 67, the World's Fair, held in Montreal in 1967, further raised Canada's stature, and drew world attention to the country's vibrant cultural development (*Globe and Mail* 1967).[2] As others in this volume have documented, this was a time of ambitious reform efforts and cultural experimentation within the Canadian political arena. Trudeau's election as prime

---

2. As the *Calgary Herald* commented, "[Expo 67] made the world sit up and take notice" (1967).

minister in June 1968 built on a campaign emphasizing confident nationhood with an effective state working to be a change agent both at home and abroad.

This sense of confidence, however, could not escape some very sobering realities in the international environment. As a member of the North Atlantic Treaty Organization (NATO), Canada participated in an alliance that was shaken by the escalation of the Vietnam War, and in which some European leaders wondered whether their interests truly coincided with those of the United States. Social protests against the war were widespread in 1968, not only in the United States but also in other NATO member states. Concerns about the impact of the nuclear arms race on Europe had already contributed to France's 1966 decision to opt out of NATO's unified command institutions (Von Riekhoff 1967). In Canada, doubts emerged over whether the military contributions and expenditures expected to maintain NATO membership were really the best use of Canada's limited resources (see, for example, Westell 1968). As Liberal politicians prepared to choose a successor to Pearson, some leadership hopefuls questioned Canada's role in NATO and called for more distance from the United States. Eric Kierans, for example, favoured removing Canada from the Western alliance (*Globe and Mail* 1968c) and John Turner called for Canada to consider advocating for international peacekeeping in Vietnam (Newman 1968). The winning candidate, Pierre Trudeau, had promised a comprehensive reassessment of Canadian foreign policy, arguing that it was in need of an update, having changed little for 20 years (Bain 1968). By and large, though, Canadian diplomacy moved slowly, bound by the gentlemanly conventions of the staff of the Department of Foreign Affairs. Given the relative stability of Canadian life at this time, there was no great urgency for change.

Suddenly, in 1968, an international event happened that required not only a quick foreign-policy response from the Canadian government, but also a public relations effort. In August 1968, Czechoslovakia was invaded by its own allies: the Soviet Union (USSR), Poland, Bulgaria, Hungary, and the German Democratic Republic (GDR). As a member of the Warsaw Treaty Organization military alliance (WTO, commonly referred to as the Warsaw Pact), Czechoslovakia's communist regime was closely connected to the Soviet Union. At the end of World War II, Czechoslovakia and its eastern European neighbours had been occupied by the Soviet Union, led by Joseph Stalin, who imposed strict Marxist-Leninist regimes organized on the Soviet model. The Warsaw Pact stood in opposition to NATO during the Cold War, and it appeared to be a united front against the capitalist West. As years passed, however, there were signs that many citizens of these countries did not accept their status as "satellites" of the Soviet Union. In 1956, the Hungarian Revolution was accompanied by sudden and intense street violence, and the uprising was put down by Soviet armed forces. While many countries denounced the violence and called for Hungarian self-determination, Western leaders conceded that the eastern European nations would remain in the Soviet bloc for the foreseeable future.

In 1968, Hungary's neighbour, Czechoslovakia, began a liberalization process known as the Prague Spring. The Czechoslovak Communist Party's leader, Alexander Dubček, fostered a climate of greater artistic freedom and expanded public debate—and tolerated calls for greater independence. In August 1968, Warsaw Pact nations (excluding Romania, which did not participate) invaded Czechoslovakia and gradually pressured the regime to muzzle the Prague Spring. Eventually, Dubček was replaced by the hardline communist Gustav Husák (Skilling 1976, 813–822). The invasion of Czechoslovakia came at a time when protests and peace movements were building throughout the world, including in Western countries. The NATO alliance was being tested by the growing criticism of the United States' involvement in Vietnam. The Soviet bloc's use of force to suppress the Czech and Slovak protesters created an international crisis that disrupted initiatives under way to improve relations between the Soviet Union and its Western counterparts.

The 1968 Czechoslovak crisis provides an interesting case study to investigate the ways in which sudden international crises can affect newly-elected governments. The invasion of Czechoslovakia caught Canada and its NATO allies off guard, creating a major setback for the evolving policy of East–West détente. This chapter has two related goals: to examine the role that Canada played in attempts to prevent and defuse the Czechoslovak crisis and to analyze the impact that the invasion of Czechoslovakia had on the Canadian polity. Following a discussion of the events of 1968, the chapter develops three main arguments. First, the Czechoslovak crisis created a strong sense of disappointment within Western diplomatic circles, as the Warsaw Pact's forceful actions suggested that the Soviet bloc could not tolerate a modest liberalization in one of its members. This realization shattered the belief that improved East–West relations could in the long run contribute to reforms within the East bloc. Second, the Czechoslovak crisis demonstrated the increased political role of Canadians of central and east European origin. Canadian organizations of Czechs, Slovaks, Ukrainians, and Poles became active in encouraging the Canadian government to admit more immigrants and refugees from Communist countries, while calling for the government to take a strong stand against the invasion. The era of quiet diplomacy in the Canadian foreign-policy community was at an end. By 1968, the world media broke stories that landed on Canadian television. A government that did not respond promptly could risk angering the many Canadians who felt strongly about international issues. A popular and outspoken prime minister, Pierre Trudeau, took centre stage as he faced his first major international event. Third, the Czechoslovak policy compelled a modification of Prime Minister Trudeau's intended plan to consider reducing Canada's commitment to NATO, and complicated the foreign-policy review that the government had only just begun.

The aftermath of the Czechoslovak crisis presented Canada with some hard choices. On the one hand, there was a strong rationale for carrying out sanctions against the Warsaw Pact nations, but on the other hand such sanctions could further isolate Czechoslovak citizens from international support. In the end, the crisis reinforced the cohesion of NATO, as member states in the Western alliance sought to demonstrate their disapproval of the Soviet Union's modus operandi in the Warsaw Pact. After 1968, the Canadian government reluctantly reopened dialogue with the east European countries over trade and other contacts. There was a sense of disillusionment that Canada and other Western nations could do little to free the east European nations, but a dim hope remained that engagement with rival countries might over time promote gradual liberalization.

Canada and Czechoslovakia before August 1968

Until August 1968, Canada's government had become cautiously optimistic about the prospects for improved East–West relations. To be sure, tensions between Canada and Eastern bloc nations continued to exist. The division of Germany, the poor human rights records of countries behind the Iron Curtain, and the desires of Canadians of Czech and Slovak origin to have contact with their family members in their mother country remained ongoing issues of concern for Canada. However, throughout the 1960s, Western leaders began to seek trade relationships and scientific and cultural ties with communist countries. It was assumed that these modest steps could eventually increase trust and promote incremental reforms in the Eastern bloc over the long term. In the 1960s, Canada stepped up its bilateral trade with east European states, who showed they were "good customers" (Bothwell 2007, 155). East European countries' diplomats invited Canada to send representatives to their trade fairs, in an effort to cultivate international ties. Czechoslovakia and Canada gradually developed a dialogue over cultural issues. In 1965, Canada hosted an exhibit at the Brno International Trade Fair (LAC 1965); the next year, Canada's exhibit was reportedly attended by 700,000 people who eagerly snapped up maple leaf pins and watched Canadian films (LAC 1966). Czechoslovakia put up a very well-attended pavilion at Expo 67 in Montreal; eschewing politics, the pavilion featured fairytales and cultural artifacts.

In early 1968, Alexander Dubček replaced Antonín Novotný as First Secretary of the Czechoslovak Communist Party (LAC 1968a). By this time, Canada already enjoyed relatively cordial relations with Czechoslovakia. In June 1967, the President of Czechoslovakia's National Assembly, Bohuslav Laštovička, visited Canada and made an appearance at the House of Commons in Ottawa (Canada 1967, 1336). Czechoslovakia had agreed to enter talks with Canada over possible restitution to Canadian citizens whose property had been confiscated through state nationalizations. This had been a longstanding sore point in Canada's relations with Czechoslovakia and other Eastern bloc states (Canada 1967, 1433). The Dubček government appeared to be more flexible than its predecessor in allowing emigration and travel to Canada; they expressed a willingness to allow more family reunification in the interest of good relations with Canada (Canada, Department of External Affairs 1968). The Canadian Ambassador to Czechoslovakia finished his posting in July 1968, and recommended that Canada pursue talks with the Czechs on improving trade terms for grain exports from Canada, as a way of helping the Czechs to stand firm amid their growing political difficulties (LAC 1968b).

Among the many initiatives that Canada's new Liberal government pursued was a review of Canada's foreign policy, considering a more independent, less ideological approach. One of the bolder initiatives under consideration was for Canada to distance itself from NATO, and particularly from the United States. Some western European leaders, especially in the U.K., Germany, and the Netherlands, feared that if Canada stepped away from NATO, there would be less leverage within the institution to counter the strong U.S. influence within the alliance (Harvey 1968). As it was, some of the European members of NATO raised concerns about the position of the United States in the Cold War. Some wanted to keep the alliance's focus squarely on European security and regarded the American foreign policy approach as too ideological. The United States' involvement in the war in Vietnam was unpopular in western Europe (Fraser 1966). Under President Charles de Gaulle, France had opted out of participating in NATO's integrated military command structure in 1966 (Meren 2012, 138). So 1968 was a moment of dissension within NATO: there was an evolving belief that the Soviet bloc might gradually evolve into more moderate regimes, if relations between the USSR and the West de-escalated. To Canada's Secretary of State for External Affairs, Mitchell Sharp, the invasion of Czechoslovakia demarcated "the end of the belief that liberalization could proceed to the point where neither the Warsaw Pact nor NATO would be necessary" (Miller 1968).[3]

The Invasion of Czechoslovakia: Canadian Response

By 1968, Canadian diplomats in Europe, and especially in Prague, had observed growing tensions between the Czechoslovak leadership and the Soviet Union. Dubček himself had openly stated that Soviet leaders were concerned that the

---

3. Sharp made the comments in a television interview on CBC's "The Way It Is," on 15 December 1968.

more open political atmosphere in Czechoslovakia might put socialism at risk (LAC 1968c). There were unconfirmed rumours that the Soviet Union was placing troops near its border with Czechoslovakia (LAC 1968d). A meeting of Warsaw Pact nations, to which Czechoslovakia was not invited, was reported to have taken place in May 1968 (LAC 1968e). This was a bad sign. Still, there was a strong belief that the USSR would not invade Czechoslovakia. This is partly because the Dubček leadership showed a brave face, projecting confidence that the path of reform was irreversible (LAC 1968f). The Department of External Affairs sent a message to the Czechoslovak Embassy in Canada instructing the maintaining of an arms-length position, to avoid any perception of getting too partial to Czechoslovakia's leadership at a time when relations between that country and its allies were strained. The Canadian authorities were very conscious of the Hungarian precedent, in which the Soviet Union claimed the West was encouraging Hungarians to defy the Soviet Union in 1956 (LAC 1968g).

When the invasion of Czechoslovakia occurred, the Soviet Union put out a statement the same night stating that the Warsaw Pact had been invited in by the Czech government and Communist Party leadership, to suppress "counterrevolution" (*Globe and Mail* 1968b). That statement was quickly refuted. The Czechoslovak Communist Party Central Committee Presidium insisted that the other Warsaw Pact states' troops had entered Czechoslovak territory without the foreknowledge or permission of that government and criticized the actions as a "denial of basic norms of international law" (Czechoslovak Communist Party 1968). Czechoslovakia's parliament issued a statement which called for the release of Dubček from custody and demanded the withdrawal of Warsaw Pact troops (Czechoslovak National Assembly 1968). Reuters was present in Prague and reported that Czech broadcasters criticized the invasion on the radio; protests included a short general strike. Rumours circulated among local Czechs that Alexander Dubček had been arrested (*Globe and Mail* 1968c). Louise Rehak, a Canadian present in Prague during the invasion, wrote that people in Prague displayed homemade signs reading "go home" or "Dubček, Svoboda." Young people were the most visible protesters, but older people cheered them on (Rehak 1968, 10).[4]

Upon learning of the situation in Czechoslovakia, Prime Minister Trudeau said: "Had the world required any evidence that the course of international events cannot be predicted with accuracy, it came forcefully in the latter part of August when several of the Warsaw Pact countries invaded another of the Warsaw Pact countries, Czechoslovakia. And had Canadians required any evidence that there are very real limitations to effective freedom of action in the

---

4. Svoboda was the surname of the Czechoslovak Prime Minister, but also means "freedom."

international arena, it was provided by this same event" (Canada 1968–1969, 16 September 1968, 65). Immediately after the Soviet invasion, a representative of the Canadian High Commission in London met with members of the British Foreign Office, as well as counterparts from the Australian and New Zealand High Commissions to discuss a possible resolution to submit to the United Nations on the Czechoslovak crisis (LAC 1968h). On 21 August, Mitchell Sharp gave a public statement which described the invasion of Czechoslovakia as "a tragedy for all peoples who prize human freedom and national independence" (LAC 1968i). The same day, the Soviet Ambassador met with Paul Hellyer (who was serving as acting prime minister while Trudeau was on vacation) (LAC, n.d.a). In New York, Canada's representative to the United Nations, George Ignatieff, participated in discussions about a possible resolution criticizing the Soviet invasion (LAC 1968j). Canada was a member of the UN Security Council at that time, and co-sponsored (with Denmark) a resolution for the Security Council to condemn the invasion of Czechoslovakia (LAC 1968k). The resolution condemned the invasion as a violation of the sovereignty of the people of Czechoslovakia and called for a peaceful settlement of the matter (UNSC 1968a). Ignatieff spoke in the Security Council on 21 August, expressing the Canadian government's dismay over the military intervention in Czechslovakia and noting that the Czechoslovak government had not requested any assistance from its Warsaw Pact allies prior to the intervention (UNSC 1968b). However, the resolution did not advance—not only because the USSR objected to the resolution, but because Czechoslovakia's Foreign Affairs Minister, Jiří Hájek, while criticizing the intervention in his country, expressed the view that the country preferred to resolve the matter through negotiations within the Warsaw Pact (UNSC 1968c).

Indeed, the invasion of Czechoslovakia put Western countries in an awkward situation. When the Soviet Union intervened in Hungary in 1956, the Hungarian Communist leader, Imre Nagy, had actually appealed to the United Nations for help (United Nations 1956). Nagy was subsequently arrested and executed (Gilbert 2015, 103–104). By contrast, the Czechoslovak reform communist leader Dubček remained in place during the Warsaw Pact occupation of 1968. Leaders of NATO member countries were reluctant to commit to a strong response that would put Dubček at risk. If the Soviet bloc suspected that Dubček was backed by the West, it could provoke an even harsher crackdown. Eventually, Czechoslovakia's representative to the UN requested that the resolution be removed from the United Nations Security Council agenda (LAC 1968l). Canada, along with the United States, the United Kingdom, and others quietly agreed not to pursue the Czechoslovak issue further in the UN General Assembly, in the interest of wanting to avoid any public action that could undermine the efforts of the Czech government to continue reform

(LAC 1968m). The issue would be dealt with in a more low-key way, to be discussed by the UN Special Committee on Friendly Relations (LAC 1968n). The Canadian Embassy staff in Prague retained contact with Czechoslovak counterparts during the crisis, who expressed appreciation for Canada's support (LAC 1968o). Montreal's mayor, Jean Drapeau, visited Prague in November 1968, which provided an opportunity for conversation between members of the Canadian and Czechoslovak governments at a time when Dubček was still trying to hold on to power (LAC 1968p).

The Soviet Union's unwillingness to back down on the Czechoslovak crisis became known as the "Brezhnev doctrine." This doctrine held that Warsaw Pact unity would be maintained, even by force if necessary (Glazer 1971). The Czech crisis had a ripple effect in the socialist world for years to come. The Soviet reform leader Mikhail Gorbachev, the country's last leader before the communist system collapsed, is said by one scholar to have been inspired by the Prague Spring, and influenced by his close friend, reformist Czech Communist Zdeněk Mlynář. According to William Taubman's exhaustive biography, the young Gorbachev kept his concerns about the Soviet invasion of Czechoslovakia to himself in 1968, but eventually became a strong advocate of non-interference in east European affairs (Taubman 2017, 53–58, 379–381). The Warsaw Pact members who had participated, and the USSR itself, eventually confirmed in writing that they had been in the wrong to invade Czechoslovakia (Soviet and Warsaw Pact 1998).

The Impact of the Czechoslovak Crisis on Canada

The aftermath of the Czechoslovak crisis revealed a growing criticism in Canada of traditional elite-driven foreign policy. Once the preserve of a small number of diplomats, foreign policy was becoming increasingly influenced by domestic politics. Citizens called for more open immigration policies, and especially for the ability of citizens and groups to sponsor refugees. Although the Czechoslovak crisis occurred during the 'dog days' of summer, Trudeau and his Secretary of State for External Affairs, Mitchell Sharp, were called upon to respond quickly, as citizen groups of Czechoslovak-Canadians requested meetings with high officials. Public protests and vigorous debates in Parliament became part of the landscape. Meanwhile, Canadians of east European descent, especially those of Ukrainian, Polish, and Slovak origin, were gathering political clout. While they represented very diverse populations and had differing positions, the various communities had built sufficient bridges with each other to be able to call for increased attention to the human rights of citizens in the "satellite countries." In addition to associations of ethnic groups, other civil society organizations became involved. The Canadian Labour Congress denounced the invasion of Czechoslovakia, as did a variety of other large unions such as the American Federation of Labor and Congress of Industrial Organizations (AFL-CIO) (LAC 1968q). Canadians of Czech and Slovak origin organized a demonstration in Ottawa upon learning of the invasion and then again a year later (LAC, n.d.b). Within 24 hours of the reported invasion, Canadian Czech and Slovak organizations held protests in Ottawa, Winnipeg, and Montreal (Raska 2018, 150–152). On 21 August, Sharp met with Canadians of Czechoslovak origin and held a press conference at which he stated that Canada was concerned over the events in Czechoslovakia (LAC, n.d.a). Even Quebec's Communist Party was reported to have promptly criticized the invasion, although the Canadian Communist Party remained silent (LAC 1968r).

Canadians also took opportunities to speak up at international forums. Canadians attending the 14th Congress of the International Council on Social Welfare, which was meeting in Helsinki on 23 August, initiated a resolution expressing "concern" over the invasion (LAC 1968s). Canada's delegation to the Inter-Parliamentary Union (IPU), which included MPs from four parties as well as Senators, participated in the debate at the IPU's Conference in Lima, Peru, in September 1968. Member of Parliament Grant Deachman spoke up at the IPU Assembly in strong criticism of the Soviet intervention of Czechoslovakia, which he depicted as a blow not only to Czechoslovakia, but to parliamentary sovereignty itself (LAC 1968t). The IPU passed a resolution criticizing the Soviet intervention in Czechoslovakia, prompting the Soviet, Bulgarian, and Polish delegations to walk out of the assembly (LAC 1968u).

Members of Parliament raised pointed questions of the Trudeau government. Opposition member Lloyd Crouse (a Progressive Conservative) asked what Canada was doing with respect to the "rape of Czechoslovakia" (Canada 1968–1969, 13 September 1968). Progressive Conservative party leader Robert Stanfield criticized the Secretary of State for External Affairs, Mitchell Sharp, for being slow to respond to the Czechoslovak events and for his excessive "detachment from the humanitarian concern for Czechs and Slovaks (Canada 1968–1969, 16 September 1968, 60). Other members of Parliament asked the government to report on measures taken to assist Czech and Slovak refugees who wished to immigrate to Canada. A role was played by Liberal Member of Parliament Stanley Haidasz, who served as a Parliamentary Secretary for Consumer and Corporate Affairs in the new Trudeau government. Haidasz said he had heard from many constituents of Czech and Slovak origins and had attended a rally organized to protest the invasion of Czechoslovakia. He noted the readiness of Czechoslovak-Canadian organizations to assist with the settlement of Czech and Slovak immigrants in Canada (Canada 1968–1969, 20 September 1968, 291–293). Sharp responded that while Canada was making every effort to facilitate the processing of entry paperwork for Czechs and Slovaks, their cases needed to be handled sensitively in order not to complicate matters for those still within Czechoslovakia (Canada 1968–1969, 13 September 1968, 18–19). The Soviet Union and its Warsaw Pact allies were depicting pro-democracy activists in Czechoslovakia as anti-state agitators, or even fascists. If Canada was perceived to be encouraging flight from the Iron Curtain countries, or to be harbouring political "troublemakers," that could presumably lead to reprisals against Czechoslovaks with Canadian relatives. Furthermore, if hard-liners within the Warsaw Pact thought that Western countries were meddling in Czechoslovak affairs, that could weaken Dubček's position.

Sharp announced in the House of Commons that the government planned to impose a variety of sanctions in response to the events in Czechoslovakia: first, to suspend all planned ministerial-level Canadian delegation visits to Warsaw Pact countries; second, to halt new government-to-government exchanges (but continue existing ones that were "purely technical, cultural or academic in nature"); and third, to tell the Soviet Union and other Warsaw Pact states participating in the invasion that relations with Canada were adversely affected and would continue to be as long as their troops were in Czechoslovakia (Canada 1968–1969, 17 October 1968, 1467–1468).

The invasion led many Czechoslovak citizens to flee the country as refugees. While many Czechs and Slovaks left the country due to political circumstances, there were also thousands who had been out of the country at the time of the invasion (for example, on vacation elsewhere in Europe), some of whom were reported to be postponing their return home until the situation was clearer. Many of the prospective refugees were highly educated and extremely talented individuals, such as musicians (LAC 1968v). Canada's newly formed National Arts Centre Orchestra expressed an interest in locating musicians for possible auditions (LAC 1968w). By 1 November, more than 3,500 Czechoslovaks had arrived in Canada, many of whom were recipients of government grants or loans. About a third of them found work promptly, and another 800 or so were given English- or French-language courses. The government reported that an additional 10,000 people had applied to immigrate to Canada (Canada 1968–1969, 31 October 1968, 2289–2290). Within six months, a total of 12,000 Czechs and Slovaks had settled in Canada (Canada 1968–1969, 21 January 1969, 4552).

Canada's program for Czechoslovak refugees was short-lived. In mid-January 1969, the Canadian government ended the special program to facilitate Czech and Slovak immigration. Czechoslovakian citizens would still be eligible, but only through regular channels. It is not clear why this decision was made; Czech and Slovak immigrants were reported to be highly qualified, in little need of government assistance, and still seeking asylum in Canada (LAC 1969). It is possible that Canada wanted to avoid the perception that it was contributing to a brain drain, which could further weaken the cause of reform in

Czechoslovakia. Neutral Austria was feeling pressure from the Soviet Union because of its openness to receiving Czech migrants and because of the sympathy of the Austrian media to Czechoslovak liberals (LAC 1968x).

As Jan Raska argues, Czechoslovaks were generally seen by the Canadian government as desirable immigrants: many were accomplished professionals. Many arrived with few belongings; some had fled on foot, others had been on vacation and decided not to return home (Raska 2018, 143–145). Czechs and Slovaks who arrived in Canada were found to be very successful at integrating into society, with many of them finding jobs quickly and building permanent lives in Canada (Madokoro 2009, 167). The vast majority of them promptly completed English- or French-language classes (Raska 2018, 171). After the events of 1968, immigrants to Canada from Czechoslovakia included some prominent individuals who enriched Canadian cultural life. Among them were the writer Josef Škvorecky, author of *The Engineer of Human Souls* and other works, who was eventually nominated for the Nobel Prize in Literature. Not only was he a celebrated author in his own right, but during his time in Canada he co-founded 68 Publishers, a Toronto-based publishing house that enabled the works of censored Czech and Slovak writers to appear in print during the final decades of communism (Wilson 2012). Another Czech who made his home in Canada in 1968 was the musical conductor Karel Ancerl, formerly of the Czech Philharmonic, who became the music director of the Toronto Symphony Orchestra (Littler 2017). The Czech author and philosopher Radoslav Selucky, who was well known in his country for political critique, also came to Canada in 1970 after fleeing to Austria when the Soviet troops invaded. He became a professor at Carleton University in Ottawa (*Ottawa Citizen* 1991). Selucky and Škvorecky both lived long enough to return to Czechoslovakia after the fall of communism, where they were celebrated by their fellow citizens.

Czechoslovakia and Trudeau's Foreign Policy Initiative

The first meeting of the House of Commons after the invasion was the opening of the first session of the 28th Parliament, and the Governor General addressed the Czechoslovak crisis in the Speech from the Throne:

> In international affairs generally, my Ministers regard the current situation as uncertain and deeply destabilizing. ... The situation in Czechoslovakia has also caused the gravest concern to the government, not only for its effects on the prospects of detente and future evolution within Communist countries, but also for its consequences for the freedom and well-being of the Czechoslovak people. For those of them who have to seek refuge in other countries, my Ministers have already taken steps to offer permanent homes in Canada. (Canada 1968–1969, 12 September 1968, 8)

The invasion of Czechoslovakia made it difficult to revisit Canada's commitment to NATO. The actions of the Warsaw Pact confirmed the Soviet Union's willingness to use force in Europe, and the crisis created pressure on NATO countries to present a strong, united bloc. While Trudeau continued to advocate a pragmatic and flexible foreign policy, it was no longer expedient to consider softening Canada's commitment to NATO. Among other NATO members, the United Kingdom argued that NATO needed to show resolve to the Warsaw Pact by maintaining its existing troop commitments in Europe (Canada 1968–1969, 30 September 1968, 557). The United States Secretary of State, Dean Rusk, wrote directly to Mitchell Sharp advocating that Canada participate in a firm collective response from NATO (Canada 1968–1969, 13 September 1968). In November, though, Trudeau said "We are not led to the immediate reaction, after the Czechoslovakian events, to conclude that we should necessarily escalate in NATO" (Canada 1968–1969, 12 November 1968, 2626). Members of the opposition Conservatives quickly pressed Trudeau in the House of Commons on whether the government needed to discontinue its re-evaluation of NATO (Canada 1968–1969, 16 September 1968, 60). On the other side of the political spectrum, New Democratic Party MP Ed Broadbent expressed the concern that a show of strength from NATO might actually discourage the Soviet Union from withdrawing its troops from Czechoslovakia (Canada 1968–1969, 25 September 1968, 468).

On 9 October, Mitchell Sharp addressed the United Nations General Assembly. "Above all," he argued:

> no international order can be founded or can exist on the self-appointed right of any government or group of governments to impose their policies on other sovereign states by force. The invasion of Czechoslovakia by the Soviet Union and some of its allies was nothing more than the assertion of a proprietary right of a great power to exercise domination over eastern Europe under the guise of a "fraternal" ideological relations. (Canada 1968–1969, 10 October 1968, 1078)

In the same speech, however, Sharp said that Canada favoured a "pragmatic and realistic" approach to international affairs, and advocated more open dialogue across the East–West divide (Canada 1968–1969, 10 October 1968, 1078–1082).

Like Canada, other NATO countries had agreed to implement mild sanctions against the WTO invading countries, such as cancelling bilateral visits, snubbing social invitations from WTO governments involved in the invasion, and discouraging tourism to those countries (LAC 1968y). The NATO countries had a ministerial meeting on 14–16 November, the result of which was a communiqué condemning the invasion of Czechoslovakia as a violation of international law (interfering in the internal affairs of the Czechoslovak nation, whose people had the right to self-determination). The communiqué noted that this event would be an obstacle to East–West dialogue on the future of Germany and reiterated that the NATO countries did not recognize the German Democratic Republic. Finally, the communiqué called for a plan to be in place by January 1969 on improving troop levels in NATO (Canada 1968–1969, 18 November 1968). The NATO Council met in November 1968 and its communiqué flatly rejected the Soviet Union's claim that the crisis was an internal matter within the Warsaw Pact (North Atlantic Council 1968). In Parliament, Trudeau said that the Czechoslovak invasion had not directly threatened any NATO member country; nonetheless, the crisis showed that European security still depended on NATO. Trudeau stated that Canada would close one of its three air bases in Germany but that it had not yet decided whether to remove airplanes or redistribute them among the other two (Canada 1968–1969, 18 November 1968, 2831–2832).

In March 1969, NDP leader Tommy Douglas called for Canada to remove its forces from Europe and emphasize NATO less; instead, he suggested that Canada play a greater role in international development. He also urged the government to consider more seriously the Warsaw Pact's proposal to have a conference on European security (Canada 1968–1969, 23 April 1969, 7878). But as Trudeau announced to the House, the government had already decided on a policy of remaining within NATO, while starting a dialogue with other NATO states on the eventual reduction of Canadian troops in Europe. He claimed that Canada's continued participation in NATO allowed the country to be part of a dialogue within Europe and to participate in the process of East–West détente. Trudeau's position did not satisfy any of the opposition parties in Parliament; Stanfield criticized it as vague, while Douglas deemed it superficial (Canada 1968–1969, 23 April 1969, 7866–7868, 7871, 7876). Indeed, under the circumstances it was hard to steer a middle course between abandoning NATO and acting as a cheerleader for it. France was attempting to do so, but in contrast to Canada, France's geographical location and historical importance meant it was unlikely to be sidelined in any conversation about European security.

Conclusion

The Czechoslovak crisis had a sobering effect not only on Canada but also on its NATO allies and other European states. Although it involved less violence than the Soviet Union's armed intervention in Hungary had in 1956, the invasion of Czechoslovakia provoked widespread outrage in the West. The pro-democracy movement in Prague had been peaceful and moderate, and encouraged by a loyal socialist regime—as a result, the Warsaw Pact invasion was widely seen as unjustified. In the words of John Diefenbaker (the former prime minister and then a Member of Parliament), "they strike against their friends" (Canada 1968–1969, 27 September 1968, 532). While the Hungarian Revolution of 1956 had been a moment when Lester B. Pearson made a name for Canada at the United Nations, the Czechoslovak crisis produced a sense of disillusionment with Canadian leadership. Canada accepted thousands of Czechoslovak refugees, but there was little that Canada could do in the short term to help Czechs and Slovaks determine their own democratic development. Despite the international attention given to the events, Dubček was replaced in 1969 by the hardline Communist Gustav Husák, who remained in power until the Velvet Revolution of 1989.

Canada's actions as a member of NATO clearly did not halt the invasion of Czechoslovakia. But did Canada's stance have an impact over the long term? One cannot be certain, but the measured response of Canada and other Western countries may well explain the fact that the Czechoslovak crisis marked the last time that a member of the Warsaw Pact invaded one of its own. In the long run, bilateral dialogue between Canada and Warsaw Pact participants may have helped ease the tensions of the Cold War. Seven years after the invasion of Czechoslovakia, in 1975, the Helsinki Accords were signed by the European states, Canada, and the United States. The accords committed the Soviet Union and its allies to the principle of non-interference in the territorial integrity of other states. Canada and Czechoslovakia maintained cordial relations until the Cold War ended.

Canada's decision to remain firmly in NATO was not a capitulation to pressure but a recalculation of Canada's interests in light of new information. Despite a renewed commitment to NATO, Pierre Trudeau continued to forge his own direction in foreign policy, and indeed he somewhat downplayed the concern about future aggression within the Warsaw Pact. In October 1968, he was quoted as saying "I am less worried about what might happen in Berlin than in Chicago or New York" (Walz 1968). In any event, the Trudeau government continued to regard Europe as being in a state of gradual evolution; the Czechoslovak crisis constituted a severe setback, but ultimately a temporary one. The final product of the Liberals' foreign-policy review, *Foreign Policy for Canadians,* had this to say:

> In Czechoslovakia in 1968, the pace of change became so rapid that the Soviet leaders apparently saw no alternative but to intervene militarily in order to maintain their control over events. That intervention naturally dealt a hard blow to détente, that is the reciprocal search to improve relations between the countries of Eastern Europe and Western powers generally. It did not, however, destroy the widely-held conviction that

there is no realistic, long-term alternative to détente, even though each side may interpret that process in a different way. (Canada, Department of External Affairs 1970, 10)

The Warsaw Pact did indeed come to an end, two decades after the foreign policy review was completed. After the fall of communism in 1989, Canada was one of the first countries visited by former dissident and new President Vaclav Havel. In February 1990, Czech and Slovak Canadians warmly welcomed Havel. The Czech President told an admiring crowd in Nepean, Ontario, that "we have a lot of friends here, people who had to leave our country" (Ward 1990). In making his visit, Havel acknowledged the friendship of Canada and also paid his respects to the Czech and Slovak Canadians who had continuously advocated for an Eastern Europe free of heavy-handed Soviet influence.

References

Bain, George. 1968. "Canada and NATO." *Globe and Mail*, 13 April: 6.

Bothwell, Robert. 2007. *Alliance and Illusion: Canada and the World, 1945–1984.* Vancouver: University of British Columbia Press.

Calgary Herald. 1967. "Expo Triumph." 28 October: 1

Canada. 1968–1969. *House of Commons Debates.* 28th Parliament, First session. https://www.parl.canadiana.ca.

———. 1967. *House of Commons Debates.* 27th Parliament, Second session. Volume 2. https://www.parl.canadiana.ca.

Canada, Department of External Affairs. 1970. *Foreign Policy for Canadians. Europe.* Mitchell Sharp, Secretary of State for External Affairs. Ottawa.

———. 1968. "Note." 12 June. RG 25, vol. 8906, file 20-Czech-1-3-USSR, part 1, Library and Archives Canada.

Czechoslovak Communist Party. 1968. "Statement by the Praesidium of the Central Committee of the Czechoslovak Communist Party." Czechoslovakia: 22–23.

Czechoslovak National Assembly. 1968. "Declaration by the Czechoslovak National Assembly." Czechoslovakia: 25.

Fraser, Blair. 1966. "NATO: Divided It Stands," *Maclean's* 79, no. 3 (5 February): 16, 26, 30.

Gilbert, Mark. 2015. *Cold War Europe: The Politics of a Contested Continent.* London: Rowman and Littlefield.

Glazer, Stephen G. 1971. "The Brezhnev Doctrine." *The International Lawyer* 5, no. 1 (January): 169–179.

Globe and Mail. 1968a. "Russians Install New Transmitters, Take Over Airwaves in Czechoslovakia." 24 August: 2.

———. 1968b. "Soviets Occupy Czechoslovakia, Prague Youths Fire on Tanks." 21 August: 1.

———. 1968c. "Would Abandon NORAD, NATO, Kierans Says." 6 February: 2.

———. 1967. "In Expo Canada Came of Age." 28 October: 1

Harvey, Alan. 1968. "React to Trudeau Hint of Change: Europeans Worried about Ottawa Attitude to NATO." *Globe and Mail*, 11 April: 31.

LAC (Library and Archives Canada). 1969. "Message from Department of External Affairs to Canadian Embassy, Prague." 8 January. RG 25, vol. 8908, file 20-Czech-1-3-USSR, part 16.

———. 1968a. "Cable from Canadian Embassy, Prague to Department of External Affairs." 2 February. RG 25, vol. 8906, file 20-Czech-1-3-USSR, part 1.

———. 1968b. "Cable 595 from Canadian Embassy, Prague to Department of External Affairs." 15 July. RG 25, vol. 8906, file 20-Czech-1-3-USSR, part 1.

———. 1968c. "Cable 402 from Canadian Embassy, Prague to Department of External Affairs." 7 May. RG 25, vol. 8906, file 20-Czech-1-3-USSR, part 1.

———. 1968d. "Cable 1284 from Permanent Mission to the United Nations (Ignatieff)." 9 May. RG 25, vol. 8906, file 20-Czech-1-3-USSR, part 1.

———. 1968e. "Cable 419 from Canadian Embassy, Prague to Department of External Affairs." 13 May. RG 25, vol. 8906, file 20-Czech-1-3-USSR, part 1.

———. 1968f. "Cable 441 from Canadian Embassy, Prague to Department of External Affairs." 20 May. RG 25, vol. 8906, file 20-Czech-1-3-USSR, part 1.

———. 1968g. "Message 5770, from Department of External Affairs to Canadian Embassy, Prague." 20 July. RG 25, vol. 8906, file 20-Czech-1-3-USSR, part 1.

———. 1968h. "Cable 4060, from London to Department of External Affairs, Ottawa." 21 August. RG 24, vol. 21594, file S-2-5080-7.

———. 1968i. "Statement by the Secretary of State for External Affairs." 21 August. RG 25, vol. 8908, file 20-Czech-1-3-USSR, part 18.

———. 1968j. "Cable 2293, from Permanent Mission to the United Nations, New York, to Department of External Affairs, Ottawa." 21 August. RG 24, vol. 21594, file S-2-5080-7.

———. 1968k. "Cable 2315, from Permanent Mission to the United Nations, New York, to Department of External Affairs, Ottawa." 22 August. RG 24, vol. 21594, file S-2-5080-7.

———. 1968l. "Cable 2394 from Permanent Mission to the United Nations, New York, to Department of External Affairs, Ottawa." 27 August. RG 24, vol. 21594, file S-2-5080-7.

———. 1968m. "Cable 3887, from Permanent Mission to the United Nations, New York, to Department of External Affairs, Ottawa." 18 November. RG 24, vol. 21594, file S-2-5080-7.

———. 1968n. "Cable 2576 from Permanent Mission to the United Nations, New York, to Department of External Affairs, Ottawa." 12 September. RG 25, vol. 8908, file 20-Czech-1-3 USSR, part II.

———. 1968o. "Cable 918 from Canadian Embassy, Prague to Department of External Affairs." 3 September. RG 25, vol. 8908, file 20-Czech-1-3 USSR, part II.

———. 1968p. "Cable 1124 from Canadian Embassy, Prague to Department of External Affairs." 6 November. RG 25, vol. 8908, file 20-Czech-1-3-USSR, part 16.

———. 1968q. "International Labour and the Czechoslovakian Events." Dispatch from Canadian Embassy, Brussels, to Deputy Minister of Labour, Ottawa. 3 September. RG 25, vol. 8908, file 20-Czech-1-3 USSR, part II, LA-141.

———. 1968r. [Cable]. 22 August. 29-13-1. RG25, vol. 8907, file 20-Czech-1-3-USSR, part 5.

———. 1968s. "Cable 356 from Helsinki to Department of External Affairs." 23 August. RG 25, vol. 8907, file 20-Czech-1-3-USSR, part 6.

———. 1968t. "Address of Grant Deachman, MP, Chairman, Canadian Group IPU to the General Assembly of the Inter-Parliamentary Union at Lima, Peru. September 6, 1968." RG 25, vol. 9065, file 20-4-7-1968.

———. 1968u. "Deachman, Grant, Letter to Mitchell Sharp." 26 September. RG 25, vol. 9065, file 20-4-7-1968.

———. 1968v. "Minutes of an ad hoc meeting held in the Canada Council Conference Room to discuss the identification and recruitment of Czechoslovak refugees of exceptional qualifications." 7 September. RG 25, vol. 8908, file 20-Czech-1-3 USSR, part II.

———. 1968w. "Letter." 9 September. RG 25, vol. 8908, file 20-Czech-1-3 USSR, part II.

———. 1968x. "Memorandum no. 671, from Canadian Ambassador to Austria to Under-secretary of State for External Affairs, Ottawa." 13 November. RG 25, vol. 8908, file 20-Czech-1-3-USSR, part 16.

———. 1968y. "Cable 2216, from Canada Mission to NATO, to Department of External Affairs." 10 September. RG 25, vol. 8908, file 20-Czech-1-3 USSR, part II.

———. 1966. "Cable 433 from Canadian Embassy, Prague to Under-Secretary of State for External Affairs." 30 September. RG 20, vol. 2734, file 950-B15-1.

———. 1965. "Letter to Minister Counsellor (Commercial) Vienna from Director, Trade Fairs and Missions Branch, Department of External Affairs." 22 April. RG 20, vol. 2734, file 950-B15-1.

———. n.d.a. "Chronology: Canadian Public Response to Events in Czechoslovakia." RG 25, vol. 8908, file 20-Czech-1-3 USSR, part II.

———. n.d.b. "Translation of an article from the August issue of the ethnic newspaper 'Novy Dom.'" RG 25, vol. 8908, file 20-Czech-1-3-USSR, part 18.

"Lester Bowles Pearson—Facts." n.d. The Nobel Prize webpage. Nobel Media AB 2019. https://www.nobelprize.org/prizes/peace/1957/pearson/facts/. Accessed 4 January 2019.

Littler, William. 2017. "TSO Makes Pilgrimage to Prague." *Toronto Star*, 10 June: E4.

Madokoro, Laura. 2009. "Good Material: Canada and the Prague Spring Refugees." *Refuge* 26, no. 1 (2009): 161–171.

Meren, David. 2012. *With Friends Like These: Entangled Nationalisms and the Canada–Quebec–France Triangle, 1944–1970*. Vancouver: University of British Columbia Press.

Miller, Leslie. 1968. "Canada Must Decide on NATO, Sharp Says, Citing Czech Invasion." *Globe and Mail*, 16 December: 9.

Newman, Donald. 1968. "Would Not Restrict Entry, Turner Says of Dodgers." *Globe and Mail*, 16 March: 10.

North Atlantic Council, Communiqué, Ministers' Meeting, Brussels, Belgium. 1968. 15–16 November. https://www.nato.int/docu/comm/49-95/c681115a.htm.

Ottawa Citizen. 1991. "Famous Czechoslovakian Writer Planned Return to Homeland." 12 March: B1.

Raska, Jan. 2018. *Czech Refugees in Cold War Canada.* Winnipeg: University of Manitoba Press.

Rehak, Louise. 1968. "Canadian Leaves Czechoslovakia, Washed Diapers to Take Mind Off Invasion." *Globe and Mail,* 26 August: 10.

Skilling, H. Gordon. 1976. *Czechoslovakia's Interrupted Revolution.* Princeton, NJ: Princeton University Press.

Soviet and Warsaw Pact. 1998. "Document No. 140: Soviet and Warsaw Pact Apologies to Czechoslovakia, December 1989." In *The Prague Spring 1968: A National Security Archive Documents Reader,* edited by Jaromír Navrátil et al., translated by Mark Kramer, Joy Moss, and Ruth Tosek, 576. Budapest: Central European University Press.

Taubman, William. 2017. *Gorbachev: His Life and Times.* New York: Norton.

United Nations. 1956. "Document A/3251." In *Official Records of the General Assembly.* Special Emergency Special Session, 4–10 November. Annex: 1.

UNSC (United Nations Security Council). 1968a. UN Security Council Proceedings, 1442nd Meeting, 22 August: 3–4.

———. 1968b. UN Security Council Proceedings, 1441st Meeting, 21 August: 18.

———. 1968c. UN Security Council Proceedings, 1445th Meeting, 23 August: 19–20.

von Riekhoff, Harald. 1967. "NATO without France." *International Journal* 23 (2): 281–286.

Walz, Jay. 1968. "Tough-Minded Canadians: Pierre Elliott Trudeau." *New York Times,* 18 October: 2.

Ward, Bruce. 1990. "Havel Optimistic about German Unity." *Ottawa Citizen,* 19 February: A1.

Westell, Anthony. 1968. "Canada to Shun New NATO Plane." *Globe and Mail,* 24 October: 1.

Wilson, Paul. 2012. "Josef Škvorecky Obituary." *The Guardian,* 9 January. http://www.theguardian.com/books/2012/jan/09/josef-skvorecky.

Chapter 15
The Libreville Conference and Federalism in Canadian Foreign Relations

ROBIN S. GENDRON AND DAVID EDWARD TABACHNICK

Abstract

In February 1968, Quebec's Minister of Education, Jean-Guy Cardinal, attended the meeting of francophone ministers of education in Libreville, Gabon. After almost a decade of disagreements between Ottawa and the government in Quebec City over Quebec's interest in conducting its own foreign relations, Cardinal's participation in this international conference represented the opening shot of the "*Guerre des drapeaux*" during which the two governments competed for support for their positions from French-African statesmen and governments. This chapter examines Quebec's participation in the Libreville Conference within the context of the Canada-Quebec dispute over their respective responsibilities for foreign affairs in the 1960s. It discusses the legacy of Libreville on Canada-Quebec relations, on the international engagement of Canada's provinces more broadly, and on the evolution of Canadian federalism over subsequent decades. The broader goal is to provide insight into the future of federalism in the context of sub-national group efforts toward autonomous foreign policies.

When Quebec's Minister of Education, Jean-Guy Cardinal, met his counterparts from France and the French-speaking countries of Africa in Libreville, Gabon, in early February 1968, it was anything but a typical event. While both provincial and federal government ministers spent much of their time in such meetings and conferences, both at home and abroad, Ivan Head, a close advisor to the soon-to-be prime minister of Canada, Pierre Trudeau, reacted to Cardinal's trip with great alarm, describing it as "one of the most serious threats to the integrity of Canada that this country has ever faced. ... It contains the seeds of the destruction of Canada as a member of the international community" (quoted in Nossal, Roussel, and Paquin 2015, 327). This fear explains

LA DERNIÈRE...SCÈNE.

DE GAULLE: "FAITES DONC UN PETIT PAQUET POUR L'AMBASSADEUR DU CANADA!"

Figure 15.1. La dernière scène": Géneral de Gaulle orders wait staff to make a small gift for Québec minister Jean-Guy Cardinal, "the ambassador of Canada," 25 January 1969. *Source:* BAnQ Québec, fonds Raoul Hunter.

why Cardinal's participation in the Libreville Conference was so bitterly contested by the federal government of Canada, which considered his invitation—received directly from the government of Gabon rather than via Canada's federal authorities—not only contrary to diplomatic conventions and procedures but a serious encroachment on their jurisdiction. A product of almost a decade of political disputes in the field of external affairs, Minister Cardinal's participation in Libreville was viewed as a huge defeat in what has been called the "war of conferences" (Granatstein and Bothwell 1991, 136) or, more often, "*la guerre des drapeaux.*" Between 1968 and 1970, the governments of Canada and Quebec engaged in an unprecedented competition for support from an assortment of French African statesmen, with the French government pulling strings from behind the scenes.

This chapter examines the legacies of Quebec's participation in the Libreville Conference within the context of the Canada–Quebec dispute over foreign policy in the 1960s and the broader history of Quebec's involvement in external affairs to that point. In the short term, the Libreville Conference caused a significant amount of tension in the Canada–Quebec relationship at a time when the nature of that relationship was being both challenged and reimagined. But in the long term, the dispute over Quebec's participation in that conference had significant effects on the overall relationship between Canada's federal and provincial governments by catalyzing the evolution of Canada's federal system to accommodate the international activities of all of the provinces, not just Quebec. Over time, the conflict and competition provoked by the Libreville Conference evolved into accommodation and collaboration in external affairs between Canada's federal and provincial governments, a development that offers lessons for other federated countries as well. As more and more subnational governments—Catalonia, Scotland, or California, for example—become more internationally engaged, the legacy of Libreville and of 1968 for Canada demonstrates that this development need not result in the entrenchment of "competitive federalism" between them and their "national" governments.

Background—Quebec Foreign Relations to 1967

Despite their absorption into the British Empire in the mid-to-late eighteenth century, French Canadians never isolated themselves from engaging with other peoples and societies in North America and beyond. As missionaries, politicians, entrepreneurs, artists, journalists, and travellers, Canada's French-speaking peoples have a lengthy history of engagement with the world outside of Quebec and Canada (Demers 2014; Granger 2005; Groulx 1962). The government of Quebec was not the first provincial government in Canada to send representatives abroad or to experience tension in its relationship with the federal government as a result. Provincial agents from Canada, Nova Scotia, and New Brunswick appeared in the imperial capital of London as early as 1866, to advance provincial interests in immigration and trade. The federal government worked hard throughout the late nineteenth and early twentieth centuries to deny these agents the ability to establish direct contacts with imperial authorities and the representatives of other governments (Smith 1975, 316–317). For its part, Quebec first sent an agent—Hector Fabre—to Paris in 1882, though, in a unique twist, he also served as Canada's official agent in France until his death in 1910. Quebec later appointed agents in London (1911), Brussels (1914), and New York (1940) in the first half of the twentieth century.

So, when the Quebec government led by Jean Lesage began to rebuild Quebec's international presence in the early 1960s following the relative disengagement of the Maurice Duplessis years from the 1930s to the end of the 1950s, its interest in international affairs was not unprecedented. Encouraged by individuals like journalist Jean-Marc Léger and university professor (and later senior government advisor) André Patry, the (re)establishment of Quebec's international presence became a key component of the Lesage government's efforts to modernize Quebec and advance the interests of its francophone population during the period that became known as the Quiet Revolution.[1] After some initial skepticism, the government of Quebec opened offices in Paris in 1961, London in 1962, and in Rome and Milan in 1965. Premier Lesage and his ministers travelled abroad frequently, including at least three visits by Lesage to France between 1961 and 1964; they also welcomed high-profile visits by foreign officials to Quebec, notably that of French cultural minister André Malraux in 1963; and Quebec began signing agreements with foreign governments, including two with France on education and cultural and technical cooperation in February and November 1965, respectively. Underpinning all of this activity was the argument that under the *British North America Act* (Canada's constitution), foreign relations was a shared responsibility between the federal and provincial governments.[2] Paul Gérin-Lajoie, Quebec's Minister of Education, developed this argument further and announced it to the world during a speech to Montreal's consular corps in April 1965. His Gérin-Lajoie doctrine asserted that Quebec's constitutional responsibility for fields such as education and culture applied not only domestically but also extended to the international arena as well—a doctrine that has formed the basis for all of Quebec's international activities ever since (Turp 2006).

Canada's federal government, however, rejected the Gérin-Lajoie doctrine and its fundamental assertion of Quebec's international competence. The Pearson government asserted that Canada had full responsibility for foreign affairs, both through the residual clause of the *British North America Act* and because it had inherited the rights and powers formerly exercised by the British government prior to the passage of the *Statute of Westminster* in 1931. It also insisted that Canada could only speak with one voice internationally (Feldman and Gardner Feldman 1984, 49). As stated above, federal opposition to the international ambitions of the provinces was not new, yet several factors intensified the conflict between the governments of Quebec and Canada in the 1960s. First, Quebec's government pursued its international ambitions at that point more broadly and with a greater willingness to challenge federal interests directly than any previous provincial government.[3] This fact, coupled with

1. In October 1961, for example, André Patry wrote a letter to Jean Lesage to encourage the premier to develop Quebec's international identity and assert its powers on the international stage (Patry 1961).
2. In 1937, the Judicial Committee of the Privy Council, then Canada's highest court of appeal, ruled in the Labour Conventions case that the federal government had no authority to implement international treaties in an area of provincial jurisdiction without the agreement of the provinces, thereby limiting both its treaty-making power and its responsibility for foreign affairs more generally (McWhinney 1979, 38–39).
3. A prime example of Quebec's newfound assertiveness in the pursuit of its international identity and competence was its ultimately unsuccessful attempt to wrest

suspicions that the federal government harboured by the mid-1960s about the ultimate ambitions of the government of Quebec and many of its officials, reinforced federal resistance to what many in Ottawa increasingly considered an existential threat to itself and the Canadian federation.[4] Second, and perhaps more importantly, the government of Quebec benefited from an international partner that was committed to advancing its international interests despite the objections of Canada's federal government. Provincial assertions of the right to establish direct contacts with foreign governments in the late nineteenth and early twentieth century had been meaningless, for example, when the British and other governments refused to deal directly with provincial representatives at the behest of Canada's federal authorities (Smith 1975, 316–317). In the 1960s, however, Quebec found an ally in France and its president Charles de Gaulle, willing and even eager to develop relations with Quebec regardless of how much it angered the Canadian government.

Different explanations have been advanced as to the source of France's interest in Quebec and the deterioration of its relations with Canada in the 1960s. Historians have argued, variously, that Canada's relations with France suffered as a result of de Gaulle's growing rejection of postwar American hegemony and the broader difficulties that undermined France's relations with the Anglo-Saxon powers (Newhouse 1970; Thomson 1988); or that de Gaulle and his government embraced Quebec in the 1960s to atone for having "abandoned" it in the eighteenth century—the so-called "Debt of Louis XV" (Courteaux 2011); or because de Gaulle had reinvented France as the champion of dependent peoples and embraced a mission libératrice following the collapse of France's colonial empire in the early 1960s (Meren 2012). Whatever the cause, from the opening of Quebec's *délégation générale* in Paris in 1961 to the signing of the cultural accord in 1965, France's relations with Quebec expanded dramatically, while the Canadian government found itself sidelined by de Gaulle and his government.

The signature moment in the burgeoning Quebec–France relationship occurred on 24 July 1967, when Charles de Gaulle stood on the balcony of

---

control from the federal government over Canada's educational assistance program for the French-speaking countries of Africa from 1964 to 1965 (Gendron 2000–2001).

4. In May 1966, Quebec's Deputy Minister of Intergovernmental Affairs, Claude Morin, told Marcel Cadieux, then Canada's Undersecretary of State for External Affairs, that Quebec wanted to establish its international identity the same way as Canada itself had done decades before, through a series of small precedents that ultimately secured its independence from Britain. Despite Morin's protestations to the contrary, this statement reinforced Cadieux's belief that Morin and his government really wanted to secure Quebec's own independence from Canada (Morin 1994, 191–192).

Montreal's City Hall and proclaimed "Vive le Québec libre" to the crowd below, a public declaration of his support for Quebec's eventual independence from Canada—an act that inspired Québécois nationalists and angered the Canadian government.[5] Over the long term, however, the cultural accord signed by Quebec and France in November 1965 had even more importance. Concluded on the heels of an earlier agreement on education signed by Quebec and France in February 1965, this was a broad agreement on cooperation in culture, science, and the arts that expanded the potential scale of Quebec–France interactions in a wide array of fields. This worried the federal government so much that in response to its imminent signing, the Pearson government pressured its French counterpart into signing a similar Canada–France cultural accord that served as an umbrella agreement covering the forthcoming Quebec–France agreement (Thomson 1988, 156). A face-saving measure, this gave the appearance that the Canadian government had authorized the growing array of direct dealings between Quebec and France. It also maintained the principle that the federal government remained ultimately responsible for all aspects of Canada's foreign relations, even those undertaken by provinces. The government of Quebec, however, had other ideas.

The Libreville Conference

By the mid-1960s, federal authorities, including Prime Minister Pearson and Secretary of State for External Affairs Paul Martin Sr., accepted that France enjoyed a "special" relationship with Quebec and that if de Gaulle's government persisted in dealing directly with the government of Quebec, the federal government could do little to stop it. Still, they had reason to believe that France represented the exception rather than the rule, with Canadian pressure recently dissuading both the Belgian and the Tunisian governments from establishing direct relations with Quebec outside of federal channels.[6] And yet, spurred by the Gérin-Lajoie doctrine, Quebec remained determined to extend its domestic powers onto the international stage. By the late 1960s, it had targeted membership in the emerging international community of French-speaking states as an

---

5. De Gaulle's *cri du balcon* angered Prime Minister Pearson in particular, though he was even more upset by de Gaulle's additional comparison of the reception he received in Quebec to that of the Liberation of Paris in 1944. Pearson's characterization of de Gaulle's intervention in Canadian affairs as unacceptable prompted the French president to cancel the rest of his trip—principally his visit to Ottawa—and return to France (Thomson 1988, 207–220).

6. In 1966, federal authorities intervened to prevent Tunisia from signing an agreement on technical assistance with Quebec, while in May 1967 the Canadian government signed an agreement with the Belgian government that required Quebec to work through and with federal officials if it wished to develop cultural relations with Belgium (Gendron 2006, 109–114, 126).

important vehicle for the development of Quebec's francophone culture and an ideal forum in which to assert its international competence. Initially proposed by African leaders like Léopold Senghor of Senegal and Habib Bourguiba of Tunisia in the mid-1960s, the idea for a community of French-speaking states grew out of the regular meetings between governments and ministers from France and its former colonies in Africa in the aftermath of their independence. Beginning in 1967, the new government of Daniel Johnson sought admittance for Quebec to these meetings. By the end of that year, Johnson along with Minister Marcel Masse and Deputy Minister for Intergovernmental Affairs Claude Morin (who later was promoted to Minister of Intergovernmental Affairs), had approached France's Minister of National Education, Alain Peyrefitte, as well as its Ambassador to Canada, François Leduc, about an invitation to the next meeting of ministers of education in the capital of Gabon in February 1968 (Zoogones 2008, 2). More importantly, they wanted Quebec invited to the meeting directly rather than through the federal government.

Quebec's interest in the emerging community of French-speaking states and its interest in relations with other French-speaking countries did not come as a surprise to the Pearson government, nor did the possibility of Quebec receiving invitations to its international meetings. In late 1966, Quebec's Justice Minister Jean-Jacques Bertrand had been invited to a meeting of the non-governmental Institut international de droit de pays d'expression française (IDEF) in Togo in January 1967, though the IDEF president René Cassin apologized and invited Canada's Justice Minister, Lucien Cardin, when informed that justice was a shared jurisdiction in Canada. In the end, Bertrand declined to go to Togo and Pierre Trudeau, then Parliamentary Secretary to the Prime Minister, went in Cardin's place.[7] As Trudeau and other Canadian diplomats and officials discovered, however, at least some French African statesmen and governments had an interest in direct contacts with Quebec: while in Togo, Trudeau had to dissuade Léopold Senghor of Senegal from inviting Quebec's Minister of Education to the 1967 precursor of the Libreville Conference. Consequently, the Pearson government came to doubt its ability to prevail in any showdown with the province and sought a compromise. In December 1967, Pearson sent a letter to Premier Johnson offering to let the province's representatives lead a Canadian delegation to meetings of the francophone community, such as the upcoming conference in Libreville, but to no effect. Johnson did not reply to the letter and Claude Morin assured François Leduc, the French ambassador in Ottawa, that Quebec would refuse any invitation that came through Ottawa (Gendron 2006, 133). Ottawa insisted on preserving

---

7. Trudeau benefited from the invitation to make a broader trip to several French African countries to explain the Canadian government's position on foreign relations and the place of provinces like Quebec therein (Gendron 2006, 122–124).

its claim to primacy in foreign affairs for all of Canada while the province insisted just as strongly on its ability to act internationally in provincial spheres of jurisdiction. Quebec wanted its own invitation to Libreville to help entrench its claims.

This dispute over invitations and representation struck other governments as somewhat absurd. Even officials within the Quai d'Orsay, France's Foreign Ministry, believed that a compromise along the lines suggested by Pearson offered a workable solution to the problem.[8] Yet in the aftermath of de Gaulle's visit to Quebec in July 1967, as long as Quebec insisted on its own invitation to the meeting in Libreville, France felt committed to delivering one (Zoogones 2008, 3–5). In the end, French influence proved decisive. Despite the efforts of the Canadian government and its diplomats in France and in Africa to prevent the invitation from being sent, they had trouble even getting to see officials in Paris or Libreville.[9] In early January, Quebec and its Minister of Education, Jean-Guy Cardinal, received the much anticipated invitation to the Libreville Conference. Officials in Gabon claimed that Cardinal had been invited in a purely personal capacity yet there was no disguising the dismay in Ottawa and the elation in Quebec. As he was returning from his last unsuccessful attempt to meet with President Omar Bongo on 31 January, Canada's Ambassador, Joseph Thibault, passed Libreville's City Hall where, with preparations for the start of the conference well underway, Quebec's fleur-de-lis flew prominently amongst the flags of the states whose ministers of education were soon to arrive in Gabon's capital.

Far from being peripheral figures at the conference, Jean-Guy Cardinal, his deputy minister Arthur Tremblay, and his director-general of cooperation, Julien Aubert, figured prominently during their stay in Libreville. They participated fully in the conference and enjoyed the same treatment and status throughout as every other participant; indeed, as Thibault reported to Ottawa, Cardinal and his colleagues were treated as if they represented an independent, fully sovereign state (Thibault 1968). In practical terms, the Libreville Conference accomplished little of substance: many discussions were held but no major initiatives or commitments were realized. And yet for the government of Quebec, its participation in the conference represented a watershed in its efforts to establish its own international competence. For the first time, Quebec had been invited

8. The French Foreign Ministry led by Maurice Couve de Mourville displayed a much greater sensitivity to the perspectives of the Canadian government than did other elements in the French government, such as the president's office in the Élysée Palace.

9. In early January 1968, President Omar Bongo of Gabon refused to meet Canada's newly appointed Ambassador to Libreville, Joseph Thibault, to discuss Canada's interest in the Libreville Conference—on the pretext that Thibault had not yet presented his credentials as Ambassador (Gendron 2006, 133).

to an international meeting on its own, independent of the federal government. That invitation made it more likely that Quebec would receive invitations to other international meetings or establish direct relations with foreign states, thereby reinforcing, if only by increments, Quebec's claim that it had the right to act for itself internationally in areas of provincial jurisdiction. The federal government attempted to limit the damage from Quebec's presence in Libreville by breaking off diplomatic relations with Gabon, hoping that such a dramatic response would discourage other African governments from dealing directly with Quebec. Rather than giving an appearance of strength though, Ottawa's response to the "crisis" struck many African governments, even sympathetic ones, as heavy handed since everyone knew that the real target of Canadian wrath lay in Paris—and Quebec City—rather than Libreville.[10]

La Guerre des drapeaux: **The Aftermath of the Libreville Conference**

What followed the Libreville Conference almost descended to the level of farce, though it did not appear that way to either Quebec or Ottawa. For the next three years, the two governments repeatedly engaged in the same arguments over invitations to a series of subsequent meetings of the community of French-speaking states leading to the establishment of the Agence de coopération culturelle et technique, the first institutional structure of what came to be called the Francophonie (la francophonie), in 1970. Armed with the precedent established at Libreville, Quebec secured an invitation to the follow-up meeting in Paris later in 1968, though this is hardly surprising since the French government organized that meeting itself.[11] For the next meeting at Kinshasa in the Democratic Republic of Congo (subsequently Zaire, now the DRC again) in 1969, however, President Mobutu Sese Seko made a special point of inviting Canada first. Quebec was invited later and only after France threatened to boycott the meeting if Quebec was excluded. Mobutu then "disinvited" the

---

10. Senior officials in Canada's Department of External Affairs engaged in an extensive discussion of the proper response to Gabon's "interference" in Canada's internal affairs. Undersecretary of State for External Affairs Marcel Cadieux urged the federal government to punish both France and Quebec, the true instigators of the crisis. However, Paul Martin argued that "… no amount of escalation will budge [de Gaulle] on the essentials of his ill-inspired policies" and that any action against France or Quebec would only make it harder to find a compromise to end the problem once and for all (Martin 1968).

11. The French government defended the invitation to Quebec on technical grounds. Invitations were sent to all participants of the previous meeting in Libreville so, it argued, since Quebec had been present in Gabon it should be invited to Paris as well (Zoogones 2008, 8).

province by insisting that Canada send a single delegation.[12] If Quebec had "won" Libreville then Canada clearly triumphed at Kinshasa, with Quebec compelled to participate within the framework of a broader Canadian delegation. Between the two conferences, however, both Canada and Quebec dispatched senior officials on tours of Africa—Lionel Chevrier for Canada and Julien Aubert for Quebec—to win friends and influence people with offers of aid. Canada continued to bemuse and frustrate African statesmen with arcane explications of the fine points of Canada's constitution and, when compelled to collaborate, Canada and Quebec argued endlessly over the composition and leadership of delegations, when delegates could speak and on what subjects, how their respective flags would be displayed, and other issues. This was *la guerre des drapeaux*: unable to resolve their differences at home, the Canadian and Quebec governments exported their difficulties and in essence asked various African governments to adjudicate between their respective interpretations of Canada's constitution.

From Kinshasa, the battleground shifted to Niamey, the capital of Niger, where two meetings in 1969 and 1970 laid the foundations for the establishment of the Agence de coopération culturelle et technique (ACCT). At these meetings, the fundamental issue at stake for the two Canadian governments remained whether and how Quebec participated both in the meetings and, more importantly, in the international organization emanating from them. The basic dynamics had not changed from the meetings at Libreville and Kinshasa: Quebec wanted to participate in the Niamey meetings and the Francophonie on its own merits, while Canada wanted to ensure that if Quebec participated it did so within a framework that recognized the overarching authority of Canada's federal government over foreign affairs. The Canadian government continued to perceive Quebec's interest in representing itself internationally as a threat to the sovereign integrity of Canada, particularly since it came from a province with a burgeoning separatist movement.

Other familiar dynamics remained in place as well, most obviously the pressure exerted behind the scenes by France, which wanted Quebec but not Canada to be a member of the community of French-speaking states. The resignation of Charles de Gaulle as President of France in April 1969, just two months after the first Niamey meeting, had little immediate effect on French

---

12. A former Belgian colony, the DRC had fewer ties to France and was much less dependent on French aid and French workers than most other French-speaking countries in Africa. It was also a federal state that earlier in the 1960s had experienced a bitter struggle against separatist agitation from some of its wealthiest provinces, including Katanga, which made Mobutu and his government more sympathetic to Canada's struggle to contain the aspirations of Quebec (Meren 2010, 113–116; Granatstein and Bothwell 1990, 136–146).

policy; his successor, Georges Pompidou, continued supporting Quebec and its international ambitions, at least in the short term. All three governments lobbied their African counterparts furiously to support their respective positions and considered boycotting the meetings and the organization if they did not get their way (Meren 2010, 117–122). Despite the continuation of "hostilities" throughout 1969, however, Canada and Quebec were edging towards a compromise.

As became evident, both Canada and Quebec had good reason to search for some sort of mutually satisfactory arrangement. With French support, Quebec secured an invitation to the first Niamey meeting (Niamey I) in February 1969, but the failure to receive one for Niamey II in March 1970 came as a shock. It indicated that Hamani Diori, Niger's president, and perhaps other African leaders, had at least some sympathy for Canada's predicament.[13] It also raised the possibility of Quebec's recent gains on the international stage being short lived (Morin 1987, 105–110). The provincial government still believed that France's influence would carry the day, but many of its leading officials such as Jean Chapdelaine, Claude Morin, and especially the new premier, Jean-Jacques Bertrand, who had replaced Daniel Johnson as premier in October 1968 following the latter's death, were increasingly persuaded that the time had come to consolidate Quebec's gains, even if that meant compromising with the federal authorities (Meren 2010, 121). For its part, the federal government took seriously the threat that Quebec, and consequently France, would boycott Niamey II. Unwilling to risk that possibility, federal officials similarly concluded that a compromise with Quebec was needed.

In the end, just as it had done at Kinshasa, Quebec participated at Niamey II as part of a larger Canadian delegation that also included representatives from Ontario, New Brunswick, and Manitoba, with the right for its representatives to speak on behalf of the province on subjects of provincial jurisdiction. The Canadian government also accepted a French-proposed structure and mandate for the ACCT focusing on cultural and technical cooperation with membership open to any government, such as Quebec, whose responsibilities encompassed these fields. These compromises involved weeks of difficult negotiations, and the Canadian government only finally agreed to the structure of the ACCT in the dying days of the Niamey II conference when Gérard Pelletier persuaded Prime Minister Pierre Trudeau that the conference was headed for failure and Ottawa would be blamed (Granatstein and Bothwell 1990, 151). Canada did gain a formal veto over Quebec's membership in the ACCT—which, politically,

---

13. Jack Granatstein and Robert Bothwell argue that the outbreak of civil war in neighbouring Nigeria over Biafra in the late 1960s had a significant effect on Diori's perception of the dispute between Canada and Quebec (Granatstein and Bothwell 1990, 140).

it could never use—but Quebec gained virtually everything it had wanted since the pronouncement of the Gérin-Lajoie doctrine in 1965. With the agreement of the federal government, Quebec became a member government of the ACCT with the right to represent itself and interact with other members on all subjects touching upon its areas of responsibilities (Neathery-Castro and Rousseau 2011, 404). Julien Chouinard, Quebec's Cabinet Secretary and chief delegate at Niamey II, signed the charter of the ACCT as part of the Canadian delegation.

The Seeds of Destruction or Competitive to Collaborative Federalism?

These were hard fought compromises largely spurred on by the federal government's concern about Quebec's growing confidence and autonomy in foreign affairs. Clearly, the federal government thought it had the most to lose, with Ivan Head's dramatic warning about "the seeds of the destruction" of Canada's membership in the international community loudly ringing in its ears. From this perspective, Quebec was not simply promoting provincial interests at Libreville in 1968 and elsewhere thereafter. Rather, it had directly challenged the federal government's authority and Canada's integrity as a sovereign country. Like many federal states, Canada generally tolerated the international activities of its subnational units, the provinces, within certain limits. Yet, when Quebec seemed to exceed those limits and threaten broader federal interests, Ottawa forcefully and actively opposed the exercise of the province's "paradiplomacy" (Lecours 2002).

Uniquely, however, Quebec was able to pursue the development of its international competence at Libreville, and thereafter, within the framework of Canadian federalism. As already noted, while most federal constitutions give explicit jurisdiction over foreign affairs to the central or federal government, the Canadian constitution is silent on this matter. So, unlike more recent examples such as Catalonia and its "Catalan Ministry for Foreign Affairs," the actions of Quebec's ministers and diplomats in 1968 were not illegal or unconstitutional.[14] Instead, they represented an example of vertical "competitive federalism" that ultimately gave way to greater collaboration.

In Canada, such competitive federalism is almost always limited to domestic issues such as energy policy (Cameron and Simeon 2002, 51) and mostly stems from the fact that "the federal government has pursued national standards in fields of exclusive provincial jurisdiction" (Radin and Boase 2000, 65). Canadian foreign policy has been, historically, a preserve of the federal government even if consultations with the provinces—both formal and informal—on issues

---

14. Spain is technically a unitary state even though it has downloaded much responsibility to its ethnically and linguistically unique sub-units.

touching upon provincial interests have become commonplace. Indeed, provincial governments recognize "federal pre-eminence" in the making of Canadian foreign policy (Nossal 1985, 207) and thus are willing to collaborate with the federal government to solve disputes. The Canada–Quebec clash over Libreville stood out precisely because it contradicted this emphasis on collaboration or cooperation that typically resulted in the harmonization of federal and provincial external interests.

As it turned out, this competition ultimately gave way to collaboration. Ivan Head's "seeds of destruction" never germinated. As Ottawa became accustomed to Quebec's presence on the international stage, such overwrought concerns dissipated. In other words, competitive federalism over foreign affairs, while noteworthy, does not represent a mortal threat to central governments and can, eventually, give way to collaboration.

The nature and form of Quebec's membership in the ACCT, for example, was worked out before the agency's first meeting in 1971 and Quebec took its seat at that conference as Canada–Quebec rather than just Quebec. Tension still occasionally bedevilled Canada–Quebec relations over foreign affairs in subsequent years, especially when an overtly separatist government held power in Quebec City. But through the agreements reached between Canada and Quebec before, during, and after Niamey II, Canada's federal government accepted the general principle that Quebec's constitutional competence extended into the international sphere. Instead of leading to further conflict, the agreement over Quebec's membership in the Francophonie represented an example of constitutional accommodation between the federal and provincial governments at a time when such accommodation proved very difficult to come by.[15] The dispute between the two governments over Quebec's claim to international competence had focused largely on symbols and appearances of Quebec's competence (i.e. conference invitations and flags) but, in substantive terms, the two governments discovered that they shared many of the same interests and could collaborate effectively even on the international stage (Gendron 2016). Consequently, as time passed, the hostility that had characterized initial Canadian responses towards Quebec's international ambitions diminished more and more, leading to further manifestations of Quebec's international competence.

---

15. From the mid-1960s to the early 1990s, Quebec's aspirations for greater affirmation of its distinctiveness within the Canadian federation and its desire for greater constitutional powers led to repeated failed rounds of constitutional reform and unity crises within Canada, including the Fulton-Favreau Formula (1964), the Victoria Charter (1971), the repatriation of the constitution (1982), the Meech Lake Accord (1987), and the Charlottetown Accord (1992), as well as two referendums on Quebec separation (1980 and 1995).

By the mid-1980s, Quebec's involvement in international affairs had become normalized enough that the Canadian government accepted its full, distinct membership in a reorganized Francophonie in the run-up to Quebec hosting its first official summit in 1987. In 2006, Canada and Quebec reached a further agreement giving Quebec a permanent representative within Canada's mission to the United Nations Economic, Social, and Cultural Commission (UNESCO) and, consequently, an official voice in a United Nations body for the first time (Paquin 2006, 321). More prosaically, over the years Quebec has opened quasi-diplomatic offices in some 28 countries around the world and has signed numerous agreements with other national, regional, and sub-national governments. Quebec's relationship with France is still especially close, characterized by a multitude of intergovernmental agreements and regular visits of French presidents to Quebec and of Quebec premiers to France undertaken with all the pomp and ceremony of official state visits. Quebec led the way in pushing provincial rights in international affairs and it remains the most actively involved of Canada's provinces on the international stage. What is more, to varying degrees, all of Canada's provinces have become active internationally since the late 1960s.[16]

If external competitive federalism on the international stage has become more common in recent years, and even "the norm" (Ahdieh 2008, 1196),[17] there needs to be an answer to calls for a "third way," a "new governance" structure or a fully realized "new federalism" in which the distinct foreign policy interests of sub-national states are taken into greater account, even when they compete or conflict with those of a national authority (Ahdieh 2008, 1188–1189). If this "new federalism" is ever to come to fruition, Canada's example may well prove useful since Canada and Quebec travelled the long road between competition and collaboration over foreign affairs decades ago.

16. Nossal, Roussel, and Paquin point out that "by the early 1980s, seven provinces were operating more than thirty-five offices on three continents" (2015, 337). They go onto to explain: "Provincial offices abroad have numerous purposes: to promote trade and investment between the province and the foreign jurisdiction; to promote provincial products and services in the foreign market; to identify local trade and investment opportunities for provincial businesses (and of course the obverse: to identify province trade and investment opportunities for local businesses). Other functions include promoting tourism, monitoring legislation and policy being considered by the foreign government that might have impact on provincial interests, acting as the first line for lobbying foreign governments when necessary, encouraging "twinning" relations between the province and the local jurisdiction, and arranging local visits for provincial politicians" (338).

17. Ahdieh points to California and other American states that have asserted independent and even antagonistic policies in response to U.S. federal inaction on the genocide in Darfur and climate change (2008, 1186, 1193, and 1196).

Other federal states may have more clear-cut constitutional arrangements giving the federal government singular authority on foreign affairs, yet they are still increasingly subject to competition over foreign affairs from their subnational units. In an obvious sense, in Canada's case, it was a lack of constitutional clarity that allowed for the movement from competition to collaboration. At the very least, this uncertainty makes Canadian federalism an interesting example for how to deal with multilayered foreign policy disagreements—better perhaps than the heavy-handedness of Madrid against the intransigence of Barcelona or the paralysis indicative of the formalized intergovernmental *traités mixtes* politics of Belgium.[18] Following the resolution of many of the issues surrounding Quebec–Canada relations in 1968, Canadian federalism has allowed for a series of tricky national/sub-national agreements. Examples include Canada–U.S. Free Trade Agreement (CUSFTA) negotiations in the 1980s, which can be viewed as a success because the federal government was able to sign off on a deal even though Manitoba and Ontario remained opposed.[19] Similarly, the adoption of the *Universal Convention on Cultural Diversity*, which initially created a major rift with Quebec, ultimately led to an agreement recognizing the province's claim to represent its language and culture internationally (Lecours 2009, 123–124). In these cases, there is a link between the successful accommodation of provincial interests in foreign affairs by Canada's federal government and its earlier conflict with Quebec over the Libreville Conference and the Francophonie. The long-term legacy of Libreville and 1968 for Canada is not, therefore, the tension or the anxiety caused by Quebec's demand for a more autonomous international identity but the role that Libreville and subsequent events played in catalyzing the evolution of Canada's federal system to accommodate the legitimate interests of Canada's provinces in international affairs. If indeed federal supremacy in foreign affairs is giving way to a new federalism, Canada is a good example of how to navigate external vertical competition while avoiding dissolution and outright dysfunction.

References

Ahdieh, Robert B. 2008. "Foreign Affairs, International Law, and the New Federalism: Lessons from Coordination." *Missouri Law Review* 73 (4): 1185–1245.

---

18. For example, the Comprehensive Economic and Trade Agreement (CETA) between Europe and Canada (2017) was much delayed and almost scuttled because article 167 (3) of the Belgian constitution requires agreement of all seven regional parliaments.
19. While avoiding assertions of federal supremacy, it was still able to sell the agreement politically because it was "careful to craft the language of the treaty in such a way that would minimize its apparent encroachment on provincial jurisdiction" (Lecours 2009, 123–124).

Cameron, David, and Richard Simeon. 2002. "Intergovernmental Relations in Canada: The Emergence of Collaborative Federalism." *Publius* 32 (2): 49–72.

Courteaux, Olivier. 2011. "De Gaulle and the 'Debt of Louis XV': How Nostalgia Shaped de Gaulle's North American Foreign Policy in the 1960s." In *France's Lost Empires: Fragmentation, Nostalgia, and La Fracture Coloniale*, edited by Kate Marsh and Nicola Frith, 43–53. Lanham, MD: Lexington Books.

Demers, Maurice. 2014. *Connected Struggles: Catholics, Nationalists, and Transnational Relations between Mexico and Quebec, 1917–1945*. Montreal and Kingston: McGill-Queen's University Press.

Feldman, Elliot J., and Lily Gardner Feldman. 1984. "The Impact of Federalism on the Organization of Canadian Foreign Policy." *Publius* 14 (4): 33–59.

Gendron, Robin S. 2016. "Education and the Origins of Quebec's International Engagement." *American Review of Canadian Studies* 46 (2): 217–232.

———. 2006. *Towards a Francophone Community: Canada's Relations with France and French Africa, 1945–1968*. Montreal and Kingston: McGill-Queen's University Press.

———. 2000–2001. "Educational Aid for French Africa and the Canada–Quebec Dispute over Foreign Policy in the 1960s." *International Journal* 56 (1): 19–36.

Granatstein, J. L., and Robert Bothwell. 1990. *Pirouette: Pierre Trudeau and Canadian Foreign Policy*. Toronto: University of Toronto Press.

Granger, Serge. 2005. *Le lys et le lotus : les relations du Québec avec la Chine de 1650 à 1950*. Montréal: VLB éditions.

Groulx, Lionel. 1962. *Le Canada français missionnaire : une autre grande aventure*. Montréal: Fides.

Lecours, André. 2009. "Canada." In *Foreign Relations in Federal Countries*, edited by Hans Michelmann, 114–140. Montreal and Kingston: McGill-Queen's University Press.

———. 2002. "Paradiplomacy: Reflections on the Foreign Policy and International Relations of Regions." *International Negotiation* 7 (1): 91–114.

Martin, Paul, Sr. 1968. Memo to the Prime Minister. 17 January. RG 25, vol. 10046, file 20-1-2-FR, pt. 1.2, Library and Archives Canada.

McWhinney, Edward. 1979. *Quebec and the Constitution, 1960–1978*. Toronto: University of Toronto Press.

Meren, David. 2012. *With Friends Like These: Entangled Nationalisms in the Canada–Quebec–France Triangle, 1945–1970*. Vancouver: University of British Columbia Press.

———. 2010. "De Versailles à Niamey: le patrimoine constitutionnel canado-britannique du Québec et sa participation au sein de la Francophonie, 1968–1970." *Globe* 13 (1): 99–124.

Morin, Claude. 1994. *Les choses comme elles étaient*. Montréal: Boréal. 1987.

———. 1987. *L'Art de l'impossible : la diplomatie du Québec depuis 1960*. Montréal: Boréal.

Neathery-Castro, Jody, and Mark Rousseau. 2011. "Quebec and La Francophonie: Quebec between Provincialism and Globalization." In *Quebec Questions: Quebec Studies for the Twenty-First Century*, edited by Stéphan Gervais, Christopher Kirkey, and Jarrett Rudy, 402–415. Don Mills, ON: Oxford University Press.

Newhouse, John. 1970. *De Gaulle and the Anglo-Saxons*. New York: Viking.

Nossal, Kim Richard. 1985. *The Politics of Canadian Foreign Policy*. Scarborough: Prentice-Hall.

Nossal, Kim Richard, Stéphane Roussel, and Stéphane Paquin. 2015. *The Politics of Canadian Foreign Policy*, 4th ed., Montreal and Kingston: McGill-Queen's University Press.

Paquin, Stéphane, ed. 2006. *Les relations internationales du Québec depuis la Doctrine Gérin-Lajoie (1965–2005): le prolongement externe des compétences internes*. Québec: Les Presses de l'Université Laval.

Patry, André. 1961. Letter to Jean Lesage. 25 October. P422 S2, 3A 011 03-02-0048-01, article 2, file 4, Bibliothèque et Archives nationales du Québec, Québec.

Radin, Beryl, and Joan Price Boase. 2000. "Federalism, Political Structure, and Public Policy in the United States and Canada." *Journal of Comparative Policy Analysis: Research and Practice* 2 (1): 65–89.

Smith, David. 1975. "Provincial Representation Abroad: The Office of Agent General in London." *Dalhousie Review* 55 (2): 315–326.

Thibault, Joseph. 1968. Letter to Undersecretary of State for External Affairs. 6 February. RG 25, vol. 10690, file 26-4-CME-1968, pt. 2, Library and Archives Canada.

Thomson, Dale. 1988. *Vive le Québec libre!* Toronto: Deneau.

Turp, Daniel. 2006. "La doctrine Gérin-Lajoie et l'émergence d'un droit québécois des relations internationales." In *Les relations internationales du Québec depuis la Doctrine Gérin-Lajoie (1965–2005): le prolongement externe des compétences internes*, edited by Stéphane Paquin, 49–79. Québec: Les Presses de l'Université Laval.

Zoogones, Frédéric. 2008. "La France, le Canada et l'émergence du Québec sur la scène internationale: l'Affaire de Libreville." *Histoire@Politique* 4 (1): 1–12.

Chapter 16
"Flowers have been getting a lot of publicity this year": 1968 and David Helwig's "Something for Olivia's Scrapbook I Guess"

WILL SMITH

Abstract

In 1968, Robert Weaver's edited anthology *Canadian Short Stories: Second Series* was published, including stories by well-known writers such as Hugh Garner and Morley Callaghan and significant new work from emerging writers. The title story from Alice Munro's debut collection *Dance of the Happy Shades* featured a publication that would see her win the Governor General's Award in the same year. Less known for producing short fiction, David Helwig also features with the early story "Something for Olivia's Scrapbook I Guess." Preceding its inclusion in Helwig's debut fiction collection *The Streets of Summer* (1969), the story positions the reader in Yorkville, a Toronto neighbourhood intimately tied to Canada's sixties counterculture. Where Joni Mitchell, Neil Young, and many others began their careers, Helwig's characters enact life at street level. This chapter examines the time and place of Helwig's story and its publication context to reconsider the symbolism of 1968 in Canadian literature.

In 1968, Joni Mitchell sang "Night in the city looks pretty to me, night in the city looks fine. Music comes spilling out into the street, colors go waltzing in time." "Night in the City" features on Mitchell's 1968 debut album *Song to a Seagull*, but the song was written and toured to audiences at live performances prior to the album's release. David Yaffe's recent biography gives Mitchell's own explanation of the song, as she introduced it in Leicester, England, in September 1967:

> It's about a night in any city where you go out and wander around listening to music. I wrote it about a place in Toronto, Ontario, called Yorkville

Figure 16.1. Hippies hanging out in Yorkville, 12 August 1968. *Source:* Frank Lennon / *Toronto Star* via Getty Images.

Avenue. It's a little village there, and there are clubs all along for several blocks and you can … stand in what I think of as music puddles, where music sort of hangs from here to here, and if you step too far over into the other direction, then you're in … a new music puddle. (quoted in Yaffe 2017, 79)

Here Mitchell evokes what Stuart Henderson terms the "scene" of Yorkville, a countercultural space in Toronto in the 1960s (2011). The experience of the neighbourhood's cultural production is documented, celebrated, and recirculated in Mitchell's song. Elsewhere, 1960s Yorkville finds expression in myriad cultural texts, from a "proliferation of magazine articles, newspaper updates, television specials, and National Film Board-sponsored studies [which] offered contradictory assessments and treatments of the scene" (Henderson 2011, 236). The dynamics of countercultural activity in English Canada, concentrated in a neighbourhood like Yorkville, challenged the reception of any fixed cultural representations of a scene. Fictional representations and media coverage alike struggled with the romantic sense of escape aligned with dropping out of society and the very real consequences such alienation could bring. David Helwig's short story "Something for Olivia's Scrapbook I Guess" is emblematic of this tension. First published in *Saturday Night* magazine in 1968, this story is probably the most anthologized prose piece by Helwig. Predominantly attached to discussions of urban identity, the meaning of the story's publication to Helwig's career has, as with much of his writing, not attracted a broad body of critical writing. A writer who completed nearly 50 books in his lifetime, as well as numerous works for television and the stage, edited collections, and broader acts of literary labour, Helwig's name, as Ingrid Ruthig notes in a recent volume of essays, "is not household and he remains underappreciated" (2018, 2). Known for his connections to Prince Edward Island later in his life, Helwig's childhood was spent between Niagara-on-the-Lake and Toronto, along with significant periods of time in Kingston and in England. This means that his overall writing practice evades any one regional attachment.[1] Yet this chapter considers how "Something for Olivia's Scrapbook I Guess" represents an evocative place and time in Yorkville and how the various actors who intervene in the event of its publication concentrate this meaning. Considering the text, its status as a prize-winning story, the reception of the story, and its anthologizing, this chapter argues that the story's multiple temporalities show how various actors and agents use it to express their vision of a Canadian counterculture in

---

1. Lawrence Matthews commented in a book review in 2004 that Helwig had often been associated closely with Kingston but that his work was being reinterpreted after relocation: "David Helwig … after decades of being a 'Kingston writer,' has now become a 'Prince Edward Island writer'" (119).

1960s Toronto and to represent Helwig's wider position in English-language Canadian fiction.

The Story

"Something for Olivia's Scrapbook I Guess" was first published in *Saturday Night* in March 1968. In 1969, the story was collected alongside a novella and other short fiction in Helwig's first prose book, *The Streets of Summer.* Book publication led to increased public discussion of the story. This was framed partially by the presentation of the book-as-object. Michael Macklem's young Ottawa-based Oberon Press published the collection. Helwig claims that Oberon does not get its due in accounts of publishing in that period: "In the mythology of the time, it is the House of Anansi who gets the most attention, as the place of discovery, bravery, new things—deservedly to a large extent— books by Atwood, Purdy, Ondaatje—but it strikes me now that it also happened because Anansi, like Coach House, was in Toronto, close to the newspaper journalists who make the choices about what's important" (2006, 131).

Part of Oberon's striking choice for *The Streets of Summer* can be seen in the work of the Canadian visual artist prominent in its presentation. The jacket image used was by Canadian painter Greg Curnoe, who had come to national prominence in the 1960s. Curnoe's anti-establishment credentials would have been fresh in the minds of reviewers, having been cemented in 1968 with the highly publicized removal of his government-commissioned artwork *Homage to the R-34.* The painting was deemed anti-American and was removed after only a week in Montreal's Dorval airport.[2] This would not have been lost on Helwig who, in his autobiography, lauds Macklem for using these sorts of images: "in the sixties and early seventies it was refreshing to see books that were designed by someone who had read them, who was committed to what was written in them, who cared" (2006, 130). Many viewed what was captured between the pages as a reflection of something evanescent.

Reviewing *The Streets of Summer* in March 1970, Don Bailey hones in on the story "Something for Olivia" as an expression of a Toronto neighbourhood now materially changed. Bailey describes the story as a "bit of contemporary history that already fits into the nostalgia slot" (282), continuing to lament, "the Yorkville of the flower children era … is no longer in existence. I can't find it anyway. Where have all the flower children gone?" (282). Bailey's remarks

---

2. The Federal Department of Transport, which commissioned the piece, claimed it was "not an appropriate display in an airport terminal." As the Canadian Press reported, "three of the panels contained written texts implying opposition to war and violence. The fourth showed a blood-covered man who, according to a department official, 'bore a good resemblance to President Johnson' lying on his back" (*Montreal Gazette* 1968).

tie into the wider feeling that during 1968 the countercultural neighbourhood of Yorkville had undergone something of a transformation. Joni Mitchell gave an interview in 1968 recognizing the shifts in North American politics, and implicitly in the scene, that affected the performance and reception of "Night in the City":

> How can I sing, "night in the city looks pretty to me," when I know it's not pretty at all, with people living in slums and being beaten up by police? It was what happened in Chicago during the Democratic Convention that really got me thinking. All these kids being clubbed... (quoted in Yaffe 2017, 84)

Henderson's *Making the Scene* sees 1968 as a turning point, using a number of sources, including the *Health of Yorkville* report published in the aftermath of a hepatitis outbreak in Yorkville, to explore the "end days of hip Yorkville" (2011, 233). Evaluating a variety of public and political observations, Henderson concludes "whatever Yorkville had been prior to the hepatitis outbreak of August 1968, and whoever its Villagers had been, it was no longer anything of the sort, and they were all gone" (233). This view is confirmed for Henderson in an interview with the journalist Michael Valpy. Valpy theorizes that Yorkville had shifted from its early days of middle-class rebellion to a different kind of youth population in its later years. Valpy recalls, "my memory is that by '68 it had definitely changed. It was more of these [wounded] kids" (quoted in Henderson 2011, 213).

Helwig's story hints at this looming change making both a wounded complex child and flower children central themes on the fringes of the social world of Yorkville. The unnamed narrator describes his own position as far from countercultural. His store is "just north of Yorkville, where Yorkville is going to expand next, that's what the real-estate man says" (1969, 152).[3] Though this shop is not commercially successful, "full of handicrafts and imported odds and ends that nobody buys" (152), it is a window onto the local populace and the drama of the story. Crucial to the action are the narrator's observations of the flower seller, Barrow Man, and his discussion of the living he is making from the symbolism of the counterculture. The narrator speculates that his profit is made at public expense, further undermining any countercultural stance. The Barrow Man had "been down at this usual spot on Cumberland selling flowers that he'd picked from parks and gardens the night before or got from florists who were ready to throw them out. Flowers have been getting a

---

3. Unless otherwise noted in the text, subsequent references to "Something for Olivia's Scrapbook I Guess" are taken from the 1969 publication in *The Streets of Summer*.

lot of publicity this year, and he sold them cheap and made enough to stay alive" (152). The judgement implicit is tempered by the fact that Barrow Man's profit is negligible. Nevertheless, the Barrow Man's capitalist role is only subverted when he brings home a young deaf and mute girl to a house on the narrator's street. Turning from sales to charity, Barrow Man provides the girl with lemonade and a "handful of Zinnias." The narrator again underscores the theft of their sourcing, noting "he must have got [them] from somebody's garden" (153) before speculating that Barrow Man carries an air of sexual threat, present in this flower giving. In the narrator's words to "neutralize what he'd done" (153), the narrator intervenes, taking more flowers from Barrow Man's wheelbarrow and placing them in the girl's hair. Two 16-year-olds who live with Barrow Man emerge to join in, placing flowers in or around the girl. Jane, another of Barrow Man's housemates, sends down paper flowers on wire to wind around the girl's wrists in what the narrator describes as a game. The end result is a curious silent tableau with the girl covered in flowers and the neighbourhood speculating who she might be. Critic Tony Kilgallin asks many questions of the story, suggesting "just how the theme switches from hedonism to Samaritanism should be carefully investigated" (1971, 33). Yet, this change is hard to pin down by virtue of the narrator's perceived bias towards Barrow Man, and by Barrow Man's own alleged speech.

Barrow Man defends himself against the gathering's insinuation that he has sexual intentions. Instead, conflating flowers themselves with joy, and in an exemption from his usual economics, Barrow Man declares: "I'm full of loving kindness. I sell flowers and make people happy. I let you crazy people steal every one of my flowers to give her. I just want to make her happy" (154). The commodity resale value of the flowers is re-signed as a show that countercultural, or at least altruistic, values have taken the fore. A party ensues with much drinking, dancing, and playing of music as a potentially hedonistic interlude before the key plot point of the story emerges. The narrator's wife, Olivia, draws attention to newspaper reports that police are looking for a deaf-mute teenage girl "who stabbed her mother to death with an ice pick in some little town in Muskoka and then hitch-hiked to Toronto before anyone found the body" (156). Despite this news, the narrator conspires with other village inhabitants to thwart the police search and hide the girl. Olivia is at odds with her husband's behaviour, suggesting that his future lay either in jail or in an asylum: "either way there, there's going to be nothing left of you around here except your clothes. Unless I keep a scrapbook of your newspaper clippings" (163). The story concludes with Barrow Man setting fire to his barrow to distract the police whilst the narrator and Barrow Man's housemate Jane attempt to smuggle the girl out of the neighbourhood. She evades even the narrator's plans, however, running away down a side street. A subplot about the narrator's suspicions that Olivia is cheating on him is only developed as far as the narrator resolving to remain faithful to her.

The title of the story hints that the narrator's actions could result in some future public admonishment, and thus become a newspaper article for Olivia's fictional scrapbook. At the same time, the likelihood that the short story is a scrapbook item perpetuates its concern with time. It is a short, detailed observation lifted from the lives of the characters who all expand outwards beyond the action of the story. The setting of Yorkville is clearly indicated and yet fiction constantly tempts us as readers to take the leap toward an imaginary geography. In this case, the events on the fringe of Yorkville remind us that the imaginary temporality of the story is explicitly about the common narrative of a countercultural scene, but also implicitly about the struggles to live and to remain within the core zone of activity that such a scene obscures.[4]

Scholar Carolyn P. Morrison reflects on the sense of vulnerability that all the characters feel within Helwig's story, in that "in this story the authorities are the enemy and the institution threatens, both personified by the ever-present 'they'" (1981, 44). The feeling that the police are a threat to both the "fleeing" girl and to the narrator hints at the climate of the times as itself a pressing force. Collective perceptions of time seem to isolate the individual, and varying explanations might be given to unpack the actions taken within the story. The narrator's instinctive feeling that the girl must be protected may stem from the girl's proximity to Barrow Man, but then subsequently the narrator easily switches rationale and wishes to see her protected from the police. Both instances speak to the tension between personal and collective understandings of time, where prior events inform the present action. The girl's alleged crimes exist within the external reality, where Olivia's media awareness rules. The allegation takes no account of any attempts she may be making to communicate otherwise in the present, where she instead registers as a deaf-mute and a complex vehicle for communication. The narrator's suspicion of the police is entwined with the news reports, highlighting a fear that civil disobedience would not be reported favourably in the media climate of 1968. In turn, the narrator fears that the presentation of the girl as deaf-mute to the authorities would lead to her detention rather than confirm her liberty.

Attempting to recall how inspiration struck, Helwig suggests that "the germ of the story came from a newspaper clipping about a young girl from Muskoka lost (or was it found?) among the hippies of Yorkville" (2006, 123). This description seems apt given the temporality alluded to in Olivia's potential scrapbook, and the shifting idea of where the young girl belongs. The notion that Yorkville in 1968 could still be a genuine space of belonging seems to challenge the

---

4. Henderson's *Making the Scene* features maps to underscore the extent of the neighbourhood influenced by countercultural music venues and coffee houses.

predominant viewpoints outlined in Henderson's study. Henderson suggests a declension where such experiments at belonging had fallen prey to poverty, violence, and illness. Fuelling this were the spatial pressures of developers attracted by the aesthetic of the counterculture and the municipal government's attempts to intervene in the village. Focusing on governmental and non-profit social agencies' attempts to provide services to those living in Yorkville between 1968 and 1970, Henderson observes an increasing mobility where villagers began to perform Yorkville outside of the geographic bounds of the neighbourhood. The disappearance, or relocation, of such villagers is also at the heart of the readerly feeling of time-lag identified by Bailey, where Helwig's Yorkville and the flower-girl motif seems to have disappeared into nostalgia. This might simply fit with the notion that the plot emerges from an old newspaper clipping. Yet both Bailey's sense of what Yorkville was or could be traffics in the same collective notions of time and action as the very fabric of the newspaper coverage. As such, Helwig's story seems to evade the stereotypes of Yorkville in the late 1960s by subscribing to neither optimistic nor pessimistic narrative. Communal housing exists here, suspicions are raised about people's true intentions, and yet somehow small, independent businesses exist alongside cooperatives. Flower power retains a presence and the eruption of parties is still possible. Any undertone of violence is contained within the realm of the unprovable or the imaginary.

Helwig attributes the success of the story not "so much its subject matter as the narrative voice, the rueful, pained, comic perceptions of the unnamed narrator" (2006, 124). The wry and distanced tone sits oddly apart from the actions so as to again upset the chronology of the story. If this is about the present, where is the narrator speaking from? If not, if this is the past, then where might the narrator's world be located? The conflicting senses of temporality are embodied in this voice and are subtly replicated in the slight editorial shifts that can be traced in the story's move from its initial publication in *Saturday Night* to *The Streets of Summer*. In the story's publication in magazine form in 1968, the narrator's opening suggestion that his wife Olivia is being pursued by a young sculptor named Harold Bettmann is cleared from a topic of conversation by the narrator remarking "still, I know better than to say anything to her" (1968, 34). In the version in Helwig's collection in 1969, this statement becomes "still, I knew better than to say anything to her" (151). The shift in tense from present to past distances us further from the actions and beliefs of the narrator and the time frame within which the events are taking place. Another significant alteration comes in the narrator's thought process prompted by Barrow Man. The initial magazine text from 1968 reads: "He thinks that sex is good for any woman at any time and place whether she thinks so or not. Maybe that's what women see in him" (34). The lack of agency afforded to the women in this scenario is restricted but seemingly attributed to Barrow Man's viewpoint. In the 1969 version the following sentence is inserted in between the two original: "Maybe he's right" (152). The second publication then leaves us with a more morally compromised narrator, who is more willing to entertain the notion that Barrow Man's alleged disregard of female agency is a viable world view.

What remains integral to the story in tone and action is the sense that the narrator is attempting to control the action but that events are happening to him. The distance between narrator and action is one suggestion (so, too, are Olivia's comments and behaviours), but the deaf-mute girl's escape from the narrator and Barrow Man's "rescue plan" shows both male protagonists as unsuccessful in achieving their goals. Echoing an assessment made by Jack Batten in *Saturday Night* in 1968 of "the new Canadian role" in fiction, Helwig's story fits a pattern of prominent Canadian protagonists being viewed as "the losers" (37). The narrator's eventual refusal to explain his actions in the story's final line could be read as more evidence of this tendency. Although connected to his refusal to consummate an affair with Jane, the narrator's concluding remark refuses meaning: "don't start asking me why" (1969, 166). This refusal deliberately opts out of the search for meaning operating within the reader's gaze, just as it abandons a payoff from the plot's main action. Nevertheless, such a refusal more accurately embodies the values attached to the counter-cultural movement, with its emphasis on independent thought and evading prescribed systems.

The Story's Publication: Helwig's Belmont Award

"Something for Olivia's Scrapbook I Guess" was first published in *Saturday Night* in March 1968 alongside an illustration of a doll with flowers in its hair taken by Canadian photographer and conceptual artist Arnaud Maggs. A caption to the image reads "Benson & Hedges Short Story" (33). Helwig had entered the *Saturday Night* prize sponsored by Benson & Hedges—and its brand, Belmont cigarettes. The prize was then in its third year, and his story was awarded second prize. The prize meant an award of $500 and publication in *Saturday Night* magazine. This little-known award gets a brief mention in Nick Mount's *Arrival*, a literary history of the period, largely due to Austin Clarke's win in the first year of the prize in 1965. Mount provides the following outline of the duration of the award and its significance: "the next two prizes went to writers never heard of before or since. In 1968, the judges decided that none of the submissions were of sufficient merit, and the Belmont Award quietly disappeared" (2017, chap. 9). Whilst three years of the awards produced few names that would have the recognition afforded to Clarke, it is too harsh to suggest that few ever heard of Helwig again. Though Ruthig makes it clear that Helwig's literary position has been as "one of those unassuming craftsmen," her assertion that his work is therefore "beyond the glare and distraction of prize culture" could also be qualified with a detailed look at Helwig's Benson & Hedges Short Story prize win (chap. 1). Helwig's story is the last story attached to the prize that emerged in print, but the win, expressed in various places as a "Belmont award" win, remains in numerous iterations of Helwig's biographical notes. Given the brevity of its existence, the significance of the award itself has faded, but there are sources that signal the important work that it conducted at the time.

Montreal's *Gazette* ran a feature in 1966 on Benson & Hedges (Canada)'s participation in arts sponsorship. In the feature, journalist Joan Fraser directly references the short-story award, suggesting "it may be only a coincidence, but the year the award was started was the year Benson & Hedges switched from losing money to making a profit" (25). Antonio Toledo, executive vice president of Benson & Hedges, was more circumspect, explaining the logic of arts funding not as a way to bring in new smokers but as "a sort of social conscience salve" (quoted in Fraser 1966, 25). Toledo sought to frame the gesture within Marshall McLuhan's ideas on the future of cultural work, advocating "the closing of the gap between art and business" and seeing it as "part of the over-all implosion that closes the ranks of specialists at all levels" (quoted in Fraser 1966, 25). The editor of *Saturday Night* magazine, Arnold Edinborough, made clear the benefits of attracting new work to its pages but was also keen to suggest that the prize was beneficial for the company as "Benson & Hedges, who make Belmont cigarettes, are always looking for creative talent since any merchandizer depends on creative advertising" (1966, 3). Whether or not Toledo's theoretical gambit or the defence offered by Edinborough holds up to scrutiny, the provision of an arts subsidy from a private enterprise as an act of public citizenship and social care is now familiar in the Canadian literary award landscape. In this case, publication and money combined to give the text and the author a larger profile.

Poet-critic Louis Dudek attended the presentation dinner at which Helwig was given second prize and reported on it in a 1967 column in the *Montreal Gazette*. Dudek reflected on the award itself, describing it as a "wily piece of promotion" and cautiously welcomed the "commercial patronage of the arts" (11). The rest of Dudek's reflection dwelled on the historic conflicts presented in pleasing patrons and on corporate and political responsibilities for fostering the arts. Public patronage was the dominant force in literary recognition in Canada at the time, and increasingly the source of support for commercial presses that published Canadian literature. But both public and commercial funding sources came with conditions, as Curnoe's commission in Montreal demonstrated. Whilst short-lived, the Belmont award's existence is perhaps most striking because, as Toledo clearly states, it alludes to the feeling that certain brands require the perception of conscience that funding the arts may provide. Reflecting on corporate subsidies for Al Purdy's A-frame house, and thus Canadian literary legacies of the CanLit boom of this period, Joel Deshaye suggests that the "source matters" when it comes to corporate funding and more so when these are "funds from corporations not usually involved in literature" (2013, 209). There are few examples as steeped in what Mel Evans terms "artwash" as the Belmont award (2015).[5] Moreover, the premise of the commercial sponsorship of awards established here foreshadows the more recent dominance of commercial sponsorship in Canadian literary prizes, such as the Scotiabank Giller Prize and the RBC Taylor Prize.

Dudek mentions the Belmont winners in passing, but surprisingly the roles of the judges are omitted from his gaze. In a full-page spread in August 1967, *Saturday Night* announced judges for the prize, framing their expertise via their prize-winning calibre:

> The judges Panel for the 1967 Belmont Short Story Contest will be Brian Moore, who won the Governor General's Award for *The Luck of Ginger Coffey* and also wrote among others, *The Feast of Lupercal* and *The Lonely Passion of Judith Hearne*
> Marie-Claire Blais, of Quebec City, who last year won the French Prix Medicis for her novel *A Day in the Life of Emmanuel*
> Under the chairmanship of Arnold Edinborough, editor-in-chief of *Saturday Night*. (*Saturday Night* 1967, 40)

The jury was made up of literary names that carried weight in this period. Moreover, they were intended to signal a cross-Canadian embrace, with Blais's residence in Quebec City countering the potential anglophone bias. The receipt of the entries was "blind," and each entrant submitted under a pseudonym. This was to ensure a significant bestowal of cultural capital via the judges' opinions of the manuscripts. Helwig's memoir unpacks the award process further and looks at the broader impact of the prize, recalling "my Belmont Award (given by a tobacco company—all the company guys are self-consciously holding cigarettes in the photographs at the award ceremony) was given to me in Montreal, and I felt at the time there was something a little strange about the details" (2006, 122). Helwig presumed there had been some shift in

---

5. One tragic comparison might be made to Gwendolyn MacEwen's *The Death of the Loch Ness Monster*, which was commissioned by "Queen Anne Rare Scotch Whiskey to mark and celebrate the Fourth International Festival of Authors at Harbourfront, October 17–22, 1983" (1983). MacEwen died of alcohol-related causes in 1987.

priorities as the first and second prize were meant to recognise English and French stories, whilst a third prize would be awarded to a previously unpublished writer. In the event, Phil Murphy, "a professional journalist from Toronto, who turns his hand to fiction on weekends" won first prize and Helwig was tied in second place with Leonard Forest's short story in French (Edinborough 1967, 3). With the help of renowned literary editor and broadcaster Robert Weaver's hearsay (who allegedly passed along the words of judge Moore), Helwig recounts what happened. Apparently, Moore had left the judging process believing that Helwig's story would receive first prize. After the event, Edinborough (as publishing editor) overruled the decision having "liked it less" and amended the judges' verdict, awarding Helwig second prize. What Blais thought about this change was never recorded. Regardless, Helwig's account from Weaver reveals how significant the award was.

The award win meant publication, which also meant that the influential Weaver had seen the story. He later republished it in a landmark book of selected Canadian stories. Kilgallin summed up Weaver's contribution to the form in 1971 claiming that Weaver "has done more for the modern Canadian short story than anyone else" (7). More recently, Weaver's work supporting young Canadian writers has been well documented by Elaine Kalman Naves.[6] In 1968, Weaver was at the height of his powers, as his CBC radio program *Anthology* "expanded from thirty to sixty minutes and moved from Tuesday to Saturday evenings ... [and] regularly pulled in between 30,000 and 52,000 weekly listeners" (Naves 2007, 44). The point was echoed in Mount's history of Canadian literature: "In 1968, when it grew to an hour and moved to Saturday nights at ten, *Anthology* had a budget of $48,000 a season. Weaver seems to have spent what he could of the money as much to support writers as to buy writing—a one-man Canada Council with a built-in audience" (2017, 119). Weaver's involvement with the anthology form was not just a broadcast one. In a follow-up to his first successful Oxford University Press anthology in 1960, Weaver published *Canadian Short Stories: Second Series* in 1968 as a "new anthology ... on writers whose work belongs to the 1950s and 1960s" (vii). Here, Weaver brought together well-known writers, such as Hugh Garner and Morley Callaghan, with significant new work from emerging writers. The volume includes the title story from Alice Munro's debut collection *Dance of the Happy Shades*, a publication that won the Governor General's Award in 1968. Other contributors, such as Mavis Gallant, also went on to greater international recognition for their short fiction. The inclusion of Helwig's story in Weaver's anthology served a canonizing function as these stories were meant

---

6. Naves (2007) provides transcripts of personal interviews with Weaver and the writers whose work was supported by his many endeavours on the radio and in print.

to represent the very best new stories written in Canada for both public and scholarly audiences. Weaver's introduction to the volume makes it clear that these generations of writers were shifting focus from "a rural to an urban sensibility," but the short précis of Helwig's story as a "description of hippies in Toronto's Yorkville area" seems to represent a reduction of the story's complexity (ix). Travelling under this basic introduction, if not the new institutional frame of Weaver's volume, likely aided the story's subsequent re-anthologizing. Helwig was also scheduled to appear on CBC's *Anthology* on a Tuesday night in February 1968, reading poetry and a short story, and giving an interview. The event promotion in the press referenced his prize win, but no recording of the episode can be located in the CBC's radio archives.[7] Attention emanating from the prize win and Weaver's patronage ensured that Helwig's story drew comment in print reviews when it was eventually included in Helwig's debut collection of short fiction, *The Streets of Summer*, in 1969. In addition, Weaver's involvement together with the prize endorsement helped to ensure that "CBC TV bought it to adapt—very badly" according to Helwig (2006, 122).[8] Badly adapted or not, this one short story brought Helwig further writerly income.

The combined force of institutional support, the cultural capital of an award, and a perception that the story stood for authentic Canadian countercultural experience explains why the story has been anthologized so many times and how it has figured as a significant moment in the development of the Canadian short story. The story appears in Tony Kilgallin's 1971 *Canadian Short Story* anthology. It was referenced in 1973's *The Supplement to the Oxford Companion to Canadian History and Literature*, which notes that the story "depicts the colours, sounds and smells of Toronto's hippie community" (Toye, 91). Morris Wolfe and Douglas Daymond's 1977 *Toronto Short Stories* includes it, as does Don Bailey and Daile Unruh's 1995 anthology *Going Home*. Amy Lavender Harris relates a different short account of the story in her 2010 study *Imagining Toronto*, in a section devoted to Yorkville in literature: "Yorkville's young runaways were not always innocents: one of the protagonists in David Helwig's story 'Something for Olivia's Scrapbook, I Guess,' for example, is a teenaged fugitive hiding out in Yorkville to avoid capture after

---

7. The "Radio Highlights" in the *Ottawa Citizen* for 6 February 1968 refers to the broadcast, noting that "Helwig won second prize in this year's Saturday Night magazine Belmont Short Story contest" (29).
8. Carol Bolt adapted Helwig's story for television in the first season of *Theatre Canada* and it aired for one week in late October 1970. It featured Tudi Wiggins and Nicky Fylan. A brief synopsis of the adaptation shows some changes from the story: "Olivia and Richard operate a successful boutique in Toronto's Yorkville, but their marriage is something else. Richard gets involved when the flower-seller Rafe turns up in the village with a deaf-mute girl who, it turns out, is wanted by the police. And the cynic Olivia has the last laugh" (*Ottawa Citizen* 1970).

allegedly stabbing her mother to death" (181). Harris's search for fictional depictions of Yorkville in the late 1960s often turns up retrospective imaginings. Those renderings published closer to "Something for Olivia" echo Bailey's 1970 review of Helwig. One example of this is a brief incident in Juan Butler's 1970 *Cabbagetown Diary*, a novel of the same period. Butler's work hints at a crueller, less compassionate Yorkville, with a narrator who is derisive of the scene "where you can watch people who watch you as you drink a fifty-cent coffee; art galleries full of modern painting that looks like the stuff we did in grade one" ([1970] 2012, 71). The ambivalent politics of Helwig's story go some way to ensure that the story remains "about Yorkville" in a certain period and also strangely outside of time.

In *Timing Canada*, Huebener emphasizes the complex process of reading temporalities in literary texts. Highlighting the broader inequalities that are perpetuated by dominant ideas of time, Huebener suggests that "individual texts, like the nation as a whole, should be understood as negotiating multiple visions of time and conflicted senses of temporal upheaval in ways that are both explicit and implicit" (2015, 18). Texts might be about time and consciously playing with the representation of time, yet they are also embedded in a wider set of temporalities in their production and reception. Distilling the common narrative around the establishment of Canadian literature as a discipline and as a public phenomenon, Mount's *Arrival* argues that "the long decade between the late 1950s and the mid-1970s saw the emergence of the best-known names in Canadian literature" (2017, 5). Mount involves Helwig in this account as an insightful commentator, not least when picking up on what Helwig suggests in his memoir: "writing is easier if you no longer believe that all the action is somewhere else" (quoted in Mount 2017, 58). For Mount, this ties into a narrative about cultural nationalism and the amplification that the centennial year of 1967 provided to Canadian readers, writers, and publishers alike. Moreover, for the Toronto-centric world of mid-century Canadian publishing that Mount highlights, the analogy in the cultural upheaval of the 1960s is symbolized by Yorkville: "the hippies of Yorkville shared with their parents, and with the politicians in Ottawa: the desire to redirect affluence into immaterial rewards" (6). But what Helwig's "Something for Olivia" provides here is a sense in which a text first published in 1968 plays a key role in representing a hinge point in local and national culture. To read the text as a work of its time we must navigate the long genesis of writing, the time the text appears to be about, and the indications read from the various print contexts from 1968 onwards. Yet, Helwig's story is an acknowledgement that contemporary actions in Canada had become worthy of attention—actions in the present of writing. For all the temporal instability in "Something for Olivia," the story is certainly not about a deep historic past.

Drawing on Huebener's provocation to look for the explicit and implicit temporalities, this chapter has taken a single story to consider both representation and the representative function that the text serves in many contexts. Helwig's adoption of a detached persona and an unclear ending contribute to the long publication life of "Something for Olivia." But as part of a debut collection, they also form a significant element in the commentary within promotional coverage of Helwig early in his career. The risk here is that such a stance is inseparable from autobiography. In the evocation of setting, place, and spirit, the focus remains on a lived, vibrant scene whose allure remains intact. Yet, in adopting the wry, distant persona, the narrator directs a gaze towards the lives of others. This seems to resonate with how Helwig has been described subsequently, as a modest, often self-effacing, presence. During the conception and writing of this chapter, from an original idea to its presentation to a fleshed-out reflection on the impact of a single short story from 1968, Helwig died from cancer at the age of 80. The obituaries reiterated his character drawn in personal and critical articles. Martin Morrow suggests that "Helwig himself never sought the spotlight and remained underappreciated, one of CanLit's best-kept secrets" (2018, B20). Yet Helwig's most easily recognizable labour was predicated on drawing the spotlight to others and in an obsessive attention to the present over the past. Shortly after his publication alongside some well-known and well-respected Canadian short story writers in 1968, as the recipient of Weaver's famed attention, Helwig initiated a project editing an annual anthology of new Canadian short stories. Helwig's work on the series ran from 1971 until 1995. Despite a slight variation of its title, and occasional changes in editors and co-editors, the series, which began in 1971, still runs to this day.[9] The ongoing existence of attention to the Canadian short story in this series owes much to Helwig and demonstrates his legacy of shining the glare of attention on others. Much of this practice stems from Helwig's experiences in publishing "Something for Olivia" in 1968.

References

Bailey, Don. 1970. "The Clark Kent Image." *The Canadian Forum*, March: 280–282.

Bailey, Don, and Daile Unruh, eds. 1995. *Going Home*. Ottawa: Oberon.

Batten, Jack. 1968. "Books in Review." *Saturday Night*, May: 37–38.

Butler, Juan. (1970) 2012. *Cabbagetown Diary: A Documentary*. Waterloo, ON: Wilfrid Laurier University Press.

Deshaye, Joel. 2013. *The Metaphor of Celebrity: Canadian Poetry and the Public, 1955–1980*. Toronto: University of Toronto Press.

Dudek, Louis. 1967. "Arts of Today Has Roles for Business Men and Politicians." *Montreal Gazette*, 2 December: 11.

---

9. For a recent account of the series' history, including correspondence with Helwig, see Metcalf (2017).

Edinborough, Arnold. 1967. "The Inside Story." *Saturday Night*, December: 3.

———. 1966. "The Inside Story." *Saturday Night*, April: 3.

Evans, Mel. 2015. *Artwash: Big Oil and the Arts*. London: Pluto Press.

Fraser, Joan. 1966. "Wham! Pow! Sock! Pop Art Meets Business." *Montreal Gazette*, 30 November: 25.

Harris, Amy Lavender. 2010. *Imagining Toronto*. Toronto: Mansfield Press.

Helwig, David. 2006. *The Names of Things*. Erin, ON: Porcupine's Quill.

———. 1969. "Something for Olivia's Scrapbook I Guess." In *The Streets of Summer*, 151–166. Ottawa: Oberon.

———. 1968. "Something for Olivia's Scrapbook I Guess." *Saturday Night*, March: 33–38.

Henderson, Stuart. 2011. *Making the Scene: Yorkville and Hip Toronto in the 1960s*. Toronto: University of Toronto Press.

Huebener, Paul. 2015. *Timing Canada: The Shifting Politics of Time in Canadian Literary Culture*. Montreal and Kingston: McGill-Queen's University Press.

Kilgallin, Tony. 1971. *The Canadian Short Story*. Toronto: Holt, Rinehart and Winston of Canada.

MacEwen, Gwendolyn. 1983. *The Death of the Loch Ness Monster*. Toronto: Tim Inkster / International Festival of Authors.

Matthews, Lawrence. 2004. "Atlantic Myths." *Canadian Literature* 180 (Spring): 119–120.

Metcalf, John. 2017. "Introduction." In *Best Canadian Short Stories 2017*, edited by John Metcalf, 7–22. Windsor ON: Biblioasis.

Mitchell, Joni. 1968. *Song to a Seagull*. Reprise CD-6293, 1998, compact disc.

Montreal Gazette. 1968. "Artist Raps Ottawa Attitude over Rejected Airport Mural." 3 April: 38.

Morrison, Carolyn Patricia. 1981. "Perceptions of the City: The Urban Image in Canadian Fiction." MA thesis, University of British Columbia.

Morrow, Martin. 2018. "Prolific Writer Was a Literary Jack-of-All-Trades." *Globe and Mail*, 29 October: B20.

Mount, Nick. 2017. *Arrival: The Story of CanLit*. Toronto: House of Anansi.

Naves, Elaine Kalman. 2007. *Robert Weaver: Godfather of Canadian Literature*. Montreal: Vehicule Press.

Ottawa Citizen. 1970. "TV Highlights." 29 October: 38.

———. 1968. "Radio Highlights." 6 February: 29.

Ruthig, Ingrid, ed. 2018. *David Helwig: Essays on His Works*. Toronto: Guernica. ePub.

Saturday Night. 1967. "The Belmont $1,000 Award Story." August: 40.

Toye, William, ed. 1973. *The Supplement to the Oxford Companion to Canadian History and Literature*. Toronto: Oxford University Press.

Weaver, Robert, ed. 1968. *Canadian Short Stories: Second Series*. Toronto: Oxford University Press Canada.

Wolfe, Morris, and Douglas Daymond, eds. 1977. *Toronto Short Stories*. Toronto: Doubleday Canada.

Yaffe, David. 2017. *Reckless Daughter: A Portrait of Joni Mitchell*. New York: Sarah Crichton Books / Farrar, Straus and Giroux.

Contributors

Jane Arscott is Professor at Athabasca University, Canada's Open University, located in Alberta. Her work concerns the election and appointment of women in public life. She advocates for a next-generation gender-equality agenda to carry forward the one produced by the Royal Commission on the Status of Women a half-century ago. Her interest in dissent, centralization and self-government, and freedom of political association is expressed in her published work, including *The Presence of Women* (Harcourt Brace, 1997), *Still Counting* (Broadview, 2003), and *Stalled* (UBC Press, 2013).

Stephen Azzi is Associate Professor of Political Management, History, and Political Science at Carleton University, where he is director of the Clayton H. Riddell Graduate Program in Political Management. He is author of *Walter Gordon and the Rise of Canadian Nationalism* (1999), *Reconcilable Differences: A History of Canada–US Relations* (2015), and the 3rd edition of the *Historical Dictionary of Canada* (with Barry Gough, 2021).

P. E. Bryden is Professor of History at the University of Victoria, and served as president of the Canadian Historical Association from 2019 to 2021. She writes on Canadian political history and the evolution of the modern state, and is the author of *Canada: A Political Biography* (2016).

Andrea Chandler is Professor in the Department of Political Science at Carleton University, in Ottawa, Canada. Chandler is the author of three single-authored books, the most recent of which is *Democracy, Gender and Social Policy in Russia: a Wayward Society* (Houndsmills, UK: Palgrave Macmillan, 2013). Her current research focuses on Canada's foreign relations with East European countries during the Cold War (1945-1989).

Laura K. Davis teaches and researches in the field of Canadian literature at Red Deer College. Her research resides at the intersections of history, culture, and literature, and her approach to the study of literature emphasizes the material and intellectual contexts in which texts are produced. Her books include *Margaret Laurence Writes Africa and Canada* (2017) and *Margaret Laurence and Jack McClelland, Letters*, edited with Linda M. Morra (2018).

Graham Fraser is Senior Fellow at the Graduate School of Public and International Affairs at the University of Ottawa. A graduate of the University of Toronto, he spent almost four decades as a journalist in Toronto, Montreal,

Quebec City, Washington, and Ottawa for the *Globe and Mail, Maclean's, The Gazette*, and the *Toronto Star*. From 2006 to 2016, he served as Canada's Commissioner of Official Languages.

Andrew Gemmell is completing his PhD at Carleton University in the School of Indigenous and Canadian Studies, with a specialization in the Institute of Political Economy. He studied philosophy at the New School for Social Research, Graduate Faculty, as well as religious and cultural studies and philosophy at Wilfrid Laurier University. His current work is a discursive treatment of the Crown in Canada.

Robin S. Gendron is Professor in the Department of History at Nipissing University. His research and teaching focuses on Canada's international history, with an emphasis on Canada's relations with France and French-speaking countries and the international activities of Canadian businesses. He is the author of *Towards a Francophone Community: Canada's Relations with France and French Africa, 1945–1968* and is writing a manuscript on Canadian mining interests in New Caledonia in the late twentieth century.

Michael K. Hawes is the President and CEO of Fulbright Canada. He is Professor (on leave) in the Department of Political Studies at Queen's University. He has also been visiting professor at the Annenberg School for Communications and Journalism at USC, the University of California at Berkeley, Kokusai Daigakku in Japan, Tsukuba University in Japan, the University of British Columbia, and the Swedish Institute for International Affairs. His most recent books are *Canada's Public Diplomacy*, with Nicholas Cull (2020), and *Canadian Foreign Policy in a Unipolar World,* with Christopher Kirkey (2018).

Andrew C. Holman is Professor of History and the Director of the Canadian Studies Program at Bridgewater State University in Massachusetts, where he has been teaching courses on Canada and the United States since 1996. His most recent book is *A Hotly Contested Affair: Hockey in Canada. The National Game in Documents* (The Champlain Society 2020).

Christopher Kirkey is Director of the Center for the Study of Canada and Institute on Quebec Studies at State University of New York College at Plattsburgh and serves as President of the Association for Canadian Studies in the United States (ACSUS).

Jocelyn Létourneau est professeur d'histoire québécoise à l'Université Laval. En 2018, il a été honoré du prix André-Laurendeau de l'ACFAS pour sa contribution exceptionnelle au champ des sciences sociales. Son dernier livre, publié en 2020, a pour titre *La Condition québécoise : une histoire dépaysante* (Québec, Septentrion).

Paul Litt is Professor at Carleton University in Ottawa. He is cross-appointed between the School of Indigenous and Canadian Studies and the Department of History.

Sasha Mullally is Professor of History at the University of New Brunswick. She has published widely on the history of health-care services, especially as such services evolved in twentieth-century rural contexts. Her book *Foreign Practices: Immigrant Doctors and the History of Canadian Medicare* (with David Wright, 2020) examines the influx of physicians during the second half of the twentieth century and the central role they played in the early implementation of universal health care. Her new SSHRC-funded project turns attention to the origins of occupational therapy and the practice of "therapeutic craft" in early twentieth-century clinical and educational institutions in Canada and the United States.

Will Smith is a lecturer in Publishing Studies at the University of Stirling and holds a doctorate in Canadian Literature from the University of Nottingham. His thesis analyzed representations of Toronto in twenty-first-century literature. He has recently published articles on the author Bradda Field, prize culture, and self-publishing.

David Edward Tabachnick is Professor of Political Science at Nipissing University. His research focuses on linking political thought to contemporary ethics and politics. A former Fulbright Scholar and Harrison McCain Visiting Professor, he is the author of *The Great Reversal: How We Let Technology Take Control of the Planet* (University of Toronto Press, 2013) and articles on Heidegger's philosophy of technology and multiculturalism, and is a founding editor of and contributor to The Ancient Lessons for Global Politics book series. His editorials have been published in Canadian and American periodicals, and he has provided political commentary and analysis in various newspapers, and on radio and television.

Michael Temelini has a PhD from McGill University, is part-time Professor in the School of Political Studies at the University of Ottawa, and has held research and teaching positions at Concordia University (Montreal), Memorial University of Newfoundland, and Università degli studi di Genova (Italy). In his research and publications, such as *Wittgenstein and the Study of Politics* (2015),

Temelini investigates dialogical approaches to politics and to struggles over recognition and distribution, notably Canadian multiculturalism and minority nationalism.

Alexandre Turgeon est présentement chercheur postdoctoral à l'Université de Montréal financé par le Conseil de recherches en sciences humaines du Canada (2018-2020). Spécialiste des enjeux politiques liés à la mémoire, il mène actuellement des recherches sur les liens entre l'histoire, la mémoire collective et les médias sociaux. Il a été chercheur postdoctoral à l'Université d'Ottawa financé par le Fonds de recherche du Québec – Société et culture (2015-2017), Killam Visiting Professor of Canadian Studies à la Bridgewater State University (2017) et titulaire de la Fulbright Distinguished Chair in Québec Studies à SUNY Plattsburgh (2018).

Ira Wagman is Associate Professor of Communication and Media Studies in the School of Journalism and Communication at Carleton University in Ottawa. He teaches, researches, and writes in the areas of Canadian media history, the study of Canada's media industries, and cultural and communication policy.

David Wright is Professor of History and Canada Research Chair in the History of Health Policy at McGill University. A specialist in the social history of modern medicine, he has published extensively on the history of psychiatry, children's health and disability, the development of hospitals, medical migration, and the evolution of Canadian medicare.

Index in English

Index en français

Mercury Series

**The best resource on the history, prehistory, and culture
of Canada is proudly published by the University of Ottawa Press
and the Canadian Museum of History**

Series Editor: Pierre M. Desrosiers
Editorial committee: Laura Sanchini, Janet Young, and John Willis
Coordination: Lee Wyndham

Strikingly Canadian and highly specialized, the *Mercury Series* presents works in the research domain of the Canadian Museum of History and benefits from the publishing expertise of the University of Ottawa Press. Created in 1972, the series is in line with the Canadian Museum of History's strategic directions. The *Mercury Series* consists of peer-reviewed academic research, and includes numerous landmark contributions in the disciplines of Canadian history, archaeology, culture, and ethnology. Books in the series are published in at least one of Canada's official languages, and may appear in other languages.

Recent Titles in the *Mercury Series*

For a complete list of University of Ottawa Press titles, see:
www.press.uOttawa.ca

Printed in March 2021
by Gauvin, Gatineau (Québec), Canada.